The Dark an

Memoirs 1

Studies in Austrian Literature, Culture, and Thought

Translation Series

General Editors:

Jorun B. Johns
Richard H. Lawson

Hilde Spiel

The Dark and the Bright: Memoirs 1911 - 1989

Translated and with an Introduction
by
Christine Shuttleworth

Afterword by Felix de Mendelssohn

ARIADNE PRESS
Riverside, California

Ariadne Press would like to express its appreciation to the Bundesministerium für
Unterricht, Kunst und Kultur, Vienna for assistance in publishing this book.

.KUNST

Translated from the German
Die hellen und die finsteren Zeiten © by Ullstein Buchverlage GmbH, Berlin.
Published in 1989 by List Verlag and
Welche Welt ist meine Welt © by Ullstein Buchverlag GmbH, Berlin.
Published in 1990 by List Verlag

Library of Congress Cataloging-in-Publication Data

Spiel, Hilde.
   [Hellen und die finsteren Zeiten. English]
   The dark and the bright : memoirs 1911-1989 / Hilde Spiel ; translated
and with an introduction by Christine Shuttleworth.
     p. cm. -- (Studies in Austrian literature, culture, and thought.
Translation series)
   ISBN 978-1-57241-154-8 (alk. paper)
   1. Spiel, Hilde. 2. Authors, Austrian—20th century—Biography.
   I. Shuttleworth, Christine. II Title.

PT2639.P55Z46 2007
833'.912--dc22
[B]   2007039228

Cover Design
Art Director: George McGinnis
Designer: Beth A. Steffel
Photographs: Courtesy Christine Shuttleworth and
Österreichische Nationalbibliothek

Copyright 2007
by Ariadne Press
270 Goins Court
Riverside, CA 92507

Contents

On the move: arriving at the hotel in Ochrid, Yugoslavia, for
International PEN Congress, 1974

Translator's Introduction

When the memoirs of my mother, Hilde Spiel, were about to be published by List Verlag in Germany, she felt the need to explain to me why she had not referred more frequently or fully to her relationship with me. After all, she had written with unprecedented frankness, for her, about her two marriages, to my father Peter de Mendelssohn and to Hans Flesch-Brunningen, as well as about other, earlier relationships of which I had previously known little or nothing. But Peter and Flesch had both predeceased her and, she insisted, some things were still too private to be dwelt upon; after all, it was her own life and not the lives of her children that she was recounting. She asked me not to be offended by the omission. In her memoirs, it is her eventful intellectual life, the political upheavals through which she moved, and her constant travels, throughout Europe and beyond, which form the main themes, as does, most strikingly of all, her lifelong dilemma as to where her allegiance belonged – to Austria, her dishonored native land, or England, her adoptive home. In a television broadcast made after her final return to Vienna, she described herself as someone with two homes, but added: "that is to say, with none." Her love, far from uncritical and to her mind only partially requited, of both these homes is the recurring theme of these memoirs.

In working on this translation, which I did not begin until after her death in 1990, of Hilde Spiel's account of her own life, I found myself intensely regretting the fact that I could no longer consult her whenever I hesitated over a phrase or reference which was obscure to me. A few years earlier, when she had asked me to undertake the English version of her biography of the eighteenth-century social and literary hostess Fanny von Arnstein, it was entirely due to her encouragement and confidence in me that I went ahead with the challenging task. From my London home, I sent her my work chapter by chapter, along with endless lists of factual and stylistic queries, which she promptly answered from her apartment in Vienna with her unvarying professionalism. *Fanny von Arnstein*, her favorite among all her books, was eventually published in England a few months after her death. It is to my brother, Anthony Felix de Mendelssohn, that I owe a debt of gratitude for his assistance in resolving a number of queries arising from the German text of the present work.

Inevitably, these memoirs contain a number of references which may seem enigmatic or esoteric to an English-speaking readership. Rather than burden the book with heavy-handed notes, I have occasionally added a brief explanatory phrase to the text, and in a very few cases made cuts where I felt that the flow of narrative or thought should not be impeded by interpolations.

I believe that Hilde Spiel's character and personality emerge vividly from these pages. She was not only an accomplished writer but a woman of great warmth, humor, elegance, energy, courage, and determination, as fastidious in her personal life as in her prose. Certainly, she had *les défauts de ses vertus*; she could be stinging and un-compromising in her judgments, often finding it impossible to put up with less than total loyalty or moral integrity on the part of others; but she could also be generous and forgiving to a fault. As she freely admitted, she had tenacious enemies as well as devoted friends. She hated to be categorized, particularly as a "Jewish writer"; I remember her face freezing with disapproval when an interviewer awkwardly began with the statement, "*Hilde Spiel, Sie sind Jüdin.*" Despite her hatred of intolerance in any form, it is noticeable in all her writings that she rarely used the words "Jew" or "Jewish," preferring some circumlocution. She was as much Catholic as Jewish, and as much a romantic as a rationalist. Aware from her girlhood of her own emotional vulnerability, she constantly strove to harden her own heart, aspiring to the philosophical stoicism she admired in her friend Nora Wydenbruck, who, as recounted in this book, when she "felt her death approaching, [...] summoned a woman friend and sat up in bed to draw up, in all tranquility, her own death announcement and a list of those to whom it was to be sent"; or in the circus manager played in a film by the French actor Raimu, who, when his daughter fell to her death from the trapeze, "tore himself out of his sorrow, mur-muring: '*La tenue!*'", an "admonition to dignity" which became her watchword. Once, commiserating with me over some unhappy love affair of my youth, she told me that whenever she had felt herself betrayed by a lover or friend she would "tear him from her heart" – a horrific image which clearly represented a painful but necessary process for her.

It may have been on the same occasion that she quoted to me the words of Hofmannsthal's Marschallin in *Der Rosenkavalier*:

> *Leicht muss man sein*
> *mit leichtem Herz und leichten Händen*
> *halten und nehmen, halten und lassen,*
> *Die nicht so sind, die straft das Leben*
> *Und Gott erbarmt sich ihrer nicht*

> ("One must be light of heart and hand,
> Holding and taking, holding and letting go;
> Those who are not so, life punishes,
> And God has no mercy upon them.")

Yet what seemed to sustain her throughout her life was her love of transient things – of beloved persons, places, or objects, which inevitably perished, were lost or irrevocably transformed over the years, lending a note of melancholy to much of her autobiographical writing.

A few days after telling her children that she had done everything in her life that she had wanted to do, and now wished only to be released from the physical and mental suffering imposed upon her by her last, long illness, Hilde Spiel died in Vienna on November 30, 1990. Her request to be buried in the cemetery at Bad Ischl, alongside her parents and her second husband, was respected; her funeral, in the bitter cold and deep snow of a winter evening, as a red sun sank below the horizon, had an austere beauty that she of all people would have appreciated.

Christine Shuttleworth

Translator's Acknowledgments

I would like to thank Ingrid Schramm and Maud Fuerst for invaluable help with picture research; Paula Gebhardt, Jeanette Haskell and Norma Munson for assistance in the preparation of the text for an American readership; Hans A. Neunzig for his help in preparing the biographical note and bibliography; and also my daughter Beckie Shuttleworth for her support and encouragement.

Thanks are expressed for the use of illustrations:

Austrian National Library, Picture Archive: pages 2, 24, 38, 118, 175 (both), 177 (both), 295, 355, 356 (bottom), 372 (both), 398, 406.
A. Bellinggrath: page 178 (bottom, left).
Foto Berger, Berlin-Wilmersdorf, Hamburgerstrasse 73: page 202 (right).
Bild-Archiv Kultur & Geschichte, Munich: page 326.
Other illustrations are from private collections. Apologies to any copyright owners who could not be traced.

Part One

1911–1946

In the dark times
will there also be singing?
Yes! there will also be singing
about the hard times,
there will also be singing
about the dark times.

Bertolt Brecht

La plus perdue de toutes les journées
est celle où l'on n'a pas ri.

Chamfort

The author's parents, Marie (Mimi) and Hugo Spiel

PROLOGUE

A Child in Vienna

In the suburbs of the city, the villages of the still recent past, the last years of the great peace lay nestled, as were they themselves in the furthest hollows of the Vienna woods. Pötzleinsdorf is first, seen but not fully discerned at the first opening of the infant's eyes; Sievering, familiar but already forgotten again by the end of the second year of life; Heiligenstadt, its parish square, a house and garden in the Probusgasse, the already unforgettable landscape of a childhood into which, before its third year had begun, the war exploded.

The apartment was at ground level. On the overgrown lawn the sun and the summer appeared to stand still. One season melted into another. There was always the golden downpour of laburnum bushes, the smell of jasmine. An apple tree grew into a double trunk not far from the ground. Above, in the branches, tents facing each other were built from rough grey army blankets, their corners fastened to twigs. Two girls and three boys climbed up when they wanted to escape from the adults: here, an only child was not aware of being one.

The war was far away. It had summoned the young father. The young mother, in a long dress of raw silk, with beaded embroidery she had worked herself, sat dreamily at the piano, her hair languishing down the back of her neck, as she sang *"schad um das schöne grüne Band,"* a favorite song of theirs from *Die schöne Müllerin*. The surging strains of Wagner to which they had found each other in the fourth row of the gallery had long since died away. Now it was time for true feeling, their own feeling, and for the music of Schubert, which came from the heart and not the senses.

The mandolin with the colored ribbons accompanied the father to the battlefield, and when he returned for a brief period of leave, he brought with him a German shepherd bitch, Vera, whose owner had fallen at Gorlice and which had adopted him. This blonde, intelligent animal bounded along the Wildgrubenweg with him; he whistled as she chased after the hazel sticks he hurled for her. Further down, the rack-and-pinion railway ran from Nussdorfer Platz up the Kahlenberg. On October afternoons, climbing down through the vineyards to the bluish twilit valley, one could see deep, dark shadows sinking in the east, where the war was.

It was just after *Fronleichnam*, Corpus Christi, when the child, her hair curled and sticky with sugar water, had left the little parish church of St. James to join the procession through the village streets, decked with birch twigs. Her eyes had been red with tears because she was not allowed to carry a statue, only a sky blue ribbon that hung down from it. Now wicker baskets and hard, metallic-colored cases in the shape of a Romanesque chapel were being packed with children's clothes, a teddy bear, a picture book. The family was going away. The destination was distant, but they were not to cross any border. When did they arrive? At what time of day? The mists of the past obscure the memory.

Flat yellow country, flat peasant houses, their mortar crumbling away. The village is Krönau, in Moravia. Part of the howitzer field regiment, whose cadre is at nearby Olmütz, are put up here. In the dusty or clayey alleyways – here it never seems to rain – are occasional riders, soldiers, carts, artillery. The officer, in his grey uniform with red lapels, swings himself up onto his horse. Once he has gone, his freckle-nosed orderly lounges, blinking in the sunlight, by the warm wall. Round about, as far as the eye can see, are fields of grain, scorched by the sun. The vegetables too are drying in the sun, peas and beans from the front garden, the green beans called *Fisolen* which constantly produce new shoots, picked by the farmer's wife, cut diagonally and scattered over rickety wooden tables and stone benches to dry. When the dog roses on the edge of the forest turn to red rosehips, they too are gathered. For necklaces? No, for stewing.

The light carriage rolls down the country road to the chief town of the district. The child rides *"Biskotterl,"* sandwiched between her childlike parents, one in grey army tunic, the other in lilac spotted voile, who are playing at being grownup, playing at having-to-go-to-war, at saying farewell and meeting again; who love each other without having to play "pretend." There is a gypsies' camp at the roadside. "They steal children from their mothers' arms" – so the child is told – dragging them out of their carriage, putting them among their own children, those creatures with flashing eyes and unkempt hair. What elemental terror! The child clings to the golden-brown ensign on her right, the green-eyed girl on her left, to whom in some mysterious, reassuring way she belongs.

In Olmütz, with its walls of imperial yellow, time seems asleep, no distant noise of battle reaches the ears of the Sunday families promenading, sitting on the café terrace, standing in front of the tall statue of the Virgin on the Buckelpflasterplatz and gazing pensively heavenwards. The brass band plays. Ice cream is eaten. There is much, but casual, saluting. The little Mama blushes as the commanding officer's wife, splendidly curved in her linen costume with the embroidered openwork hem and swaying straw hat, graciously addresses her. The child rocks to and fro to the strains of the *Walzertraum*. The straw with which she has been drinking a fizzy blonde lemonade becomes a conductor's baton.

Unforgettable how yellow everything was there: the houses, the sun, the Sunday, the lemon ice cream, the lemonade. The village is a paler shade than the town, dusty and sallow, but the fields of rape blaze in the summer heat. The child's aunt, as young as her Mama, has come to visit from Vienna. Mimi and Lonny: two giggling girls, netting and embroidering sofa covers, dressing and undressing the child as if she were a china doll. One morning the father appears with a gold star at his collar and whirls his wife and sister around with glee, showing them his officer's commission. The child is beside herself with excitement, jumping on and off the bed like a shuttlecock, hugging her mother and incessantly shouting: "*Frau Leutenant, Frau Leutenant!*"

In Cracow it was winter. The cadre was now nearer to the front. In those blue, glass-clear days it was as if one could hear a distant roar of cannons. The green onion-shaped towers, the tall grey angular buildings stood silhouetted against the blue. It could not have been cold at first, for at the party in the officers' casino there was a tombola in the open air. Stalls with blue and red wooden necklaces, painted statuettes, candied fruit. There were living creatures among the prizes – chickens, rabbits, caged birds, a cock pigeon. It was only the pigeon the child longed for, with his rose-colored neck, the blue-green feathers of his back. Only the pigeon! But the tombola turned, with every so often a flourish of trumpets, and everything disappeared from view, at last even the yearned-after pink, iridescent green, fluttering, nodding bundle of feathers. The festival was over. Tearfully the child listened to the imperial hymn, saw the ladies in their ostrich-feather hats and the bareheaded gentlemen rise and stand straight as candles in patriotic reverence. Gone, gone the pigeon, gone the tombola and the fanfare. Lost and gone with the town, the Emperor and his hymn.

Glass-green, snow-blue January in Poland. With no grandmother far and wide to advise the young mother, the child wore short socks, even at the skating rink. The ice skates glided over the crunching ice; a fall would scrape the skin from one's reddened, frozen knees. The wind clattered. The sky had a cutting clarity. All the more sheltered, as if inside a scarlet heart, was the plush chamber of the Krongold ladies, with whom the lieutenant's wife was staying with her little girl. Scarlet the carpets and wallpaper, the door curtains and the armchairs. The Krongold ladies, two sisters and their mother, were voluptuous and white. Their white bodies floated in the bathtub. Steam filled the bathroom, which had been partitioned off from the kitchen. The child was allowed in, sitting on a little wicker chair, for the parents had entrusted her to the ladies in order to attend a ball at the casino. Kleinrock, the Galician orderly, brought sausages from the mess. The ladies, sweetly scented from their bath, disapprovingly watched him carry in the unclean food in an army dish.

The child's terror of the man in the cape must be recorded. In that winter of the war he went about in Cracow, or rather stood silently on dark corridors, and when a woman entered the stairwell he would strike with his knife. The nights were full of unheard screams. Ever nearer, even on the next street corner, his shadow had been spied. The Krongold ladies muttered about him in the child's hearing. Suddenly blood began to flow inside the scarlet heart. The child's red, frozen legs in their short socks began to tremble, her nose was running; by evening she was feverish. Shaking with fear, she lay in bed listening to her father playing his mandolin and singing Russian songs which had drifted over the border.

"Kleiin-rock! Where is that mooncalf? *Pshia krev!*" He curses in Polish. The child is ill. Kleinrock is sent for the doctor. The child no longer sees the stocky, bearded man. She is walking through the door into the dark house. A cape opens, a knife flashes. Then again it is one of the voluptuous sisters whose white flesh the man is slitting from top to bottom. In a feverish nightmare the child reveals what the Krongold ladies revealed to her. Whispering behind the door curtain. The father is shouting in the fierce tones of a lieutenant. The ladies, outraged, argue with him. Slowly the restlessness dies away, the fever is over. It is March. Snow melts, dripping from the roofs. The army leaves its winter quarters. In the evening, before the journey back to Vienna with her Mama, the child for the first time hears grownups weeping.

Grandfather is dead; the Virginia cigar will not be passed to her again to pull out the straw and take a puff herself; the bulbous silver box of throat lozenges lies unused beside the cigar-case. Who will now call the child his "little sunshine"? It is always November. On the *Ring* a funeral procession moves along, but it is not Grandfather who is being carried to his grave; he was buried days, weeks earlier. From the bay window in the Wollzeile, between the black-clad Aunt Lonny and the black-clad Grandmother, the child sees the funereal horses pacing in the distance. Plumed hats and brass-band music. Pale shadows in the drifting autumn fog. Could they have been grey horses? They must have been black horses, but they stay in the memory as greys.

The child's sky grows even darker. Fear, cold, and hunger move into the house in the Probusgasse. The gas burns low and less often. Water freezes. Oh for the prickly dried vegetables of that yellow summer! There are no rosehips in Heiligenstadt either; they disappear from the bushes overnight. She eats *Wrucken*, woody turnips. She eats grey polenta. Her cheeks are swollen by mumps. She has an irritating cough. Chest and throat are full of phlegm. A little coat has been made from the rough grey tent-blanket, to which Mama has sewn a fluffy white collar. Father, long ago made up to first lieutenant, has not been seen for an eternity. Without the box of *Speck* that Rühr, his new "mooncalf," brought from the Ukraine she would perhaps be mortally ill by now.

November again. Then one day her father was at the door, in army green, his fur coat hung over his shoulders, hollow-cheeked, his eyes flickering. It seemed as though he was not at all happy to be home, as though he felt unspeakable sadness in the arms of his loved ones. The bitch Vera slunk around, cowering in constant fear of his

The author's parents (center), with two other officers and their
wives on the Kaiser's birthday, Olmütz, 1916

bad moods. The war was over, but what was beginning? Not so young
any more, no longer on horseback, conquered, humiliated, his
inheritance from Grandfather all spent, the man in the shabby
uniform had to knock a future together for himself from splintered
wood.

The child came home from school singing a song:

> *Die noblichen Herr'n*
> *mit die goldenen Stern'*
> *die müssen jetzt d'Straßen aufkehr'n.*

> (The noble gentlemen
> with the gold stars
> now they must sweep the streets.)

The door sprang open, the father stormed in and slapped the
child's face – once, twice, left and right. The child stood speechless,
terrified to the depths of her soul. What had happened? It was over!
For I was I. And a new era had begun.

1

Aura and Origin

At certain moments, during an evening at the Salzburg Mozarteum or in the foyer of the Vienna Konzerthaus, I sense it again, quite close at hand: the breath, the perfume, the aura of my childhood. In the war years, and for some time afterwards, before the hectic forms of Expressionism had begun to emerge in everyday life too, architecture, furniture, women's clothes, their jewelry, lamps, and vases were of a reassuring, almost Biedermeier-like simplicity. The luxuriant blooms of the *Jugendstil* had fallen away. There remained modest wreaths and garlands on the walls, among which, as in the appliqué decoration over the entrance to the Café Bazar in Salzburg, plump putti clasped each other like those in the ceramics of Wally Wieselthier.

If Otto Wagner had once overcome historicism through a change of direction towards the unpretentious harmony of the Biedermeier, there was now no trace of the often monstrous Klimtian ornamentation to be discerned in the Wiener Werkstätten, whose utensils, patterns, porcelain, and bookbindings still defined the taste of the day. In those two musical institutions, unscathed up to the present day by art deco, functionalism, or the *Empire* style of the Third Reich, there still hang the glass chandeliers of my youth; the buffets and toilets are still indicated in black or gold by the curving italic characters of my childhood books. There, and only there, I feel taken back to the awareness of life of the late Francisco-Josephine era which came to an end with the gunshots at Sarajevo in 1914.

Wardrobes, beds, console tables, sewing table and chairs in my parents' bedroom were all blonde. The great wardrobes, which came back into my possession in a roundabout way after my return to Vienna, now stand in my cellar in the Cottagegasse. They are decorated with modest fluted moldings and brass fittings, apart from which they are austere and very commodious. The long dresses and costumes which my mother wore up to the beginning of the twenties did not have to trail on the wardrobe floor, and there was room enough on the shelves for her batiste linen with its threaded ribbons. I often sat with my homework at the little sewing table while she took her afternoon rest; the scratching of my pen, it seemed, pleasantly soothed her into slumber.

The rest of the furniture too at the garden apartment in Heiligenstadt, where everything possible was painted or lacquered white, gave hints of Josef Hoffmann, whose designs were now the models for even third-rate manufacturers. I remember my father's dark-stained desk, the floral-patterned armchairs. My mother's evening gown, her pointed bronze-colored shoes were inspired by the picture which at that time was reproduced as a print that hung in many bourgeois households: a lady in a shimmering green dress, dreamily absorbed in music. I have forgotten the artist's name.

My mother's maiden name was Marie Gutfeld, and she came from a family which exemplified the development of a cultured stratum of people of Jewish origin, of their entry, already complete, into the social structure of Vienna. The earliest ancestor of hers of whom I have any knowledge was a learned man, who had become at the age of thirty-five the leader of his community in the little town of Nikolsburg and not long afterwards the chief rabbi of the region of Moravia. Markus Benedict had been born in 1753 in the Hungarian county of Somogy and had sat at the feet of great Talmud scholars first in Nikolsburg, then in Fürth, and finally in Prague before he began to rise in the religious hierarchy.

I have learnt from a history book that in his later life Markus Benedict took up the study of Hebrew grammar, and of the major philosophical work of Moses Maimonides and the writings of Moses Mendelssohn. This "hero of the spirit," as the historian Hugo Gold calls him, "while observing religious matters with the greatest rigor, did not scorn profane culture. He had very modern views and, unlike many other great Talmudists of the time, by no means considered it impermissible to speak and write German correctly. It is typical of his commendable liberalism that, in his plan for a course of studies for candidates for the rabbinate, he proposed that, together with their strict rabbinical education, pupils who had passed their eighteenth year should privately study all the grammar-school subjects, learn

Latin and German, and take a public examination, in order subsequently to study philosophy." Mention is also made here of the "innumerable miracles, and even supernatural powers" ascribed to him, and in his own lifetime he was "revered like a saint."

Markus Benedict died in 1829 at Karlsbad, the spa he used to visit in the summer to take the waters. His son Jakob, born six years before the turn of the century, moved to Vienna. During the *Vormärz*, the period leading up to the revolution of March 1848, he must have settled there as a merchant. One of his grandchildren, my great-uncle Gustav Singer, *Hofrat* (court councilor) and chief director of the Rudolfspital in Vienna, was able to give me more information about this Jakob, but above all about Jakob's father, his illustrious ancestor: "He was a confidant of the late Emperor Franz, a fact commemorated by an inscription in Hebrew characters on a rocky plateau in Karlsbad, opposite Pupp. Emperor Franz met him on the promenade in Karlsbad, shook his hand, and walked with him for a while. This relic has now probably been destroyed by the Nazis. But I remember that, the first time I was with Archduke Eugen in Karlsbad, I drew his attention to this inscription... I believe that it was in honor of this ancestral distinction that I was promoted to the rank of a sort of lord-in-waiting [*Kämmerer*]."

In the middle of the Second World War, in January 1941, when I was beginning to write a novel about the last decades of the previous century and had asked my great-uncle for family recollections, his answer reached me from the country hotel Selsdon Park. This former stately home had become a luxurious residence for gentry who hoped to escape bomb attacks on English cities among the gentle Surrey hills. "His Eminence," as my father used to call him, the former personal physician of Archduke Eugen but also of the sinister prelate Ignaz Seipel, long-standing Chancellor of the First Austrian Republic, was living in exile with the same elegance and dignity which had been his as a leading light of the Vienna school of medicine. Long ago converted to Catholicism and married according to its ceremonies, in his letter he recalled, not without pride, those forebears whose creed and lifestyle he had abjured:

"Grandfather Kopel B. was a respected Viennese citizen who founded an important silk business. He was, however, more of a scholar, famous for his witty lapidary sayings, and a man of exemplary character, particularly strict in his demands for correct commercial behavior. He attributed the rise of his house not only to the favorable times but to the active support of his wife Luise (Deborah). She was in her youth a beautiful, exceptionally shrewd and energetic woman, who spent her working life alternately sitting at her desk and lying in childbed. Despite her swarm of children, she directed the administration of the business, engaged and supervised staff, and went on business journeys." Such active participation on the part of a woman, wrote my great-uncle, "was at this time – the mid-nineteenth century – most unusual."

"Nevertheless," he added, "this woman, who spoke *Hochdeutsch* [standard German] and was very cultured and well-read and whose circle of friends consisted mainly of politicians, kept her household in brilliant order (her cuisine was famous and distinguished) and brought up her children according to modern principles. She had excellent teaching skills, employed French and later English governesses, and also paid great attention to physical education. All the children were accomplished athletes, ice-skaters, swimmers, and dancers; my mother was a famous swimmer and diver. They lived in a huge old patrician house (on the Wieden, Pressgasse), and the ruling spirit of the house was good old Viennese gaiety.... My grandfather is associated in my mind with the memory of a splendid collection of clocks and watches and a drawer full of beautiful gold snuffboxes. Grandmother too took snuff, and she had a valuable collection of lace. The image of the family was one of cozy, idyllic dignity."

I can still remember that famous swimmer and diver, my great-grandmother. She was one of the nine daughters born to Luise Deborah. Their names – Netti, Kathi, Fanny, Fevi, Tini, Gini, Rosy, Pauly, Eugenie – have been preserved, unlike the names of the six brothers and of those who did not survive early childhood out of the total of twenty offspring. Fanny, later Singer, lived as a widow in Döbling, the district of Vienna preferred by my maternal relatives, and as a very old lady in the Hotel Elisabeth in Baden, near Vienna. I was taken to family gatherings there by my mother; we traveled on the Baden electric railway, peaceful even in wartime, but made perilous on the homeward journey by drunken fellow travelers. The matriarch, her hair covered by an old-fashioned bonnet, was enthroned among her brood in the well-appointed hotel room, where she ordered coffee and *Torte* to be served. The joker among them, Leo, a lawyer, constantly made her laugh like a young girl. She had no notion that two of her sons, Gustav and Leo, would both attain the rank of *Hofrat* and become experts in their respective professions, still less that they would both become totally absorbed into Christianity – at least until the advent of Hitler.

Fanny Singer had married off her daughters in good time, thus postponing by a generation a similar absorption into the world around them. Irene's marriage took her to Budapest. Melanie, my mother's mother, did not, as originally planned, marry the coal baron Gutmann, but had to be satisfied with a luckless man called Adolf Gutfeld. It worked out badly. After the wedding night in the Grand Hotel, she ran away from him, was sent back by her parents, resigned herself to her marriage, was occasionally unfaithful to Adolf – once with the captain of the paddlesteamer *Franz Josef I* on the Wolfgangsee – and left him as soon as their children, Marie and Felix, were grown up. She had a romantic nature, loved pink and sky-blue ribbons, played Schumann and Chopin on the piano, and cherished all those *Jugendstil* trinkets that we despised and advised her to throw away. Luckless in her turn, she struggled through life with the grudging help of "His Eminence" and a small income of her own. Despite the cheerlessness of her life, she often showed a great sense of humor.

My mother left her parents' home early. But Felix, after a long imprisonment in Russia, which lasted long after the war had ended, finally obtained a doctor's degree in law; unable to find a post as an articled clerk, he continued to live in a small room of the house in which he had grown up. He read, wrote, and brooded; turned to Socialism; and sought after earthly, religious and cosmic truth. "From my seventeenth year onward," he confessed to his friend Otto after a failed suicide attempt in 1925, "I was incessantly and untiringly concerned with constructing some sort of world view for myself." He immersed himself in many inquiries, including those of rhetoric, "as I eagerly studied the book of Deutero-Isaiah, Demosthenes, and Cicero, as well as the lectures of Bossuet, Bourdaloue and Mirabeau, Pitt, Burke, Macaulay and Brougham, Lassalle and others, and allowed them to influence me." In the Russian prison camp, he had produced "treatises on the nature of rhetoric, on the theatrical, on the tragic, the comic and the sublime... on classicism, romanticism, and decadence."

He wanted to develop a theory of art anchored in philosophy, to be called "phenomenological aesthetics."

Felix's letter to Otto (who was unknown to me), twenty-four pages long and preserved only by chance, is a heart-rending document of unfulfilled talent, unproductive depth of thought, high-flying ideas which were never realized. All the lectures he gave in Russia, where he was caught up in the wake of the revolution – 1919 in Irkutsk-Ratarejnaja, later in Omsk and Moscow – then later in Vienna, around 1923, at a conference in Döbling of Communist party stewards, which he thought "unsuccessful," on the subject of "Spartacus or Gracchus? Revolutionary Mass Movements in Ancient Rome"; all the translations of poems "from Greek, Latin, French, English, Hungarian and Middle High German originals" are lost, submerged in the maelstrom of the twenties, the years of hunger.

A silent, pale man, Felix would sometimes visit us for half an hour, as long as his tram ticket (which permitted a change of trams) would allow, give me a book of poetry, perhaps by Villon, stroke my cheek, and depart once more. In October 1935 he was imprisoned for six weeks in the penal camp of Wöllersdorf by the *Ständestaat* (the authoritarian regime of 1934 to 1938). Toward the end of the following year, when I was already in England, he disappeared forever. As he confided to someone, he was going to "look for God in Spain." He became a medical orderly, and fell on February 20, 1937, at the Jarama, a river near Madrid.

My mother, a beautiful dark girl, remained unaffected by such turmoil of the soul and the times. She had inherited a cheerful wit, good taste, musicality, and a certain dreamy indolence which sometimes, though not in her case, goes along with or precedes a tendency to inward contemplation. Unlike her brother, she was easygoing, as long as she was unscathed by fate. She was fervently attached to Vienna, and after all journeys and holidays she yearned to be back in her own city. She had a well-shaped little nose, a finely cut mouth. Her girlfriends called her Mizzi, and the name, from Arthur Schnitzler's play *Countess Mizzi*, matched her temperament. My father called her Mimi, as I later did myself.

When she met my father, she unresistingly fell into line with his inclinations. These were natural science; high-altitude mountain walking; music, above all that of Wagner, Schubert, and Mahler; and his friends in the *Couleur*, a liberal students' association. If she only respected, rather than shared, his knowledge and his own contributions to chemistry and engineering, if she did not join him in climbing the Dachstein but only the less demanding Alpine peaks, she did follow him to the fourth row of the gallery at the *Hofoper* and to the ladies' evenings of the *Suevia* student corps.

My father, Hugo Spiel, must be imagined as a sturdy man of medium height, resolute in his features, with two deep scars from youthful duels to the left of his chin. He was capable of unspeakably tender emotion towards people, animals, and music, but also of sudden attacks of rage and, if perhaps it was a case of protecting a woman from a lout, of sheer violence. Before my birth, he had fought a duel with pistols. On his honeymoon, he all but drowned before my mother's eyes in a whirlpool in the Danube. In his mountain walks, he constantly left the prescribed paths and made hazardous detours, all but plunging to his death. He was a member of a student corps and later wore the uniform of an imperial-royal reserve officer as if it were a second skin; at the same time, he was a thinker, a researcher and inventor, who spent days and nights over his experiments and analyses of them, and recorded them in his tiny, neat handwriting – a man full of thirst for knowledge but equally a man of action, no less aware of his physical than of his intellectual potential. His *Schmisse*, or dueling scars, which at first sight gave him the appearance of a swashbuckler, were later to preserve him from undeserved disgrace.

At the time when some Viennese began to be distinguished from other Viennese, Hugo Spiel was one of those who suffered from the disgrace of their origin. How it came about that such a man such emerged from his ancestry is indeed not easy to explain – for one thing, because so little is known about it. He and his sister Leonie were certainly not related to a Georg Heinrich Gerhard Spiel, who published a National Archive of the Kingdom of Hanover in 1819, nor to the families of the few existing bearers of this name in his native city, who included advertising consultants and police officers but also physicians and eminent psychologists.

Three photographs from the possessions of my aunt Leonie or Lonny, pronounced Loni, provide some sparse information. One, taken in Vienna in 1897, shows an elegant gentleman in a fur coat for city wear, and top hat, with a fair or greying moustache: my great-grandfather Spiel, then aged sixty-three. A second photograph, taken in September 1916 at the Hallstätter See, shows his son, my grandfather Jacques, beside his wife Laura and his daughter Lonny in a full-length dirndl in front of a backdrop of the little village. Two months before his death, his roundish face with the dark moustache has a composed expression; in his hand he holds the stub of a Virginia cigar; the checked cap, worn with his town suit, emphasizes the country holiday setting.

That is all. Where did they come from, the Spiels, on what was their middle-class existence founded? I do not know. My grandfather Jacques imported lace and other accessories from Paris and often traveled there; this much is certain. Hence, probably, the French form of his first name, which is given as Jakob on my baptismal certificate. Presumably this branch of the family had been resident in Vienna for some considerable time. Grandmother Laura alone came from the East, although it is no longer possible to establish where. My father, who was unwilling to confirm this fact, nevertheless sometimes told stories of riding in coaches and on horseback as a little boy on the estate of his maternal grandfather. The family had clearly been well-to-do, living on their own land. When I read the memoirs of Salka Viertel, in which she described her childhood as the daughter of the great landowner of Wychylowka in Galicia, I was reminded of my father's recollections, few and hesitantly conveyed.

The family in the East was called Birnbaum, a name which sounds better in its Sephardic form, Pereira. Did they emigrate there from Portugal in the dark and distant past? The answer lies in the depths of oblivion. A third, yellowing photograph conjures up my grandmother's brother, Heinrich, about whom only three facts are preserved: he was a doctor of medicine, he was homosexual, he took his own life. In the picture, he is seated in a café, with a cheerful expression, reading the newspaper. None of the distinguishing features supposedly found in people of his origin are to be discovered in him either: he could be a department head in the Ministry of Transport, reading a report on the opening of a new railway line in the crownland of Croatia.

No one in my family, of those I am able to remember, was outwardly religious. As a child, I was unaware that my faith was not that of my forebears. My father, perhaps in his student days, had become a Catholic. In this, he was unquestioningly followed by my mother, both of whose uncles had already converted to Catholicism. They were married in church – only a few months, there is no denying it, before I was born. "His Eminence," as head of the maternal clan, was against the union of his twenty-year-old niece with the recently qualified doctor of chemistry and technical sciences, who also appeared to have seduced her. When it became clear that this was the case, they were married.

I grew up with the other children at the Heiligenstadt primary school following the Christian festivals and went to see the manger scene in the church at Christmas, celebrated my first communion, attended May devotions in honor of the Blessed Virgin, took part in the Corpus Christi processions. There was only one thing I did not understand. When I went for walks in the inner city with my grandmother Laura, it seemed to disturb her that I made the sign of the cross when passing one of the many churches. Was this necessary? she asked me once. Yes, certainly, why not? And she left it at that.

Student identity card, 10 November 1932

2

School of Sensibility

At the Tivoli amusement park in Copenhagen, masked figures, their faces painted white, were capering on the little stage: a Columbine, a Pantaloon, a Harlequin, performing something I could not understand. I felt uneasy. I was seven or eight, and sitting beside my fostermother, the Danish colonel's lady, of whose language I already had some command, but who also liked to talk to me in a very Nordic *Hochdeutsch*. Two children, hardly older than me, were crouching on the bench in front of me, whispering together in an idiom which was familiar to me, yet I could not tell what they were saying. Suddenly a shudder ran down my back, as I realized they were speaking in Viennese dialect, like my school friends in Heiligenstadt. But I no longer belonged to them; I could express myself in Danish and Frisian, but the elemental sounds of my people were foreign to me.

A premonition of future terror – and for me, who was later to go into voluntary exile, perhaps worse than that. I have never forgotten that moment, although, once I returned, I was instantly at home again with the accents of the Vienna suburbs. I had gone to Denmark with the help of a "Campaign for Officers' Children," and that was why I had not been sent like other young charges to farmers in the country, with their milch-cows and chicken runs, but to a military family in the capital, to the retired Colonel Lundsteen and his wife Agnes, Willemoesgade 23, Entrance II. They were an elderly couple, full of kindness, whose adult sons and daughters sometimes looked after me; yet I was alone, alone with this tall, grey-haired, distinguished-looking, and rather taciturn pair, who gave me *rote Grütze* – red fruit pudding – to eat, taught me to make my own cocoa in the evening, lavished care and attention on me, but could give me only help, not the love I had received to such a generous degree from my young parents.

During the Second World War, London children were removed

from the capital for longer or shorter periods, some by sea to America, others to quieter areas in their own country. It has been said that many of them were left permanently damaged by the experience. After our apartment was bombed, we entrusted our own four-year-old daughter to a teacher's family with several other children, living in Cambridge. She stayed there for six months, during which I, also temporarily in the area because a second child was on the way, often visited her or took her to stay with me. Nevertheless, she believes that this is why she still suffers today from anxiety about separation, from timidity among strangers, from fear of groups with which she is not associated. In a similar situation I fared better: I seem to have accepted stoically that for a short time, which I had been promised would be a limited one, my world would be a different one.

During this winter of 1919-1920, I was taken to friends of the Lundsteens, in beautiful wood-paneled houses, where fires blazed from the hearth and we were served quantities of fish and seafood. One day we visited a childless couple in Charlottenlund, in whose rooms dolls were seated everywhere on chairs and sofas. Some were as large as babies, others were little girls my age; their porcelain heads had cheeks lightly touched with pink, eyes that opened and closed, little mouths all half open as if they were about to speak. My fosterfather, the Colonel, jokingly put his cigar-stub between the lips of one of the dolls. Their friends were horrified. We were just about to make a hasty departure, then someone changed the subject.

At the carnival I was given a costume to put on and allowed to go down to the street, where children and grownups in masks were milling about in confusion. This too was terrifying; but it left no "spots on the mirror of my soul," as Marie Bashkirtseff called it, but simply stayed in my memory, as little else has done from this half-year in Denmark. My strongest memory of this time is of the Colonel's elderly mother, to whom I grew much closer than to her son or daughter-in-law. She must have been a cultured old lady. On her shelves were books in many languages, German ones too, all the books of Hanns Heinz Ewers, *Alraune, Die Gred*; I skimmed through them and remembered their titles. The old lady venerated Napoleon, and her passion communicated itself to me. I used to stand for a long time gazing at his miniature in an oval frame, a watercolor that showed him still in the blue uniform of the *petit caporal*, whitefaced, with thick dark hair. I too adored him. This incredible feeling made my farewell to Copenhagen hard for me and accompanied me for a long time on the journey home.

There was still famine in Vienna. Though not as chubby as the *Wienerbørn* who had been fattened up on the rich Danish meadows, I came back refreshed and rested. This did not last. And my first experience was one of bitter sorrow. Vera, our beloved bitch, had been stolen. Our maid Lisi whispered to me that people were stealing animals for food, a totally unbearable idea, which lingered for many weeks. Then my father went to a local dog breeder and bought a little German shepherd called "Diemo von der Wildgrube"; we were to keep him until he died in his fifteenth year. My father had found work with the group for "property demobilization," an institution which for an indefinite period of time had the task of disposing in various ways of army surplus equipment. The scientific magazine he had edited before joining up, which promised to keep his job for him, had long ago ceased publication.

I had not yet been cast out of the paradise of the Probusgasse. But the day came when, as we refused to leave of our own accord, the landlord had us evicted. Lisi piled our goods and chattels onto wheelbarrows and prepared to move them to the third district. I was taken for a while to the gigantic apartment in the Wollzeile, where Grandmama Laura, Aunt Lonny, and the faithful Anna Peterka, who once cradled my father on her knees, had stayed behind. Two of the many rooms had been rented. In the bay-windowed, hall-like room from which I had watched the funeral of Emperor Franz Joseph, I was allowed to sleep on a chaise longue under a shelf containing ornamental porcelain figures; nobody had any inkling of my fear that they might fall. The two ladies sat in the bay window netting and embroidering, ringing for Anna when a glass of water was wanted. I sat crouched on the Persian carpet, half under the piano, leafing through the great grey volumes of Viennese songs and dances that Eduard Kremser had begun to publish in the year of my birth. Soon I was able to sing the songs, for Aunt Lonny accompanied me on the piano when I asked her.

Our move to the fourth floor of Stanislausgasse 2 marked the end of my childhood. One hurdle remained for me to overcome, small bundle of nerves as I was at the time, growing up without siblings. On

28

a train journey one summer day between Hallstatt and St Gilgen, where we were visiting friends, a piece of food went down the wrong way and I succumbed to a swallowing phobia which lasted over half a year. Treatment for a nervous disorder was tried; a professor of speech therapy gave me electric shocks. Nothing helped. I would and could swallow only mushy foods. In the end, I was sent to the Pirquet children's clinic. Losing myself in the crowd of small patients, I began to share postwar food with them: rice with potato salad. Cured, I returned to the Stanislausgasse, and on the balcony, to celebrate my recovery, I consumed a frankfurter sausage just like the one I had thought was going to choke me.

Adulthood had not yet begun, only an uncertain state of transition. Young as I was, I was caught up in the deceptive momentum of these postwar years. My parents, like the "new people" they aspired to become, threw themselves into the *Anbruch*, the new dawn, the awakening into a better, a republican, a democratic age. A fortnightly periodical was actually called *Musikblätter des Anbruch*; it introduced the atonal, not yet twelve-tone, composers. My father joined the newly founded Society of the Intellectually Active. He befriended the artists and bohemians of the Café Museum and Café Pochhacker, and in particular, the impressive cabaret performer, caricaturist, theater designer and collector of historic weapons Carl Hollitzer, a member of the circle of the recently deceased Peter Altenberg. Hollitzer used to sing with his powerful voice in the Reissbar: *"Ich bin der arme Konrad, nun komm ich mit dem Spiess* [I am poor Konrad, here I come with my spear.]" Among the artists we frequented were Merkel, Harta, Jungnickel, Carry Hauser. We bought a tiger's head from Jungnickel – where on earth did we get the money? From Carry Hauser, my father bought a charming, slightly cubist Madonna, with frost-blue fingertips. The picture hung over my bed in the white-lacquered nursery until, at nearly twenty-five years of age, I felt able to abandon this close connection with my parents.

In the evenings, they went to fancy-dress parties and masked balls. Inflation had set in, millionaires seemed to spring up out of the ground and banks went bankrupt, no one had any money any more, many had no work, and yet in Vienna people danced the nights away, and the less certain they were of being able to buy next day's dinner, the more wildly they danced. My father had set up a laboratory in the attic at the Stanislausgasse, where he conducted experiments of various kinds. Soon he founded a little "electrosynthesis" company in order to evaluate his inventions. However, because he still had to work and support us, he became a junior partner in a chemical firm. A folding artillery telescope had been left over from the "property demobilization"; later I was to use it for a particular purpose from the high balcony of our apartment. My mother, like all the ladies of her acquaintance, used to stroll up and down every morning between Sirkecke and St. Stephen's Cathedral, on the lefthand side of the street – the right-hand side was reserved for the stunningly beautiful *cocottes*. In the afternoons she played bridge. My father's earnings were never sufficient. But at *Fasching*, the carnival season, we joined in all the festivities.

According to custom, we all went to the carnival together, but married couples immediately split up and spent the night of the ball with strangers. The war had loosened up middle-class behavior; one owed it to oneself to appear desirable to strangers, to go to the limit in the close embrace of the tango, though usually no further. The day after a masked ball, Mimi received a bouquet whose splendor and size eclipsed any other flowers ever placed in our shimmering vases. A Herr von Doderer, a dancing partner of my mother's the night before, had had them delivered by messenger. My mother was endlessly teased about the odd name of her beau. The following summer, my mother and I visited the Döbling open-air baths. We were reclining in the meadow when an angular young man in swimming trunks came up to Mimi and bowed ceremoniously. She was embarrassed to meet him again in bright sunlight, and even more so to introduce him to her twelve-year-old daughter, who had not inherited her own slender beauty and, moreover, whose existence cast doubt on her own youthfulness. My first meeting with the author Heimito von Doderer did not rise in my memory from the depths of the past until some three decades later.

As I have said, my mother's nature was lighthearted. Every morning a hairdresser called – her name, reminiscent of the characters of Nestroy's comedies, was Umlauf – "Runaround"; she visited all the ladies in turn to curl their hair with tongs. Maids of all work, Lisi, and later Marie, who stayed until we left Austria, looked after the whole household. Nevertheless, by postwar standards we were poor. At the end of every month Marie would leave little misspelt notes on my father's desk reading "bite um den lohn" ("please may I have my wages"). As was customary in Italianate Vienna, Mimi had a *cicisbeo* or gentleman friend, whose name, as it happened, was Otto Umlauft. He was the son of a famous geographer, cartographer, and astronomer, whose atlases we used at school. "Uncle Otto" was a tall, leonine, very handsome man, a decisive figure of my childhood and youth, and the head of the house of Rikola, which published modern literature in those first postwar years. Apart from the classics and my father's favorite writers, beside Heinrich Mann's *Der Untertan* and Romain Rolland's *Maître Breugnon*, the smoking-room bookshelves contained the works of Leo Perutz, Otto Soyka, and Robert Müller, but also those of Joris-Karl Huysmans and Joséphin Péladan. I read them all at the earliest opportunity.

At secondary school – for the time being the school founded by the *Frauenerwerbverein* (Viennese Women's Employment Association) – I had a number of friends, but soon had to suffer a new experience of rejection. Stella Werner, dainty and delicate, shared my first literary pleasures. She was there when a slightly deformed boy of our age recited the whole of Rilke's *Cornet* (*Die Weise vom Leben und Tod des Cornetts Christoph Rilke*) to a small group of precocious children in a basement room. And with her, I read the whole of Schnitzler's *Reigen* (*La Ronde*), dividing up the roles, over the telephone (my number was U12033, but I have forgotten hers); it took nearly an hour, but cost no more than a short conversation. Our parents were out, and it was thus that endless dialogues could take place. But all this came to an end one day. Another schoolfriend invited me to a birthday party. She lived in a small *Palais*, or mansion, in the exclusive district of Wieden, unspeakable luxury! Uncle Otto collected me, and, with all the scorn of the intellectual, said to my parents when we got home: "The child has been at the house of *Schieber* [black-marketeers or crooks]." I innocently repeated this at school next day and was ostracized by the whole class. My diary, hidden in the drawer of my desk, was dragged out and read aloud: anger, pain and profound shame.

Not till the following year did I have a new friend: Eveline, daughter of the big industrialist and patron of the arts Carl Ritter von Taussig, whose wife died young and whose mistress, as was well known to the twelve-year-old, was the magnificent Betty Fischer: she was once the young Emperor Karl's mentor in love and now ruled as prima donna at the Theater an der Wien. From my great-uncle Leo's box I saw her there in all the operettas of the "age of silver." It was with Eveline, a slim, blonde, very pale-skinned girl, that I now shared my newly awakened fondness for the theater. She was strictly brought up and allowed to attend a play only in the company of an adult. I was allowed to go alone to the Burgtheater, the Deutsches Volkstheater, the Theater in der Josefstadt, theaters with standing room at the back. Max Reinhardt had just taken over the direction of the last-named theater and was presenting *The Merchant of Venice* with all of the well-known Thimig acting family. For the first time since seeing Napoleon in Copenhagen, I was gripped by a strange feeling when Rudolf Forster's Antonio bared his white chest and challenged Shylock to take his pound of flesh.

At the Burgtheater there were still great names from the prewar era: Reimers, Zeska, Devrient, Bleibtreu, as well as the nasal-voiced young hero Raoul Aslan, and Else Wohlgemuth, beautiful beyond all measure. There was uplifting German drama, but also Raimund, the creator of naive fairytale delights. But my first great passion was kindled in the Deutsches Volkstheater by Alexander Moissi, who often gave guest performances in Vienna. He was considered the successor to Josef Kainz, whose death my mother, already engaged to be married, mourned in September 1910 in words of sentimental sorrow: "sun and steel were in your eyes. It seems unimaginable that you are no more, your art was carved deep into my heart" – words that I read now, written in faint pencil on a sheet of paper that she kept for the rest of her life.

It was Moissi's name that was carved into my heart. Of Albanian-Italian ancestry, a lyric and heroic tenor of the dramatic stage such as one can hardly hear today, he was our Hamlet, our Oswald in *Ghosts*, our Gottwald in Gerhart Hauptmann's *Hanneles Himmelfahrt*, the heartrending Montezuma in Hauptmann's *Der weisse Heiland*, Shaw's Dubedat, Philipp in Richard Beer-Hofmann's *Graf von Charolais* and those great Tolstoy figures, Fedya in *The Living Corpse* and the wandering lad in *It Is All His Fault*. He took us into a seventh heaven with Goethe's "Mailied," and into a state of profound melancholy with Verhaeren's "Novemberwind," translated by Stefan Zweig. Klabund (Alfred Henschke) called him "the most bewitching

Singspieler of the German language." People fell hopelessly under his spell.

Moissi touched the nerve of the time, the torn, the social and human suffering, the Russian in us all at that time in Vienna. He was a friend of Tolstoy's daughter and granddaughter and often visited Yasnaya Polyana, first in Tsarist Russia and later in the Soviet state. The fate of the humiliated and injured was brought home to us too by the expatriate Russian Jushny's little traveling company "Der blaue Vogel," which appeared twice a year at the Volkstheater. Unforgettable was the scene called *Der Leiermann*, with an organ grinder and two emaciated figures, one of them a shivering girl of our own age. It was only through the medium of the stage that we became aware of the existence of war invalids, of the unemployed, of the starved beggars on every corner, and learned to feel pity for them.

During those years we were subject to violent contradictions, to shattering, banal, and ridiculous sensations, as if plunged alternately into hot and cold water. A multiplicity of worlds opened up to us. At ballet school, not yet ten years old, we were trained in the first positions and in tripping along on pointe. Later we were encouraged to perform expressive dances, as still carried out gently and gracefully by the Wiesenthal sisters, and in the style of Maenads by their successors Gertrud Bodenwieser and Gertrud Kraus. We were expected to perform ecstatic movements, for which we still lacked the inner motivation. At the ice-skating club near the Konzerthaus, however, we floated along with a certain grace, whenever we managed to complete a figure eight without deviating from our path. The glittering expanse, the arc lamps, the black firmament above us gave us the feeling of taking part in a spectacle, supernumeraries in a pantomime or a ballet like the *Puppenfee*. Two divinely beautiful sisters and their even more beautiful mother, all blonde and dressed entirely in white, with the appropriate name of Engel, seemed to me the main characters in this shimmering pageant which continually circled around me on ice skates and in which the audience were at the same time the performers.

In autumn or in early spring the city breathed out a melancholy which took hold, not of adolescents only, but of these most powerfully. In the little grey streets, the leafless parks, even more in the great deserted squares in front of mansions now uninhabited, except perhaps for a shivering bureaucracy, we sensed the isolation, the impoverishment of the former imperial capital. Summer weeks in the country, by Carinthian lakes or in the Salzkammergut, lifted our spirits. Quite early on, in Hallstatt, I had written my first poem about the morning sun, the twitter of birds, the church bells. Now, at the house of the teacher Grossl on the edge of the village of Pörtschach, where I was sent to stay year after year while my mother was at the bathing beach of the fashionable Hotel Werzer and my father was climbing with his dog in the Lienz Dolomites, I lay for many hours reading and dreaming on the hot tarpaper roof of the Grossls' boathouse, thinking of names I might assume when I was famous: Hilla Spila, Hille Syla. Teacher Grossl played on the out-of-tune piano: "*Servus du, flüstert sie ganz leise.*" And another boarder, a young customs officer from Gera in Thuringia, gave me my first kiss, on the cheek. My second, the following summer, when I was thirteen, was given me by a man of such exceptional beauty that I never forgot him: the Yugoslav consulate official from whom I was collecting a visa for a journey to Bled with my grandmother, and who was inspired to this gesture by my admiring gaze.

The dark and the bright had the same effect on my nature. Once we interrupted our holidays in our own country and traveled to Italy. In Viareggio we stayed in a pension two streets away from the sea. And yet, that endless blue, at first perceived with fear by this child of the Alps, that blindingly white sand! The landlady had a little daughter, Fernanda, who incessantly tried to teach me the "r," rolled on the tip of the tongue, of her native language. "*Dí buona sera. Sera.*" At last I learned it and never lost it again. And then, late in the afternoon, a long black car drove slowly down the street. People ran to see, Fernanda dragged me outside. "*Il maestro!*" was the cry. It was Puccini. For a second I saw his vigorous, masculine profile, his high-combed black hair. One day in Venice on the way home was as intoxicating as it was exhausting. Fierce August heat, foul smells from all the canals, dripping clotheslines, my mother close to fainting, our feet sore from walking. And yet, what a backdrop! I expected to come across Antonio the merchant and Shylock at every point in this theatrical scenery.

In the following winter came a nocturnal experience which at first deeply disturbed my soul. I woke up to a full moon; snow lay on the roofs. Irresistibly drawn to the window, I believed I could see a human figure on the ridge of the roof opposite. Yes, it could not be otherwise. He lay half stretched out on the slate slope, seemed to move, perhaps towards the abyss below. A moonlight sleepwalker, for certain; I had read of such things. I opened the window, not daring to call to him, but unable to return to my bed, though I was shivering in my thin nightdress. This may have lasted an hour or more; in the end I must have collapsed drowsily to the floor. Next morning all became clear: it was a dark patch where the snow had melted, probably from the hot smoke of a chimney. All this was, if possible, only surpassed by the mortal terror a year later, when a small earthquake passed through Vienna and my father made two incredible pronouncements: "How wonderful it is when nature comes into the room," and "Now we must be prepared for the aftershock"; and then calmly went to bed, while I trembled all night long in expectation of the next tremor.

Three figures surface from my memory, spectral and grotesque, as if invented by the Austrian writer and artist Fritz von Herzmanovsky-Orlando. "The lady with the wasp-waist," who walked along the streets to the inner city at that time when the *garçonne* style was prevalent, was dressed in the long robes of the turn of the century, heavily rouged, with an extravagant coiffure. Her waist was so tightly laced that two hands could have spanned it – one could not imagine where her internal organs could find room, how the blood could circulate to her lower body. Unlike her, the old woman who suffered from elephantiasis was not to be met on the streets. She would sit on a park bench, almost completely filling it. Despite the monstrous circumference of her body and limbs, she was good-humored. How the slightly built husband beside her had brought her to this place and how he intended to take her away again were equally mysterious questions. And finally there was Countess Triangi, probably an aristocrat only by marriage, who appeared, absurdly costumed, as an unintentionally comic solo entertainer in cheap amusement halls. What an embarrassment for the family! They would no doubt have liked to change their renowned surname.

In Vienna, as in Venice, theatricality was always breaking in. And yet there were tensions between the feigned and the everyday reality. At the theater, I was emotionally shaken; at the Frauenerwerbverein secondary school, I was deeply bored by the teachers; at home, I was constantly confused by the variety of manifestations which my parents liked to adopt. My mother, who otherwise took little notice of me, nevertheless sat sternly at the piano with me for an hour every day to supervise my practicing. My father appeared particularly sensitive and introverted when he sat at the same piano in the evening to abandon himself to the prelude to the third act of *Tristan* or the "Illusion" monologue of Hans Sachs in the *Meistersinger*, but I could not quite take him seriously in his role as the "old gentleman" of the Suevia – all that talk about duels, about *Leibfüchse* and *Burschen*, about *quodlibet* or "miscellaneous" evenings of *Salamander reiben* – drinking general toasts involving an elaborate ritual; all the jingoistic Germanic romanticism which referred to the black-red-gold banners of the liberal uprising of 1848, and yet was more national than liberal – as I could only guess at that time.

At certain times, when they had been wounded in fencing duels and dared not go home, the *Leibfüchse* (junior members of the student fraternity) Grabner and Haas stayed with us for a few days. Recently, I read in a Viennese newspaper of the death of "Dipl. Ing. Otto Freiherr Haas von Hagenfels, *wirkl. Hofrat i. R.* [a title given to a retired civil servant]" and was reminded of how he helped me with my mathematics homework while his scars were healing. The imperious Uncle Otto, who, although an academic, did not belong to the fraternity, observed the infantile rituals of the physicians, lawyers, and architects among its members with noticeable irony.

I did not get very far in music, although I took part in a school concert organized by my teacher Moriz Lampel, who had once rapped my father's and Aunt Lonny's knuckles with his ruler. I was allowed to play a quartet with three other little girls, a Spohr polonaise. I had hardly mastered a Mozart sonata with some approach to perfection when it was found that the ceiling of our dilapidated apartment had to be supported for years to come on huge piles, and the piano had to go. In those years of ever-increasing struggle, my father would in any case have had little time for the intoxication of evenings at the piano. But he did try – broadcasting was then in its infancy – to call forth music from a lump of quartz with the help of a movable needle. This proved unrewarding, and we had no gramophone yet. There remained to me books and the stage. But anyone who reads a great deal will one day begin to write.

Still at the Frauenerwerbverein, I surprised the teacher of German language, whose name was Czerwenka, by my unconventional interpretation of her essay subjects. Once we were told to describe a famous genre painting by Carl Spitzweg. But the image of the long-nosed poet in his attic, holding an opened red umbrella over himself while sitting in bed because of the rain leaking through the roof, held little charm for me. Instead I thought up a few sketches, instant pictures which I ascribed to his imagination. One was called "A Castle in the Vendée"; the characters were people in rococo dress. This idea was unlikely to have occurred to Spitzweg's poet. Frau Professor Czerwenka said that, although my work had not followed the prescribed theme, I could read it out to the class. My classmates listened, for the most part baffled. This was perhaps the beginning, although I did not know it.

My love for Moissi led to a disaster which in the end proved a blessing. Not content with cheering for my hero at the stage door after every guest performance, I wanted to see him just once as he arrived at his villa at Dornbach. One morning, when his arrival from abroad was expected, Eveline and I stayed away from school; we made our way to the suburb and waited there for hours, but in vain. At home I was met by my father, ready to mete out judgment, but so gently and with such obvious amusement that I could not help laughing through my tears. The tears were for Eveline, since the Ritter von Taussig, informed that morning of our misdeed, had already telephoned my father in a rage, declaring that he would no longer tolerate my harmful association with his daughter. Then, before Eveline's eyes, he trampled underfoot all her Moissi gramophone records. For the sake of the Frauenerwerbverein's founder and patron, my parents were put under pressure to remove me from the school, and this was done.

I was not to lose Eveline forever. During the war I met her in London, in ATS uniform, which was very becoming to this tall, slim, silver-blonde young woman, and later occasionally with her husband, an English colonel whom I found more distinguished and at the same time less pretentious than her father. After that she disappeared from my life for years. I did not want to go to another school, but rather to the Academy for Dramatic Art. Not yet fifteen, gaunt, highly strung, and far from pretty, I stepped onto a platform to recite the monologues of Schiller's Joan of Arc and Hebbel's Klara. "On! On, my heart! Crush yourself so that not one more drop of blood can escape." It was pitiful. Rudolf Beer, the director of the Volkstheater and one of the examiners, called me down into the auditorium. "My dear child," he asked," what would you do if we did not accept you?" Instead of threatening suicide, I replied sheepishly: "Go on studying and perhaps go to university." "Quite right, go ahead," he replied, and sent me away. My relieved parents registered me at the school of Dr Eugenie Schwarzwald.

Crossing from Naples to Capri, 1936

3

Becoming a Person

Every November 12 at the Frauenerwerbverein school, we had
sung the national hymn of the republic: *"Deutsch-Österreich, du herrliches
Land, wir lieben dich* [German-Austria, you glorious country, we love
you.]" At Eugenie Schwarzwald's school in the Wallnerstrasse, in
rooms designed by Adolf Loos, we sang at every possible opportunity
a song which the "Fraudoktor" hoped would instill trust in the future
in her students:

> If hope is green, I have won half the battle,
> If joy is in blossom, victory is mine,
> If my luck has not run out altogether,
> Truly, I am content in my heart.
> Cares and worries I will drive away,
> whoever asks me, to him will I say:
> If hope is green –

and so on. Today it is usual to regard the First Republic as an ill-
starred organism, doomed from the start to founder before it achieved
its national identity. Our experience, over a long period of time, was
different. Since our elders did not mourn the monarchy, neither did
we. The loss of an empire did not trouble us, for then, in the twenties,
we believed we had exchanged it for Europe, indeed for the whole
world.

> Indians, Japanese and Eskimos,
> The world belongs to us all and the world is wide,
> Frontiers are for the old,
> Us they cannot hold,
> Freedom and friendship are our goals.

This too was taught at the Schwarzwald school. For us, the frontiers fell in the songs of the *Wandervögel*, the German ramblers' association, found in the *Zupfgeigenhansl* collection or the *Jugendrotkreuz*, whose colorful monthly magazines, often adorned with cheerful drawings by the *art nouveau* painter Franz Cizek, put us in touch with the children of all nations. After all, the worst years seemed to be over. This republican Austria was young and fresh to us now, not doomed by any means. Our fathers too, who not long before had gone to war out of loyalty to the Emperor, had meanwhile accepted the situation; they considered the poverty and unemployment which were still in evidence, the inflation which had only recently been conquered, as merely the birth pangs of the republic, and put their faith in the solidarity of other democratic countries, in the League of Nations, in the universal desire for peace and in European unity.

In 1926 Richard Coudenhove-Calergi called the first Paneuropa Congress in Vienna. We children sat in the circle of the Konzerthaus, believing every word the speakers uttered. I myself was in my last year at school, and on the national holiday in November, I was allowed to give the Republican Address in front of the whole school, in our own great, light-filled assembly hall. Even though I cannot now remember a single sentence of my speech, I certainly managed to come up with a declaration of faith in, and love for, this state system. This was a year after the burning of the Palace of Justice, a year after that fifteenth of July in 1927 when the republic, for the first time since its founding, was shaken by a bloody confrontation between the people of Vienna and the administration. The outraged workers, inflamed by the acquittal of some right-wing murderers, their numbers swollen by an uncontrollable mob, against the intentions of their more prudent leaders, attacked the seat of Austrian jurisdiction, and the chief of police had them gunned down by case shot. Eighty-nine people died, and hundreds more were injured.

Certainly we were naïve. Certainly we knew far too little about the continual tug-of-war between the two great groups in the land, the Socialist camp of Karl Renner, Otto Bauer, and Theodor Körner, and the Christian Social Party, which was headed by a prelate, Dr Ignaz Seipel. This Seipel, whom my great-uncle Gustav had brought back to health after the assassination attempt on him in June 1924, was federal chancellor of Austria. The capital was ruled by the "Reds," with Karl

Seitz, a man of great dignity, at their head as mayor of Vienna. We had no inkling of the daily petty political battles between ideologies and ideologues, of attempted and unsuccessful rapprochements, for whose final failure, according to individual interpretations of history, the blame is lodged by posterity with one party or the other.

On the upper floors of that house in the Wallnerstrasse, at the front of which, in the Herrengasse, was the Café Herrenhof, the haunt of the literati, we still moved for quite some time in a climate of purity, goodness, and humanity, a climate of the most beautiful illusions. The Fraudoktor, one of the most energetic persons of her age, would certainly have dismissed the illusory side of her character and her influence, and persisted in her evergreen hope. But the truth was that she could not be wholly aware of the signs of the times, otherwise, she would have been unable to carry out her philanthropic and pedagogical work. It was not until the moment of the *Anschluss* with Germany that she had to tear the blindfold from her eyes. In 1939 she wrote from Ascona to the writer Felix Braun in London, who had praised her past achievements: "What if ten thousand Viennese whose children's lives I have saved shout 'Heil Hitler!' as long as Felix Braun says 'Evoë Genia!' to me? It gives me courage for more work." Only in that passing phrase did she betray her bitterness. And she gave herself confidently. She died, of cancer and deadly disappointment, the following year.

In 1895, born in Polupanowka on the Russian frontier of the monarchy and brought up in Czernowitz, the Fraudoktor had wanted to take up German studies in the West. Women were not yet admitted to the university of the Austrian capital, so she went to Zurich and sat in the lecture theater as one of three women students among one hundred and fifty men. After obtaining her doctorate she opened her first educational establishment in Vienna – "girls were to learn everything there that men knew, while remaining sweet, modest, maidenly, housewifely," as she unrepentantly described it in retrospect decades later. Like most truly emancipated women, she had little time for feminists of the shriller variety. One of her classes included three famous men's future wives, who themselves became well known in their own right: Helene Weigel-Brecht, Alice Herdan-Zuckmayer and Elisabeth Neumann-Viertel. But her progressive school alone did not satisfy Genia Schwarzwald. During the First World War, she initiated an abundance of good works, a campaign to take children to the country, community kitchens, Friendship Aid, Aid to the Elderly. Her closest friends, social reformers like herself, were in Scandinavia – Karin Michaelis, Elsa Bjoerkman, Anna Lene Elgstrom - but she was in touch with people of good will all over the world.

The Fraudoktor also recognized artists of genius before anyone else had done so; she engaged Schönberg, Egon Wellesz, Adolf Loos, and the latter's protégé Kokoschka as teachers in her school and gathered important, or at least likable, people around herself in her city apartment and during the summers at various places in the Salzkammergut. To her students, even when they were no longer taught by her personally as I was, she was, despite her sometimes overpowering energy, a model of neighborly love and courage. What she possessed, what she preserved in herself in the face of the increasingly dark situation, was, in her own words, a "black optimism... a cheerfulness which one builds up with great effort, dragging the bricks along in tears; for the world will not deliver the materials to you."

I was becoming a person, then, at her school, where friendships which influence lives were being spun. For fear that I should become too learned, too eccentric, too much of a bluestocking, my parents sent me not to the *Gymnasium*, but to the parallel *Frauen-Oberschule*. Here, apart from the usual educational subjects and modern languages, I also learned cookery, needlework, and child care. And as I had voluntarily been studying Latin for the last few years, my *Matura* (the Austrian school-leaving examination) qualified me for university entrance. Meanwhile I made friends with two girls who, while they did not further my precocious intellectualism, in their quite different ways did help me to become aware of my physical being.

Maria, a charming, boyish creature, was already at fifteen a budding swimming champion and later a record-breaking athlete. I went with her to the Dianabad, an open-air pool where one could not only swim but also watch swimming competitions and games of water-polo. Two members of the Jewish sports club Hakoah turned up there one day, sturdy young fellows called Fritz Thorn and Fritz Kantor, one of whom was to become my lifelong friend, the other my lifelong enemy. As water-polo players they battled valiantly against swimming clubs such as Vienna, WAC, and Danubia, but most vehemently against the reputedly Nazi club EWASC. Conceded superiority, at best, in coffee-house debates, they were also keen to demonstrate their equality in sport. Even so, both these young men were just as happy in a few years' time to sit at the marble tables of the Café Herrenhof as to disport themselves in the swimming-pool. The one who became my friend accompanied us on our Sunday skiing expeditions.

It was to Maria that I owed not only the athletic activities we undertook together, but my own impulse to become involved in them. At the Austria swimming club – not Maria's club – I won a minor competition, a triumph on the same level as the perfectly played Mozart sonata. Soon I was drifting down the middle of the Danube, where it is at its deepest and calmest, from Zeiselmauer down to Kritzendorf, with other companions, our clothes fastened to our arms in rubber bags. In winter we got up early to catch the first train at five o'clock on the Aspangbahn railway to reach the skiing districts around the Semmering. We climbed up the Stuhleck for two hours, our skis on our shoulders, often through snowstorms, to make the descent from the Bettelbauer. Skiers today, conveyed to the heights eight times a day by ski lift to race down the swarming pistes, know nothing of the glories of traversing deserted snow-covered forests, of the challenge of narrow defiles winding steeply down to the valley.

I have already used the word "beautiful" too often; I have applied it to my mother, to the actress Wohlgemuth, to the ice-skating Engel sisters. I cannot help it, I must use the same word for Hansi Mahler: she was beautiful. When I based a character on her, outwardly hardly changed, in one of my novels decades later, a leading critic made fun of the adjectives, "enchanting and lascivious," that I applied to her, of her "square, jeweled monocle," her room, with its "odor of scent, stale smoke, faded flowers, and slept-in sheets." How he would have mocked if I had described her as a young girl, as eccentric, as corrupt, as stylistically mannerist as could have been demanded, among other things, by the *Zeitgeist* of Vienna in the 1920s. Even then she had her monocle, though not the jeweled frame. A face of regular features, deep blue, somewhat short-sighted eyes, her black hair cut in an Eton crop. Outrageously unconventional clothes, designed by her less pretty sister Grete. At fifteen Hansi was already sleeping around, something the rest of us did not do until much later. Her luxurious room in her parents' apartment – her father, an elderly lawyer, was a consultant and representative of the world of the operetta – was frequented by several concurrent lovers; one was a Monsignor of the rank of count, related to the royal family.

Sometimes Hansi affected lesbianism, called herself Hans and boasted of having seduced the pretty chambermaid of the house. She did not even spare her younger brother Fritz, who committed suicide at seventeen. No one – including myself – was immune to her erotic aura. Her life was played out almost exclusively indoors, among soft cushions, dimmed lights, little tables on which stood cocktail glasses. Her foolish mother, completely besotted with this precocious schoolgirl, would serve up her favorite dessert, banana slices in cherry brandy, to her and her girlfriends. A greater contrast to our classmate Maria could not be imagined. And yet their circles touched even outside school, for life in Vienna was and is interlinked in the most curious way, in a kind of intellectual and social incest.

On April 2, 1927, at three in the afternoon, I went to the Theater an der Wien with Hansi to attend a student production of the Bundesrealgymnasium. The program consisted of four playlets: two by Georges Courteline, one by Averchenko, and the last a one-act piece by Egon Friedell and Alfred Polgar, *Goethe*, in which the old prince of poets is shown as knowing much less of his own life than a professor of German literature and taking a student's place in an examination, causing him to fail. The third play, after the intermission, was Courteline's *Der gemütliche Kommissär* in the version by Bernard Shaw's translator Siegfried Trebitsch. An overgrown boy in a cycling cape came on stage and began to speak. The self-confidence of the sixteen-year-old was breathtaking. The program told us that the role of Monsieur Floche was played by the schoolboy Hans Békessy.

We made his acquaintance. Soon he became Hansi's lover, and the following year he was my comparatively platonic friend (the term *demi-vierge* was characteristic of the time). I have never been able to understand what induced this youngster – to many an arrogant brat, to others, surprisingly, a grown man – to renounce my beautiful friend and turn to me. I had begun to get myself up a little more fashionably and had a few admirers, but in Hansi's circle my role was that of a colorless, subservient lady's maid. That early spring when I played her false – for without her knowledge her Hans, sometimes gently mocked, but always her jealously defended property, had become mine – that spring was the first for me without melancholy, the first that was full of happiness.

Can anyone who reads this take seriously the experiences of two semi-children of sixteen and seventeen? They call it puppy love, but never again have I felt what I was capable of feeling then. We walked in the Vienna woods, the ice was breaking up, liverwort grew in the damp grass. Everything was a beginning, everything was poetry. Hans too, apparently so hardened, was swept along by my uncompromising devotion. Hans Békessy, called Jáncsi by his mother, in those days already possessed that smooth charm which was later to become unctuous. He had long gangling limbs, slightly protruding eyes and ears; the latter were eventually corrected, if too late for me. I will not say that I was as blind to his flaws as Titania was to those of the transformed Bottom. I saw the flaws but was unaffected by them.

The year before, Hans's father had been driven out of Vienna with the help of Karl Kraus and thereafter worked to clear his name in Budapest, by means of a periodical called *Békessys Panoptikum*. Only one issue appeared, in April 1928, with contributions from Franz Blei, Anton Kuh, Robert Müller, and others. Hans knew very well that Emmerich Békessy had been as artful a journalist as he was an unscrupulous blackmailer in velvet gloves, but he stood by him and wrote a *Matura* thesis on Heine in which he poured scorn on Kraus, but which was read by no one but his teachers. He took me to hear an extempore speech by Anton Kuh, a new version of the talk on "Zarathustra's Ape" which Kuh had first given in 1925. Again, supporters of Kraus sat in the Mozartsaal of the Konzerthaus, loudly heckling Kuh's brilliant improvisation.

Emmerich Békessy had courted Vienna's high society and then denounced it, or not, according to whether he was paid for his silence. His son, while still at school, was a confirmed or at least a presumed Communist. On that November 12 in 1928, when I was giving the Republican Address in the hall designed by Loos, he was doing the same for a workers' group, which was willing to receive instruction from the young gentleman who was so well informed about Marx and Engels. And yet he often took a taxi to school from the apartment he shared with relatives in Dornbach – Moissi's district. And he sometimes slipped into the role of a Schnitzler figure, for example when he hired a *Fiaker*, a hackney coach, at Baden near Vienna and had us driven to the Helenental, just like a latter-day Anatol with his still unconquered mistress. Five years later, before I went to England, I met him wearing the uniform of the *Heimwehr* (the right-wing militia), a feather in his hat; at that time, he was head of the Austrian Fascist state press office's photographic department. A bundle of contradictions, yet in his early days he was no cynic, but was touched by idealism, perhaps even a poet. His first novella, *Rache der Scham* (*The Revenge of Shame*), written under the pseudonym Hans Habe (by which he later became known) and presumably never published, was a conscientious attempt at psychological inquiry into an apparently inexplicable crime.

The year of my seventeenth birthday, which fell in October, was a decisive one, a year of rapid maturing. Soon, invited by my favorite among the two water-polo players, I began occasionally to visit that Café Herrenhof around the corner in the Herrengasse, in the same building as the Schwarzwaldschule. There, at the tables, or in the *Loge*, as the circular seating along the walls of the great hall of the coffee house was called, we sat with the clever and witty Ernst Polak from Prague, who had been divorced from Kafka's Milena three years earlier. As the result of a misjudgment by Margarete Buber-Neumann, posterity was to be unjust to this man, an industrious banker and late student of Schlick. Other figures in this group included Ernst Stern, another tame philosopher, as well as draftsman and wrestler, a powerful young man who liked to draw complicated arabesques on the marble tabletop and called them "Art, or The Beautiful"; his lover, Susi Joachim, a delightful dancer; and the satirical poet Peter Hammerschlag, a respectable doctor's son, who exacted a tribute of one schilling out of my sparse pocket-money of five schillings a week; not to mention the celebrities who sometimes turned up in the *Loge*.

The other water-polo player, Fritz Kantor, was meanwhile commuting between Prague and Vienna. Soon his first novel, *Der Schüler Gerber hat absolviert*, was to be published under the pen name Friedrich Torberg. There was as yet no conflict between us, for I was a nobody, younger than he, still at school, modestly silent most of the time, but he was already holding forth at Polak's table. Over the next few years we saw each other, sometimes daily, at the coffee-house, went to see films together, and were friends in a careful, vigilant, and

– apart from a single incident on New Year's Eve – dispassionate manner. We never used the more intimate *du* to each other. And when my first book was published by the same firm, and soon received the same literary prize as his, our lifelong war began. "Ritze ratze, voller Tücke/ für die Kati auf der Brücke" ("Scritch-scratch, full of tricks/ for Kati on the bridge") was his dedication to me of his second book in February 1933.

I have been jumping ahead. I was still in the top class of the less distinguished of the two Schwarzwald schools – sometimes at the stove, cooking according to a prescribed diet, sometimes sewing hats or blouses, sometimes in the roof garden looking after the little ones on Montessori principles, while the proud *Gymnasium* girls, copies of Ovid under their arms, smiled pityingly at us. Our tuition in the sciences, in mathematics and languages, was, to be sure, equally excellent – how could it not be so, under the direction of the Fraudoktor? She herself was no longer teaching. Shy of seeking her particular attention, I did not visit her during her consultation hours. I was completely absorbed in my private realm, my flirtations, male and female friends, sport and books, and had only marginal knowledge of the Vienna salon of the Schwarzwalds or their summer guesthouse on the Grundlsee. I was not one of her circle of privileged "children."

Yet she was among us daily, if only to receive petitioners from all strata of the establishment in her office during the late morning, like the Marschallin at her levee in the *Rosenkavalier*. One room at the Wallnerstrasse was occasionally occupied by the young Count Helmuth James von Moltke, one of the many in her circle who were of a humanistic way of thinking. On one occasion, she wandered through all the classrooms in the middle of lessons, followed by the radiantly handsome Moltke, who carried a tray of bonbon glasses, presenting each schoolgirl with a chocolate. This little interlude was received by us, as well as by our teachers, in the intended spirit: as a sign that no activity could be so serious that it could not profitably be interrupted by a moment of light-heartedness. The young German good-naturedly joined in the fun. And yet the memory of this harmless little scene is now heartrending. For Helmuth von Moltke, head of the Kreisauer Kreis, the resistance group of army officers against Hitler, was executed in January 1945, and nothing, nothing could ease the pain of this death and of the year of torment that preceded it.

She was an early role model, this Genia Schwarzwald, even from a distance, with all the little tricks and vanities that even the noblest benefactors are prone to. Shortly after I left school, I was summoned to see her, because the political commentator and editor of the *Neue Freie Presse*, Emil Kläger, was looking for a school leaver to take part in an unscripted radio talk on young people's problems. My teachers had recommended me to her. The Fraudoktor let me in, failed to recognize me, and hastily went into the anteroom to find out my name from her faithful assistant. Then she returned, gave me a hug and spoke to me as if we had always been close friends. The radio program was broadcast and attracted a good deal of attention because Kläger refused to reveal the identity of the "unknown eighteen-year-old." But all this belongs to another life. My leaving school was not the turning-point; that came a year earlier, a year after that joyous early spring. It was the break with Habe which plunged me from all the heavens of blind faith, a wound to my soul that would never heal, although its author soon became demythologized and unimportant.

My beautiful friend Hansi, taking a belated revenge, drove my susceptible seducer into the arms of a little serpent of the salons, a niece of the singer Mimi Kött. But I myself gave him his marching orders at the first sign of infidelity. Perhaps this was rash, but I was more concerned about losing my self-respect than my lover – a pattern which throughout my life has proved to be the right one. Nevertheless, I have no idea how I got through the next few months. During the summer, as a guest of Maria's parents in the country, in a beautiful, spacious baroque mansion, furnished in palatial style, I cried myself to sleep every night over young Békessy's love letters, which were spirited in style and manifested noticeable literary pretensions. It was probably not for him but for my own squandered emotions that I mourned. At that time we were all reading, as well as Gide, Cocteau, Giono, the fashionable French poet Paul Géraldy. His volume *Toi et moi* included a poem which seemed to affect us all. We were not, it said, in love with another person but with love itself. We believed it while not wanting to believe it.

I wallowed in my pain, but this too was overcome by literary means. For the moment, I had to concentrate on my *Matura* thesis for my revered German teacher Alfred Nathansky. It was on "Die Jugendgestalten Wassermanns" – "the youthful characters of Jakob Wassermann." Today it still seems to me not a bad piece of work. Later I sold the manuscript to a student in Bialystok, who gained her doctorate with its help. And if in these memoirs, as far as possible, I do not mention my published works, let alone enter into a discussion of them, I may at least mention my forgotten children that never saw the light of day. It seemed out of the question that I should pass my *Matura* with distinction, since my intelligence did not stretch to mastering higher mathematics. Then the prosperous father of another school friend, a cousin of the humorous writer Roda Roda, paid for his daughter Maydie to be coached in mathematics, and I was allowed to attend these lessons. Our tutor was a Communist of noble birth called Paqueni, a tall, ugly, awkward young man who immediately conceived a violent passion for me. He spent his hard-earned cash on presents for me – a camera, a gramophone – which I dared not refuse when he threatened suicide. This went on for some time. For some reason, we never called him anything but "The Man."

Meanwhile, my friendship with the second water-polo player intensified – Fritz Thorn, who in later years used the byline f.th. for his newspaper articles on the arts. He started his career as a color chemist and graphic artist. After I had successfully passed the *Matura*, thanks to the efforts of "The Man," I began my studies at Vienna University in the autumn of 1930. I soon abandoned the German studies which had been my original choice, went to lectures on art history and comparative religion, and finally signed up for the lectures of Moritz Schlick and Karl Bühler.

Moritz Schlick, 1930

4

Model, World View and Bloody Politics

A child plagued by cosmic fears, a young person distressed by the contradictory theories and ideologies constantly presented to me, I found myself all at once freed from chaos. Every morning, day after day, in the great lecture hall of the Vienna school of philosophy, I felt enlightenment, reassurance, confidence, a plan for life emanating from the person of a truly wise, truly good man. Moritz Schlick loved and often repeated Kant's saying that David Hume had awakened him from his "dogmatic slumber." As a student in my first term, this was how I perceived my own experience. Although the norms of thought of logical positivism had certainly already in some respects been superseded, it appears to me in my old age that to disparage them altogether as shallow, banal, one-sided, as the new obscurantists and despisers of critical reason are now doing again – just as the "mythologists of the twentieth century" did in Schlick's lifetime – is one of the saddest developments of these times.

If the man regarded as the head of the "Vienna Circle" had not appeared to me from the first moment as humane, modest, cautious in the extreme in the presentation of his radical views, would I have followed him less willingly? Perhaps so. Yet the charisma of a teacher is part of his teaching; it makes it more accessible, less strenuous to approach, but if a spirit of kindness and philanthropy is present, it also lends enhanced credibility. A zealot railing against God, against Plato, against Nietzsche or Marx would have aroused our mistrust, or even repelled us, from the start. Our gentle mentor convinced us of the clarity and sincerity of his thinking through the force of his own clear, sincere personality. In his moderate manner, by removing from philosophy the metaphysical cobwebs of many centuries, by urging us to caution in the face of any *a priori* observation, but also to the precise examination of every alleged political patent remedy, Moritz Schlick saved us in good time from pursuing many false tracks such as those followed by the late-converted adherents to the "God that failed," the Koestlers, Silones, and Spenders.

Although the ethics of logical positivism, most attacked by its opponents, set up no axioms of life and considered moral behavior to be possible only on the grounds of utilitarian principles, Schlick, through his own example, taught us valid codes of decency and reciprocal respect. To my own surprise I have never felt the need for any others, whether based on religion or ideology. He had no wish to remove the support of religion from the devout among his students; he allowed them space for their faith, as long as they did not insist that the unprovable could be proved. And while the Austrian Socialists of the time, unlike for instance the British Labour Party, were Marxist in outlook and therefore espoused a historic materialism which he rejected because of its dogmatic nature, he did recognize their great achievements in the field of the people's welfare.

Every morning, before he came to the lecture hall, Schlick used to go riding in Vienna's great public park, the Prater. It was the only relic of his aristocratic upbringing, about which he kept an embarrassed silence, as he did about his connection with the family of a count, with his maternal ancestor Ernst Moritz Arndt. Much more manifest was his friendship with Bertrand Russell and A. N. Whitehead, whom he resembled not only in his way of thinking, but also in his personal character. Along with the critical attitude he had learned from the great empiricists Locke, Hume, and Berkeley, went a tolerance which John Milton had been the first to demand and practice. Born in Berlin, married to an American, Schlick bore a greater similarity to the offshoots of England's grand old educated classes than to his own compatriots.

Schlick's seminar was the meeting place for the most acute and intelligent minds of Vienna and was by no means open to all students. Ernst Polak, the lord of the *Loge* in the Herrenhof, a venue of similar exclusivity, was admitted, as was Thomas, a younger brother of Peter de Mendelssohn and a prospective physics graduate. At nearly fifty years of age, Polak had obtained his degree with Schlick with a thesis, "Critique of Phenomenology through Logic". Thomas von Mendelssohn was a man of exceptional scientific talent. As soon as I began to attend the seminar, the limitations of my own understanding became only too clear to me. That I was incapable of the higher degrees of abstract thought was something I had discovered through mathematics at school. What "The Man" (Paqueni, my tutor and admirer) had been able to teach me was forgotten and lost again once the examination was over. When mathematical logic was the subject at Schlick's seminars, I managed not to fall by the wayside but tried to press ahead as far as possible, although I constantly found myself coming up with a crash against the walls of my ability to understand: a salutary process, which saved me from spiritual arrogance.

There were obviously some of my father's brain cells or genes which I had not inherited. But the world of formulae in which he was so much at home seemed to me the purest, cleanest, most untroubled of realms, and I envied him his ability to move around in it so freely. I was presumptuous enough, however, to write to him in Frankfurt – where he had been summoned for half a year to redevelop some chemical businesses – to press my newly acquired opinions upon him. He must have replied that there was "no metaphysics without the formation of concepts," a remark with which I disagreed. His justifiable response was that, if one wanted to discuss philosophical matters, it was necessary first of all to agree on the definition of the terms to be used. "Metaphysics for me," he continued, "is, and I believe I am in agreement with the current interpretation, neither a religion nor a *Weltanschauung*, but a realm of thought and research which lies between the exact sciences – which we may for brevity call physics – and pure philosophy. It includes those areas which cannot yet be opened up by the laws and methods of the physics of today, but with which we must concern ourselves in our thinking, in order to come closer to them and slowly bring them to readiness for strict scientific investigation. All great new discoveries in both fields lie dormant in this realm."

This last sentence seemed too succinct for me, obstinate as I was, and other objections of his were equally unacceptable to me: "If we used numbers or algebraic symbols instead of words for thinking, speaking, and writing, their relationship would emerge in the form of exact, compelling formulas, independent of the individual. Unfortunately, or fortunately, this is not the case. Thought is not objective, but, however much objectivity we try to exercise, it is somehow weighted by emotion or purpose, and influenced, colored, by the thinking personality." This problem, I thought, had been eliminated by the logical positivists in their distinction between meaningful and meaningless statements. At any rate, another passage from his long letter of March 1931 seemed to me worthy of consideration:

"One of the most important metaphysical questions is whether there is not a principal, as it were organic or physiological, obstacle to grasping the process of philosophy, or, let us say, of thought in general, with scientific clarity. Can the human mind analyze itself, be at the same time tool and object? Would it not for this purpose need to become finer, more penetrating, better able to command space and time, to be able to de- and transubstantiate itself? Perhaps what we call death is this process of transubstantiation, perhaps the corporeal–sensual has to disappear so that the spirit may find its way toward the supersensory, the absolute, which of course would mean that our beloved individuality would be lost." This last phrase in the subjunctive mood suggests that my father had not yet completely cast off the religious concept of a bodily resurrection or at least the survival of the individual after death.

My father soon returned to Vienna, his future again uncertain. I rather doubt whether our ideological conversations were continued at home. In their daily contacts both parents and children are more inhibited than in letters. In any case Schlick's influence upon me, although the most significant, was not the only one to which I was exposed at that time. Professor Charlotte Bühler, in a discipline which she called *Lebenspsychologie*, life psychology, graphically depicted the course of a human existence. According to this depiction, from the straight vertical line of childhood there grow out, with increasing age, protuberances representing friends, relationships, interests, which become ever more diversified and intensified, until in mature years a narrowing begins again, and in the end an almost leafless tree appears. It is not quite like that, in my own experience. But from the age of eighteen, I have found the increasing ramification as stimulating as it has sometimes been overpowering.

The Frau Professor is standing on the platform giving a lecture. Charlotte Bühler – slim, dressed in black, with short dark hair – employs elegant movements of her hands to emphasize the points in her lecture, which she delivers in a rather crisp, very North German tone. The student in the dusty lecture hall, which has not been renovated since 1884, suddenly notices that the professor's long white fingers end in nails lacquered blood red. This was one of the most revolutionary impressions of my first term, a concise and vivid image of the emancipated woman, such as we were never given by the Fraudoktor, with her ideal of the amiable, modest, and housewifely schoolgirl. Charlotte Bühler was a professor of less than one year's standing, but she was self-confident, as if it was clear to her that she represented the new, postwar woman. To my folksy fellow students, sitting around stuffily in their traditional dirndl dresses, there was something not quite right about her. Soon they wandered off in another direction to their German studies.

Proving one's own worth in the circle of the Bühlers was easier than at the Schlick seminar. Here experimental psychology was practiced; the atmosphere was friendly, practical and fairly basic. Karl Bühler was certainly an imaginative and sensible, as well as kindly South German, from Meckesheim in Baden. A fellow student once told me an unpleasant story about a visit to Edmund Husserl; the latter had Bühler's book *Die Krise der Psychologie* (*The Crisis of Psychology*) lying open on his desk and was using the wide margins of the pages for making notes, which he would then tear off. Ernst Polak rightly picked a quarrel with the phenomenologist with the help of logic. Studying with Bühler brought honor and profit. Before me, Karl Popper and Jean Améry were his students as well as Schlick's.

What Bühler, that kindly and trusting man, did not know was that nearly all his assistants were in analysis with one of the great Freudian scholars such as Heinz Hartmann or Siegfried Bernfeld. He was certainly open to discussion, for example allowing the Freudian René Spitz to speak at his seminar, but in his opinion the "principles of Freud's basic assumptions contained in the desire for function and the desire for satisfaction" were inadequate for the "understanding of the fundamental processes of life." He himself, with Charlotte's support, saw life "primarily through the perspective of the creative principle." But he was also open to ideas coming from the circle of individual psychology and encouraged the plan of young Paul Lazarsfeld, the son of a woman friend of both Alfred Adler and Victor Adler, to set up an institute of social psychology. With Bühler's help and that of a few enlightened industrialists, a research center was attached to the Psychological Institute of the university, which not only investigated problems such as that of unemployment, but also undertook market analysis in order to support itself. In the course of my studies I did some work there.

In 1919, while still at school, Paul Lazarsfeld, with his friend Ludwig Wagner, had founded the Union of Socialist Secondary School Students. The Industrial-Psychological Research Center, as it was now called, was staffed predominantly by left-wing workers. Here I met Marie Jahoda, Hans Zeisel, and Gertrude Wagner; here I made contact with the youth officials as well as with the lower ranks of the SDAP (Sozialdemokratische Arbeiterpartei or Social Democratic Workers' Party). Years earlier, as I now read to my own astonishment in my desk diary of May 30,1930, I had joined a Socialist torchlight march at half past eight in the evening in the Ringstrasse. And my father wrote to me from Frankfurt in November of that year: "I was not too delighted *primo loco* by your demanding that Mimi should vote for the Sozis. I do not know if I would perhaps even have done so this time myself, for tactical reasons, I know too little here of the situation, but M. wrote to me that you have become a passionate supporter of the Reds, which makes me fear that you may continue to support them from the party and agitation point of view, which I would very much regret, in view of the long discussion we had at one time on this point. As far as Mimi is concerned, it was very bad form to put pressure on her to cast her vote for the Socialists."

No, I did not join the Party, not yet. But if not "*primo loco*" a political animal, I was soon caught up by the spirit of the time and of my city, where the advantages of Otto Glöckel's educational reforms, Julius Tandler's welfare facilities, and the financial strategy of Hugo Breitner, which made possible a whole range of domestic and artistic activities, were clear even to young people. We were influenced too by our reading of Dostoevsky and Tolstoy, which arose from our interest not only in Russia itself but also in its presumably successful liberation of the poor and oppressed. We knew nothing of the murder of the kulaks. We admired Lunacharsky, the People's Commissar for Culture, who occasionally visited Vienna, and above all Alexandra Kollontai, the guiding intellectual force of the Russian women's movement and fighter against sexual taboos, a person as rebellious as she was fashionable, whom we considered to be successful, although she had long fallen from favor with Stalin and had been pushed aside into various diplomatic posts.

It was for emotional rather than rational grounds that we were moving to the left. Russian songs from the first uprising in 1905: *"Zar Nikolai erliess ein Manifest/ Den Toten ihre Freiheit/ Die Lebenden in Arrest"* ("Tsar Nicholas issued a manifesto/ Freedom for the dead/ Arrest for the living"); Richard Dehmel's "Arbeitsmann" ("Working Man"), who needs only one thing "to be as free as the birds are – only time"; Alfons Petzoldt's poem of the dead worker, *"Meine Not ist zu Ende und all meine Qual, köstliche Erde hüllt die ruhenden Hände, und mein Leib ist worden ein leuchtender Sonnenstrahl"* ("My hour of need and all my torment have passed, precious earth covers my resting hands, and my body has become a brilliant ray of sunshine"). And soon there were the songs of Bert Brecht, which we read in the volumes of *Versuche*: *"Da musst du den ganzen Staat/ Von unten bis oben umkehren/ Bis du deine Suppe hast"* ("You will have to turn the whole state/ Upside down from top to bottom/ Before you get your soup"). Those who have never felt in this way in their early years need not be trusted in their old age. Nevertheless, we did not become Communists. Even the young painter Alescha, who painted my mother's portrait and afterward often came to tea and played folk songs from all countries, but above all those of the Slavs, despite all his love for the Russian soul felt he belonged to the Socialists. And even "The Man," Paqueni, who claimed to be an admirer of the Bolsheviks, avoided the Communist party.

This dear, kind, selfless man, together with his sister, who was equally gaunt and bony, but also slightly sour in her manner, was later to fall into the snares of the Nazis. I found this out the first time I returned to Vienna after the war. Another friend of my youth ended up the same way. In my last year at school, I had started a correspondence with a German student, Lutz Hannemann. One day he actually turned up, very much the Berliner, rather dashing, but nevertheless a declared Socialist who, unlike others in my circle, found my father's loyalty to his dueling club utterly ridiculous and strengthened me in my left-wing sympathies. What was it I liked about this Lutz? What induced me, during his semester in Vienna, to rattle through the countryside clinging to him on the pillion of his motorcycle, and then to hold philosophical conversations with him in some *Gasthaus*? I do not know. And that was all that happened between us. Apart from his repeated, tersely formulated if vehemently uttered affirmations of feeling for me, the whole thing may have been attributable to the stimulus of his North German vitality and acute precision, his North German wit and, yes, his charm. A premonition – if in the form of a parody – of my first husband, Peter. After Lutz left, we exchanged hundreds of letters. I destroyed his when I heard that Maria had seen him, soon after 1933, wearing a storm trooper's uniform.

Another messenger from Berlin had appeared at my parents' home about 1930: Otto Schneider, born in Vienna, a pre-eminent intellectual of the Weimar period, once editor-in-chief of the *Musikblätter des Anbruch*, now redolent of the spirit of the house of Ullstein, where he was editing a magazine, and of the Romanischer Café. With his pale, intense face and razor-sharp profile, he could have sprung from an illustration in the avant-garde journal *Der Querschnitt*, which I used to read sometimes. I was about to leave school. He advised me to move to his own exciting city, where future prospects were so bright; he tempted me with his piercing gaze, scenting potential in me, promising all sorts of things, and like those other Viennese women, Vicki Baum and Joe Lederer, like the budding literati from all over Europe, I was within a hair's breadth of following the call of this magnetic metropolis – where I would only have experienced with them the years of their agony. Something preserved me from this. I stayed "behind my tiled stove," as Peter called it later, and, in summer, on my little balcony.

This balcony was on the fifth floor; it towered over the houses opposite, in any case distant; in between were trees and gardens, not my territory. So steep was the downward view, so far did it protrude into nothingness, that the urge, the adolescent death wish, to fling myself from the edge, constantly came over me. It proved to be resistible. The view distracted me from it. Some hundred meters to the right lay a great courtyard belonging to the furniture company Portois & Fix, where occasionally there were military exercises – the *Heimwehr*, the *Schutzbund* (the left-wing militia)? – not the army, at any rate – and in the evening, the old Austrian retreat was played. In the distance was the whole range of the hills of the north-westerly Vienna woods, an impressive sight that somewhat made up for the loss of the Heiligenstadt idyll. The little balcony, on which the sun beat down so fiercely that the dog Diemo preferred to keep away from it, had barely room for more than two or three chairs and a small table for my typewriter. Much typing was done here, from my fifteenth year onward, much reading, sitting, and lying outstretched, much eating of bread and butter with mustard, and less coarse food as I grew older. And when it grew dark, that folding telescope from the property demobilization group was put into service, allowing glimpses of figures and goings-on in the brightly lit windows opposite, not in the manner of Doderer's character, the official Zihal, but of an intimate nature: girls taking off their blouses, married couples having arguments, bourgeois tragedies emerging like shadows from the rooms. Curiosity about how other people live their lives.

There was music from the smoking room, and later, after "The Man" had given me a little grey wind-up gramophone, also in my room. The piano had to go one day, and was replaced by radios. My father liked above all to listen to broadcasts of classical music; I, who had been dragged since early childhood to concerts given by the pianist Alfred Grünfeld and the violinist Bronislaw Hubermann, had less room in my heart for such music at that time. Amid my white nursery furniture, I played recordings of the soul seductresses of the twenties, the rough and the smooth, Sophie Tucker and Lucienne Boyer – "The Man I Love" and "Parlez-moi d'Amour" – but also what we considered the wildest sounds of modern times, "Forty-Second Street," "Big City Blues," and "Puttin' On The Ritz." My father would enter the room and listen with an indulgent smile. He had already made the acquaintance of true Dixieland jazz around the middle of the decade, and praised it to the amazed Viennese in an article which was actually published in the *Neue Freie Presse*.

At night I read – what did I not read! My father introduced me to *Reineke Fuchs* and *Die versunkene Glocke* before I could decipher them myself. The first book he gave me was Faraday's *Chemical History of a Candle*. In a volume, *Till Eulenspiegel*, which I still possess is the childish inscription "Hilde Spiel, six years"; and after the name, repeated by means of a toy printing set, "No. 15"; so I already had at least fifteen books. My first reading was a mixed bag: *Leatherstocking* and Nathalie von Eschstruth, Jules Verne and Karl May, Felix Dahn's

Battle for Rome and Eduard Stucken's trilogy *White Gods*, the *German Holiday Book* and *The Good Comrade* with their foreign-seeming Low German or Wilhelminian colonial-patriotic stories such as "The Vollrads in the Southwest" – though I despised the little girls' weekly magazine of similar origin, *Das Kränzchen*. Soon there were Gustav Freytag's *Soll und Haben*, whose characters I saw almost tangibly before me, and, touchingly closer to me, Else Feldmann's *Löwenzahn*, a novel of poverty in Vienna, a beloved book, now out of print.

I read all these together with the true, the great writers, assigned at school or discovered for myself. From the collection at home of which I have already spoken, I progressed first of all to the French who for a long time dominated my world of youthful feeling - Balzac, Flaubert, Zola, certainly – but more the newer writers, Jean Giono with his *Jean le Bleu*, the bible of my sensibility, as I called it. Gide, Cocteau, Carco, Radiguet, Charles-Louis Philippe, Eugène Dabit. They still stand on my bookshelves. The English writers came much later. Before them, inspired by the Café Herrenhof, there were Kafka and Herzmanovsky-Orlando, who at that time belonged to us all.

Opinions differed on Karl Kraus. The two water-polo players idolized him and everything he approved of. They read aloud Else Lasker-Schüler's *Tibetteppich* as though it were a prayer. Fritz Thorn gave me a little volume published by Insel Verlag, Albert Ehrenstein's *Tubutsch*, illustrated by Kokoschka. I went to Kraus's readings with Thorn, just as I had gone to hear Kuh's polemic against "Zarathustra's Ape," with the young Békessy. An ambivalent attitude could hardly be avoided here: admiration was mingled with skepticism, even mockery. Who, as a young contemporary, could evade the stern linguistic dictates of Karl Kraus (I have long acknowledged the fact that he still looks over my shoulder today as I write), the grandiose perversity of his polemic, the brilliant mimicry of *Die letzten Tage der Menschheit* (*The Last Days of Humanity*), the pathos of *Die letzte Nacht?* But it would never have occurred to me to reject Heine and Hofmannsthal, Bernard Shaw, or every line that Stefan Zweig or Werfel ever wrote, just because Kraus despised them. I could not bring myself to react with anything but embarrassment to the arias of the *Grossherzogin von Gerolstein*, which he liked to render in a croaking voice.

But what was I writing? Poems – one, my first published work, appeared in the periodical *Tag der Jugend*; a story, "Der kleine Bub Desider," a little in the manner of Peter Altenberg, which was published in the children's supplement of the *Neue Freie Presse* in October 1929 in three installments, although it could not be considered for an award in the newspaper's literary competition, "as the author is already over eighteen years old"; then a number of short stories, published mostly in the evening edition of the *Presse*, often under pseudonyms, "Grace Hanshaw" and "Jean Lenoir," when I felt they were rather lightweight. Nearly thirty titles are recorded on an old list; most of them are lost. There was also a serious attempt, a psychologically tormented novella, *Begegnung im Trüben*, which was seen by Robert Neumann and which he found of enough interest to encourage me to embark on a full-length novel. When I had completed the novella after great agonizing, Neumann put in a word for me with the publisher Paul Zsolnay, but insisted on tightening it up thoroughly himself before it was sent for typesetting. I wept bitterly at the interference. This sort of thing would happen to me often enough in life, said Neumann unpityingly. How true.

Meanwhile, however, I had to earn a living, for as usual money was in short supply. I reported to a Frau Dr. Kernegg, the editor of a women's magazine called *Der neuzeitliche Haushalt* (The Modern Household). I worked there by the hour, wrote, edited, learned about the production of this childishly unsophisticated periodical. After a humiliating morning trying to sell advertising space, I immediately gave up this duty. One day, an absurd German-American called Herbert William Herzog appeared like a comet in Vienna, planning a daily paper in English (to be pompously entitled *The Continental Times*), got Thorn, myself, and others to bring out a free first issue, made me an offer of marriage which reduced me to laughter, and promptly disappeared forever from the city, leaving behind countless debts, including our salaries - an episode of which the only relic is an impressive business card.

For Christmas 1929, Thorn gave me a little pocket calendar-diary and wrote on the flyleaf: "This calendar is so small because it is not to become a banal diary of aphorisms and because you are only to record that events have occurred. Your *attitude* to them must be altered over and over again – your whole life long." From then on, I have always kept calendars of this kind, up to the present day. Many dozens of them have survived, containing not a single aphorism, but many feelings. On March 21, 1933, it is true, I only noted laconically that I had been to the publishers in the morning, had been given the first copy of my book, *Kati auf der Brücke*, and was upset because the paper was too thin and as a result the book looked too slim. "Nachm. F. Stelle." ("Afternoon R. Institute.") This was a visit to the research institute for industrial psychology, where I now sat every day producing statistics. One month later – the first good reviews had come out; even Torberg had said "nice things about Kati" – I entered my conviction that the book was "honestly, honestly bad." Soon afterward, I wrote a "suicide poem," "Der Tote," which I found simply beautiful. The fluctuations of adolescence, its extravagant despairs and joys persisted for some time. It was not in Vienna but in London that I became an adult.

If at that time a young woman of twenty-one – as I was that May – went on a journey alone, the whole family, parents, grandmother, and friend, would come to see her off at the railway station. I had had a book published, I was being sent to Zurich to conduct a survey on Bally shoes for the research institute, but I could not depart unaccompanied. In decent, honest Switzerland I immediately lost a sapphire ring, which I left in a washroom. It had been given to me by Mimi and was the only precious stone I ever owned in my life. I spent four weeks in the Confederation, working with Nellie Kreis, an Austrian resident in Switzerland; through her cousin Ninon, she was related to Thomas Mann, and later, in Geneva, in wartime, became the companion and loving nurse of Robert Musil. At her house one day, I met Else Lasker-Schüler, who seemed to me to have sprung from a Ringelnatz poem, raven-like, warped, disheveled, strangely attired and adorned. Nellie lent her my novel. It was, Lasker-Schüler announced on a postcard in huge upright letters, "written with a pen of silver." The postcard has been lost. Who will believe me now?

From Zurich, which had a calming effect upon me, like a well-ordered toybox, I traveled to Paris for the Pentecost holiday. A "business trip," arranged by Kuoni – I have never toured the city more thoroughly than during those three days. And I will never forget the intoxication, the fever of bliss I experienced. I arrived at night and checked into a hotel in the Rue de Caumartin, and then, according to my pocket calendar, wandered the streets and boulevards between half past two and half past three in the morning - to the Opéra and back to the Madeleine, to the Place de la Concorde, to the Louvre. I gazed from the countless blazing lamps of the Concorde up to the Champs Elysées, I bent over the parapet of the bridge toward the river, I sang, I danced, I laughed and "wept with joy." I felt transported to the red plush salons of the *belle époque*, I conversed with Frédéric Moreau and Lucien de Rubempré. In the daytime, we were taken the length and breadth of the city from Montmartre to Montparnasse, we drank a glass of champagne at eleven in the morning on the sunlit terrace of the Trocadéro opposite the Eiffel Tower, we stood beneath the windows of Sainte Chapelle – what an unearthly gleam! – and in front of the fine spray of the fountains of Versailles; we ate ice cream at Fouquet and visited the Rue Mouffetard and the *bals nègres* of the Rue de Lappe. Whit Monday: "Evening Café de la Paix. Farewell. The world is dying." And so back to Zurich.

Four weeks in Switzerland, and I dreamed only of Paris. In Vienna, I immediately borrowed a novel by a young German for the sake of its title, *Paris über mir*. The book enchanted me. I wrote a letter to the author, Peter Mendelssohn, in Berlin and sent him a copy of *Kati*. No reply. During all the months that followed, while I studied, did market research, wrote short stories and worked on a new novel, to be called *Der Sonderzug* (*The Special Train*), I thought only of how I could get back to France. I painted watercolors in the open air with Fritz Thorn, I sat in the "Heho," as we called the Café Herrenhof, with him and Torberg, whenever Torberg came to visit from Prague. I rather enjoyed the local fame my book had brought me, and on one occasion felt I was on the brink of life as a true literary figure, when Robert Neumann invited me to dinner in the Hungerbergstrasse together with Hermann Broch, Torberg, and a German writer called Stock. Steffi Neumann, still influenced by the Youth Movement, sat there defiantly in her woolen cardigan, depriving the occasion of its ceremonial quality. But this was restored by Broch's authoritative manner.

In the new circle of friends that I had joined, I took part in improvised theatrical performances, attended little concerts given in private houses where the composer Erich Zeisl simulated whole symphonies by Bruckner and Mahler on the piano – one seemed actually to hear the horns and woodwinds – or tried my hand as a member of the choir in the mass he was currently writing; I had my portrait painted by the artist Lisel Salzer and saw the painting exhibited at the Hagenbund (it disappeared during the Anschluss); for a time, I visited our sick Diemo in the veterinary hospital, and dashed off to the cinema to do research for my doctoral thesis. But again and again, I felt that consuming nostalgia for Paris.

At the Café Schottentor, opposite the University, during those years one used to meet people who for some reason avoided the Herrenhof, among them Elias Canetti, the Freudian disciple Siegfried Bernfeld, and Albert Fuchs, the "son of a good house," as he later called himself in his autobiography. Fuchs was pale, sickly, and a Communist. My novel, perhaps I myself, pleased him; he heard of my wish to travel to Paris again to do research for my work in progress, *Der Sonderzug*, and as he wanted to go himself for a few weeks, he supplemented my limited resources so that I could make the journey with him at the beginning of September. It had been a platonic arrangement, which, however, soon led to difficulties because, although Fuchs respected it, he was still resentful. So, in my blissful happiness – the first hotel was actually called "Paradis" – I still had my reproachful escort by my side. It was not by chance that I gave the character inspired by him in my book *Der Sonderzug* the prosaic name of Kalk.

For a month, often without Albert, I traversed the city, still totally captivated. At the second-hand bookstalls I bought slightly battered copies of Cocteau's *Rappel à l'ordre* and Breton's *Manifeste du surréalisme*, the latter inscribed with "respectueuse hommage" to a Dr. Nussbaum, as well as three wonderful Japanese woodcuts on fragile rice paper. I sometimes dined formally with the writer André Chamson, a slender, elegant official in Daladier's foreign ministry, whom I had met through a letter of recommendation from Robert Neumann; otherwise, I usually ate frugally at the Dominique, where there was borscht and "pain à discrétion," and where I met the beautiful and melancholy Elisabeth Janstein, a journalist reporting for the *Neue Freie Presse*. She took me along to a banquet held for foreign correspondents – we were served *caneton à l'orange* and champagne – and expressed her annoyance over the invasion of the so-called "*Chez nous.*" This was a reference to the German immigrants who had been swamping Paris since Hitler's rise to power and, still unpracticed at emigration, kept complaining to the French about how much better everything had been "*chez nous.*" There was an apocryphal story about a former Berliner who was said to have exclaimed, while watching the July 14 parade: "Our German army used to march more smartly!"

In the evenings, at the Dôme, the Select, the Rotonde, or the Coupole at the Montparnasse junction, these mournful figures lamented over their lost homeland. And even Albert's friend, the biochemist Erwin Chargaff, who decades later in his American laboratory was to make important discoveries about the composition of DNA, and to be cheated out of the Nobel Prize, wept for the Institute of Hygiene in Berlin, where one could work so much more efficiently than at the Institut Pasteur.

At the Hotel Namur in the rue Delambre, around the corner from Montparnasse, the center for artists as well as exiles at that time, I met people who, in altered forms, reappear in *Der Sonderzug.* The events of those September weeks, the Stavisky scandal, the murder of a young girl, all became material for my book. After my departure, which I approached in a state of "petrifaction," as I called it, in order to bear the pain of farewell, I worked on this book for a whole year, lived with it, saw it as my comfort and my support. More than half a century later it still seems inconceivable to me that it was never published, a child – not my only one –carried to full term, but stillborn. A few days' stay in Zurich on the way home relieved the contrast between the effervescence of Paris and the dull stagnation of Vienna. There, at least, one could see Cocteau films, enjoy Erika Mann's refreshingly cheeky "Pfeffermühle" at the Niederdorff – this political cabaret was the subject of my first ever theatrical review, for the *Neue Freie Presse,* which printed it in October 1933. Then, back home, once again the round of these unimaginably full days, from University to research institute, to coffee houses and the countless friends, several of whom I saw every day. When did I work, when did I write? I do not know. Yet poems and stories were produced, and the beloved, hopeless novel continued to grow.

In December, I was nominated for the Literature Prize of the City of Vienna and had to present myself to the brother of Julius Reich, who founded the prize which still bears his name. After visiting Professor Emil Reich, I made a note: "malicious little man." However, I have no memory of the meeting. Torberg received the prize before me, for his *Schüler Gerber*. He was not pleased that a second precocious blossom from the Herrenhof, and one from his closest circle at that, should receive the same honor. But these were all trifles, games on the edge of the abyss which was beginning to yawn ever more visibly. On New Year's Eve, I recorded: "I am so terribly afraid of the new year." In fact only six weeks still remained before the end of democracy in Austria, six weeks to civil war, the destruction of the entire left-wing movement in the country and the foundation of the Christian *Ständestaat*, the authoritarian regime, whose clerico-fascist structure cannot be denied even by its present-day apologists.

In this solipsistic report, I have not spoken of the advent of the Nazi regime in Germany, except in connection with the "*Chez nous*" in Paris. The fact that my first novel was published on the day of the Reichstag fire at first obscured the historic event for me in favor of the private one. But soon I became aware, even more because of my surroundings at that time, what had begun that day and was threatening us too. Since that March of 1933 which had made unlimited power possible for Hitler, Austria's democratic rights too had been lost, if in a far less spectacular manner. Little Chancellor Dollfuss, making use of a parliamentary irregularity, had dissolved the National Council and since then had ruled with the help of a law on wartime economy which had never been repealed, from the time of the old monarchy. The First Republic was in fact already finished, the opposition lamed, if not yet beaten.

So for one short year a political life began for me, in addition to everything else that was happening. I joined the Social Democratic Workers' Party; I attended protest meetings against the seizure of power in neighboring Germany, in defiance of right-wing groups of all kinds, Nazis, *Sturmscharen*, and *Heimwehren* at home. We shouted slogans, we sang "Brothers, to the sun, to freedom," and raised our fists high. I was, as I still believe, on the right side. And yet, while I experienced the warmth of the like-minded crowd around me as pleasant and comforting, I still felt a slight shudder at the loss of my individuality. Since the destruction of the SDAP after February 1934, I have never joined another political party.

On top of this, there was my love for a Socialist editor which had suddenly surged up during the previous March, and which was as violent as it was finally unhappy. He was in charge of a supplement of the *Arbeiterzeitung* and wrote commentaries under the pen-name "Hafis"; he was a total "political animal," a man completely absorbed in the events of the time and the day, who allowed himself no private, let alone emotional, relationships. After reading my book, in which, God knows, I did not ignore social problems and revolutionary ideas, he asked smilingly but firmly: "What are you trying to prove?" As far as he was able, which was little enough, he returned my feelings, but we saw each other seldom, talking mostly on the telephone, only to find that editorial conferences, party events, meetings, negotiations made it impossible for us to meet. This went on for a whole year, in secret and outside my work and my circle, and became inexplicably heightened with the rise of political tension.

Many a time, after taking leave of my friends, I would telephone him from a public phone booth in the building of the *Vorwärts* printing works; the number, which I have never forgotten, was B 23 0 87 – in the fifties I put it into a novel. He was not to be reached, he was at the typesetters, at a meeting, or he came to the telephone and told me very tenderly that he could not see me, or he arranged to meet me in some out-of-the-way coffee house where we were unknown, not arriving till it had closed and I had to go home, or he suggested meeting after midnight at the Café de l'Europe on the Stephansplatz, which was open at all hours, and where he was discussing the situation and future policy with a group of comrades. I was allowed to sit at the table, tolerated if disregarded, until three or four in the morning; he would escort me home, for he came from a good middle-class family and in his way was certainly very fond of me, then he would go all the long way home to his own apartment, exhausted in mind and body, only to plunge into politics and journalism again the following morning. A handsome man, his mind always elsewhere, unattainable even when I stood on the doorstep in his silent embrace.

My fear when the *Vorwärts* building was temporarily occupied on February 8, 1934, was above all for him, and even more so my despair when, four days later, between eleven and twelve in the morning, the clocks in public places were stopped, every light in the somber rooms and dark corridors went out, and the streetcars stood motionless on the Ringstrasse. "It is civil war," I wrote that evening in my calendar. "Now I will never see him again." And so it was. While during the next few days the city was shaken by shots from cannons and howitzers, while municipal buildings were reduced to ruins and bloody battles raged around Vienna's railway stations, workers' homes, public pools, and schools, while everywhere tanks and trucks clattered through the streets, laden with soldiers ready to shoot, and the general strike was inexorably paralyzed, I was running around trying to find Hafis. He had disappeared; perhaps he was a member of the Socialist "shadow committee" founded on February 15 under the leadership of the editor-in-chief of the *Arbeiterzeitung*. Then I learned that he had reached Prague and was in safety. As early as the 16th a house search had taken place at the research institute. I was sitting in the front room when the little *Heimwehr* troop broke in, led by *Ingenieur* Messinger, a member of my father's student corps. He looked at me and without a word went into the adjoining rooms with his men. Although in the last one, Lazarsfeld's office, there were bookshelves holding the works of Marx, Engels, Kautsky, and others, Messinger made no arrests and stormed out. A few days later, when as it happened I was not there, another troop appeared at the institute and dragged off every member of the staff to the prison on the Elisabethpromenade.

On February 20 – everything was over, many hundreds of workers and Socialists had fallen, thousands were wounded and more arrested, their leaders, those who had not already fled, tried at improvised courts-martial and nine of them summarily hanged on the orders of the justice minister, Kurt Schuschnigg – we heard Verdi's *Requiem* played on the radio. We felt it as a lament for our companions, and the events of the past week as the end of our world. No one believes those for whom February 1934 was a more dreadful turning point than the Anschluss. When, after years of fighting in Spain, Madrid fell to Franco, a woman in a group of exiles in London was reproached for not weeping. She said: "I wept for Barcelona." We wept that February. What happened four years later was terrible, but predictable for all those, myself among them, who had not deliberately closed their eyes to it. That is why I, like several of my friends, like Robert Neumann and Stefan Zweig in those early days, wanted to leave Austria after the civil war. But first I wanted to complete my studies. My life in the meantime was to be a provisional one.

5

Time of Contradictions

Worse than provisional, it was a time of blurs and smudges, as I once described those last years before the Anschluss. German émigrés and native Austrians were coming to Vienna to escape from Hitler, while Viennese, repelled by the regime at home, were leaving for London or Paris. At Alma Mahler-Werfel's salon, literati such as Ödön von Horváth, Franz Theodor Csokor, and Carl Zuckmayer did not shrink from socializing with members of the government of the *Ständestaat* and the dubious creators of cultural and educational policy of the *Vaterländische Front* – the "Fatherland Front." But Csokor had yet to learn that at the premiere of his play, *The Third of November 1918*, the touching scene including the Jewish regimental doctor Grün would be cut. In many respects, people were at pains to keep pace with, even to pre-empt, the principles of the neighboring dictatorship. Up to 1936 there was seething unrest among the underground, the Nazis, still officially banned, carried out minor acts of terrorism, and Jewish university students were beaten up. After Schuschnigg's pact with Hitler in July 1936, the ruling party demanded a declaration of faith in *Deutschtum*, Germanness, while the influence of the officially illegal party was seeping into all areas of politics and culture.

I experienced only the first half of that sad five-year period, but I too was moved by its distortions, its half-measures, and its confusions. From the start I realized that one cannot live on the "heroic" or "tragic" plane, as Arthur Koestler was to call it, for all twenty-four hours of the day. On that 16th of February when I was so nearly arrested, Torberg had arrived in Vienna from Prague, and the following evening, as I noted in my pocket calendar, I went to the cinema with him to see Greta Garbo in the original English-language version of *Grand Hotel*. This was an example of what Bertolt Brecht in his *Mother Courage* calls the "islands of peace" in war. I did, to be sure, ask myself how it was possible "to be yielding, as if made of elastic feathers," and how "everything could still go on," and I felt I could "never be happy again." But there was still comradeship among friends, close cohesion, although driven underground. Whatever help could be given by the little group that had formed at the research institute was given now, and we were all involved.

Albert Fuchs, who had stayed for months in Paris, had set out on his return journey after the outbreak of civil war, in order to pursue his activities in secret. At the beginning of April, he took me to see a woman friend at whose home other like-minded people had already gathered. For a whole evening at Litzy's apartment in the Latschkagasse we sang the forbidden battle songs of Brecht and Eisler. At some point, a slim young Englishman emerged from a room, to be introduced as her lodger. His name was Kim Philby. Soon afterward he and Litzy married and traveled to London, where I later saw them both again. Long before this secret gathering, which succeeded only in blinding us temporarily to our powerlessness, we had already made the acquaintance of a few other visitors from England. For the last six months, a teacher of economics, Hugh Gaitskell, had been living in Vienna in order to take part in a seminar held by the great political economist Ludwig von Mises, whose apartment was in the Wollzeile below that of my grandmother. As a bonus, Gaitskell found that he was enjoying his stay. "There is probably no place in Europe," he wrote to a friend, "where the women are so attractive and their morals are so loose." But at Christmas his girlfriend Dora arrived in Vienna – and in any case, Gaitskell, as I knew him then, would not have taken excessive advantage of the loose morals of the Viennese girls.

The events of February 12 affected Gaitskell deeply. The "son of a good house," like Albert Fuchs – in fact probably a "better" house, for his father had been a senior official in Burma and lived in a small mansion in Rangoon with his large family and twelve servants – he too had become drawn toward the underprivileged and oppressed. The best education possible in England, then as now – Winchester and New College, Oxford – had led Gaitskell first toward humane, then to liberal, and finally to Socialist convictions. As early as 1926, the year of the General Strike, at the age of twenty-one, he had aligned himself with the workers. Now, from the very first day of the civil war, he had placed himself at the service of the lost cause. He managed to get the British Labour Party to send several observers to Vienna without delay: the young lawyer Elwyn Jones to keep an eye on what happened in the courts and prisons, the trade unionist Walter Citrine to make contact with the underground party members, and the Scottish writer Naomi Mitchison, to concern herself with the families of those who had fallen or were under arrest.

They all brought funds for the relief of those in greatest need, partly contributed by the Labour Party, partly by the Quakers, with whom both Gaitskell and Jones had connections. What was wanted were lists of those needing help, but such lists could be compiled and passed on only in secret, for they revealed the names of those who still counted themselves members of the Socialist movement and hoped for support from it. Our Marie – Marie Weihs, my parents' domestic help and my confidante, indeed my ally, from early on – had been for many years an SDAP member and knew most of the members of this party and of the *Schutzbund* in our district. With her, behind the backs of the "master and mistress," my parents, I organized regular contacts between those in difficulties and their helpers. Once again, while on my way to the university with a bag full of lists of names, I narrowly escaped arrest; a woman just in front of me was searched, but nothing whatsoever was found on her. Many of my friends and colleagues at the research center were to remain in prison for weeks or months, the longest serving being Ludwig Wagner in the Elizabethpromenade. I took him some of my most beloved books, such as Dostoevsky's *The Insulted and the Injured*, thus losing them forever.

Wagner's wife, Gerti, Lazarsfeld's closest colleague after Marie Jahoda (who was also in prison at that time), had introduced me to Hugh Gaitskell, Dora Frost, Elwyn Jones, and also to Naomi Mitchison, the rebellious niece of Lord Haldane who stayed briefly in Vienna, did beneficent work in all the parish halls, returned home, and in the same year had her *Vienna Diary* published by Gollancz. It was dedicated in German to "the unvanquished comrades, in solidarity and love." We, the little band, continued to meet for months with our British friends, sat with them in the Opiumhöhle (Opium Den), the favorite evening venue of the *bohème* of the day, and on Sundays took them to Greifenstein to sunbathe and swim on the left bank of the

Danube. Gaitskell, whom we all called Sam, could never quite detach his mind from the many, often dangerous tasks he had taken upon himself at this time – courier services to the SDAP leadership in exile at Brno, missions on behalf of *Schutzbund* members who were wanted and in hiding, whom he was to smuggle out of the country – and always seemed rather serious, shy, and inhibited, or perhaps he was just incurably reserved in the manner of the English *haute bourgeoisie*, with which I was not yet familiar. Dora cheered him up and encouraged him. And Elwyn Jones had the gift of being able to forget all such worries and cares of the time on such evenings and Sundays.

Elwyn, the son of a Llanelli steelworker, had managed, through a combination of talent, industriousness, and scholarships, to get into Cambridge to read law. His surname, he explained to us, was so common that if you stood in his college quad and called "Jones!" all the windows would be flung open. Elwyn was cheerful, rosy, and inclined toward flirtations which never revealed the degree of his emotional involvement. We said a melancholy farewell to him after a sherry party he gave on June 25 for all his friends, helpers and sympathizers – including the American John Gunther, who wrote a novel decades later, *The Lost City*, about the Vienna of the civil war. Hafis was lost to me; my relationship with him had cast a cloud over that with Fritz Thorn; and I liked Elwyn. It would have been possible at that time for our flirtation to turn into something more serious. But when all was said and done, Elwyn, the Welsh steelworker's son, had his inhibitions too.

We exchanged a few letters after that. Elwyn's are not preserved; I only have a draft of one of mine, and cannot even remember if it was posted. It is written in execrable English. "Do you know," I wrote, "that I really hated you and began to forget purposely your nice crabb-red face and your charming 'what?' in moments of astonishment?... Dear Elwyn, don't excuse about not having read my book. I'm not a bit interested in it any more, since I'm writing the new one. It's always the same: you worry about it for more than a year, and it gets you down more then a hundred times, and if its finished and driven out to publicity, its no more your own and you can read it half a year later like any other one. I'm sorry about Naomi Mitchison, you know, that I liked the Diary in the most important parts. Isn't my Englisch very bad? If you'll happen to write me once more, try to write a little bit more distinctly, if you please, otherwise it's like walking through thorns!" Three years later, I saw Elwyn again in London, in Gray's Inn, at a party given by the influential left-winger D. N. Pritt, his mentor in legal matters. At his side was Pearl Binder, whom he married soon afterward. The research institute was closed, the work in the underground movement gradually came to a halt. I was back at my studies with renewed zeal, working on my new novel, writing short stories, making notes for my thesis.

One morning I boarded a boat on the Danube and went on a day's journey to Budapest, where my mother's beloved cousins, the Erdëlyi and Udvarós families, lived. They were charming, hospitable people, who took me in for a week and showed me their city. At night, on both sides of the bridge, it was almost as beautiful as Paris. By day I discovered on many of the houses, so similar to those of the Viennese *Gründerzeit* (the Founding Epoch), archaic, even barbaric shapes and ornamentation, relics of the deeply rooted Turkish taste. Yet my aunt Stella – a figure like those of Klimt – loved German classicism and lived in its spirit. Her son Hans, my young second cousin, enthusiastically translated for me the poems of Petöfi and Endre Ady, which he knew by heart. Sitting in the Café New York, strolling on the Fischerbastei, I noticed old gentlemen with humorously spiritual faces of great character. Many decades later I recognized this facial type in Julius Hay and Tibor Déry, even in that astute man of letters Ivan Boldiszar. The plump playboy's face of Imre Békessy – whom it did not occur to me to look up – bore not the slightest resemblance to them.

On my return to Vienna I met Hans Habe by chance in the street; he looked away in embarrassment. The year before he had been "Europe's youngest newspaper editor" and had published a flowery review of my novel in his Sunday paper. Now he was wearing a *Heimwehr* uniform with wearing the cockerel tail feather in his hat. I heard that his father's former connections with Christian Socialist politicians had earned him his position in the national news agency.

The weather was hot. Lying motionless for hours in the sun at the public swimming pools in Döbling and Hietzing, one could forget the cares of love, the torment of writing, the hopelessness of politics. At the Hietzing pool I won the second prize – an African necklace of carved horn – in a contest for the best suntan. A rich Egyptian sent me a message that he would pay handsomely to spend a weekend with me on the Semmering – he too was obviously convinced of the "loose morals" of the girls of Vienna. Sometimes one could laugh and relax; it was only by living from time to time on a "trivial level" that one could manage to ignore the threatening reality: the small mortar explosions continually set off by the still illegal Nazis around the University, in the Votivpark, or on the terrace of the Café Schottentor; their subversive activities, directed from Munich by Hitler's commissar for Austrian affairs, Theo Habicht; the machinations of the minister Emil Fey.

So it was that the events of July 25, 1934, came as a shock for which I was totally unprepared. "Midday," I noted in my calendar, "the first reports of a Nazi coup." And then: "Dollfuss †." I had little cause to lament his death and not much time to think about the consequences of this first attempt to seize power in Austria, for my personal life was once again intruding into public events. The day after the murder of Dollfuss, I met Peter de Mendelssohn in the Café Schottentor – or was it the Café Landtmann? He had come from Paris to visit his brother Thomas, whom I knew from Schlick's seminars and the Café Herrenhof. Peter's wife, "Tschu" von Tschirschnitz, growing tired of the privations of exile, had left him to return to her father's estate in the Hanover area. As he told me one day much later, he had met Claire and Yvan Goll at the Gare de l'Est, and they asked him why he was traveling to Vienna. "I'm going there to marry a girl called Hilde Spiel," he replied. At that time, he knew only my book, of which he had never even acknowledged receipt. And although I informed my calendar as early as the beginning of August that Peter was "definitely the man for me," the one to whom I wanted to commit myself, it took another two years, and much, much more was to happen in between.

Soon after this entry in my calendar, emotionally crushed by the conflict which Peter's appearance had provoked, particularly with Thorn, I fled from the city to St. Wolfgang, where the composer Erich, the lawyer Susi, and the painter Lisel had booked into various small hotels. They were reassuring company. During the day we swam, rowed and painted watercolors by the lake, in the evening Erich Zeisl conjured up the entire range of instruments of Beethoven's Pastoral Symphony on the out-of-tune piano at his boarding-house, to the accompaniment of a thunderstorm outside. On August 16 – I like to confirm the reality of what happened by means of these precise dates – Lisel and I made the acquaintance of two Belgians, the Walloon Paul Delpire and the Fleming Richard de Kriek. They were touring Europe in a little Ford – considered as chic and amusing at that time as the Mini was some thirty years later – in the company of the much older Monsieur Byloës, and by chance our paths crossed. Within a few days a strange interplay of feelings developed, a constant changing of partners which took place with as much ease and lightness as in a ballet, if at certain moments not without a touch of melancholy. The Belgians drove to Vienna, returned to St. Wolfgang; we spent an evening together in Salzburg; then they left, as we thought, forever. But I was to meet them again.

In Vienna there were more serious complications to deal with. "Both men wept," I noted on a page of my calendar. How emotional we all were in those days! From time to time, almost like a *diabolus ex machina*, my friend-enemy kept reappearing. "Torberg put pressure on me in his dreadful way." Eternities later, on a rainy afternoon, under the canopy of the Café Bazar in Salzburg, I was sitting with Ingeborg Bachmann. As the rain dripped down close to our table, she told me of an evening with friends when Torberg had tormented her verbally and reduced her to tears of impotent rage. On September 24, I completed *Der Sonderzug*. Then I "finished," first with Peter, the next day with Fritz Thorn. And at the beginning of October I left for Paris with this very same Peter, as well as an assistant to Professor Bühler, Käthe Wolf, and my fellow-student Lotte Reiter, to attend a congress on scientific films led by Jean Painlevé: my third, not the least momentous visit to that city.

At first I, like Peter, whose *Paris über mir* I had recently reread, stayed at his beloved Hôtel des Grands Hommes on the Place du Panthéon, which plays its part in his book. It had been his home for years. But thanks to the extreme fluctuations to which my feelings were subject at that time, I walked out onto my balcony at half past three one morning and stared at the Panthéon in a state of the deepest depression. Later that morning I moved in with my Viennese friends at a hotel in the Rue de Rivoli, and the following day, at a bar in the Palais Royal, I did after all say a touching farewell to Peter, who was going to Saarbrücken for the election. A letter from Richard de Kriek reached me in Paris, asking me to come to Brussels. That indeed was impossible. In between, I had disagreements with Käthe and Lotte, who rushed off between conference sessions to go window shopping in the fashionable Rue du Faubourg St. Honoré, an activity which I despised. Meanwhile, I wandered about in the wretched back streets of Belleville and Ménilmontant, for me the true, traditional, politically but also artistically more relevant Paris.

After another stopover in Zurich, I was back in Vienna. And now began the process of weakening, of slow but inevitable corruption – one among many reasons why I felt I must emigrate as soon as possible, leave this Austria of the *Ständestaat*, for fear of becoming corrupted myself. After the war, in a radio discussion with Gottfried Benn, Peter explained the necessity of emigration from a country which had become totalitarian by saying that it rendered impossible "the retreat into a false compromise." If a person blocks a path for himself "of which he knows that outwardly it is convenient, but inwardly will take him to hell, then this cannot be in vain." And he added: "We are all particularly weak people, inwardly as well as outwardly, we are all exposed to the most disastrous temptations every day, temptations of a political, intellectual, moral nature, whatever they are. The important thing is to cut off the avenue to these temptations." And this was exactly how I felt at that time.

The temptations came from an unexpected source. Hansi, that beautiful, corrupt creature, whose younger brother had taken his own life – perhaps because of incestuous love for her – had already been married once, to the sculptor Felix Weiss. Now she was the companion of a publisher, Ralph A. Höger, a dark, gaunt fellow who financed his enterprise by shady means. Through him, the profitable but sinister influence of Mussolini's Italy upon Austria seeped through into Peter's and even into my private sphere. Höger, although an original, was in a certain sense so characteristic of the lifestyle and attitude in clerico-fascist Vienna that I give him more attention here than he deserves.

A Catholic by conviction, at the same time a voluptuary and playboy, he used to travel by taxi from one to another of the seven churches in which, by old Viennese folk tradition, people visited the Holy Sepulchre set up there on Easter Saturday. Going on pilgrimage to Mariazell with Hansi, he took with him a small whip, which the chambermaid, having unpacked his suitcase, suggestively laid upon his pillow. Even after marrying his Jewish lady, he still spoke in a friendly manner of Hermann Goering, whom he described as a former drinking companion. On the other hand – for the truth was always elusive where Höger was concerned – this companion may have been Goering's younger brother Albert, at the time estranged from Hermann, who lived in Austria and was to vote against the Anschluss. Playing off Hitler's various ministers against us may have been only one of Höger's notoriously bad jokes. The money for his firm at any rate came from Milan or Turin; no one knew from whom or to what purpose, for he published nothing which could justify the financial contribution from Italy – no politically colored literature, only literary works of a totally acceptable kind.

It was not only I who offered a book to Höger for publication; Peter too was to do so. At that time Peter was in Saarbrücken with Prince Hubertus von Löwenstein, taking part in the election campaign for the Saar to remain under the protection of the League of Nations. In between, he repeatedly came to Vienna, where meanwhile another phenomenon of the time in Austria, the twilit figure of Klaus Dohrn, had settled with his young wife Anneli. He edited the weekly journal *Der christliche Ständestaat*. Klaus came from a highly respectable German family of landowners and scholars; he was the grandson of Anton Dohrn, the great zoologist and builder of the marine research station in Naples, and the son of the noted patron of the arts Wolf Dohrn, who founded the garden colony of Hellerau and persuaded Peter's father among others to settle there. A highly intelligent intriguer, he fell under the influence of the Austrian Right and edited a polemical newsletter directed against the neighboring Nazi dictatorship, but from the point of view of the Schuschnigg regime. With Peter, I went to visit his former schoolfellow. At the bedside of Dohrn's little daughter Beatrix stood a Princess of Braganza, whom he had persuaded to be her godmother. There we also met, as I noted, a "Jew-devouring SS man." *Qui mange du fascisme, en meurt.* Peter too was distressed by this encounter.

Nevertheless, as one of the first émigrés, Peter discovered in the Saar, under Löwenstein's influence, his nationalistic, as well as violently anti-Nazi, feeling for Germany; in his utopian exuberance, he would have liked to imagine it as a democratic state under the

Prince's leadership. His own mother as well as his youngest brother – like him, in strict terms scarcely endangered by the fact of a single Jewish grandfather, but branded as a result of the name he bore – and a half sister were still living in Hitler's Third Reich. Peter should have borne this in mind, but did not, as was proved by his commitment in the Saar. At any rate, his book about the minnesinger Oswalt von Wolkenstein, with which he was now occupied, was to be published by Höger under the pseudonym Carl Johann Leuchtenberg. This was Höger's wish, and Peter knew that he would find no other publisher for his ambitious attempt to describe, in a thoroughly archaic German, the life of the medieval Tyrolean knight, soldier, and wandering minstrel. This massive work attracted enthusiastic reviews in Nazi Germany. And in the autumn of 1936 my father, in his admiration for this literary tour de force, which accorded so much with his way of thinking, approved my decision to marry Peter.

But for the present, the fateful year of 1934 was approaching its end. On New Year's Eve an odd thing happened. A wild bunch – as I can only call it – of young people, students, artists, persons of uncertain ways of life had been asked to a party in the family home of a woman painter, a friend of Lisel's. It was a collector's house, full of beautiful paintings and costly porcelain. The guests got drunk and some became unruly. Just after some of them had been admiring the portfolios of Hiroshige prints, there was a sudden crash of delicate wine glasses; someone fell against some Chinese plates hung on the wall, shattering them on the floor. Amid the rattle and clatter, I fled into a smaller room and unwittingly found myself alone with Torberg, and somehow I, the hated bluestocking, the pirate in his waters, found myself in the embrace of my friend-enemy. It could have been a natural occurrence, only a little side step in the minuet of emotions such as we all used to make. But Torberg the man could not deny Torberg the intellectual. He abruptly pushed me away, looked deep into my eyes and said questioningly: "*Frau?*" What an embarrassing situation! It took me several days to get over it.

January began badly. On the 7th the publisher Zsolnay rejected *Der Sonderzug*. It was, I recorded, "the greatest disappointment of my life," and so it has remained, in my professional life at any rate. A lost illusion, no less so than the end of my first love affair, and just as indelibly engraved on my consciousness. Marie Bashkirtseff's "spots on the mirror of my soul," which she had wanted to keep un-blemished, had now appeared on mine as well. Nevertheless, I labored on at a story which I had begun to write "under the influence of Julien Green." At home, there were money problems, and another presumed suicide attempt by my uncle Felix; it then turned out that he had been arrested. One evening I was at Hansi Höger's again in the role of a chambermaid, before she set off for the Opera Ball, "as beautiful as a fairy." On January 28 I went to a reading given by Thomas Mann. And because it was Mann who, far ahead in the future, was to cause me to fall out once again with Torberg and who was to dominate the last ten years of Peter's life, I would like to repeat here my naive comments as a member of his audience:

A well-groomed gentleman with a white-edged waistcoat – quite the Hanseatic citizen. Too thin below the waist, though, and the trousers a little too short. An indescribable presence! The charm, music, and gesture of his public speaking! Incomparable. His pronunciation, thank God, is South German, with a very slightly clipped *Reichsdeutsch* accent. So effortless, warm, nice, and kind in everything, perhaps rather like Schlick at his most wonderful. A paternal manner when he watches his dog with a look of amusement and pleasure. At the end – he reads for a long time, from half past seven to a quarter to ten, with an intermission – at the end, he closes his book sharply, in the middle of a gently flowing passage, and says, "Well, that's enough now," and goes. The audience demands five encores. Finally he raises his hands: "Now let me go, children, and go home sensibly, as I am going to do." A few descriptions from *Joseph in Egypt* are "melting." The most beautiful about the Sphinx. For hers was *permanence*, a *false eternity*."

Höger did not want to publish *Der Sonderzug* either; he preferred the idea of a little summer book that I had in mind. The following month he accepted my outline, but insisted on a title which annoyed me, because it sounded "cinematic, like something by Vicki Baum." It was not until 1986, when the little book came out for the third time, that I managed to get rid of the title. And soon I regretted putting my delightful experience with the Belgians of the previous year onto paper; I also regretted the lightness of touch requested by the publisher. At the end of March: "Oh Flaubert, Julien Green, Giono, Giraudoux – I am writing a pot-boiler, a piece of flim-flam that doesn't even make sense – forgive me." I am well aware today that Colette would have handled it better. But the little volume was praised by Hermann Hesse. On April 4, two events took place which were typical of my intellectual and emotional range at the time. In the afternoon I saw the "wonderful, wonderful film *Resurrection* based on the Tolstoy novel"; in the evening I met an Italian diplomat, Tino Martinelli, at Höger's, and promptly went "alone with him to the Sanssouci-Bar."

Tino was about forty, a man like a tree, handsome, tall, mustached, and a fascist by conviction. Presumably he was in charge of the secret service at the Italian embassy, for he was the head of the passport control section, whose duties, it was said, included espionage. Weeks later, he informed me mockingly what information was held in the Austrian police dossier on my father; not only was there still such a thing, as in the days of Emperor Franz, and still is today about every citizen of any note in the country, but even the emissaries of the Mussolini protectorate had unobstructed access to it in the *Ständestaat*. Not only this, but the details were inaccurate. My father was described as a Socialist. I told Tino, "He is a liberal; I am the Socialist." Perhaps this was a dangerous remark to make, but Tino, although an animal, did have a spark of decency. "An animal! He is an animal! An animal!" was the repeated cry in my pocket calendar. Today he would be described as "macho," a sadistic eroticist, but then again he would show childish enjoyment at a boxing match, an opera performance by a touring Italian company, or an excursion to Heiligenkreuz in the southern Vienna woods. There would be wild eruptions in a hotel where rooms were let by the hour; then the following morning a messenger would arrive at my parents' apartment with fifty dark red roses, which were placed on my white cot.

"No, there is no aesthetic armor against 'the fascistic'" – so I read in an essay, "Dangerous Feelings," in the weekly magazine *Die Zeit*. I was helpless, entranced and appalled by this man; I called him a coachman, a horse, I wrote a short story called "Das Pferd Hyazinth" (The Horse Called Hyacinth) in which a mythologically transfigured

Tino collides with another horse in London's Rotten Row, falls and is killed; at his side I allowed myself to sink ever further into the swamp of those times. By day – having finished my little book – I went to Schlick's readings, presented to the Bühler seminar the outline of a "theory of representation in film" which I was trying to develop in my thesis; Schlick's assistant Friedrich Waismann was among the listeners; "Bühler delighted"; there was even talk, probably jesting, of a "new Lessing." In the evening, my life was one of dissipation, mostly in the Högers' company; Hans Békessy came along as well, now luxuriously established in Vienna after a lengthy stay in Geneva as a correspondent for the League of Nations, married to a new, well-to-do wife, a divorced Mosse, and editing a weekly paper. We gadded about from one *Lokal* to another – the Kerzenstüberl, Berta Kunz's, the Sanssouci-Bar, the Kaiser-Bar, Reiss-Bar, and Rotterbar – drinking too much, wisecracking, surrounded by the new masters, the elite with the cockerel feathers in their hats. Not even the purest snow of my Sunday skiing expeditions could cover up the grime of this kind of morality, and it was only for a brief period that I stayed oblivious of it. One day, I encountered Thorn in the street. He "stared at me without speaking."

When did I actually do any studying? I was writing stories – I had already completed forty of them – and working on my thesis. I sat in the Café Schottentor, opposite the university, in whose little front garden the illegal Nazis' mortar bombs were going off again this spring. There were Nazi riots even in the *alma mater* itself. Once, I arrived on the scene as a Jewish student was beaten up and thrown down the University steps, to lie bleeding at the bottom – a horror which became for me, who was to emigrate the following year, symbolic of everything that happened in 1938. In the Schottentor, we were looked after by the red-haired waiter Herr Ignaz, who later turned out to be a secret helper of the persecuted, though he lacked the dignity of the head waiter Herr Hnatek or the heavily obsequious charm of Herr Albert, a waiter at the Herrenhof. For a long time I heard nothing from Peter. We learned that he was spending the summer as a house guest of Hubertus Löwenstein at Schloss Matzen in the Tyrol, settling into the character and history of Oswalt von Wolkenstein.

In June my little summer novel was published. Soon afterward, I met by chance the publisher to whom I owed the stains on my soul, Paul Zsolnay. "Dear Hilde, this is a book I would have published too," he said. There was no answer to this but a rueful smile. August came. I wanted to go away. With very little money, I traveled to Belgium, in the face of Tino's wrathful protests. In his unpredictable way, having come to terms with my departure, he announced that he wanted to deposit money for me at the Brussels branch of CIT, the Italian state travel agency. I proudly declined the offer. On arriving in Brussels, I went to stay with my school friend Maydie, who had moved there on her marriage; I had no plans to contact Paul and Richard, preferring to avoid further complications. But, as so often happened during those years, I seemed to attract unexpected encounters as if by magnetism, or perhaps the magnetic pull came from the other direction.

Strolling on the Avenue Marnix, I saw a car stop at the edge of the pavement. It was the little Ford, with the two men in it. They were together again for the first time after many weeks of separation, and traveling in Richard's car – Paul had had a Mercedes for some time. They were planning a journey to Venice in three days' time. They were thunderstruck to come across me "*par hasard*" in Brussels. During the short time before their departure, I was continually with one or both of them, at the Exposition, in the Rue Haute or the Rue Zérézo. "Richard is enchanting. Conversations about *sensibilité*." In between, I went to the great Impressionist exhibition, which left me "almost dazed." On their last evening we all had dinner together in a country restaurant on the main road out of the city to the east. And again the magnetism worked. As we approached the car – Paul's Mercedes this time – to drive back into town, we were hailed by the driver of a foreign car, who looked out of the window to ask for directions. It was Baron D., Maria's husband. Then Maria jumped out of the car and we embraced.

It was only in my old age and long after his death that I realized that women did not mean much to Paul Delpire; he only liked to caress them gently like puppies, like smooth little marble figures which are pleasant to stroke. He married late in life. Unlike his friend Richard, he did not take part in the resistance against the Germans, but became involved with them to a certain extent. His apartment in the Rue des deux Églises was furnished in exquisite taste; he generously offered it to me when he left with Richard for Venice, and I lived there for a week. "I am living the life of a highly cultured young Belgian gentleman," I noted. In his library I found and immediately read Gide's *Nourritures terrestres* and a wonderful book from which, contemptibly, I refused to be parted, Paul Drouot's *Eurydice deux fois perdue*. I did thank its owner for it as profusely as I was able. From the little radio on his bedside table I heard the beguiling strains of Paul Whiteman's swing band from across the Channel, for Delpire, like most of his generation, was at that time Anglophile to the highest degree, and his radio was permanently tuned to the BBC.

In the end I swallowed my pride, went to the CIT office, and withdrew the four hundred Belgian francs Tino had transferred there for me. I traveled to Bruges, to Ghent and Ostend, where, over port and cheddar in a little bar, England seemed close enough to reach out and touch. I visited Antwerp with Hélène Yelin, an Egyptian friend of Paul's and Richard's. In Stenockerzeel, I attempted to gain admittance at the residence of the Austrian imperial family, but they were on holiday at Juan-les-Pins, and the butler merely pointed regretfully at the seven Habsburg descendants' raincoats, hanging in graduated order of length in the hall of the little lakeside castle. I learned that these disinherited members of an ancient dynasty had settled in this little Belgian backwater. Six years later, in May 1941, when Belgium was occupied, I wrote an article for the London exiles' newspaper *Die Zeitung* in which I wished myself back in its "great peace." I recalled everything which had fascinated me that summer – the country fair at Pepinster, the Grand' Place in Brussels, the city where "French wit mingles with Netherlandish energy," the painters of the Flemish school and the new Flemish painters de Godelaer, Van Vlasselaer, and Devos, the convent of the Beguines in Bruges. "What unearthly quiet! If ever anyone, oppressed by the harsh sounds of life, longed for some indefinite place of refuge in the future – this was where it could be found." And I closed, in a melancholy vein: "Nostalgia for these things is more than nostalgia for Belgium. It is nostalgia for a Europe which has learned how to live in peace."

On my return to Vienna it began all over again, the intoxication, the poverty, the inner turmoil. "I am too afraid of unhappiness to be unhappy." The expression "*Wedekindergarten*" was used, but actually we were all much too old for this to be valid. Tino tormented me, loved me, lied to me. On October 3 the war in Abyssinia began, and Signor Martinelli was constantly busy at the Embassy – I preferred not to know with what. On October 9 I finished my thesis, handed it in and promptly took an oral examination, which I passed. Peter turned up and in turn was also drawn into the dubious hurly-burly. With him, the Högers and the Békessys, we went to a new night club called Sonjas Plüschsofa – Sonja's Plush Sofa – which had been opened by German immigrants. In between: "In the morning I studied Leibniz," and the next day: "In the morning I studied Kant." Echoing Schiller and Byron, I lamented: "Twenty-four, and I have done nothing for eternity!" At the end of the month, I found out that the apartment where Tino had sometimes entertained me with scampi, which he cooked himself, *insalata mista*, and wonderful red wine, belonged to an elegant woman journalist, and that he was not only her lodger but also her lover.

The delusion had lasted for seven months. Perhaps it was not quite a delusion, for Tino later told the Högers: "I loved the Spiel girl very much, but for me she is dead. I can put up with bad behavior, but not stupidity." My alleged stupidity lay in refusing to see him again when I found out about the situation which he had underhandedly kept secret. It was like a scene from an operetta – as in that cliché of the genre, the angry farewell at the end of the second act before the intermission, to be followed by the reconciliation in the final act – when a friend of the house, on my instructions, announced to the unsuspecting visitor: "Fräulein Hilde is no longer at home to you." In retrospect, the scene gives me as much pleasure as the one in *Polenblut*, when the soprano Betty Fischer, playing Helena, after taking revenge on Count Boleslaw, played by the tenor Hubert Marischka, hurled at him the words: "*Herr Kraf, wir sind kitt*" (Count, we are finished).

Operetta and cheap literature: at that time, my enjoyment of these was unfortunately not unclouded. But the break gave me new energy. I studied as if possessed. In the middle of December, I passed my examination, with unanimous praise from Schlick and Bühler. A week later I went "out on the tiles till four in the morning" with the Högers, Torberg, and Robert Neumann. These contradictions, this dancing on the edge of the volcano, seem to me to reflect very clearly the Vienna of the thirties, just before the arrival of Hitler.

6

The Last Year

If I were to go on describing my life at a leisurely, measured pace, as I have done so far, with the same wealth of melismas and discords, this book would become intolerably long. Soon I must begin to condense more ruthlessly, and discard completely much that appeared important at the time, but now seems trivial. The more closely my account approaches the present, the less I need to describe the times themselves, as distinct from the private destinies that followed in their wake. The climate in which I grew up, however, is largely foreign to my younger contemporaries. The emotional and moral needs that oppressed us during the first half of the century present themselves very differently today.

Young people like myself – constantly wavering between extremes of emotion, deeply at odds with themselves, extravagant in behavior yet introverted, helplessly at the mercy of external forces, cheerful in the face of despair and skeptically confident, committed to high moral principles and yet so weak, so easily seduced, in everyday life – such young people can be imagined only against the insecure backdrop of the twenties and thirties. How a man like Robert Neumann, who had made a new life for himself in London soon after that bloody February, could return again and again and, as I observed in my pocket calendar, enjoy the night life in the heart of the *Ständestaat*, along with such dubious figures as Höger and Békessy; how my beloved Hafis, as well as Ernst Fischer, now a "revolutionary Socialist" and, like him, living in Prague, could turn up in Vienna for short, more or less secret visits, one to be found at the Högers', the other at Anna Mahler's salon, along with all the *Heimwehr* officers: all this is hard to explain except by the fascination of that city, even in its shimmering putrescence.

Even Peter de Mendelssohn, always a man of an upright, very

Germanic – in a good sense – way of thinking, occasionally found himself sinking into this mire. "Is art more important than principles, or are principles more important than art?" he was to ask in later years. "Is art worthy of consideration if it is nourished by the sacrifice of principles?" In 1952 his answer was unequivocal, as it could not have been in 1935. However, he had understanding for his earlier attitude: "*Todesverachtung* [contempt for death] is a word. In our time, there has been many a brave spirit under tyranny to show that it is not an empty word. Some have been capable of it; many have proved that they were. But it is not given to all. Those to whom it is not given have the final resort of exile." But what if there is no fundamental difference between the place of refuge and the tyranny from which one has fled? Even Karl Kraus regarded Austrian fascism as a "lesser evil," and anyone who could experience its more slackly implemented constraints as a relief had already forgotten what true freedom was.

"To cut off one's own retreat" – Peter's solution was equally valid for me. I was ready to adopt it, but only after I had completed my studies. I still had to pass in a subsidiary subject; I had chosen ethnology, although it was taught by the nationalistic Professor Oswald Menghin, who was to become rector of the University immediately after the Anschluss. Peter, on the other hand, had decamped from Paris after that Tyrolean summer and followed Hubertus Löwenstein and his entourage to London. In December he came to Vienna again, though not with the sole purpose of renewing his relationship with me. On Christmas Day, he read to me from his completed manuscript of *Wolkenstein*, which he was about to deliver to Höger. The book immediately reminded me of de Coster's *Ulenspiegel* or even Grimmelshausen. The following day, it was my friend-enemy's turn: "Evening with Torberg, whose novel is dreadful." This can only have been *Die Mannschaft* (*The Team*), and certainly I was not unbiased in my judgment. My last New Year's Eve in Vienna was celebrated in the Högers' luxury apartment in the Biberstrasse. A footman who reminded me of Leopold, the servant of Ochs von Lerchenau in *Der Rosenkavalier*, waited on us in white gloves. A fortune teller informed me that in the coming year I would travel abroad, across water.

And already, just as in that Viennese *La Ronde* which we were all reliving, the next gentleman was about to appear on the scene. On the first Sunday in January, I drove with my parents and their friend Dr. Tafler, a lawyer working for the Creditanstalt, in his car to visit another member of the student corps, who owned a little villa in Neuhaus, in the hilly Triestingtal. In the evening, as we sat in the Markus family's pleasantly rustic living room, more visitors arrived, an architect and his wife. I was thunderstruck, for Willi K. and my passionate tormentor of the previous spring were as alike as two peas in a pod. "K. is another Tino, but at the same time the best, most childlike, and purest of men. Happily married." Nevertheless, he seemed to have been struck by the same *coup de foudre*, though not for months did this erupt into a tempest. For the time being, we did not see each other again.

During the weeks that followed, while I was familiarizing myself with the basics of ethnology, new encounters were taking place in the inner city of Vienna, as if in a ceremonious or even feverish quadrille. In the Café Herrenhof, Peter and Torberg sat at the same table, while Jakob Hegner from Hellerau appeared at the house of Klaus Dohrn, who was still editing the anti-liberal, Catholic organ of an "authoritarian *Ständestaat*, Fascist in character." Charlotte Bühler's assistant Käthe Wolf had broken off her secret analysis by the Freudian Hartmann, having at last entered into a satisfying relationship, with a Count Auersperg. I argued with Walther Hollitscher about Elias Canetti's recently published novel *Die Blendung* (*Auto da Fé*), to which I preferred Giono's *Que ma joie demeure*. And when I gained my doctorate, I danced in the Kaiserbar until four in the morning with a visitor from Paris, Reggie Raffles, the partner of Mistinguett, and with Robert Neumann. My success was celebrated in early February with great pomp, telegrams, and bouquets, if not *sub auspiciis presidentis*, as that custom had been abolished. In the Café Schottentor opposite, according to another custom, the waiters, led by Herr Ignaz, formed a guard of honor and shouted in chorus: "Congratulations, Frau Doktor!"

Many things were now changing for me, though I made no major decisions. From one day to the next, I gave up my green fountain-pen ink for plain black. I had my blonde hair tinted back to its natural dark color. Hardly realizing it, I experienced my last *Fasching* in Vienna at the costume ball of the Secession, where I flirted with a splendid white-haired gentleman with the untranslatably reversible name of

Bergrat Fluss (Mining-Company-Director River); and in the early hours of the morning I saw the poet Josef Weinheber leap onto a table and make a speech in support of the Nazis. Yes, this was in 1936. And then, completely exhausted by nights of alternate studying and frenzied nightlife, I took my skis and traveled alone to Kitzbühel, where I checked into a modest hotel.

Two and a half weeks of glorious mountain air and extreme physical effort washed away the rituals and excesses of Vienna. I read in my calendar: "Three hours of painful ascent of the Hahnenkamm. Descent of the Kaserer. Courageous"; "Morning, dashed up the Hahnenkamm. Difficult descent of the Ochsenhorn"; "At Hofbrunn on the Bräuenalp I met my handsome *Bergrat*"; "On the Kitzbüheler Horn with the crazy Baroness. Most difficult climb."

Every day I forced myself to achieve some physical feat and I felt more and more relaxed, more liberated from the oppressive atmosphere of the city. This too was a "last time"; there was to be no skiing in England. Once, in the evening, I went to the Kitzbühel casino, won six schillings and immediately left the building. I have never had a mania for gambling like Dostoevsky, Tibor Déry, or Torberg. Before my return to Vienna, I visited the painter Alfons Walde in his studio, full of innumerable, almost identical snow scenes featuring flat, monochrome village houses and roofs and plump peasant women in Tyrolean costume; I called on the physicist Hans Thirring, as eminent as he was modest, and Harald Dohrn and his wife, who had emigrated temporarily to the Tyrol, touchingly unpretentious, decent people, closely related to the enigmatic Klaus Dohrn.

Back in Vienna, in disgust at the grey heavens, the grey streets, I took refuge in a bronchitis attack. And in a premonition of the changes that the year was to bring, I nestled ever more cozily into my old nursery room. "Feel very well protected. Strong feeling of affinity with my parents." It was early spring. I was writing a novel, with which I was not to get very far, and because my heroine was a medical student I made repeated excursions into neurology, psychiatry and anatomy. I went to lectures by Pötzl and Hoff, where schizophrenic patients were paraded in front of the students. In the anatomical institute, I watched the dissection of the torso of an old woman – once and never again. The sight was horrendous. I would never be any good as a doctor. Two new mentors – today they would be called gurus – appeared during the weeks and months that followed; I called them the Magus and the Docteur. The Magus was fifty-four, a gaunt private scholar with the deeply wrinkled brow of the thinker, a vegetarian, a *Mystagog*, a universalist, from a family of rich industrialists, who lived alone with his old mother in a *Jugendstil* house on the Wieden, and every morning went to the Nationalbibliothek. Here I must anticipate: after spending his exile concealed in a Trappist monastery in Belgium, he returned to find the whole of his enormous library for sale in the bookstalls of the Josefsplatz. He did not get back a single volume.

I had met the Docteur at the Bühler seminar; he was the Freudian scholar René Spitz, who already lived in Paris at that time and had become quite Frenchified. Because I was not planning to leave Austria until the autumn and needed money until then, I accepted his offer to employ me as something between secretary and colleague. The Docteur was working on some analytical project, I can no longer remember what, but, as with Berthold Viertel later on, we hardly ever got any real work done. He would begin telling me stories; he was amusing and instructive and liked to show off in front of his listener. Behind every conversation, palely blending into the background, as with Käthe Wolf, hovered the father figure of Sigmund Freud. I had read his most important works but had graduated in philosophy without ever having been questioned about him. Once, with a thrill of reverence, I saw Freud himself near his summer residence in Khevenhüllerstrasse in Pötzleinsdorf, a small gentleman in greenish walking clothes, with breeches, and leggings of cloth wound round his legs in strips, like puttees.

The Magus wanted to convert me to mysticism. This was impossible for a student of Schlick's. But I sat at his feet – often with Stefan Possony, who decades later was to be a member of the Pentagon brain trust – listening to his art-history discourses, his interpretations of visual symbols, his gnostic and cabbalistic instructions. When the Magus suggested that I should join him on an artistic tour of Italy in the summer, the plan did not seem too outlandish to me. At Easter I traveled to Neuhaus again with my parents. And here the situation sparked off by that *coup de foudre* at the beginning of the year at last resolved itself. On the first day it rained.

The air on the little hill was less biting than in the Tyrol, but just as pure. We ate our Easter ham in the well-heated parlor, but when the sun came out, we walked in the woods. Willi, the architect, was dressed in country style, with a colorful embroidered waistcoat; in the corridor of the comfortable Curhotel d'Orange, and under the spring trees still dripping with rain, we became close to each other. How could Willi's astonishing resemblance to Tino be explained? Somebody had once suggested that Tino's name was not Martinelli at all, that he had a Slav name such as Vukovic, and had been born in Pula in Istria, the former military harbor of the monarchy, with its ancient Venetian past. Perhaps this was an Austrian manifestation, an amalgam of Croat and Italian ancestry, which he may have had in common with Willi and to which both men owed their tall, powerful stature and grace of movement. Recently, Tino himself had made renewed attempts to curry favor with me, sent me messages through the Högers, and even, when we met by chance near his embassy, caught hold of my hand and spoke to me in an insistent tone – "he was unshaven and horrible, I laughed at him." Now his image, within the same contours, had been overpainted with a different facial expression and finally blotted out altogether.

Meanwhile, my relationship with Willi was doomed to failure from the start. This good-hearted man would never have been capable of leaving his wife, and I myself would not have wanted him to do so. What it would have been like to spend the Hitler years in Vienna under his protection became evident to me after the war. A temporary love, then, which he lived through with desperate passion and constant feelings of guilt toward his Elsa, presumably more painful than happy for him. We would meet in a little apartment and he would bring me delicate tearoses or books – *Pierre et Luc* by Romain Rolland, and Kurt Hamsun's *Mysterien*. It was beautiful, peaceful, sometimes melancholy. We both suspected that all this would probably end with the summer.

On June 22, 1936, I traveled to town on the number 71 streetcar, and by chance glimpsed the headline of a newspaper over my neighbor's shoulder: "The philosopher Moritz Schlick shot dead." Even today I sense how my knees became weak, my head dizzy. Involuntarily my tears coursed down, there in the overcrowded streetcar. I got off and leaned for a long time against a house wall. It was the deepest of sorrows that I had yet experienced, not to be compared with the earlier pains of love,. I wrote one of the first tributes to this great man (it was published by the *Neue Freie Presse*), in which I called him the model of humanity for us all – "no one could have been unaware, not only of his clarity of thought, but also of his desire for decency of moral feeling." But the *Ständestaat* press immediately distorted his image.

The weekly *Die schönere Zukunft* (*The more beautiful future*) gave him the following obituary: "The Jew is a born a-metaphysician; what he loves in philosophy is *Logozismus*, mathematicism, formalism, and positivism, all qualities which were united in Schlick to the highest degree." And a "Professor Austriacus" forecast that Schlick's murder would "lead toward a truly satisfying solution of the Jewish question." All this, at a time when the Nazi party was still illegal! In the *Linzer Volksblatt*, the authentic clerico-authoritarian tones could be heard. Schlick was said to have corrupted "the fine porcelain of the national character," "the native children of the soil, the noble growth of the intellectual reserve of strength of our farming community." Declared to be a "*Muss-Jude*," his truly liberal attitude attributed to "Austro-Marxism," he became branded as a guilty murder victim, whose murderer was in reality innocent. This man, Hans Nelböck, a university-educated peasant's son, classed as a "schizoid psychopath" by the hospital director Pötzl, had committed the act out of unfounded jealousy, but explained it later as an act of revenge for the loss of his religious faith as a result of Schlick's teaching. This saved him from the death sentence. He was put into the mental hospital of Steinhof for three months and then served a two-year sentence. Six months after the German invasion, he was released.

The decision to leave Austria was one I had made long ago. I was living in a sort of limbo. The question was, where should I go? The Docteur – who on one occasion, shamming illness, received me in pajamas and an oriental dressing gown – argued in favor of Paris. The Magus was of the opinion that I should first travel to Italy with him, and postpone the decision till the autumn. I did not need to fear any erotic approach by this ascetic man who seemed interested only in my spiritual development. In fact, it was only once, on Capri, that he lost his composure, and that not without reason. Meanwhile he provided me with sources for Karoline von Günderode, whose biography I was tempted to undertake, and advised me against the "novel about a red-haired woman" which I was also contemplating at the time. An entry in my calendar, shortly before our departure, reads simply: "Torberg incessantly abuses me" – where, and about what, remains unclear. On the last day but one, I met Willi. He gave me a present of more symbolic significance than practical use at that time of year – an umbrella. In the evening, I was visited by Joe Lederer; she was a novelist, famous at the time, who had returned from Berlin to Vienna, and we had become friends. On Sunday, July 5, I left for Venice with the Magus. I had saved up the money I had received for my work for the Docteur, and was otherwise not quite without means. Certainly, the Magus, a rich private scholar, took the responsibility for all the additional comforts of the next six weeks. But we traveled modestly, in third-class train compartments or by local bus, staying in little hotels or pensions that were clean but by no means luxurious, and living on a mostly vegetarian diet, although the Magus did not stand in the way of my occasional wish for more substantial food. Thus, after six weeks, every so often making shorter or longer stops, we gradually got as far as Naples. We spent many hours each day in churches and art galleries.

We had no need of Goethe (who in fact often made derogatory remarks about Italy) to make us fall under the spell of "the land where the lemon trees bloom." Who, particularly in the time before mass tourism, could resist that beauty and easy way of living, these relics of ancient greatness and dignity? The man with whom I was to share the second half of my life went into ecstasies whenever he stepped onto Italian soil. *Haec est Italia, diis sacra!* was his first greeting. To be sure, at that time it was the land of Mussolini: the land of the blackshirts who strutted everywhere like peacocks; of the puffed-up *bersaglieri* with their cockerel feathers who had become the model for our *Heimwehr*; of the hubristic heroism which broke down in all the world wars, but found itself confirmed by the victory recently achieved over the poor, helpless Ethiopians. But did all this in any way cloud our enjoyment? To be honest: not very much.

While we admired the charming little Duchess in the Uffizi or Donatello's young David in the Bargello, while we stood spellbound in front of Cimabue's St. Francis in Assisi or looked out from the little temple of the Clitunno over the Umbrian landscape and the grove of the gods, the Duce's regiments were already arming to take part in the Spanish Civil War. In the visitors' book which lay open in the Marchese Guglielmi's villa on the island in Lake Trasimeno, the names of General Franco and his whole family were inscribed. Italian troops were now planning a return visit to fight alongside his army. We, however, continued our investigations of this country that was still so blessed, although ruled by the accursed fascists. In Passignano, by the lake, the *segretario politico* and the lawyer sat in the café in intimate conference with Dottore Cohen, but on the opposite shore the young flight officers were being trained for service in Spain. I met one of them, Mario, and danced half the night away with him.

How does one, later on, come to terms with such memories? Someone like me writes a book about them. I was already dreaming one up during my travels; it was to be called *Licht in Umbrien* (*Light in Umbria*). In England, where it came into being and was first published, the title was changed and the story placed a year earlier, but everything I experienced during those summer weeks went into it, and more that I invented. In it, I gave more attention to the political background than we had done at the time, but everything had been stored in my subconscious and came to light at the right moment. On July 11, the very date on which I had attended the ball in Passignano, an agreement between Hitler and Schuschnigg was signed in Vienna by the German ambassador, von Papen. The Magus read the news in the Italian papers and, without outward emotion, announced to me the imminent end of Austrian independence. The Chancellor had now dismissed the *Heimwehr* and its leaders, who had become irksome to him, but while he was now playing the strong man, he was said to be still too weak to make use of his breathing space. The Magus realized and explained all this to me, yet it did not occur to him to abandon his house and great library in the Mayerhofgasse. For the time being, we were traveling farther south, through Umbria and the Abruzzi to Rome.

Why portray yet again what I have already described *con amore*? "Wine olives sun laurels," runs the note in my little calendar, and "Perugia, the most beautiful city of my life." Perhaps it still is. We spent eleven days there, and walked as far as Assisi one night, arriving in the grey of dawn. At the summer university, we met Spaniards, Germans, Dutch, Swiss, and French, as well as two American girls who begged us to look up one of their friends in Rome, a young writer called Alberto Moravia, who had caused a stir years ago with his first novel *Gli Indifferenti*. But when we arrived in Rome from Aquila on the first of August, we were told that Moravia was on Capri. We were even given the address.

In recent days the Magus, although he had not only guided me through the Vatican, through many churches, the Forum and the Colosseum, the Capitol, and the Quirinal, but also taken me to distinguished restaurants such as the Fedelinaro, had often seemed unfriendly and irritable, as though this trip had not quite worked out as he had planned. He was, after all, although by nature practically a recluse, not exclusively a man of the spirit, and less undemanding in his needs than I had thought and he had caused me to believe. A man of fifty-four – good heavens, an old man to me then! But I had deceived myself and perhaps also failed to consider his feelings in various ways. Nevertheless, he did not lose his patience, and gave only slight hints of ill humor. After six days, we decided to cut short our stay in Naples and travel to Capri. The crossing was calm. Unsuspectingly we disembarked on the wrong side of the island. Nobody lived on the Marina Grande. But by evening, we were sitting in the café on the piazza above.

In reality, the Magus had no grounds for complaint. Without earning it, he enjoyed the camaraderie of the young people who surrounded me everywhere. How else might an eccentric confirmed bachelor, withered, dried up, and arrogant, even dismissive in manner, in the awareness of his intelligence and education, have gained effortless access to people of my age, such as I encountered in every spot or town in Italy? It was the same on Capri. As soon as we arrived, we left a message at Moravia's lodgings to say where we might be reached. At first he failed to find us: "The stupid boy at the hotel got the message wrong." On the following day he did not appear, but I met a girlfriend from Vienna and borrowed some money from her, for I wanted to stay a few more days.

In the Bar Tiberio we met the painter Jakovlev, who knew Moravia. Something was in the air; the Magus, probably gifted with second sight, had no wish to stay around and brusquely announced his departure for the island of Korcula, where he wanted to meditate in solitude. I shed tears of shame for the hurt he had inflicted on me, and I on him. On the morning of August 10, I accompanied him to the boat for Naples. Then I myself enjoyed a day of solitude in Anacapri. Toward evening I found a message from Moravia at the hotel and climbed the endless steps to the piazza. The bar was full of young people joking in all languages; in their center was Moravia, who immediately drew me to his side. He had a square-cut, unhandsome face, whose expression confused and captivated me; against the background of a deep somberness, laughter lit up his face again and again, exaggerated, even hectic, and yet overshadowed: a contrast I was to encounter again decades later in Thomas Bernhard.

When, unexpectedly, Moravia leapt up and announced his intention of walking me home, I noticed for the first time that he was slightly lame in one leg, though he still moved along with great speed, almost at a run. On the steps to the Marina Grande, he slowed down, and stopped at a dark corner. That night I noted in my little book: "*Amour*," next day: "*Le parfait amour de détresse.*" I had dropped into French because it was in this language that we talked and later wrote to each other. The days that followed passed much as before. I went swimming, explored the island, and only toward evening sought out my new friends. Their wild, witty conversations were often incomprehensible to me when they slipped into their rapid Italian. Much about them struck me as uncanny and fascinating, as did, above all, Moravia himself. One of his companions, Prampolini, had a pronounced limp, much more disabling than that of Moravia; the pair of them, walking together across the piazza, gave the impression of a tragic farce.

At the age of twenty-two, in 1929, Moravia had written his first novel, *Gli Indifferenti*, and become famous overnight. The American women we had met in Perugia had read the book; I knew it as little as *Le ambizioni sbagliate*, which had come out in the spring. In fact I knew nothing about him, and learned about him only by our direct contact: his bitterness, his cynicism, his black erotomania. To this day, although I saw him again on several occasions, and in the meantime familiarized myself with his work, I am not sure what to make of him. That profound seriousness, that dark, solemn brooding, those long pauses in which he appeared to gaze within himself as though he were searching for the primeval slime of creation! And yet he may have been thinking of nothing more than a feminine curve or hollow, for it is evident from his novels and stories how much he is obsessed with sexuality. In the *Indifferenti* there is not a single word to remind the reader of the fascism of the current day. Moravia himself, indeed, a potential victim, spent the end of the war in hiding, and finally became a Communist, a delegate to the Council of Europe, a traveler to Russia, president of International PEN. But who was, who is Moravia really? I do not know.

On Capri, for the short duration of this *amour de détresse*, I had become enchanted by him. The constant alternation in him between sudden gaiety and profound silence fascinated me. The name "Grave," which I gave him in my Italian novel, might or might not match the basic mood of his nature. When I came across him again in Rome after the war, the man I met was the highly successful author of *The Woman of Rome*, known to all by the name "*L'Orso*." He may have appeared unsociable, morose, even bearishly gruff in the company of people who bored or repelled him. There was coldness in his nature, even in his passion. The sudden brightenings of his mood had become rarer. Ten years earlier, he had been capable of more tender feelings; this was clear to me on the evening of our farewell, as it was from the letters I continued to receive from him for weeks afterward. These were to fall victim to the passage of time.

By the middle of the month, I was in Vienna again. "It is beautiful here, cool, pleasant and ordered." I admonished myself: "No nonsense with Peter." Thinking daily of Moravia, I traveled with my parents to the Salzkammergut, to Mattsee, where Peter had taken lodgings, newly arrived from England but already decked out in the local costume. Some of the Löwenstein minions were in the area. Volkmar Zühlsdorff, who used to be known then, half jokingly, half seriously, as "*das kleine Gräflein*," the little Count, briefly fell in love with my mother. On a walk in the woods, over-excited as I had not been for a long time, I wreathed myself with flowers like Ophelia and talked in a fanciful way. Peter lacked frivolity and was incapable of falling in with my mood. Nevertheless, a future shared with him seemed inevitable. I began to write my novel about Italy. We spent a day in Salzburg at the Festival, at an exquisite performance of *L'oca del Cairo* and the *Pauvre matelot*. It had long been a settled thing that I was to leave Austria in the autumn, so my father made no objections to my departure for London, to take upon myself the precarious fate of the emigré. But as for marriage to Peter, he advised against it. At the same time, he was already calling me the *Maulrappin* – after the clan of the Maulrappen, the ancient occupants of the castle Wolkenstein in Peter's book, which he loved so much.

By the end of August, everything was decided. But Peter could not agree with my father's counsel; he was determined that we should be married. We departed in different directions. And then, according to my journal, all the characters of my drama made their appearances on stage once more, before the curtain fell. "Willi telephoned three times." Hafis turned up at Hansi's, on the same evening as Klaus Dohrn: a strange pair of guests. A first letter from Moravia, which pierced my heart. I lamented to my calendar, in a mixture of English and French (and I cannot defend myself, even to myself, from the charge of affectation): "Oh, gloomy man who takes everything seriously and *s'en fout de tout.*" In between there were constant outbursts of turmoil and doubt. "How will it all work out? And my splendid suffering? And all this love?" Even up to the last moment my friends tried to talk me out of leaving: "Hansi furious, prophesies all sorts of dreadful things." "The Magus makes infernally malicious remarks about my marriage." "Willi, haggard with anxiety," sent "many red roses after a moving farewell in the evening street." But Tino wrote a mocking postcard, also signed by Hansi, in which he wished me *"molti bambini ebraici."* I read Goethe's *Wahlverwandschaften*, worked, packed my things. On October 24, I left Vienna.

Until the end of 1946 I made no more entries in my journal. But the weeks that intervened are engraved upon my memory. First I traveled, by the night train, only as far as Munich, to introduce myself to Peter's mother, Gerta von Cube, as her future daughter-in-law. At that time, thanks to her unimpeachable ancestry, she was still living in the Third Reich, unchallenged though reluctantly, with her youngest son, who had been called up for military service despite his Jewish grandfather, whose name he bore. It took me one long day to become acquainted with the repellent features of this regime. During those years, at any rate, in Munich, rural manners prevailed over elegance. In an aroma of *Weisswürste*, mustard, and cabbage I walked through the streets; brownshirts, jackboots and girls of the *Bund deutscher Mädel* – the German Girls' Association – with their hair in long plaits were everywhere. I had left my luggage at the railway station, and sat down briefly in the park, where I unsuspectingly powdered my nose. The hostile glances of the passersby bored into me. I wandered on, and found myself near a military barracks, where a man in uniform ordered me to raise my hand in a Hitler salute. Should I enter into long explanations? I gave the salute.

In the afternoon I met Frau von Cube in the Carlton Teeraum – Hitler's favorite establishment. I suspected that, after Baroness von Tschirschnitz, I might not be altogether welcome to her as a daughter-in-law. In a slightly reserved but not unfriendly manner she began to warn me: against Peter's violent fits of anger, his changeable moods, the unaccountable temperament inherited from his Baltic forebears. Gradually softening toward me, she told me stories of his childhood and youth, his defiance, his truancy, how he eventually became so intractable that he was packed off to a boarding school. Much was left unsaid, but there was much I had already learned. We said our good-byes politely, if not cordially. Separated from her second husband, Frau von Cube saw no reason to stay in Germany any longer than necessary. Before the war began she had already left, leaving behind property of great value, including a collection of "degenerate" paintings which would be priceless today, acquired from Peter's father in Hellerau.

That evening I traveled on to Paris, where two friends, Lili and Vera, recently returned from London to their little hotel on the Left Bank, awaited me. I stayed with them for two days, while they explained that the Channel was actually wider than the Atlantic Ocean, that England was nearer to America than to Europe, and that here in France they felt as if they were at home in Vienna after their weeks in that strange land – a useful preparation. On a grey afternoon I took the boat from Dieppe to Newhaven – the longest route I could have chosen; I never did so again. It was a rainy, stormy crossing. I crept into the belly of the boat, feeling miserable. On the already darkened quay, after the embarrassing questioning by the immigration officer, stood Peter, in a tall, wide-brimmed thirties hat, the collar of his trench coat turned up. Just for a moment my courage deserted me.

We boarded the train for London. In the little compartment, a steward offered us sweet, hot, milky tea in paper cups. There was a smell of cigarette smoke, Virginia tobacco, Lucky Strike cigarettes just as in the Paris Métro, but somehow different, quite different, truly foreign.

7

Welcome to London

A winter without snow. And yet I feel the cold more than I ever did in Vienna. Fog, drizzle, rain, gales. The damp cold penetrates through all the cracks, through all our pores; the sliding windows let in a draft; a skylight in the bathroom stays immovably open; the radiant heaters in the fireplaces formerly used for coal hardly warm the rooms; there is a musty smell throughout the house.

We were living at 59 Linden Gardens, a quiet street forming a crescent off Notting Hill Gate. Even in our second-floor apartment, we could still hear the rumbling of the Central Line trains, every seven minutes from half past four in the morning until after midnight. The gas meter had to be fed with sixpences or shillings. When we had none, we put in foreign coins or buttons. Once a month, the collector would call, open the meter, silently sort out the worthless tokens from the solid British silver and say dryly, without reproach: "That'll be seven and three." The slight shiver of the floorboards at the growling of the Tube, the money-guzzling gas meter – these were things I already knew from the Elisabeth Bergner film *Escape Me Never*, which I had compared with the novel by Margaret Kennedy in my dissertation. Now it had become my own reality.

Around the corner in Notting Hill Gate was a delicatessen run by Mr. Jennings, a pale, portly, middle-aged man, whose cultured English I was able to follow, although I had difficulty with the Cockney speech of all the other shopkeepers, the bus conductors, and tradesmen. Mr. Jennings' "Continental" wares had nothing in common with the French pâté, German liver sausage, and Austrian potato salad familiar to us. Nevertheless, we bought most of our food from him, or from the Express Dairy opposite, which, moreover, gave us credit. In the immediate area there were also a tiny bookshop and a few "cafeterias," in which unspeakable horrors were served: baked beans and spaghetti on toast. We were pleased to find that the two "pipi-Kinos," or fleapits, as Peter called them, showed good old films, rather than the Hollywood epics handled by the big distributors. On the corner of Palace Gardens Terrace stood a newish block of apartments in the Art Deco style, Broadwalk Court, with which we would all have connections for decades to come.

As for us, Peter and me, we lived in a furnished apartment rented from a Mrs. Mitchell, our share consisting of a bedroom and a living room, in whose furthest corners we set up our typewriters in order to write our novels: Peter's *All That Matters* and my Italian book. In a third room was Hans-Jürgen, one of Prince von Löwenstein's vassals, also known as "the boy" or "the Master." He was an angelically beautiful, musically gifted child of the Berlin slums, and was within a few months to marry a grand English heiress called Madge, then living at Broadwalk Court. Then there was "the little Count," "Count" Zühlsdorff, who often put in an appearance at mealtimes.

Notable for his absence, however, was Prince Hubertus zu Löwenstein-Wertheim-Freudenberg, Count von Löwenstein-Scharffeneck, who had recently departed for the United States, where he had founded the American Guild for German Cultural Freedom the previous April, to get this organization on its feet. In his name and that of the Guild, Peter had written a *Memorandum on the Foundation of a German Academy in New York* and had now become the Prince's London deputy. For this he was to receive a regular though modest salary. But although, as he assured my father, payment had been guaranteed, we waited in vain for a remittance from America, and the postage Peter had to lay out for the voluminous correspondence entrusted to him was a heavy burden on our sparse budget. It was perhaps as some sort of comfort, though not as a recompense, that Hubertus's younger brother Prince Poldi acted as a witness at our wedding, where we were forced to exchange brass curtain rings instead of gold ones.

In the vocabulary of our circle, the little world of Notting Hill was characterized as "pleasantly *louche*." But beyond that world, by way of Kensington Gardens and Hyde Park, lay Marble Arch and everything that began there, the navel of an empire, still intact at that time, of unimaginable might and splendor. As soon as we left our own district, London's streets seemed truly paved with gold. Again and again, we marveled at the hotels and mansions of Park Lane; the gigantic, venerable department stores of Oxford Street; Piccadilly Circus with its statue of Eros, from which invisible threads appeared to radiate in all directions as far as the Antipodes; Mayfair and Belgravia, the abodes of the rich; all the noble Georgian façades, all the expanses of green. And everywhere the milling crowd of exotic figures, splendidly dressed Indians and African tribal chieftains – though otherwise there were few black faces, for there was as yet little immigration from the West Indies. We were overwhelmed by the sheer size and diversity of this city. That we belonged there, were at any rate tolerated there – even though we had to apply to Bow Street police station for residential permits every three months, and await their extension in fear and trembling – was a joyful, even an uplifting thought. I, who had been touched in my childhood by the imperial grandeur of old Austria, felt as if I had been taken back to the years before the First World War.

On the other hand, we were poor. It was only thanks to the little Express Dairy on Notting Hill Gate that we did not starve when our pockets were empty. We could live for a few weeks on milk, eggs, bread, mealy sausages, and tinned vegetables, although we could not indulge ourselves in these too much or too often because, after all, one day we would be gently requested to settle our bill. All the other good things of life were beyond our means when we were in such straits. The rent was sometimes paid by the "Master," whose fiancée would "lend" it to him. Then a small check might come for one of my short stories, translated into English by Peter and published by the *Daily Express*. Or Zuckmayer, who was still living in Henndorf in Austria, would turn up and hire Peter to work with him on a film script. Once Bruno Frank gave us eight pounds to save us from the abyss that was threatening us yet again. Instead of paying off our bill at the Express Dairy we went straight off to have dinner for one pound at the Royal Palace restaurant. I was learning a lifestyle from Peter which we later characterized as "brinkmanship": always on the brink of a precipice, always on the point of falling to our ruin.

We were leading an in-between life – between pretensions to nobility and a *vie de bohème*; between English friends, from Eric Dancy, an intellectual gone to seed, to Sir Philip Gibbs, the popular novelist and benefactor, and the former leading lights of German-speaking literature, who had settled down here, perhaps in slightly more comfortable but comparably modest circumstances. At the apartment of Stefan Zweig, who had temporarily rented his beautiful rooms in Hallam Street to Robert Neumann – complete with Zweig's own secretary, Lotte, later his wife – there were gatherings which today would be quite unthinkable; for hours on end, writers read aloud to each other from their works in progress, and listened respectfully while others read. This practice was usual up to the outbreak of war, but was kept up after the war only among small groups, and gradually replaced by individual reading tours, which were easier to endure. Here, among the émigrés, it lingered on for some time.

Max Herrmann-Neisse shunned such gatherings, at which Bruno Frank, Zuckmayer on one of his occasional visits, Neumann himself, and Peter took the floor, although I never did. Sometimes we visited Herrmann-Neisse at his comfortably furnished apartment, where he and his wife formed an odd *ménage à trois* with the jeweler Sondheimer. The strikingly beautiful Leni and the bald, deformed little man who had often sung her praises in writing shared a bedroom, while Sondheimer kept in the background. I was startled by the gesture with which Leni, preparing to go for a walk in Hyde Park with Herrmann-Neisse and us, jammed her husband's hat onto his bald pate – with the utmost affection, yet also with a certain mockery, as if he were a circus clown. Herrmann-Neisse had spoken for us all in his verses: *"Wer mich zu entehren glaubte / wenn mit freveldem Befehle / er das Heimatrecht beraubte, / ahnt die ewig lenzbelaubte / Heimat nicht in meiner Seele."* (They who sought to dishonor me / When with sacrilegious command / They robbed me of my rightful home / Know nothing of the homeland in my soul / Eternally leafy with spring.)

Such were our dealings with the past. Set against these were our entry into the English language, into the written word, and finally into the community of writers in this country. In this respect, Peter progressed much faster than I did. While living in Paris he had had the courage – supported by considerable linguistic talent – to write in French, and now he was venturing into English with his novel *All That Matters*. Eric Dancy, his friend from the *quartier latin*, now back in London, helped him. In January 1937, the publishers Hutchinson, who had already published a translation of Peter's *The House of Cosinsky*, accepted his new book. For a time we were free from the worst of our worries. Most of the literary exiles did not consider for a moment abandoning their mastery of German, which they had to a greater or lesser extent achieved, for the sake of writing in the English language, which they could learn only with great effort, and must inevitably use in a simplified and stilted manner. Indeed, they would never even have considered it possible. Peter, however, was firmly resolved upon this course and urged me to follow his example. Close to tears, I complained bitterly on the telephone to Robert Neumann: "Just when I was beginning to gain confidence, when I was developing my own style, I have to – " He interrupted me with the same cheerful relentlessness with which he had used his own discretion in cutting my first novel: "Our ancestors were burnt at the stake – surely you can manage to learn to write in a different language?"

How does one learn to write? By reading. We immersed ourselves in the poetry, the essays, the journalism of the English thirties, an exceptionally stimulating, indeed exciting time for literature. A new generation had appeared on the stage: like all the important figures in politics, art, and the professions at that time, they were nurtured, challenged and fostered by the universities of Oxford and Cambridge. Auden and Isherwood, Spender, MacNeice, Rex Warner, John Lehmann, and Cecil Day Lewis were the "pink intellectuals," some of a deeper shade, Red enough to go to Spain and offer their services to the government forces. Some of their contemporaries, handsome and talented young men such as John Cornford and Virginia Woolf's nephew Julian Bell, fell in the Civil War. Auden and Isherwood, Spender and Lehmann, who were attracted by boys, followed the temptation of easy erotic relationships in Berlin, where they experienced the feverish agony of the Weimar republic, or in the Vienna of the February battles – morbidly fascinated by the European tragedy, wherever it was at its most visible.

In their poetry, their breathless prose, we detected the voice of the era. We admired their political commitment, however much it might be articulated, as in the case of Auden, in a highly discriminating choice of words, an elitist tone to which at first we did not find it easy to relate. It was only a fashionable version of the varying private languages of Oxbridge, but for some individuals it led to the creation of an outstanding body of work. The current form of the novel, on the other hand, was by no means foreign to us, schooled as we were in the "*Neue Sachlichkeit*," the "new objectivity." During one of the first weekends after my arrival, when I opened the Sunday papers – for which money always had to be found, for they were our true teachers, in those early years and perhaps for ever after – I read the reviews of Stevie Smith's *Novel on Yellow Paper*. Her book seemed not so far removed from the sensitive emanations of female narrators in the German-speaking area, such as Joe Lederer, Irmgard Keun, or Viktoria Wolf, perhaps even myself in my own early novels. Rosamond Lehmann's *Dusty Answer* had come out some time earlier, but was still considered one of the cult books of the day. A genius such as Virginia Woolf, meanwhile, was incomparable and stood alone.

The *Observer* and *Sunday Times* were not our only teachers; the weeklies too, above all the *New Statesman* and *Time and Tide*, the latter edited by women, offered models of the art of critical and contemplative writing. In all these, we found the names of Desmond Shaw-Taylor, James Agate, Raymond Mortimer, and of the younger talents, Philip Toynbee, T. C. Worsley, Cyril Connolly. We studied them first: their daring opinions, their brilliant insights, their smooth turns of phrase, their ironic allusions, their nimble wit. Then we turned to their predecessors, masters of the essay form such as Lamb, Hazlitt, Walter Pater, of whose existence we had hardly been aware, although we had been under the spell of the great English novelists. We came to understand that simplicity was not the same as facility, that to be concise was not to be flat, and comprehensibility was the result of laborious crystallization.

We still, it was true, lacked the general background, the soil from which sprang this singular imagination, this vivid illustrative power and energy, these allegories and analogies. They were clearly to be found in the early years of these authors. It was not until we had children of our own, growing up in England, that we caught up with the English childhood we had failed to experience at first hand, and from the rhymes and songs, the absurd and comical stories and verses of Lewis Carroll and Edward Lear, from A. A. Milne and Beatrix Potter, we won the knowledge we had needed to understand all the references and allusions which were obvious to the inhabitants of this island, though not to us.

So far so good; we were slowly making ourselves at home in the world of English literature. But how to acquire the much more essential precondition of life in this country, a knowledge of English manners, of the English way of life? Here is an example. In the spring of 1937, a young publisher and his darkly beautiful wife had invited us to dinner with a few of their friends. At about half past seven we arrived at their house in Tite Street, Chelsea. Our hosts opened the door, showed us into their drawing room and offered us drinks. They were smartly dressed, as one dresses to receive guests, behaved in a calm, relaxed manner, talked to us about this and that, without a hint of impatience. We sat chatting, finding the atmosphere pleasant and only slightly curious about the fact that no other guests had yet arrived. After more than half an hour, one of the two rose, I can no longer remember if it was Peter – our host Peter – or his wife Dorothy, and said with an apologetic smile: "Please forgive us, we will have to break up the party now; our friends in Kensington are expecting us soon after eight."

We had come a week early. "Next Saturday" meant not the coming Saturday, which was "this Saturday," but the following one – a semantic misunderstanding. But this couple (he a product of Winchester and New College, Oxford; she the daughter of a titled military correspondent of *The Times*), far from pointing out our social faux pas, had helped us over it in the most tactful way. The consideration for foreigners that they showed on this occasion, as they did in all things, was undoubtedly bound up with a certainty, inborn in the British, that nothing else was to be expected from the non-British, with an unshakeable belief – unshaken to this day, even by the loss of an empire – in their own self-evident superiority. We had to come to terms with this, and we did so for the space of three decades.

This was the first lesson then, the first of many; it was from this couple, above all from Dorothy, or "Dodo," that we – or rather I, for my husband's arrogance and long-since-acquired cosmopolitanism forbade him to consider this necessary – learned the rules of behavior among the educated or perhaps only the elevated classes in the United Kingdom. We had already grasped the basic principles: don't fuss; don't ask personal questions; don't touch the teapot (this was reserved for the hostess); tea in first, milk after; understatement and stiff upper lip. Now we were initiated into the higher mysteries. They concerned the right accent, the necessary codes and formulas of colloquial English, but also the consideration and courtesy, the fundamental goodwill, as well as the constantly maintained reserve toward one's fellow human, insofar as the latter was admitted to one's sphere in the first place. Not wealth, but name and education played a certain part here. But, here too, British norms were the ones that counted. Dodo's husband, who was the head of a leading London publishing firm and in the highest bracket attainable in the field of literary knowledge, had never heard of either Lessing or Kleist and had probably never read any German author apart from a little Goethe. Yet he was certainly familiar with the most obscure poets of the *grand siècle* in France.

At Oxford, and above all at Cambridge, there were at that time many Soviet sympathizers and even secret supporters of the stamp of Kim Philby, who incidentally came from a good family and had known Dodo since their youth. Even Peter, the publisher, and his circle were not Conservatives but, if anything, on the "wrong" side of the Liberal Party. There was no doubt about it - the spirit in the land was on the Left. The exceptions were Conservatives or right-wing radicals such as T. S. Eliot, Ezra Pound, Wyndham Lewis, and Roy Campbell, who were not taken seriously as political thinkers, but regarded rather as exotic geniuses. The sons of bourgeois families were proud to be published by Victor Gollancz's Left Book Club. Recently, Tom Harrisson, "to find a way out of mass misery, intellectual despair and an international heap of ruins," had founded the sociological movement "Mass Observation." He and his friends went to Bolton, near Manchester, a town of *petit bourgeois* and industrial workers, to study their habits and customs, just as Lazarsfeld and his colleagues had done in Marienthal. As long ago as 1845, Disraeli, in his novel *Sybil, or the Two Nations,* had described the dichotomy of British society – in reality far more complex – into the rich and the poor: "Two nations between whom there is no inter-course and no sympathy; who are as ignorant of each other's habits, thoughts, and feelings, as if they were dwellers in different zones, or inhabitants of different planets." We had heard Ted Bradley, a Communist agitator and a powerful speaker, denouncing this very state of affairs: "Just look at them, the children of Belgravia and the children of the East End! You can tell without being told: Baldwin's child – worker's child. Chamberlain's child – worker's child." He could just as easily have said: "Gaitskell's child – worker's child. Harrisson's child – worker's child." For the offspring of one British nation, who were now beginning to take upon themselves the misery of the other one, bore, and were to continue to bear, no resemblance of any kind to the other in their way of life.

Once, at the house of D. N. Pritt, the Labour MP, who was also the best-paid barrister in London, we found ourselves among the left-wing elite. Here, amid the Victorian furniture, I met not only Elwyn Jones, now very much the "coming man," but also the Soviet ambassador Maisky and such impressive figures as the biochemist, geneticist, and Marxist J. B. S. Haldane, nephew of a viscount, co-editor of the Communist *Daily Worker*, Chevalier of the Legion of Honor, and a leading light of the venerable Royal Society. If the expression "the Establishment," which was coined by Henry Fairlie in the fifties, had existed at that time, it could have been applied to the pillars of the Labour Party in all its ideological shades. Haldane's sister was Naomi Mitchison, who had come to Vienna in February 1934 with Elwyn to help the workers. I met her again at the London PEN Club, which offered émigré writers cordial friendship, every kind of help, and something that came close to a feeling of being at home.

What the PEN Club did for all of us cannot be sufficiently praised. This association, founded as a dining club by an actively charitable woman novelist and the noble John Galsworthy, became not only a focus for all the most important writers – with the exception of the "Bloomsberries" – but at that time of upheaval it was also a harbor for many: first the Germans, the Austrians, the Czechs, then the rest of the refugees from Hitler's Europe. They were all taken to the hearts of a succession of motherly women and selfless men, made welcome, and from then on incorporated into the community until they were able to found their own centers for writers in exile. When International PEN held its seventeenth congress in London in the middle of the war, it was attended by writers from thirty-five countries. We, who had arrived on the first wave, were introduced to PEN by Robert Neumann, who had already won for himself one of the kindest of helpers, Henrietta Leslie, the mistress of Glebe House in Chelsea, a great lady and a true patron of writers and at the same time, in Neumann's mocking words, a tireless "knitter of novels."

Henrietta, with her wonderful blue eyes and greying hair,

imposing of stature though slightly disabled by a hip complaint, became, next to Dodo, my closest English woman friend up to the time of her death. I was a frequent teatime visitor to the Vine Room in her ancient house, a circular winter garden in which a single vine spread its leaves up to the glass cupola, where we were looked after by her charming maid who bore the Dickensian name of Dorrit, and where a whole world opened up to me – a world also inhabited by the other influential figures in the English PEN. They were Fabians, Liberals plain and simple, liberal Socialists such as G. D. H. and Margaret Cole and the Pethick-Lawrences, or were occasionally attracted to Moscow in all innocence, like the gigantic Welshman Clough Williams-Ellis and his wife Amabel, who was a Strachey. They included former suffragettes, as well as male feminists such as Lord Pethick-Lawrence. They fought, loudly or quietly, some, like the recently deceased John Galsworthy, against the infringement of legal rights and the accumulation of dead capital; others, like H. G. Wells, against the encroachments of the state; or, like the Bradford-born J. B. Priestley, against the poverty in the Midlands and the north of England. The most active among them were Margaret Storm Jameson, president of the London PEN during the decisive years, and the taciturn, austere, unassumingly self-sacrificing general secretary Hermon Ould. In no other country had I encountered such a group of true humanists and tolerant moralists. Their breed has largely died out in the England of today.

In spite of all their support and generosity of spirit, we remained for a long time incidental and marginal beings in relation to them, and finally became so once again, after we might for some time have expected to move closer to the center of things. Meanwhile, it was 1937, and at the beginning of April we had to move. Mrs. Mitchell had given us notice, and soon, because she, as principal tenant, had not paid the rent, the bailiff removed all but the most essential furniture from the house. I was sent in search of accommodation. In a brand-new building, Winchester Court, on the corner of Kensington Church Street, I found a tiny but delightful apartment: two rooms, bathroom, and "kitchenette." The decision to take it was a reckless one, for the rent was ten pounds a month, on top of which we had to pay installments of three pounds to the Times Furnishing Company for the furniture. We had to ask the bank for a loan. At least we could be sure of paying the rent, for recently Peter had been taken on as second-string London correspondent by two Czech newspapers, the *Prager Tagblatt* and *Lidove Noviny* of Brno, for which he was paid exactly ten pounds a month. The senior correspondent was Peter Smolka, who later became a legendary, controversial figure. He was about my age and I had known him since his thirteenth year, in a circle of students of the Kundmann *Gymnasium* or secondary school, which was also attended by Bruno Kreisky. He used to edit "The Voice of Youth," a supplement to the magazine *Die neue Jugend* (*New Youth*), which had been founded by the publisher Erwin Barth von Wehrenalp. When, in 1926, we had together attended the foundation congress of the Paneuropa movement, the fourteen-year-old Smolka had commandeered my seat in the overcrowded box at the Vienna Konzerthaus, with the excuse that after all he had to write up the event for his newspaper. Soon after taking his *Matura* examination he married and traveled to England, where he secured the desirable post of London correspondent of the *Neue Freie Presse*, the post he still held when I met him again, many years later. Always in the know, he was aware of the imminence of Austria's downfall and had decided to work for the Prague newspaper rather than the Viennese one. He needed an assistant, and it was Peter de Mendelssohn who, to his shame, but with favorable consequences for his later career, took on the job.

Smolka was a friend of the Soviet Union – we always knew that. Amazingly enough, the extent of that friendship did not become clear to me until 1987, when Anthony Glees's book *The Secrets of the Service* was published. Half a century earlier, Smolka had published an illustrated book about the Russian polar regions, entitled *Forty Thousand Against the Arctic*, and dedicated it to "T. G. S." – his newly born son, Thomas Garrigue Smolka. When he acquired British citizenship shortly before the outbreak of war, the Foreign Office spokesmen, who had frequently supplied him with press information, asked him: "How do you like being British, Smolka?" He answered: "I don't like the way you are squandering my Empire." In 1940, by now renamed Peter Smollett, he was summoned by the head of the Russian department at the Ministry of Information and awarded the OBE, after which he returned to Vienna as correspondent of the *Daily Express*. Here, after some time, he became ill with multiple sclerosis, but with endless courage, endless energy, though finally paralyzed below the neck, he built up an industrial firm, sold it at a profit, and with Kreisky's help founded and edited yet another periodical, *Austria Today*, until his illness overpowered him. What might have lain behindthese activities – a second, secret life for all those years – has still not been fully revealed. With all his inconsistencies, Peter Smolka was one of the most remarkable persons of this century that I ever met.

Smolka set up the London office of the *Prager Tagblatt* in a room belonging to *The Times*, then still in its traditional building in Printing House Square. Here stood a teleprinter which unceasingly chattered away with the whole international news service of *The Times*. Here I too was to spend many nocturnal hours with my husband at times of crisis, taking down, in my hardly decipherable shorthand, telephone messages from Prague which in turn gave insights to *The Times* about the situation in central Europe. One evening, a very slender, very tall man entered this room. He introduced himself briefly as Hans Flesch, and politely, even modestly, requested some literary advice or other. It cannot have been a recommendation to a publisher, for some books of his, written in English under the pseudonym of Vincent Brun, had already been published by Jonathan Cape. Whatever it was he wanted, it was vaguely granted. Then he took his leave with the same hesitant politeness. Hardly had the door closed behind him when I said to Peter: "What a nice man. Do run after him and invite him round to us." He did so, and later often said, half as a joke, half in earnest, that he wished he had not.

The invitation was to Winchester Court, for we soon began to gather friends around us there on Sundays. The strange household at Linden Gardens, with the frequent "boyish quarrels" between the "little Count" Zühlsdorff and the "Master," Hans-Jürgen, was quickly forgotten. The "Master," the handsome Berlin slum-child, had meanwhile married his Madge with great pomp and grandeur at Brompton Oratory, wearing a grey frock coat and top hat, with a no less extraordinary mixture of English Catholic aristocracy and a few selected German émigrés turning up at the reception at the Rembrandt Hotel. Soon afterward the princely couple, Hubertus and Helga Löwenstein, arrived from America, and we entertained them in our new apartment, elegantly ignoring the financial sacrifice this involved for us. Hubertus "read to us from his novel. They stayed until half past one and said it had been the most beautiful evening they had spent in London." The following day, we went to a Chinese restaurant with them and the little Count.

All this, and on April 17 our first encounter with Shakespeare in English: Olivier's *Henry V* at the Old Vic. The authentic Elizabethan, whose characters could easily be English people of today, was revealed to me. It simply revolutionized all my previous ideas of Shakespeare – even Moissi's Hamlet. What more could London offer?

And yet homesickness – fanned by the profoundly Austrian personality of our new friend Flesch, who was only nine years younger than my father and, like him, a former member of the imperial artillery – drew me back to Vienna. Others, such as Stefan Zweig and Robert Neumann, as well as Hafis and Ernst Fischer – these two, admittedly, illegally and with political motives – frequently made return journeys out of exile to the *Ständestaat* and by no means regarded these visits to the much-loved, much-hated city as a burdensome duty. "I had reserved the right," wrote Ernst Fischer in his memoirs, "to interrupt my stay in Moscow repeatedly in order to go to Prague, where I was not so far from Austria." Only a few succeeded in tearing themselves away completely from their homeland, as long as it was not irrevocably lost to them. The pull was too strong. I obtained a passport full of swastikas, valid until September 3, 1939, which, after my marriage to an *Auslandsdeutscher*, a German abroad, was issued to me without any objections in the "lion's den," Ribbentrop's consulate in London. And so, before the month was out, I went "home" – for this was what Vienna still was to me.

How to understand such ambivalence, how to explain the contradictions with which one sometimes lives so unthinkingly? I had finally escaped "Austrofascism," as I had resolved to do since the February uprising, and despised it no less since settling in the birthplace of modern democracy, from an authoritarian republic to a monarchy under parliamentary rule. Yet my occasional return visits to my contaminated, as well as highly endangered homeland made me happy. I went for walks in the Vienna woods, drove to the tiny wine-growing village of Thallern with my parents to eat the famous *Backhendel* (roast chicken), and to the Eisvogel in the Prater; I was invited by a prosperous "old gentleman" of the Suevia to his villa in

Hinterbrühl for "caviar and white burgundy," and also to Neuhaus –
"I saw Willi for a moment. Doesn't hurt at all"; I swam at Greifenstein and in the Kahlenberg pool; went mountain climbing on the Rax
by way of the Kantnersteig; saw many of my old friends, Maria, Lisel,
even Fritz Thorn; and in between sat at the white nursery table in my
old room, Carry Hauser's Madonna with the ice-blue fingers above
my head, writing my Italian novel, in which I had already got as far as
Perugia.

In London, in my absence, the coronation of George VI had
taken place; the Philbys held a grand party, attended not only by the
Smolkas but by Dodo and her husband Peter (Kim was on holiday
from Spain, where he was active as a "war correspondent" on
Franco's side); emissaries from all corners and ends of the Empire
were streaming into the capital during that bright May. I was happy to
miss it so as to be in that deceptively cheerful land of mine with its
subterranean seething and sloppily authoritarian regime, where I
danced on the edge of a volcano, or more precisely at Hübner's in the
Stadtpark at five o'clock tea. "Nobly the world goes to ruin" is an old
Viennese saying. Even my parents, who were by no means free from
material cares, not to speak of political ones, seemed to enjoy all these,
mostly fairly inexpensive, pleasures while suspecting that they would
not be able to do so for much longer. But they were not prepared to
face this suspicion, let alone to act on it.

At the beginning of July, as I was finally preparing to leave Vienna
again, the reality of the tragic present, which everyone here was
evading, forced itself upon us. A confidential report from Paris
brought the news that my uncle Felix had been wounded in Spain,
perhaps killed. As it happened, I had already arranged to meet Peter
in Paris a few days later. My mother, in despair, traveled there with
me. We found out from the Spanish committee that Felix had fallen
near Madrid as early as February, in his first engagement as a medical
orderly. To comfort Mimi, we took her with us to Bandol, where we
had planned to spend a sort of belated honeymoon. My father joined
us there, and he and my mother stayed with us in an elegant little
hotel, Le Goëland. They accompanied us on bus journeys down the
coast, to Toulon or Marseilles. Peter and I, on our own, visited Lion
Feuchtwanger at nearby Sanary. I noted: "The émigrés' conversations
excite me" – as though I were not familiar with them. From the

Mediterranean heat we returned to an autumnally cool London, where the results of our recklessness stared us in the face. The table was heaped with bills. We were deeply in debt. I abandoned my novel, as it did not help the situation, and looked around for work. In the Café Herrenhof, they used to say that if you broke open a fresh roll, a Frischauer would jump out. There were a father and five sons of that name. The most successful of the brothers was Paul, a constructor of historical novels. At the time, with typical foresight, he had set up his workplace in London. He and his jolly Slavic wife Mariza had a kind of salon in their apartment, a basement, but close to the south end of Kensington Gardens. There we were to meet Arthur Koestler, once he had escaped the Malaga death cell and custody in London, as well as the plump, fabulous Moura, Baroness Budberg, the former mistress of Gorky and now the companion of H. G. Wells. I will never forget a conversation with the two of them, in which Koestler, quarrelsome even then, denied the existence of any significant writers in the Berlin of the Weimar republic, and we and Moura Budberg named Kästner, Mehring, and Brecht in spectacular refutation of his view.

Frischauer paid me to type his manuscripts, up to forty pages a day. And soon I was also employed by Berthold Viertel, who had turned up at Smolka's, a legendary father figure for Peter from his youth in Hellerau. I would go to his house in Hampstead and take dictation from him, but then we would start to gossip; he sparkled with a succession of anecdotes and brilliant ideas, and his novel remained a fragment. "My unwritten novels," Viertel told me and Peter, "are much better than your published ones." "So are ours," we replied with some justification.

I worked as if possessed, putting in many hours at the typewriter, washing, cleaning, cooking, helping out in the *Times* office, and inviting guests as often as we could afford. Slowly our standard of living began to improve, although Frischauer and Viertel were tardy payers. We had acquired a delightful tabby kitten. Our "charlady" Mrs. Parker came once a week; her first action, still wearing her edifice of a hat, was to polish the brass knob on the front door. I bought flowers and a vase, recording this as an exceptional luxury in my calendar. In September, that great old man Thomas Masaryk died in his native Czechoslovakia, then still free, and I was sent to the equally venerable Henry Wickham Steed, England's great expert on central Europe, to ask him for an obituary for the *Prager Tagblatt.* In November, despite all distractions, I succeeded in finishing my Italian book. At this time there was thick fog in London – a real "pea souper," as we heard it called.

And then, at the end of December 1937, still drawn by the invisible thread over land and water, I returned once more, one last time, to Vienna. A day in Paris with friends, a night journey by train over the Arlberg, mountain air, forest air, snow air through the briefly opened window; I breathed the breath of home, I entered the white-painted nursery and became absorbed into it. Just as, eight months earlier, I had tasted a distillation of decades of summer joys, I now savored the essence of my many Viennese winters of years gone by.

Wandering on skis in the mountains on Sundays, spending long evenings in the smoke-filled coffee houses, the Schottentor and the Herrenhof – sitting in one with Canetti, the analyst Siegfried Bernfeld, or Albert Fuchs, in the other with Torberg, who was being conciliatory at the moment; going to hear Lotte Lehmann in the *Rosenkavalier* at the State Opera and the new program at the cellar cabaret club Literatur am Naschmarkt - everything seemed to proceed as before, as if I had not, for a long time, been leading a different life. Before Christmas Eve, which we celebrated *en famille* with carp, cooked by Marie, and the decorated Christmas tree, Peter arrived from London to join in the festivities. Time and space seemed suspended, unconnected to the outside world. Long afterward I was to hear the Doctor's cry of horror in Marlowe's *Doctor Faustus*: "Come not, Lucifer!" And then I remembered: it was with such a stifled, fearful, inner cry that we experienced all this up to the sixth of January 1938 – the day of the now conclusive, irrevocable separation. Before this, Peter dared on one occasion to break through the beautiful deception. One evening, alone with me and my parents, he declared that Austria was not to be saved, and implored them to prepare for their departure to a place of safety. My father had for some time, like many other chemists during those years, been working on the production of synthetic rubber, and was involved in a patent dispute with ICI. A settlement was considered possible. Very well, said Peter, arrange the settlement. Just get out, as quickly as possible, leave this city, this country. My mother declared that she could never give up

Vienna, her beloved suburb of Döbling, her friends. Peter told her: "The SS will march through Döbling; your friends will betray you, or they will be in dreadful danger themselves." Mimi, even more emotionally stirred than I was, burst into tears, refusing to listen, to believe, to know anything. To spare her feelings, the subject was changed, and was not taken up again.

From London, from the *Times* office, I frequently telephoned "home." My parents too telephoned, and sent money, for once again we were hard up. In mid-January Peter's *All That Matters* was published. "One does not notice it very much," I wrote, "sitting here at home." Home was here too, in Kensington Church Street! My clever uncle Gustav had already turned his back on Vienna; he lived with his wife in the Connaught Hotel, for he was not short of money. Emil von Hofmannsthal, a cousin of the poet, was another harbinger of the Austrian exodus.

On the twenty-fifth of January the aurora borealis was seen in the sky. Here as in Vienna this was interpreted – even by me, the student of the rationalist Schlick – as a warning sign, a bad omen. But my parents were still refusing to look truth in the eye. During those weeks, Baron Franckenstein often invited us to the embassy. This man, whose heroic features belied his gentle character, a precious relic of the monarchy, now a loyal representative of the republic, gathered the Austrian community around him, perhaps hoping to unite those who, here too, had already split into two camps. Jan Masaryk, the Czech ambassador, was also initiating discussions of the situation in small groups. People huddled together before the oncoming tempest.

On February 12, Schuschnigg went to Hitler. The skepticism of reports reaching London had clearly not penetrated to Vienna. In the notes in my calendar, I was already giving Austria up as lost. On February 20: "Listened to Hitler speech from 12 to 3. Count Huyn quite broken." It was he, our dear friend, who was to announce after the Anschluss, "This planet is uninhabitable," and take ship for South America. Then events began to pile on top of each other. In Graz, according to *The Times*, swastika flags were seen everywhere. Five days later, Schuschnigg was still uttering soothing words on the radio. These must have completely reassured my father, for when I pleaded with him at last to think seriously of leaving, he replied that there was not the least cause for concern. On the contrary, the country stood behind the Chancellor. Only yesterday there had been a grand reception at Schönbrunn: all the chandeliers were lit and shining with candles. My father, who had always been so rational, was actually going into raptures over this beacon of the wretched regime. I, who had emigrated out of sheer abhorrence of that regime, had so far succeeded in resigning myself to the fact that my parents still lived under it. But this, this utter naiveté, this total blindness in the face of danger, robbed me of my composure. Meanwhile it was spring in London. We walked in Kew Gardens. "A pleasantly subdued day. The smell of violets. A warm breeze blowing in the streets. And the cherry trees are coming into blossom." Once more, for the last time, we sought refuge at the Austrian embassy. Even the shy and withdrawn Stefan Zweig was among us; we were saying farewell to the house in Belgrave Square, not to Franckenstein, for he had not the slightest intention of returning to Vienna. On the evening of March 11, Peter summoned me to the *Times* building. Hour by hour we experienced the events of that night as they occurred. Scrawled across the next few days in my calendar are the words: "It is horrible and unbearable. My parents are in the line of fire. The devil is in charge."

The end of the month, bright spring weather, the sunshine warmer than ever before in March, and if a piece of our world had fallen into the abyss, we were still alive. "I am thinking about a Viennese novel," I noted. 1938 had come upon us, and I was escaping sixty-five years back into the past. In mid-April, my Italian book was accepted by Hutchinson. The next day, we traveled to Paris for Easter to visit Peter's father, *der Rabe* (the Raven), as the family called him. We also saw my friend Vera Schenk, who had married the painter Berthelot, a handsome Modiglianian figure, whose famous kinsman, the chemist Marcelin Berthelot, was buried in the Panthéon. We met Peter's translator, Denise van Moppès, in the Deux Magots, and departed again on Monday. In London, beside the chattering teleprinter, we were at the mercy of our familiar grief.

All the same, we sometimes invited guests or visited our protector Sir Philip Gibbs, who had helped us to extend our work permits for another year. One evening we pulled ourselves together and went to a production of *Falstaff* at Sadler's Wells, a cheering performance. Then we decided to have something to eat at Piccadilly Circus. There we encountered a demonstration by Mosley's Fascists, singing the

With Peter de Mendelssohn

Horst Wessel song and giving the Hitler salute. I nearly fainted. "If it were not for Peter," I wrote in my little book, "I would poison myself. Oh, horror!" In Karl Kraus's phrase: "All these things can be, while all these things can be!" There is no better description of the weeks that followed March 1938.

In London, writing "my Italian novel," *Flute and Drums* (1937)

8

Winter of Our Discontent

"'Tis war! 'tis war! O angel of God, protect/ And intercede!/ Alas, 'tis war – and I desire/ that it be not my fault!" It was not our fault, nor that of most people on the enemy side, or so we must hope, yet nearly all on that side later resented the fact that we had been among the victims, not the culprits, and that in no circumstances could the slightest responsibility for the horror of so many years be laid on our shoulders. How could we ever be forgiven for this? How could we hope that one day in the distant future, when once again we would tread our native soil or even settle down on it, this gulf between those who stayed at home and those who had left or, more often, been driven away, might not yawn again at any time, to the astonishment or horror of those who might perhaps have thought that the alienation was over forever?

In the scant eighteen months which separated the Anschluss from the outbreak of the Second World War, decisive events had taken place on all levels, from the high political to the private sphere. The historical course of events is well known. 1938 was the year not only of Austria, but also of Czechoslovakia – at first only the harbinger of its fall, of the days of Munich. Like all the contemporary history of the age, these events directly affected all personal destinies, but our own in a particular way. Before Chamberlain's meeting with Hitler, people in London were already seriously expecting war; gas masks were being distributed, trenches dug in Hyde Park. But for us, who were living mainly on our income from the *Prager Tagblatt*, the betrayal of the Czechs affected not only our spirit, but also our very existence. Jan Masaryk promised us the "protection of the embassy" in the event of hostilities. But he could not have protected us either from bomb attacks or a German invasion, and the state in whose name he made this promise had as little future as the only German-language newspaper which was still not *gleichgeschaltet* (voicing the official line). If we ever experienced England in a moment of shame, then it was on the day of Neville Chamberlain's return from his last meeting with Hitler. On the weekly newsreels we saw the "man with the umbrella," that distorted image of the English gentleman, waving the ominous agreement as he descended from the aircraft and proclaiming proudly that this was "peace in our time" – at the price of the Sudetenland. The jubilation in the land, the headlines about this illusory promise distressed us deeply. There were certainly other English statesmen – Churchill, Eden, Duff Cooper – who perceived the worthlessness of the agreement and only hoped that it would provide the ill-armed kingdom with a breathing space. We knew little about this. We read of the triumph of appeasement politics, of the joy among the "Cliveden set," the aristocratic circle of which Lord Astor's country house was the center, and where Ribbentrop was a frequent visitor, of Mosley's parades in the East End, where the slogans chanted by his followers were drummed into the heads of terrified tailors and shoemakers: "There's going to be no war, there's going to be no war, there's going to be no bloody war and the Jews won't have their war."

We summoned all our resources, our connections with English friends and with the generous Ferdy Kuhn of the *Washington Post*, who offered to obtain visas for the United States, to rescue my parents and bring them to England. They hoped to have overcome all the hurdles and obstacles involved by the summer. Making plans which, as usual, overstretched our means, we decided to meet them in Paris, but then – *navigare necesse est, vivere non necesse* – we immediately traveled once more to Bandol and Sanary, where we learned that my parents were stranded in Zurich without any money; they had been refused entry to France. We sent them the last of our money and returned to London. Finally they arrived. Apart from a few pieces of furniture, pictures, books, and suitcases with personal belongings, they had left behind everything they ever possessed. These things, sent by road and prepaid to England, were confiscated in Hamburg, expropriated and sold at auction. Gone with them were the rest of my library, gone Carry Hauser's Madonna with the ice-blue fingers, gone Moravia's letters in their little gilt box. Who weeps for carpets or linen chests? One weeps for photograph albums, for the piano arrangement from

Tristan and Isolde, with the thumb mark at the top right-hand corner of the prelude to the third act, where the page was turned.

In the course of the year those Austrians who had traveled to the end of the martyrs' path from the British consulate in Vienna, by way of the inhuman authorities at home to the immigration office at the English ports, found refuge in Britain. My father's sister too had succeeded in entering the country with the help of the Quakers. Following the example of our old Bohemian cook Anna, who had once cradled her on her knee and with whom she shared her life up to the end, my Aunt Lonny had recently become very religious and was a frequent churchgoer. She was taken into the household of the Anglican Canon Mace in the cathedral close at Winchester, and soon felt at home with that good and kind family. The suitcases containing most of her possessions, including notebooks, books, and keepsakes, were stored in a warehouse in the City of London and went up in flames in the first major German air attack.

My only close relative to remain behind in Vienna was my grandmother Melanie, who was neither able nor willing to emigrate. Before being taken to the concentration camp of Theresienstadt, where she died – no one knows in what circumstances – at seventy-three, she left her silver tableware behind for my mother, entrusting it to her loyal maid, and removed from her ears her most precious possession, the diamond studs she always wore, to give to her brother Leo's wife. At the side of this faithful woman, my "Tante Grete," Herr Hofrat Siebert survived the Hitler years and after the war was able to take my children, his great-grandniece and great-grandnephew, to the Café Zauner in Bad Ischl. But I will never be able to forget my grandmother's gesture, which reminds me of the historic women who are said to have exchanged clothes on the way to the scaffold.

When Czechoslovakia was invaded and the immigrants came from the "protectorate" to the British Isles, the conscience-stricken English immediately founded a Czech Relief Fund and looked after the refugees on a grand scale. I remember a reception at the London PEN to welcome writers from Prague and Bratislava (Pressburg), held at Henrietta Leslie's Glebe House, which was also used as a fund-raising occasion. Fritzi Massary, who had married the late Max Pallenberg, thus enabling him to acquire British citizenship, came as a guest of honor, an elderly lady, no longer a great beauty, but still full

122

of charm. It was on this evening that a professor's wife, Mrs. Rose, loudly protested against the presumption of certain exiles in making use of the English language. This was the only time in all those decades that we were confronted with such chauvinistic arrogance. The Austrians received help from the good people of PEN, but not from officialdom. The news photographs of the Heldenplatz in Vienna had convinced the Western world that the whole country had enthusiastically embraced its invaders. A barmaid, questioned by the interviewers from the research organization Mass Observation on what she thought of Hitler's march into Austria, had replied: "Oh, I'm not fussy." The whole of Great Britain seemed hardly perturbed by the fact that the successor state to an empire that had been independent since 1804 had been annexed by those who were then laying waste to the German Empire founded in 1871. There was no collective support for those unfortunates who had found themselves unable to share in the supposed general rejoicing. For the time being, they had to set up an Austrian Self-Aid group, which was supported by their own noted artists and scientists, including Siegfried Charoux, Georg Ehrlich, and the superlatively lovable historian of ideas, Hofrat Friedrich Hertz, a man who epitomized old Austria. Oskar Kokoschka came to London from Prague before the end of the year, and attended the first meeting of the Austrian refugees as one of their own.

Soon, under the honorary patronage of Sigmund Freud and the former ambassador Franckenstein, an Austrian Centre was founded, which had its own little theater, "Das Laterndl," whose productions were attended by all but the Social Democrats. Its leading figure, Oscar Pollak, like his émigré party colleagues throughout the world, pursued a policy of continuous Anschluss to a re-democratized Germany – right up to the Moscow Declaration of 1943, when the Allies made the independence of Austria one of their declared aims. The factional battles in the shadowy realm of the exiles were carried to a ludicrous degree. Pollak forbade the poet Theodor Kramer to read his poems at the Laterndl. Kramer was faced with a severe moral dilemma. Yet the urge to reach an audience, in the absence of a readership, finally prevailed.

1938 was a difficult year. A year of waiting for the catastrophe, feared yet at the same time desired, because there was no other way of removing the specter of Hitler's rule from the world. Private difficulties, the financial needs of our extended family, were getting out of hand. My father, dependent on the scanty financial support of the Woburn House refugee aid organization, was continuing his long-standing patent dispute with ICI, but there was no prospect of conquering this Goliath. His partner in the patent he had developed for the production of synthetic rubber had already moved to DuPont in New Jersey, and my father too was offered a post. But the U.S. immigration formalities were protracted, and when, in the first year of the war, all the papers and the necessary funds for the journey had finally been obtained, my father, with many others, was interned on the Isle of Man. The places on the ocean liner had already been booked; they were lost, and he returned from internment two days after the last Cunard liner had departed, and all non-military shipping across the Atlantic, infested as it was with U-boats, had been suspended.

In October 1938 Peter had crossed the ocean on the little *Champlain* and spent seven weeks in New York. He visited his publisher, stayed with friends whom we had met only the summer before at Bandol, established all sorts of useful relationships, and returned, with his usual incredible linguistic adaptability, sporting a slight American accent, which soon disappeared. Nevertheless, he was determined – we were determined – to sit out the coming war in Europe. It would have seemed like desertion – although the Englishmen Auden and Isherwood and even Elisabeth Bergner by no means considered it dishonorable – to leave the sinking ship while others, less directly concerned in the resistance to Hitler's tyranny, were risking their necks.

But then, how could one abandon a country in which things such as this happened? On Christmas Eve a huge hamper from Fortnum and Mason was delivered to us at Winchester Court, full of bottles of wine and a variety of delicacies, from an unknown donor. When we inquired who had placed the order, we were told most emphatically that the client had insisted on strict anonymity. So our gratitude was not only to one, but to all our English friends. We saved the feast for New Year's Eve, when we invited a number of Viennese guests, including Hans Flesch-Brunningen with his companion Tetta, and Ernst Polak, who was like an orphan in London without his Café

Herrenhof. My father forgot his worries, "sang songs and recited poems" – which ones, I can no longer remember. The mandolin had disappeared with the rest of his possessions.

The urge to sing did not last long. That winter, my father, a man of fifty-two, again dishonored and stripped of dignity, as he had been twenty years earlier, tolerated in his adoptive land but incapable of once again building himself a new future – that winter he habitually sat by the gramophone playing his innumerable recordings on shellac, the Schubert Quintet in C major and the "Wegweiser" song, sung by Alexander Kipnis: "*Was hab ich denn verbrochen, dass ich Menschen sollte scheun?*" ("What crime have I committed, that I should flee from mankind?") My mother, now light-hearted, now melancholy, took over my little household and called back all the dishes that Marie had prepared for us over so many years, with the help of a farewell present, Alice Urbach's gigantic cookery book *So kocht man in Wien* ("How One Cooks in Vienna").

What induced us, in this breathing space before the outbreak of war, to think of bringing a child into the world? It was Peter's zest for life, his most irresistible characteristic as a young man, which carried me along with him. On his first appearance in my life, he said to me, "When are you going to come out from behind your tiled stove in the Stanislausgasse?", repeating it until I agreed. I myself, though not lacking in energy, was always secretly plagued by existential fear, and without him I would have failed to make many decisions which later turned out to be the right ones. It was right to start a family, in the teeth of all adversity. Later we simply would not have gotten around to it. And once there was one, there was the possibility of a second. My baby was to be born at the end of October 1939. But first, in February, my Italian book, *Flute and Drums*, saw the light of day. "Miss Spiel's talent remains individual and delicate in the strident cacophony of the time," Louis Golding had written as a recommendation – he was a noted novelist of the time, long before the Nobel Prize winner of the same surname – and its reception was gratifying. In Ireland, the novel was placed on the index of prohibited books. This actually contributed to its success.

I will not succumb to the temptation to quote from reviews to substantiate my account of this first encouraging reception of my work in England. Reading Hans Tietze's book *Die Juden Wiens* (*The*

Jews of Vienna), which I had brought with me, I toyed with the idea of a new, historical novel. It was Tietze, too, who sparked my interest in Fanny von Arnstein, whose biography I later wrote. But contemporary world events left me no time for long-term literary activity. By March, Czechoslovakia had already ceased to exist as a state, and we in turn lost our livelihood. Peter Smollett was prepared for this. He acquired and reactivated a rundown news agency – with what funds, I do not know – called Exchange Telegraph, and in this enterprise too relied upon Peter's assistance. When war broke out, the agency was taken over by the government and run by the Ministry of Information via Portugal. My Peter became its director, after Smollett had transferred to the Russian section of the ministry.

For me, coinciding with the attacks of nausea caused by my pregnancy, there began a time of intensive effort to make travel arrangements for friends still caught in the trap in Vienna and now also in Prague. Negotiations with the Quakers, with Woburn House, with the appropriate authorities – these took up the greater part of my day for months on end, leaving me exhausted and depressed. The result was shattering defeat. I managed to save only one couple, an old comrade of Peter's, the publisher, writer, and philosopher Paul Roubiczek and his wife. They found refuge at the University of Cambridge. As a result, I was soon able to reap an unexpected reward for my efforts. In early summer, already heavy with child, I constantly sought the coolness of the nearby park. Once, as I sat on a bench, I saw my once so beloved Hafis passing by with a companion. I turned away so as not to be recognized. He was in transit from Prague to America, where he had been sent by the Reuters agency. Much later, I learned that in the midst of the war, working for Reuters in Palestine, he had died in a road accident.

In July I spent some time alone in an old rectory at Fowey in Cornwall. Here I, the follower of the rationalist Schlick, was forced to believe in ghosts. Toward evening, lying between two open windows in the master bedroom, while reading a book, I was startled by the sensation of an invisible presence, which flew in at the left-hand window and, after circling the room, out again at the right. The rectory was known to be haunted. In Britain, even rationalists learn to come to terms with inexplicable materializations. The noted humanist philosopher Kathleen Nott, who was to become my friend, had seen an apparition during her studies in the common room at Somerville College, Oxford. It was the figure, as large as life, of a nun, whose violent death in that place during the previous century was documented. Well, perhaps scientific knowledge will one day find an explanation for such phenomena.

During these months, I used to wander around the Kensington Church Street area, up to Campden Hill Road and through the side streets, past all the little old houses which seemed so much more desirable to me than the apartment in brand-new Winchester Court. One of them was the object of all my longings. It was number 18 Aubrey Walk, and it was for rent. I could already see myself there, with my husband and child, behind the well-proportioned façade, with open fireplaces on whose mantels the invitations and Christmas cards would be lined up, with a little front and back garden, like my friend Dodo's house: the perfect English lifestyle. I mourned for that house for a lifetime. Things turned out differently. On September 3, we heard Chamberlain's announcement of war on the radio. My doctor, Dr. Altmann, the brother of Lotte, who was to marry Stefan Zweig and go to her death with him, made it clear to me that all the hospital beds in the capital were now to be kept free for those with war injuries, and a country nursing home was the only solution. I went to Cambridge, and did not return to my beloved Kensington.

I sat in an armchair on a lawn in St Peter's Terrace, on which stood a mulberry tree, one of only two such trees in Cambridge, whose fruit fell heavily to the ground to lie in the dark, purple-stained grass. I was now being looked after by the Roubiczeks, who lived in that little house, the property of Peterhouse college. Thus the next few weeks passed, a tranquil time. Once I was called before the foreigners' tribunal and reclassified as Grade B because I had left my home years before Hitler and was therefore not an immigrant. I had to hand in my camera and promise not to go within twenty miles of the sea. But soon afterward I was given Peter's Grade C status and was allowed to take photographs again. On the last day of October our daughter was born. The flickering light of a coal fire; stoneware hot-water bottles at the soles of my feet; the smell of Dettol: these became as evocative to me as Proust's madeleine. There was porridge for breakfast and shepherd's pie for lunch. At the same time, Peter left Winchester Court and moved into a larger apartment in the suburbs with the help of Flesch, who was living nearby with Tetta in an almost subterranean garden apartment. It was not for its own sake that we chose Wimbledon, but because we believed ourselves to be safer from air attack in that more thinly populated suburb than in the inner city. This turned out to be an illusion.

I spent at least a third of my life in that beautiful, green, utterly bourgeois district. In all that time, we were never invited into a single English household there, never became involved in the social structure, in spite of the fact that my daughter and son went to the local schools, run by Ursuline nuns and Jesuit priests, until boarding-school education proved to be more advisable. Not only foreign, but also Catholic among the Anglican Britons! And since we only went to church to have the children christened and confirmed, this community too was denied to us. A little lower down our street, The Downs, Sebastian Haffner lived with his family. We hardly ever visited even him. A year after the outbreak of war, London was a very dangerous place to live in, yet whenever we were overcome by loneliness, we would drive for miles to Chelsea, Kensington, or Hampstead, where almost the whole German-speaking immigrant community was to be found within a narrow radius.

Although there were hot summers, above all that dreadful first one, which put an end to the "phony war," the "*drôle de guerre*," I think of the war as if it had been one long winter. I still catch myself saying, "During the winter we had one kitten after another," or "We spent almost the whole winter in front of the radio-gramophone." That indeed was how it was. In the three-story concrete apartment house there was no air-raid shelter, so we stayed in our ground-floor apartment even during the most severe air-raid warnings. In between, we played records or listened to Beethoven symphonies on the radio – since those days that heroic music has never again moved me so passionately. But our consolation, again and again, was Schubert. For a long time, my parents lived with us; for a long time, too, we barricaded the windows with mattresses and slept on the bed frames. At the height of the Blitz, in November 1940, Peter sent me with our little daughter to Oxford, to stay with Teresa Carr-Saunders, the sister of my daughter's godmother Madge. She was married to the director of the London School of Economics and lived with her family in an ancient mansion by the Isis. Among her best friends were the highly aristocratic, but also Catholic and Socialist couple Frank and Elizabeth Pakenham, whose eldest daughter, the beautiful, proud Antonia, was then about eleven years old. I have told the story of what happened at Water Eaton Manor in a short story, "Auf einem anderen Stern" ("On another star").

The nightly attacks on London by German bombers continued for months after my return. While the rest of us, buoyed up by the stoicism of the English, managed to remain calm and felt no need to hide in cellars, and Peter, while the wildest battle raged in the skies, continued to write his novel *The Hours and the Centuries*, my anxious mother was in a constant state of nervous tension. When she seemed to be on the verge of total breakdown, we made an appointment for her with a well-known psychiatrist. The night before had been particularly noisy and threatening. When we arrived at the doctor's apartment near Primrose Hill, his housekeeper opened the door to us and said in contemptuous tones: "Dr. X left for the country early this morning." Mimi caught my eye, and we both burst out laughing. Her sense of humor, rather than the words of encouragement she had been hoping for, restored her courage – at least for a while.

Before the Russo-German pact came to an abrupt end through Hitler's invasion of the Soviet Union, we had, in fact, as calmly as possible, given ourselves up as lost. "I don't know how we are going to win the war," said my father, identifying himself as a matter of course with the British by whom he had only recently been interned, "but now we cannot lose it any more." Until then, we had fully expected a German invasion in the course of which we would be seized and executed, and only hoped that our daughter would be safe in the care of the nuns. After the shift in emphasis of the conflict to the Eastern front, the air attacks, particularly during the daytime, became less frequent. We ventured into town more often. I began my historical novel set in Vienna – writing in English – and went to do my research in the domed Reading Room of the British Museum. To sit there under the green reading lamp, reference books heaped up on the desk, totally suspended in space and time, yet feeling part of the community of all those who surrounded me, lost in a similar transport, in that huge hall, was an incomparable pleasure to me. Sometimes a few of us would leave our seats and go together to sit in the windowless café, to talk about matters as unrelated to the temporarily extinguished present as were our studies. Now and then I would chat with the Hungarian Baron Ludwig Hatvány, a friend of the "Red Count" Károly, who had the manner of a *grand seigneur*. Once I asked about his children. "I hardly ever hear from them," he said dismissively. "Anyway, they are much older than me." The English PEN occasionally invited us to events at the Institut Français. I noted a tea party with H. G. Wells, Alfred Kerr, and Robert Neumann. In autumn 1941 the Luftwaffe were beginning to pay us more frequent visits, and the Atlantic was a wildly threatening expanse, when this association of writers – so wonderful there and then –held an international congress in London. Peter and I were asked to help with the preparations. Wells presided, and J. B. Priestley chaired several sessions. John Dos Passos and Thornton Wilder had come from America. More than thirty-five nations were represented. Although we had been active in English PEN for a long time, Peter was considered a representative of the German exiles' center, along with Erika Mann, Alfred Kerr, Richard Friedenthal, and others, while I belonged to the Austrian one, like Canetti, Koestler, Kramer, Joe Lederer, and Anna Mahler.

The proceedings were lively; minor literary battles raged, just as if the whole world were not in flames. Salvador de Madariaga started a quarrel with H. G. Wells, whose account of the Spanish conquistadors in his *Outline of History* had outraged him to the highest degree. Robert Neumann accused Jules Romains, then still International President of PEN, of former close connections with Ribbentrop and Laval, and Raymond Aron defended his compatriot in heated language."This touchiness of the French!" I noted in my calendar. Erika Mann drew up a re-education program for the Germans, which some thought a little unrealistic. And Peter gave a well-received talk, "Writers without language," closing with my favorite passage from Drouot's *Eurydice deux fois perdue*: "*Les mots ne me consolent plus.... Les phrases ne me sont plus rien. Et pourtant elles sont près de nous toujours; elles ont des secrets bien plus subtils que la pensée; elles sont l'ouiement des sirènes, le sourire des fées; il faut qu'elles chantent pour que je vive.*"

In the middle of the war we became British citizens. Despite this Peter still had to wait two years for the honor of being elected to the PEN executive committee, because, after all, he was "not an Englishman." Mrs. Sims, one of our long series of home helpers, upset us deeply when she explained her departure from our household with the words: "sometimes I felt I was not in England, I was in a foreign country." This formidable woman had once entered the living room as music was ringing from the speaker, and cried: "The *William Tell* Overture? My pet aversion!" Yet I had become fond even of Mrs. Sims and in vain tried to persuade her to stay. With each of these women, I hoped to establish the sort of relationship that had existed with our Marie, our Anna in the Wollzeile; I tried to make them my confidantes, wooed and spoiled them. Yet they remained politely distant, and after a while they left us. Mrs. Parker of our Kensington days, "Blackie," Violet, Mrs. Williams, Mrs. Stenhouse, Miss Webb – I wept for each and every one of them.

A bright spot in this endless winter was the *Français libres*. We immediately found access to them, through Peter's translator Denise van Moppès, who had also emigrated, and her brother Maurice. The Free French livened up the London scene; even in the days of the blackout, they celebrated the fourteenth of July in front of the Petit Club Français in St. James's Place, soon to be called Little France in the vernacular; they alone were provided with the tart Algerian red wine that no one else could buy. On their first *quatorze juillet*, I too danced to the accordion music in the open air until late into the night, mostly with a little lieutenant in the Marines, who commended himself to me with the words: "*Dans la nuit tous les chats sont gris.*" And I, proud of my knowledge of colloquial French, replied: "*Et les sous-officiers de la marine.*"

We read the magazine *La France libre* to our great profit. There Raymond Aron had published a brilliant analysis of the German character in connection with the Siegfried myth. Only a thin layer, a kind of veneer, covered the primitive barbarian instincts of the Germans – or so he attempted to prove. I do not know whether this essay was included in the translated collections that were later published. Certainly Vercors, in his book *Le Silence de la mer*, published soon after the war ended, was more subtle in portraying the contempt of the French for their conquerors and occupiers. From time to time, Peter, and later I myself, succeeded in having pieces published in this excellent periodical for exiles. It was the same with Cyril Connolly's *Horizon* and the *New Statesman*, that house journal of the English intelligentsia up to the 1970s. Not a week went by without a mention of Kafka or Koestler in the *New Statesman*. Kafka, long known from the English versions by Edwin and Willa Muir, now seemed to be the only writer to do justice, in terms of parables, to a truth hardly any longer to be communicated in realistic terms. And Koestler, with his *Darkness at Noon*, directly influenced England's excessively unconditional acceptance of the Soviet system in gratitude for the lives rescued with the help of the Red Army under Stalin.

We ourselves, in our geographical isolation in Wimbledon, remained virtually unaffected by the concentration of German-speaking exiles in North London. Flesch too, in the throes of marital difficulties, of internment and subsequent employment by the BBC, had left Wimbledon. In diametric contrast to the settlers in Hampstead, we were considered arrogant apostates who had become assimilated to our English surroundings. But we simply found the nostalgic meetings of the exiles, who even at their most cheerful moments were predominantly concerned with the past, less exciting than, say, an evening with Gordon Turner; he was a well-to-do man, past military age and surrounded by handsome youths. Joe Lederer and her woman friend kept house for him, and his guests included Cyril Connolly and other London intellectuals, including the cosmopolitan Hatvány.

Certainly, we continued to see our earlier friends, and worried about problem children such as Theodor Kramer. From time to time we visited the Laterndl, where we saw performances of works by Jura Soyfer, who had perished in Buchenwald, and the cabaret poets Peter Preses, Rudolf Spitz, and Hugo Königsgarten, who had all reached London, and later Nestroy, Anzengruber, and Schnitzler. And once, at the German *Kulturbund*, we attended a Berlin-style cabaret. But both Peter and I were only nominally members of the two PEN centers of writers in exile, which had been founded respectively by Robert Neumann and Rudolf Olden, while the politically committed *Kulturbund* attracted us as little as Club 43, an association of aesthetes. In all these groups, Flesch, the sociable philanthropist, despite being an Austrian and a novelist writing in English, at times led the proceedings.

On one occasion British and central European standards merged for us in a curious manner. Members of the London PEN had been invited to the Czech House for an afternoon event where, in the presence of T. S. Eliot, his poem "East Coker" was read by the poet Ambrosová in her Czech version, to an accompaniment of Czech music. Eliot sat with an impassive expression. I rashly remarked to Henrietta Leslie that for me those magnificent lines, delivered in the language of our beloved cooks and tailors, had not only a strange, but unfortunately also a comic effect. Henrietta sat bolt upright, struggling for words. Then she cried out indignantly: "You – you *Herrenvolk*!" Let no one be deceived: the memories of home, which we suppressed with difficulty, kept breaking out. I dreamed of Heiligenstadt, of walks in the Prater with our dog Diemo, long dead, of the contours of the Salesianerkirche on the Rennweg, and had a nightmare of suddenly waking up in Vienna, a stranger among enemies, with English money in my pocket, an outlaw. In conversations with my laughter-loving mother, whose sense of humor and poetic imagination were more strongly marked than her rational logic, we remembered certain characters in her beloved Döbling, like the basket weaver Frau Werner, whose homespun sayings had been collected by my grandmother Melanie: "*Wer wohnen will, muss sich kümmern*" ("If you want to make a home, you must make an effort"); "*Der schlechteste Mann ist besser als die besten Kinder*" ("The worst man is better than the best children"); or, when asked what she planned to do as a widow: "*In allen Parks wird man mich sehen*" ("I will be seen in all the parks"); and why, after her constantly ailing husband had finally passed away, she continued to prepare the most elaborate dishes: "*Na hören Sie, was in meinem Magen kommt!*" ("Well, listen, what goes into *my* stomach... !") In the window of the little shop, there had always hung a notice with the inscription: "*Holde Wesen/ dichtet Körner/ gute Besen/ bei Herrn Werner*" ("Fair creatures/ in the poems of Körner/ good brooms/ from Herr Werner"). That touching love of German literature! But the laughter soon had to stop; the thought of the fate of Frau Werner, as well as of *Grossmama*, aroused uncertain and all the more tormenting fears in us. Besides, our ability to assimilate to the English lifestyle deserted us completely when it came to Christmas customs. To celebrate the festival on Christmas Day instead of Christmas Eve, to light the Christmas tree lights during the daytime, not to sing our own songs as well as the beautiful English carols, were things impossible for us. By our daughter's third Christmas, we had already taught her to sing "*Ihr Kinderlein kommet*" ("Come, little children").

In February I had to have an operation. And soon afterward – much too soon in my doctor's opinion – I found myself expecting another child. It was a difficult pregnancy, ominous from the start, but it went to full term. At the beginning of 1943, in the luxurious London Clinic, after a protracted labor of several days, the misfortune which could have been avoided in any humble general hospital took place. My doctor, a former leading light of the Berlin Charité, was not around when suddenly everything began to happen very fast, and the nurses did not dare to intervene as any midwife, any intern would have done. When the leading light arrived, the baby had already suffocated. A girl. I had wanted to call her Brigid. The days that followed were the worst of my life. Instead of comforting me, Peter expected me to comfort him. And I felt as if I had failed at the decisive moment.

At that time, the Luftwaffe's squadrons were again visiting us every night. Recently they had scored a hit on a school and killed forty children. Around the corner from us lived Garda, née Countess Stollberg, with her Jewish husband and two children. Her brother was serving in the Flying Corps. She wondered whether perhaps he was in action over London. When, in the following year, a cluster bomb fell over the nearby Ridgway, her house too was partly destroyed. Now innumerable families, above all from working areas, were again gathering in the depths of the Underground, on the platforms of the Tube; rather than subject themselves to the danger of bombs, they led a makeshift existence camping on mattresses and sacks of straw in the densely crowded, steamy proximity of their companions. Returning at night from Victoria Station to Wimbledon, one had to climb over outstretched legs, inadequately covered by rough blankets, crawling children who had escaped from their mothers, snoring old men - scenes from Dante's *Inferno*. Henry Moore made drawings of them. How could they all sleep amid the thundering of the trains? But they were even more terrified by the howling and flashing of defensive action and the crash of falling bombs.

We lived in our suburb without any friendly contacts, except those, which were not exactly intimate, with Garda and her husband. But we were supported by the goodwill, the consideration and helpfulness of all around us, from our neighbors in Wimbledon Close to the housewives with whom I stood in line for hours at the shops of the beefy butcher Higgins and the popeyed fishmonger Burgess. And yet, despite all the solidarity that exists even between strangers in times of emergency and in which we were included as a matter of course, a distinction was always preserved. As Great Britain had always described itself as "*of* Europe" but not "*in* Europe," so we were well aware that we were "*in* England" but not "*of* England." Nevertheless, like our fellow citizens, learning from their composure, we overcame as steadfastly as possible the anxiety of each day, with difficulty keeping ourselves and our cats well fed, pursuing our duties and gleaning encouragement from the broadcasts of the BBC.

We were reassured by the sonorous voices of the announcers, above all that of Stuart Hibberd, who reported both catastrophes and triumphs in the same calm tones; amused by Tommy Handley's hilarious *ITMA*, peopled by modern versions of Dickensian figures, whose catchphrases were quoted throughout England; given hope by the songs in defiance of Hitler, such as "When that man is dead and gone/ We'll be dancing down the street/ Kissing everyone we meet"; and uplifted by the eleven national anthems of the Allies and the governments in exile represented in London, which resounded ceremoniously before the news every Sunday morning. Those which moved us most were the "Netherlands Prayer of Thanks"; the "Alexandrov" hymn of the Russians – yes, certainly, the Soviet Russians; and of course "ours," "God Save the King." When it rang out in the theater before the curtain went up, when the recording was played in the cinema at the end of the last performance and the picture of the pale, smiling King, his cheerful, chubby Queen, and the two little princesses appeared on the screen, we rose to our feet with all the others, deeply moved by the feeling that with this nation, and the humanity of its ruling house, we could not go under.

Moreover, this winter of our discontent, in retrospect one long, damp, cold, gloomy, and oppressive season, in which we longed for rain or fog because they kept enemy aircraft away, was not without its moments of brightness. "There's peace in war as well," says the army chaplain in Brecht's *Mother Courage*, "it has its peaceful spots. You see, war satisfies all needs, it has to, or it wouldn't last." Our "peaceful spots" were invitations where the guests were many and various, such as a reception at J. H. Lothar's (he was the publisher of the German exiles' newspaper *Die Zeitung*), where the hook-nosed Lady Oxford and Asquith pocketed Peter's beautiful new pocket flashlight – indispensable when going home in the blackout – and Oskar Kokoschka came up to me, took me by the chin and said in his native dialect: "*Du hast a herzig's Gfriesl*" ("You've got a bonny little face"). There was sailing on the Norfolk rivers and Broads with John Arrow, a colleague of Peter's at the Ministry, and his wife Joey, jolly people and great drinkers, with whom we went on pub crawls and drank innumerable pints of mild and bitter. There were evenings in the New Theatre, where the bombed-out Old Vic company – Olivier, Richardson, Peggy Ashcroft – gave wonderful performances of Shakespeare, Webster, Congreve, and Ibsen.

And there were weddings during the war. Ernst Polak, himself almost a cult figure in London as a former friend of Kafka's, married the beautiful Delphine, daughter of the late baronet Sir James Reynolds. The dark little Denise van Moppès married John Butler, a blond giant from Nebraska. Around forty, she had recently complained that she was bored with love: "*Ça ne vaut pas la peine de se déshabiller.*" Then, after the United States had finally joined the war and sent their troops over – "overfed, oversexed, over-decorated, and over here," as they were characterized by the ungrateful English – this young man too had arrived in London. Hungry for culture, his soul seeking the England of his compatriot Henry James and the France of Proust, he was enchanted by the allure of the Parisienne Denise. Four weeks after the liberation of her city, Denise returned to France. "*Tu sais bien que les français sont méchants,*" her cousin Maurice warned her. "*Tant pis!*" replied Denise. Momô himself followed her and a couple of years later was stabbed to death on the Place Pigalle. John too had himself transferred to Paris, and at the end of the war a little son was born. Denise called him Rémy, after the child in Peter's *The Hours and the Centuries*, written during the Blitz.

Much had happened before Paris could be liberated in August 1944, and far too much happened after that. In February, that fatal month, a cluster-bomb had fallen on our part of Wimbledon toward midnight, partly destroying Garda's house and hitting an old people's home directly opposite us. Twenty-five people were killed. I can still hear today the shrill, high-pitched screams of the severely injured victims. Our little block of apartments had withstood the full impact, but the air pressure had crushed inner walls, splintered the wood, and shattered all the glass. Peter and I had helmets on, because we were going to leave for the fire station as soon as the sirens started to wail. The air raid came too fast for us. After the first bombs had struck, I had time to run into our daughter's bedroom and bend over her. Then came the earth-shaking explosion opposite. The wall at the side of the crib collapsed, falling, thank God, in the other direction. My leg was injured. Peter's upper lip was split; the blood pouring, he ran to the nearest doctor, who stitched the wound without anesthetic. All the residents of our building sat around together in the entrance hall for a while, until the all clear sounded. Conscious of having escaped danger by a hair's breadth, we found relief in hectic gaiety.

To see our tomcat Ha'penny, who had disappeared in the turmoil, returning the next morning, carefully picking his way with his little paws through a sea of broken glass, was an unforgettable experience, as was the sight of my new strawberry-red blouse, nailed to the wall by splinters, looking like some kind of scarecrow. The huge oleograph of Van Gogh's nurse holding the ribbons of a baby's cradle, which till now had hung protectively over my bed in place of Carry Hauser's Madonna, was peppered with holes. All the rooms except one were uninhabitable. We took our little daughter away, back to Cambridge, our place of refuge, to a doctor's family where there were several other children. The shock of the night of bombs, her wounded father, the separation from her parents were things that perhaps she never succeeded in banishing from her soul. On the sixth of June the invasion began, and eleven days later the first pilotless aircraft appeared over London. Hans Habe, in his smart American uniform, had invited us to dinner at the Savoy. We stayed too long. As we came out of Wimbledon station toward midnight, countless aircraft clacked over our heads, a sound like that of a hundred diabolical sewing machines. It was not the bombs, but the shower of metal that rained down from the defensive artillery that made us flee again and again into shop doorways; our journey punctuated by minute-long pauses, we finally traversed the endless Wimbledon Hill Road and the Ridgway as far as The Downs.

Soon afterward I too went to live in Cambridge, for a third child was on the way: conceived among bombs, to be born among bombs. I stayed at Eden House, Eden Street, the home of a German woman scholar, a professor's widow and the friend of Adam Trott zu Solz. In her wide-ranging library I found and read the works of Walter Pater and Meredith. I often spent time with my little daughter, but she was better looked after at the Vernons', among their children; "Miss Gerda," the domestic help, a refugee from Berlin, looked after her lovingly. On September 10, I returned to London, although Peter had warned me that a new weapon was about to be deployed against us. In the early morning hours after my arrival we were awakened from our sleep by the ear-splitting sound of the first rockets landing on London and the echo of their breaking through the stratosphere that followed.

When our son was born at ten in the evening in the middle of November, there were two flying-bomb attacks in the area of the London Clinic, and a rocket landed near enough to shake its walls. By that time our baby had already been moved down to the cellar. Up in my room, in my joy over my child, I took little notice of the V1s and V2s, Hitler's weapons of revenge. As terrible as the rockets were with their double thunder, we learned to adopt a stoic attitude toward them. One could not predict when and where they would land, and neither warning nor defense was possible, so we simply paid no attention to them. As was the practice in the mildly damp English climate, even in winter, I would wrap my little son up well, put him outside the house door in his carriage for some fresh air, and go shopping with my daughter. We were all "in God's hands," whether we believed in him or not.

In December 1944, Peter, who had been detailed to SHAEF (the Supreme Headquarters Allied Expeditionary Forces) after the dissolution of Exchange Telegraph in Lisbon, was sent to Paris in uniform. In Luxembourg, he narrowly escaped Field Marshal von Rundstedt's attack through the Ardennes. On Christmas Eve, in thick fog, which no longer deterred the rockets, he returned. He had much to tell about the sensations of that winter in Paris: about Anouilh's *Antigone* and Sartre's *Huis clos*, which had already been performed under the Germans, and Claudel's *fumisterie*, as he called it, *Le Soulier de satin*, with Jean-Louis Barrault, with a set by the great set designer Christian (Baby) Bérard. At the same time, the Allied forces were engaged in a bitter struggle with the Wehrmacht in the Ardennes, and London was groaning under the rockets and "doodlebugs" (flying bombs). The ridiculous was as close to the tragic as to the sublime.

138

When Paris fell, the Francophile aesthete Raymond Mortimer, so it was said in Fleet Street, exclaimed: "I must kiss a Frenchman today!" Soon the literary dandies on each side were to reunite.

During the months that followed, while I looked after the children with the help of my German-Jewish help Beate from Kupferdreh, but also often visited the British Museum to study the Romantics, Peter was constantly being sent to France. When, at the end of April 1945, an early harbinger of the recently forged brotherhood, the Surrealist and freedom-fighter Paul Éluard, came to the Institut Français in London, Peter went straight there from the airport. Together with many other guests we celebrated the German capitulation at Charing Cross, in the home of Kingsley Martin, the editor of the *New Statesman*, to which we had both become contributors. And next evening, together with hundreds of thousands of Londoners, we wandered dizzily through the city whose lights were allowed to flame up again after five and a half years- Piccadilly Circus, Trafalgar Square, the square in front of Buckingham Palace, on whose balcony the King, Queen, and little princesses appeared, in uniform or in blue, and lastly Churchill, who did not wave or give his victory sign, but simply bowed to the crowd. "For he's a jolly good fellow," we sang. Never before or after have I experienced such a collective intoxication of happiness, never again such certainty of being at home here and nowhere else.

The euphoria ebbed. The routine of everyday life returned. No more danger from the skies, but money problems, food problems, worries about my parents, as before. Peter was soon off again, this time to Germany and the resurrected Austria, to set up the first contacts with writers and journalists for the SHAEF Information Services Control. Among others, he tracked down Erich Kästner, at Mayrhofen in the Tyrol, the summer home for many years of my father's parents. On a brief return visit in June, he brought me a branch of jasmine from the Mirabell park in Salzburg, which instantly brought tears to my eyes. Hans Habe, whom he bumped into in Bad Nauheim, gave him an enormous, slightly grubby American parachute for me; it was of nylon silk, which could be used for making lingerie.

I found it difficult to get used to Peter's repeated absences. Once I went to spend a few days with Dodo in the country, at her seventeenth-century cottage, Mousehall Mill. Her children and mine drove around in a little pony cart and swam in the mill pond. In the evening Dodo showed me her little treasure casket, inherited from her grandmother: Elizabethan coins and ancient, slightly discolored jewelry. Her ancestors on her grandmother's side had lived in the same house in Wiltshire since the thirteenth century. "If only I had a family," I wrote in my calendar, "so deeply rooted in the land and in history."

My poor father was once again without means, as had happened so often during the war, and was facing ruin. Everything seemed to have conspired against him. After the failure of his attempted emigration to America because of his internment, he had experienced only disappointment and humiliation. A man in his prime who had gone into exile with inborn or acquired courage, he had for a long time found no suitable work and had been living in agonizing dependence on his son-in-law. During the worst years of bombing, this close family community had held firm; then it was dissolved, and this upset him to the point of depression, since he loved his little granddaughter more than anything else. We had found my parents a small one-bedroom apartment in Broadwalk Court in Notting Hill and continued to support them as best we could.

My father spent his time clearing away rubble from bomb sites, until he finally got a job with the Ministry of Supply as a laboratory supervisor in Leeds, far away from his loved ones, and then as director of research elsewhere. At long last, his technique for producing synthetic rubber was attracting attention, and he was employed in this field. For a while, his prospects seemed to have improved. The famous Professor J. D. Bernal had taken him under his wing and had suggested recommending him for membership of the Royal Society. It never happened. The rubber plantations in the Far East were reclaimed; he was no longer needed and was simply dismissed, at the age of fifty-eight.

During that hot June my father desperately roamed the streets of London trying to find some work, and again took a job clearing away rubble, until I found out about it and intervened. But I myself was often short of funds, for Peter, with his usual equanimity, had not made sufficient provision for us, and I, occupied in translating *The Hours and the Centuries* for a Swiss publisher, was not in a position to earn money. Grasping at straws, my father came up with the idea of trying his hand as a translator himself. In view of "the glorification of compulsive behavior in the heresy of National Socialism," he considered Vardis Fisher's *Darkness and the Deep*, a semi-scientific, semi-poetic book about prehistoric man, particularly suitable for translation into German. It is with shame and grief that I now read the letter in which I advised him to save himself the trouble, and instructed him patronizingly about the "economic laws" of the "literary world" which were foreign to him. I would have treated him more gently if I had understood then that his life was over, that exile was killing him as surely as a German concentration camp would have done.

One Sunday in July 1945 I was wandering along the edge of Wimbledon Common with my father, pushing my little son, whom he now also loved, in his pram, and holding my daughter by the hand. We walked peacefully for about half an hour; I was accompanying him to the bus stop near the windmill on the Common. Five days later, he was dead. In the midday heat, returning exhausted to the little apartment in Broadwalk Court from yet another vain search for work, he had, reckless as ever, got straight into a cold bath. My mother found him there, lifeless. Peter, who was not there to help, to comfort – "it is as if he did not exist," I wrote – learned the news only weeks later. Mimi and Lonny, my father's wife and sister, sat around weeping helplessly. I had to borrow money for his cremation. The second night after his death, a storm raged, as loud as the worst of the air-raids. I thought of a passage from his favorite *Florian Geyer* by Gerhart Hauptmann: "Where is one the first night after death?" "At St. Gertrauden." "Where is one the second night after death?" "At St. Michel." It was as if my father was saying farewell to us amid thunder and lightning.

On August 2, Peter returned, full of his successes and adventures of every kind, not noticeably shaken by what had happened to us in the meantime. On the sixth, we went to visit Kingsley Martin and his companion Dorothy Woodman in their cottage in Essex, and spent the day there. Toward evening we heard on the radio that America had dropped an atomic bomb on Japan. We were deeply stirred – no other term can be used. I thought of my father, whom the news would have roused to enthusiasm as a scientist, but still horrified as

In the Kahlenberg meadow, Vienna

a moral human being. Kingsley Martin announced: "This means the end of the war." And to us: "I expect you will go back to your own country now?" Then we knew, though we did not admit it to ourselves, that nine years of assimilation into the English world had been in vain.

In 1955

9

Leap to the Mainland

But where did we belong? Who were we still, what had we become? Never during the war, when half of Europe crowded together in the beleaguered island, had such questions been asked, never had we doubted that we were counted among the British, the Allies, or feared that we would not be taken up by their community. Now, with the mainland opened up to us again, when people in exile were faced with the choice of returning to their places of origin, tearing up once more the roots they had put down with such difficulty, or sinking them even more deeply into the soil of their second home – now we were put to the test. Kingsley Martin's automatic assumption that we would slip off our newly won identity like a pair of worn-out slippers at first seemed devastating. But what happened was unexpected and astonishing: never before or afterward would we feel such close attachment to the British as during the three years that followed, never feel so accepted by them as on that mainland, but in the shelter and protection of their army.

On the instructions of SHAEF, Peter had gone first to France, then to Germany. SHAEF was under the command of General Eisenhower, with a mixture of personnel who could be deployed here or there according to need. When SHAEF was dissolved in July 1945 and replaced by separate military governments, this deployment persisted for a time. The troops of the three Western powers that moved into Berlin in the first week of July 1945 were accompanied by information control departments. The press officer for the American section was the British civilian Peter de Mendelssohn. The letters he wrote me that summer from Berlin were headed "Information Control Division, US Forces European Theater" and bore the stamp "On active service."

Anyone working for the Allied forces at that time had to wear a uniform, and so Peter had been given the "assimilated rank" of major and the appropriate insignia – just as I was, when I flew to Austria the following year, rather belatedly as a war correspondent. For the time being, I stayed at home in Wimbledon, and in the course of that July on whose thirteenth day my father had died, three long reports arrived from Peter, from which it was clear that, apparently through some oversight of the military postal service, he had not received my own letters and had no idea what had happened. He could not know that his missives, each several pages long, partly written as aids to his memory, would read very differently to me than he had assumed.

These letters, ten in all, which he wrote to me from Berlin to London up to the time of his temporary return in August, then again in September, now have some documentary value. They describe vividly how it felt to revisit the most severely damaged German city, apart from Dresden, twelve years after he had left it during the fever of the Nazi takeover; now it was in ruins, and he himself a member of the conquering powers. "Berlin is boiling in the smoldering summer heat," so he described it to me, in English of course, two days after my father's death, "and the stink that rises up out of the canals and river branches of the inner city, in which thousands of decaying corpses are still heaped up, this sweetish, nauseating smell which penetrates everything, really begins to make one feel ill... In a few days the whole city will have become one single sewer. And as with almost everything about it one can only say: there has never been anything like this, anywhere."

In Zehlendorf, however, where Peter was most comfortably looked after in an unscathed villa, surrounded by birches and chestnuts, or in his office in Milinowskistrasse in the same beautiful suburb, he was distant, at least in space, from the horrifying reality of the other districts. From here, one evening, at the invitation of some high-ranking Russian officers, which Peter's immediate superior, the American Lieutenant Colonel Leonard, had accepted for both of them, they drove to a mansion house in the Grunewald district, where, in long suites of rooms and on the spacious garden terrace, a strikingly beautiful, white-gowned lady with roses in her hair received an astonishingly varied throng of guests: "Musicians, singers, theater and film people, big and small, pretty and very pretty girls, political intellectuals and intellectual politicians, resistance fighters, more

Russian and American officers. All the others are Germans, Berliners." And soon Peter ran into the director Jürgen Fehling, a young actor called Meisel whom he had known earlier, and a painter who told him about his Russian campaign to Stalingrad and back.

"I was bombarded with questions about London by Fehling and his friends... Fehling used to be married to [the actress] Lucie Mannheim and now wanted to know all about her life and career... 'Was Paris badly hit? Not at all? Thank God!' cried the little actor, with burning eyes and damp temples. 'That is one comfort. I don't think I could have survived the destruction of Paris!'" They wanted to know what Zuckmayer was doing, where Werfel was, and whether Thomas Mann was coming back - oh, and why not? Heavy, sweet red wine from the Caucasus was served; all the languages of the world were spoken. By special favor of the Russians, the lady of the house, a German musician, had acquired as her residence this little mansion, from which a high-ranking SS general had fled only a few months earlier. Peter naively asked me to ring Smollett in London and give him the message that he was in Berlin and was fascinated by Smollett's friends, the "Russkies."

In my mood of desperation, I could not suspect that this first glimpse of the former enemy country, this first direct insight into a lifestyle that was unique and unrepeatable – that of the four victorious powers at the center of the German defeat – was at the same time a preview of my own future existence in Berlin. If my eyes had not been dimmed with grief for my father, my mind not hardened against the bizarre events that Peter, unconcerned about my own situation and mood, described to me in detail during those weeks, I might have recognized their significance. But at first I was appalled by the ease with which he seemed to have mingled with that "astonishingly varied throng" and immediately resumed old friendships with Berlin artists who had obviously emerged unscathed from the Third Reich.

"Much of what you describe," I wrote in answer to his first letter, "disgusts me – like the little actor who could not have survived the destruction of Paris... You know how tolerant I am, how ready to compromise, how unwilling to hate. And I understand that it is difficult to resist people who still speak the same language in cultural matters – but I find it intolerable, quite intolerable, that one is simply supposed to forget so much suffering and torment, the dark years, all the martyrdom, hunger, annihilation, just because, on a certain level, one no longer nourishes any desire for revenge, or because no one that one meets is recognizably guilty... When I think that for years I gave Ch. a goodnight kiss without knowing whether next morning I would find her alive or torn to pieces, or remember the night when A. was born, or the helplessness of the old émigrés, or when I just look at the faces of ordinary people on the Underground, careworn and furrowed with trouble and anxiety, then something in me resists these fraternizations over Caucasian wine." I admitted: "Perhaps there is no other way. But if so, then the whole world is nauseating, a meaningless and valueless place where unspeakable pain and courage are simply poured into the gutter like a bucket of stinking water in order to purify the air. I don't know, but somehow I am glad that I don't have to meet any Germans yet. The results are too devastating."

Lonely and isolated in my London suburb, in deep mourning and still not recovered from the cruelties of the war, I could hardly feel differently; I saw things rigorously and one-sidedly, not as they are in reality. Peter in Berlin, on the other hand, was subject to the most confusing feelings. Only now, rereading his letters, am I struck by the crass contradictions in the attitude of a former German, who unthinkingly uses the derisive American nicknames, "Krauts" and "Heinies," for his ex-compatriots, but at the same time speaks with reverence of Fehling as "one of the greatest and most talented people in German theater," and clearly shows a more burning interest in the problems of the German nation than any Englishman or native US citizen at any time.

Joachim Barckhausen, who visited Peter, was his closest friend years ago, once a proud Pomeranian *Junker*, now a man broken in body and soul, whom nevertheless he harshly dismissed when Barckhausen could not understand that Peter had no intention of settling in Germany again. "But Jochen, in the last twelve years I have lived a whole life, a life that has absolutely nothing to do with your life and the life of Germany. My affections, my loyalties are elsewhere. Can you really expect me to throw all that away?" Jochen asked: "But why did you come here if not to help build Germany up again?" Peter answered: "I came here because my government instructed me to do so. And also, because I am interested in the condition of this country in a completely unemotional way. And above all, to make my own small contribution to the certainty that this nation which has murdered my friends, driven my family into misery, devastated the world I loved, destroyed the civilization for which I lived and for no reason shattered the windows and walls of my home, will leave me and my people in peace from now on and for all time, and that's the end of it."

His friend went away even more broken than when he had arrived; they saw each other twice more and then never again. The worst thing for Peter was that Jochen had lied to him. The anti-British film *Ohm Krüger* had been based on Jochen's book of the same name, but Jochen had turned the facts around and claimed to have written it after the film in order to "make careful corrections" to the historical shortcomings of the film. But Peter had read his book – "the worst, most opportunistic, shameless, impertinent and nasty besmirching of England that there could be" – and seen the film only recently at a private showing. Such encounters were not likely to shake his sense of belonging to his second home. Nor did a visit to the Russian zone together with the American Michael Josselson, a Russian-speaking lieutenant, and Shura Baer cause him any mental conflict.

In the pretty little town of Strausberg, not too far from Berlin, by a lake, was the boarding school where Peter, side by side with Heinrich Ledig-Rowohlt, had spent the last years before his *Abitur* (the German school-leaving examination). Walther von Mendelssohn, a brother of his father, who for his part passed through any number of camps and prisons in France during the war, had taught mathematics and physics there and survived the Hitler era safe and sound. His only son, however, had fallen at the retreat from Voronezh, it was believed on his nineteenth birthday. It was with strange feelings that Peter saw photographs of the nice young *Wehrmacht* soldier, whom he had not known as an adult, placed all over the living room. But Aunt Grete not only lamented the death of her son; she complained bitterly about the Russians, "these dreadful barbarians, going all over the country stealing and robbing and murdering and destroying." And these "terror attacks" (from the West) out of the air!

To her – not to his uncle, who arrived some time later – Peter explained that what the Germans had done to the Russians, Poles, Dutch, Belgians, and Greeks had been no less dreadful; no less dreadful to be bombed night after night by one's own fellow-countrymen, to "pull one's innocent child out of a mountain of glass and rubble at two o'clock on an icy February morning." When his uncle finally asked helplessly, "How is it possible that it could come to this?" Peter was shaken by his total naivety and felt boundless pity for this man who had not even realized why he had to suffer so much. "It became clear to me that Hitler had really ground these people down, physically and morally."

What Peter was "instructed to do" in this, his first phase in Berlin, or rather what he himself wanted and was able to achieve, in a memorandum of nearly one hundred pages to his highest superior, General McClure, was the founding of the first newspaper to be licensed by one of the Western Allies, in this city where until then only the Soviet powers had given out licenses. It was something he had longed for intensely in his earlier life as a junior contributor to the *Vossische* and the *Berliner Tageblatt*, "to found a newspaper after my own heart in Berlin," and now it became a reality. With the greatest effort, he had the half-destroyed presses of these newspapers in Tempelhof put back into service, and there even ran into a former courier of the *Tageblatt*, a strange omen for him. And after a strenuous search, he found what seemed to him the ideal licensees for his *Tagesspiegel*: Erik Reger; Walther Karsch; the *Reichskunstwart* (guardian of the arts for the Reich) of the Weimar Republic, Edwin Redslob – "one of the most charming and delightful old men in Germany, a very old friend of my father's" – and Heinrich von Schweinichen, a paper wholesaler and something of an eccentric. The first issue of the newspaper came out on the twenty-seventh of September. To start with, it alternated three times a week with the official organ of the American military regime in the same publishing house, the *Allgemeine Zeitung*, edited by Hans Wallenberg, who soon became a friend. It was not until November that the *Tagesspiegel* became a daily, and Wallenberg departed to take over Hans Habe's job as editor-in-chief of the *Neue Zeitung* in Munich. This, the most important of the American newspapers in Germany, had an arts section edited by Erich Kästner, whom Peter had tracked down in Mayrhofen.

In September, too, there was significant news from Berlin. "On Friday morning we all went to the big victory parade... I was squeezed into the middle of a crowd of British, American and Russian soldiers and saw everything quite clearly." All the army bands were playing, the French one right in front of Peter, "it was a hell of a noise and quite wonderful." Then came the infantry of all four Allied powers, a thousand people from each nation, but the most impressive, everyone agreed, were the British. "It was the Desert Rats who marched past, unbelievably solemn, modest, restrained, and yet with a discipline that came from within, one noticed that, not forced on them from outside." The French "had no tanks, only a few lousy armored wagons and a few trucks they had borrowed from the British;" then came the Americans; and "as the high spot, the Russian Stalin tanks, fifty of them. They are absolute monsters... really terrifying, because they are completely closed, not a single face to be seen, they were totally inhuman, just gigantic houses of steel, painted dark green, rolling by there with those enormous projecting gun-barrels."

On the platform stood Zhukov, "a stocky little man with a pot belly and a nice friendly smile." He was covered with medals – "Goering had nothing on him." No Eisenhower – General Patton came instead; no Montgomery, but there were ten French generals, full of their own importance, who went round shaking hands with everyone as if they had won the war all by themselves. Zhukov made a speech, and a nervous little British officer translated it, stammering hopelessly. "Do all British officers stammer? Isn't there one who doesn't?" And then there appeared "a very highly polished Frenchman who translated the speech into the most beautiful French, full of *gloire* and *victoire*, and the people just lapped it up. And that was the parade. A memorable day."

Soon afterward Peter was ordered to accompany the American Brigadier General McClure to the opera – the old Berlin State Opera, now housed in the Admiral's Palace in the Russian sector. Four of them drove up in the general's Cadillac, to hear a heavenly performance of *Orpheus and Eurydice*, during which it was possible to forget where one was, and with whom. Afterward, luckily, the general, rather than wanting to go to a night club, took his three companions to his house at Wannsee – "a lakeside villa which used to belong to Heinz Rühmann, the film actor, who is a great Nazi" – how easily these things were said then! They drank whisky on the terrace, it was just beginning to get dark, and then had a magnificent supper with a choice 1933 Rhine wine, and talked until half past eleven, discussing the problems of the Allies. "We are locked in with the Russians on all levels." The general was unwilling to let Peter leave, but the British guests slowly began to find it suspicious that he got on so well with the Americans and did such useful work for them. The British now seemed to Peter to be "the wrong team here. What a mess they make, these conceited little majors with their blond moustaches and Cambridge accents."

Thus the changeable Peter. In England, meanwhile, I was battling not only with grief and money worries, but also with an increasing inner unrest, because my life seemed to be slipping away from me, while the new era seemed to be denied me. When Peter returned for a brief stay, I noticed from his coolness, his absent-mindedness, and lack of involvement with our difficulties that he was far away in his thoughts and, in spite of his beloved children, wanted to get back quickly to the Continent, where history was being made and the future of Europe, even of the world, was being worked out. Now my most passionate wish was to make the leap to the mainland as he had done, if only for a short time. Peter was already gone when our little son was christened – Flesch was godfather, thus for the first time taking on the role of a substitute father, which he was often to adopt thereafter.

At some time during this period I was contacted by an old acquaintance, who gave me some remarkable information about life in France during the occupation. It was André Chamson, to whom I owed the only good meals I had eaten in Paris and who now turned up in London – a hero of the Resistance, as he gradually revealed. "I had remembered him as an exceptionally handsome, sturdy Frenchman," I wrote to Peter, "typical of a Foreign Office official. Perhaps I had idealized him, or my ideas of masculine beauty have changed, but now he seems to me rather unprepossessing." Chamson invited me to dinner at the "Speranza" in the Brompton Road, and I gave him a clothing coupon so that he could buy a tie that had taken his fancy at Harrods.

"He was in action south of Paris," my letter continued, "and then retired to a little mansion in the unoccupied zone together with the best pictures and *objets d'art* from the Petit Palais, whose curator he was. When the Germans occupied the rest of France, he joined the Resistance. He raised a battalion, Malraux raised two more, and the two of them fought side by side in the Maquis, in the famous Alsace-

Lorraine brigade... When he heard of the death of their comrade Jean Prévost, he said to Malraux: Give me the first German prisoners we take and I will have them shot for Jean Prévost. Malraux said: You shall have them. But when they arrived, he did not have the heart to do it."

I asked Chamson what he thought of Jean Bruller, whose book about the silent Resistance, *Le Silence de la mer*, had caused a tremendous sensation when it was published under the pen-name Vercors. Chamson said: "We all knew Bruller before the war, and we kept saying, let's give Bruller a chance. Whenever a new literary periodical was founded, we said, let's give Bruller a chance. Then, when the Resistance had its own publisher and magazines, all the contributors wanted to use pseudonyms. Then someone said: What will the Germans do? They will go to Curtius and ask him, who wrote this? And Curtius will say: Debû-Bridel, Michaux, Emmanuel, Paulhan. What will be the use then of writing under pseudonyms or anonymously? But Bruller, the unknown one, took his chance and finally had his success."

The summer was over. In September, with my little daughter, leaving my son in the care of the faithful Beate, I went back to Potter Higham. My friends John and Joey Arrow received us lovingly in their little riverside cottage and on their boats, *Bird* and *Forester*. We played darts in the pubs and sailed in a regatta. Once the main mast broke, falling on my head, and I was praised for not making a fuss. On the return journey, in Cambridge, we saw that symbol of the old British Empire, Queen Mary, the Queen Mother, wearing her famous toque and a magnificent ankle-length gown, descending the steps of the Fitzwilliam Museum. When I was with the Arrows, with Dodo and her family, with Henrietta and the PEN, I was part of the English social structure. But the prospect of traveling to the Continent in the not too distant future was beginning to emerge more and more clearly in conversations with Kingsley Martin.

Here I must hark back. That right to permanent settlement in his country that the *New Statesman*'s editor had thoughtlessly denied us had actually been conceded to us in his own magazine. Peter had for a long time been contributing political essays to this favorite periodical of the English intelligentsia, as it was then and remained for many decades, and I had succeeded in reaching its important literary pages with the publication of an essay on Alain-Fournier's novel *Le grand Meaulnes*. "I never managed to make the Books in General page," Kingsley had said to me jokingly in August 1944. From now on, and for a while longer, I received words of praise from many respected literary figures, which still have the power to comfort me for the lack of regard I now encounter from London intellectuals. And however un-English it may be to blow one's own trumpet, I would still like to quote what seemed to me, after the endless years of apprenticeship, an accolade to a writer who was an immigrant into the English language.

G. W. Stonier, whose little volume *Shaving through the Blitz* I loved and who was now involved in the *Statesman*'s arts section, had thanked me for sending in the Alain-Fournier essay, "which Mortimer and I have read with great enjoyment." If I would like to add something about the author's correspondence with Rivière, they would "with pleasure publish it in the center pages or under the "Books in General" heading" – and this was promptly done. The following year Cyril Connolly, the editor of *Horizon*, wrote to me asking for a report on the arts in Vienna: "I read your review of *Le grand Meaulnes* with great interest when it came out, and wondered who you were. I would like to say that I thought it was an excellent piece of work."

A few months later, in January 1946, V. S. Pritchett, the great storyteller and essayist, assured me that the *New Statesman* would "have pleasure in publishing" my article on Marie Bashkirtseff, "which we like very much," only asking me for a little information about English versions of her diary. He then thanked me for supplying these details and gave his opinion that the essay was "delightful" and complete in every way. He only wanted permission to alter the sequence of a list of Marie's admirers and place the name of Barbey d'Aurevilly, whom I had mentioned, at the beginning – "I hesitate to make this pedantic suggestion to you. The article is admirable." And to complete this list of the pundits of the day, I must also mention Philip Toynbee, who referred in the *New Statesman*, a week after the publication of the *Grand Meaulnes* essay, to my "admirable criticism."

The course seemed set for my reception into the ranks of literary journalists. But it was not to be. As my third example of a *Frühvollendeter*, a writer whose genius flowered only for a short time (though in this case it was not cut off by death), I had chosen the first incarnation of Hugo von Hofmannsthal, "Loris," and written an essay on him which failed to find favor with the *Statesman*'s cultural editors. Their regret at not being able to publish it referred to the subject rather than the treatment; in England, Hofmannsthal was known only as the librettist of Richard Strauss's operas, and even now no one was prepared to recognize him as a poet. I resolved to bring out a first British edition of his prose writings, managed to interest the publishers Methuen in the project, and made contact with the Hofmannsthal family. Their agreement was obtained, but every translator I found and suggested to them was rejected by the friends of Gerty von Hofmannsthal, who was living in Oxford, as unequal to the task of conveying the linguistic finesse of the poet. Finally, Methuen lost patience, and despite all my efforts this early attempt to introduce Hofmannsthal to the English literary consciousness failed.

The last months of 1945 dragged along agonizingly and endlessly. I trembled with impatience to see Europe again. In September, Peter Smollett went to Vienna as a *Daily Express* correspondent. After receiving a high honor at the end of his activity as leader of the Russian section of the Ministry of Information, to my astonishment he gave up the persistent and, as he thought, hopeless battle for recognition of the English identity he had acquired, and decided to return to Vienna forever with his family. I did not recognize political motives in this decision. And perhaps I could even understand it when my beloved Dodo told me in her charmingly malicious way that Smollett, invited by her husband to the Junior Carlton Club, had appeared in "gaiters." "Gaiters, I ask you!" As if he had inevitably condemned himself to the role of a "dago," "frog," or "Jerry" – the last expression being the comparatively gentle, almost respectful British term for the German enemy. For myself, for us, I, perhaps once again led astray and seduced by my journalistic success, still hoped for a more gracious acceptance.

Was all this then to be in vain – the long-standing intimacy with the intellectual life in London, the close friendships, the personal contact with so many writers in and outside PEN, with Stevie Smith and her former companion Inez Holden, with Eleanor Farjeon, Margaret Storm Jameson, Philip Hope-Wallace, and many others? This was, after all, my world; I no longer had any other. During those

154

weeks, I once saw a second, private drama unfolding in the front row of the mezzanine at the New Theatre, while Peggy Ashcroft was on stage as the Duchess of Malfi. There sat Cecil Day Lewis, whom I admired so deeply, a subtly attractive man and a fine poet, and the ravishingly beautiful novelist Rosamond Lehmann conducting a highly emotional conversation, and paying no attention to the play. Finally, wavering between my observation of the bloodthirsty drama on stage and the restrained, sensitive, tragic scene in the audience, I became aware that Rosamond Lehmann had risen from her seat in a flood of tears, whereupon the couple left their seats in the middle of the performance. Could anyone understand that such testimony, such insight into the private involvements on the literary scene in London allowed me to claim a closer attachment to it than its protagonists would ever concede?

When Peter, having completed his work in Berlin, traveled to Nuremberg in November to report on the trials of war criminals, I pressed ahead energetically with my efforts to return to Vienna. Kingsley, who now knew me as a critic, but did not know if I could deliver usable material on social and political conditions in liberated Austria, was halfhearted in his efforts to obtain permission from the military government for my journey. But Peter's colleagues helped, and in the new year, at the end of January, accredited by the *New Statesman*, in khaki uniform, with the now inaccurate description "War Correspondent" on my armband, I was in Croydon boarding a battered old Dakota aircraft which would take me to Vienna via Brussels and Frankfurt. I was flying, no, leaping right into the center of the mainland; five years of winter were now, with this flight, this leap, finally over. The flight made me free as a bird, brought me out of the confinement of the island to the land where such as I had been *vogelfrei* – outlawed – and were so no longer.

Later I was to describe in writing much, though not all, of this first return to Vienna –not enough of how affectionately embraced, how protected and well looked after by the British military system I felt from then on, and continued to feel for several years. Here in my native city, in the heart of the third district, where I had spent the second half of my life before my emigration, in a little baroque *Schloss*, I entered into the lifestyle of the Middle East force, which had a long and bloody war behind it and was now determined to pass the remaining time as comfortably as possible before returning to the civilian life they longed for and yet feared. They had earned it. There were few professional officers among these young people who had been detailed to Public Relations in Vienna, the press office in the *Salmschlössl*, the little Salm *palais*. Some themselves came from great families, like Robin Muir, who was engaged to a daughter of the Duke of Marlborough. They soon began to fraternize with the Austrian "aristos," and hungry princes such as Tassilo Fürstenberg, or princesses from equally grand houses, were daily to be seen as midday guests at the *table d'hôte*. The current master of the house also came from an elevated sphere; he was Lieutenant General David Heneker, well known as a composer of light music and delightful musical comedies before being called up. They all had perfect manners and the relaxed composure of people who had a superhuman effort behind them and were satisfied with its outcome and, indeed with themselves.

I learned new words and phrases: "admin" – everyday administration, from that of our quarters to the provisions and care of every description within the army structure. "Movement Control" – the military travel bureau, with whose help one could wander throughout Europe, particularly the British-occupied areas; "to wangle a travel order" – to get hold of the necessary authorization; "to swan around" – to travel about when this had been achieved; "bumf" – all the tiresome forms to be filled in and stacks of written instructions to be followed; "NAAFI," the store and canteen where one could buy everything that was available, from egg powder and hot, sweet, milky tea to the packets of thin paper tissues called Kleenex. These little all-purpose handkerchiefs were a sensational invention of the Americans, "which they graciously shared with their British allies, so that the latter would not have to make a special journey to the U.S. troops' PX stores to track them down. And finally the "old-boy network," a camaraderie on which one could rely in Trieste and Klagenfurt as much as in the third and thirteenth districts of Vienna, not to speak of the entire British Empire.

As if in a diving bell, I floated within the protection of the army in the grey dreariness, the miserable ruined landscape of the conquered city. The city did not feel "liberated," for the four occupying powers were a burden which weighed more or less heavily but always perceptibly upon her, and the occupants, in four different uniforms, of the jeeps which constantly rattled through the streets wore alien, unfriendly faces. For myself, dizzy with the most contradictory feelings during this return after eight years, the sight was a reassuring guarantee that here at least no physical harm would be done to me. However much I grew back into my Austrian surroundings later in life, this initial situation after the war that had been lost and won was to form a chasm between me and my fellow citizens that would never close again.

In the diving bell I was Mrs. de Mendelssohn, then "Hilda" – for the final vowel of my name was unpronounceable for my present compatriots, as it was to be later for my English granddaughter. That I had been sent here by the *New Statesman* made an impression on the press officers, as it did on the other correspondents. My closeness to Sam B., the pleasant, cultured Welshman who was to be my frequent escort during the next few weeks, to David Heneker and his beautiful, gentle wife Gwenol, and to Eric and John and "Chalky" White strengthened me in my daily new, disturbing, and confusing re-entry into the reality of Vienna.

I cannot recount yet again what I wrote about this time, in English, the year after my return, with the help of my diary notes, and while the immediate impression was still fresh in my mind. The book was to be called *The Streets of Vineta* – not a very original comparison, and one much used since that time. It was never published in England, and it was only when the German version finally appeared that the *Times Literary Supplement*, in a fit of hyperbole, spoke of a "female Proust of Vienna." Be that as it may, I can only refer in brief terms to my schizophrenic state of mind during those weeks - the arrival at Schwechat airport in rain, mud, and black snow, the four cemeteries that lined the road, those ghostly metropolises of a city possessed by death, then, soon after, past the Stanislausgasse that had once been my home, and the church of the Salesians with its wonderful, unforgotten contours.

I cannot attempt to evoke once more in all their details what places from the past I revisited during those days, up to the origin of my oneness with Vienna, which can be precisely identified as the parish square in Heiligenstadt. The people I saw again – these memories too are painful to me after all the time that has passed.

There were the two faithful members of our former household, Anna and Marie, more companions than servants, in their modest apartments still steadfastly, perpetually loyal to their *Herrschaft*, the employers who had become their true family. Then there was the self-styled resistance fighter whose party insignia had been so recently discarded, comfortably installed and plentifully supplied with food parcels by émigré friends, laughing, always laughing over the dead bodies, even over that of my friend Annie Gadol, who had been executed, and whose husband was the murdered Manjo Peczenik, whom he perhaps even knew at the Café Herrenhof. How extraordinary that, so many decades later, my disgust for those who managed to "arrange" things for themselves in those times of disaster is even more violent than against the naive henchmen of that repulsive regime.

But on the other hand: there were the new directions in the arts, the optimism for the future in the midst of starving people, in the town hall, where the Catholic Communist Matejka, as councilor with responsibility for the arts, under the influence of his friend Kokoschka reclaimed the "decadent" artists (at least in spirit), encouraged young artists to reject National Socialist realism, and obtained grants and jobs for ex-servicemen and those released from concentration camps. The gatherings at the home of Peter Smollett, who had settled in here, as yet without his family, where I met the "cultural officers," Viennese without exception, of all the occupying powers, and my old friend Hans Weigel. The premiere, soon after my arrival, of the ideological drama *Barabbas* by the same Weigel. The editorial conferences of the magazine *Der Plan*, where Otto Basil explained Kafka and Surrealism to the writers of tomorrow. The Theater in der Josefstadt, from which Hans Hilpert – who was believed to have conducted a "concentration camp on holiday" like Gründgens in Berlin – had departed, and which was now directed by two men of irreproachable character. One of these was Alfred Ibach, a German, impressive and exceptionally likeable, with whom it proved impossible not to become friends. His wife was the image of the actress Grete Mosheim, whom he had loved, but was forced to lose to emigration. Two years later I was to weep – yes, weep over Alfred's death. And yet one day it was suggested to me that he had been employed as an "Aryanizer" by E. P. Tal, the publisher of Hans

Flesch-Brunningen's first books. Ah, wilderness! A wilderness which will never be explored to its limits.

In politics I soon ran into Ernst Fischer, and when my report on Vienna had appeared in the *New Statesman* I was violently criticized by G. E. R. Gedye, its prewar Austrian correspondent, and by Oscar Pollak for my recognition of his influence. Retrospectively, all this looks like one great conspiracy, for Smollett had advised me to go to the Communist state secretary for education and art and question him about his activities. Now that it has been fairly conclusively proved that Smollett, my childhood friend and our most important source of support in exile, had passed on secret information to the Russians during his time at the Ministry, my impartiality and innocence seem called into question. But at that time, it was only my feeling for quality which allowed me to perceive Fischer, the poet and thinker whose greatest faux pas, his anti-Tito stance, still lay ahead of him, as the most interesting figure in the government at that time.

With Sam, who wanted to enter the art market when he returned to civilian life, I went to the Galerie Würthle. There were drawings by Egon Schiele for sale at twenty schillings each, a sum I could just about have managed. Incomprehensibly, I, who had long been aware of the artist's importance, did not buy a single sheet, but advised Sam to acquire a Schiele oil painting, which he felt was dear, but not too dear, at 2000 schillings. I wonder today if he ever disposed of it or still owns it. Sam also bought a picture by Josef Dobrowsky, my old prewar crony, who insisted on portraying me twice in pastels. The Dobrowsky unfortunately was not to appreciate as astronomically as Schiele's works. We spent evenings together at the apartment of Paul Schöffler, the bass-baritone, whose pretty little girlfriend Hannerl let herself be courted by the officers of the Salmgasse in order to get hold of oranges and coffee for the much admired singer. It was great fun at his place; Erich Kunz, the best Figaro, Papageno, or Leporello in Viennese operatic history, fooled around at the piano with the bass Manowarda, and Schöffler's velvety, dark voice was fascinating even in speech. At the Theater an der Wien, where the State Opera ensemble performed every evening, we experienced what must have been some of the most perfect Mozart performances of all time.

And then, while I was still sitting over my piece for the *Statesman*, its co-editor, Richard Crossman, burst in on me. He had turned up at

Smollett's toward midnight with a secretary and immediately tried to dissuade me from writing a general Viennese report. I was to travel to Carinthia, where an explosive situation for the British had developed: that subterranean stream toward Palestine of Jewish refugees rescued from Polish death camps, which the British administrators of the mandated territory were trying to prevent by all possible means. Crossman hated the Foreign Secretary, Ernest Bevin, who had strictly, even cruelly, defended the limitation worked out in 1938 of a homeland to be created for the homeless Jews even after the genocide of the majority of them, and wanted to see the reasons for its revocation discussed in his paper. So I traveled south, to the land of my childhood summers, to what was now the displaced persons' camp near Villach, where a man called Jossel showed me "the remains" of his people and made it clear that they had to leave Europe because it had become for them no more than one great graveyard. I was to describe their "Trek to Palestine" in an article in the *New Statesman*, justifying their desperate efforts without revealing in detail what these were.

Not only in the Jews' camp, but also in those, not far away, which contained other DPs, or displaced persons, desperate conditions prevailed which it was hardly possible to remedy. These poor people who had been transported, having escaped either death or forced labor, were in many cases too demoralized to be able to make use of the freedom they had won by the end of the war. Certainly, the British commandants did their best to encourage them to keep themselves clean and to feed them adequately with the support of the UNRRA (United Nations Relief and Rehabilitation Administration), but since they knew that their future was uncertain, and – like, for example, the Ukrainians, whose leaders took them to join the German troops – rightly feared disaster, they had little will to live. What a contrast to these settlements of uprooted people was the comfort of the Carinthian press quarters! Here, as everywhere, the occupying powers requisitioned the most beautiful villas for themselves, and so I found myself living at Dellach on the Wörthersee in the spacious home of Ferdinand Porsche, the Volkswagen magnate, as I later lived in Munich in that of the publisher of National Socialist specialist literature, and my own future publisher, Heinrich Beck.

I absented myself for a day from the idyll of feather beds, peasant

furniture, tiled stoves, and embroidered cushions to drive to Udine
with the cook to buy provisions. In the Villa Porsche we ate exquisite
food. While the diet at the *Salmschlössl*, not very imaginatively
assembled from the sparse NAAFI supplies and a few black-market
sources, was still so nutritious that even the high aristocracy, as I had
noticed much earlier, gratefully and frequently accepted invitations to
dine there, the Carinthian press camp had culinary ambitions. Several
times a month Movement Control supplied the little Italian chef with
a travel order to the small Friuli market town, and he would return to
Dellach in the jeep with the most wonderful cheeses, ham, and fresh
foods which he then transformed into gourmet dishes. For me, this
journey was more than a day trip to a region of simple but abundant
delicacies such as we had not known since the beginning of the war.
I was once again in the country which was for me, as for so many
Northern Europeans, the most beautiful and the dearest, the one
whose soil, sun, people, and monuments I was always to consider
consecrated to the gods, as did my second husband for the whole of
his life.

My last two weeks in Vienna were spent in a state of great inner
turmoil. This was evident from my letters to Peter, their envelopes
now bearing the inscription "From Mrs. de Mendelssohn / British
Press Camp / British Public Relations H. Q. / Vienna / C. M. F."
Right from the start, I tried to explain to him what this return meant
to me: "On Saturday afternoon I walked around Heiligenstadt, in the
melting snow about half past four, in the twilight, and it was a
hundred times more heartrending than I had ever expected. I went
into the little parish chapel and simply wept. You had better not read
this to Mimi. But the English here are a heavenly antidote, and the day
after, yesterday, I drove to Grinzing and the Kahlenberg with a
charming major and we talked a lot about English literature and
Sitwell and Bowen on the way to the Leopoldsberg, past the day-
trippers and the American skiers on the slopes of the Vienna woods,
and that evened things out again in a pleasant way."

What plagued me was not only my wavering between past and
present, but also my bad conscience, because I had left Peter alone
with the children, although with adequate help, and on top of this was
enjoying these exciting weeks so much, on the one hand the double
life of the political and cultural reawakening of Vienna – the

ministerial press conferences, the evenings at the theater and opera, the Philharmonic concerts, the private parties – and, on the other, the parties in the *Salmschlössl*, the dinners with Sam, David, and Gwenol at the Hotel Sacher or the Palais Kinsky. "Is it very bad of me? I was so starved of pleasure, and I did so love dancing and drinking and going out and having fun, before we settled down and became bourgeois. Can't one try to loosen up a little now? It's all so simple as soon as one gets out of England. But only *with* the English, I can't say it often enough. The nice ones are really so tremendously nice and charming, and I do like being with them and living among them so much, these decent, well-mannered, jolly, witty people." And then, at the end of the letter: "Without the difficult years, this triumphal emergence from the war would not have been possible. It was a bloody time, but it was all worthwhile, wasn't it? Let's not miss the opportunity to enjoy the advantages. Life is so short, let's have a little fun as well as hard work."

Peter's letters crossed with mine, and both took so long to arrive that a real dialogue was impossible. With his first, he enclosed a sheet covered with our little daughter's touchingly awkward handwriting. Her letter began: "Dear Mummy, when are you going to come back from Vienna? I would so like to know." What greater persuasion could I have needed to return home? Peter himself was magnanimous: "I hope so very much that you are living through good and interesting days and discovering within yourself everything you thought had been buried or even lost over the years. Here at home everything is all right and in good shape."

And then Peter described a big party at the *New Statesman* and everyone he had met there, Hugh Gaitskell and Victor Gollancz and Dick Crossman, who had congratulated him in detail on his reports in the *Observer* on the Nuremberg trials. Dorothy Woodman too, Kingsley Martin's life-partner, and "a young man called Denis Healey," the chairman of the foreign section of the Labour Party, eulogized him and asked him to join a committee which was to make recommendations to the government as to what should be done with the "Nuremberg documents." "I agreed, and Woodman said, oh, but you aren't a member of the Labour Party. To which I replied: yes, of course I am, and so everything was settled." And so Peter was obviously prepared to join a political party for the first time in his life.

Then, according to his account, he promptly went to the next meeting of the Wimbledon Labour Party, and liked it very much. "Now at last I am gradually beginning to feel that we are getting involved in something, I mean in the community, and becoming part of it. This is the real thing. I believe there is nowhere else where I could be even half as happy and reasonably contented. England fits me like a glove. I would never again contemplate going to live with you in any other country. It would be suicide. Let's hold out for a few more years, then we will be so deeply rooted in the circles where we belong that everything connected with our émigré problems will be washed away. Things will go well for us here."

Thus Peter, on the second of February 1948. If only things had been that simple! At that time he was convinced. But a few days later, I heard from him that the Control Commission for Germany had offered him another job, which he would probably accept, although he detested the whole idea, because he did not want to leave London and would prefer to refuse if only he knew how to get out of it and what he should do instead. Looking back, it seems to me that this was one of those fatal turning points in life, one of those existential thresholds, the crossing of which determines the course of the rest of one's life. With the decision not to struggle through on the spot and complete the process of integration, but to go to Germany – even if this time on behalf of the British –the ultimate return, decades later, was already built in. The fateful moment had been missed. For after our three years away, all the positions and offices had been filled by the whole generation of native Britons who had meanwhile returned from the war, while we had been taken over once more by the German language, even the German world, whether this was what we wanted or not, and we never really found our way back completely into the British world, although we were to continue writing in English and vegetating in our London suburb for a long, long time afterward.

But it was my fault too. I wanted to break my chains. On the seventh of February, 1948, I wrote to Peter that I was firmly convinced that at the time there could be no "fuller, more exciting, more entertaining life" than under the aegis of the military government and that it already seemed hopeless to me to return to England where, as I had read, the fat ration had again been restricted and even bread was to be rationed, "back to an existence of boredom and lack of enthusiasm, when I too could be achieving something and working somehow or other, not just you... Now you will certainly regret having let me come over here, because I have seen what life can be like when one spends one's days on real things, not just planning meals, but I suppose that was unavoidable. I am sick, sick of it, this housewife's life! That doesn't mean that I won't come back to it, because it is my duty and I chose it. But it is a terrible sacrifice."

Nothing was further from my mind, however, I immediately added, than regretting my emigration. And then comes a passage in my letter which today may evoke disbelief and even disapproval from my Austrian compatriots: "I am sure that I would not want to be Viennese for anything in the world. It may be all right for someone like my mother, who is content with the endless delights of the well-known and loved atmosphere, with the familiar streets and the Vienna woods and the beautiful churches and the marvelous weather. But for someone who needs a bit more than that, just the Western way of thinking for a start, it would be unbearable. A stay in Vienna would be completely impossible for me if not together with the British, to whom one belongs and with whom one associates. Everything is pleasant here except the attitude of the Viennese, who are either Nazis (admittedly with the sting removed) or charming, politically absurd *Volkspartei* members, or prosaic, bourgeois Social Democrats, or doctrinaire Communists, or charming but absurd Communists. That, more or less, is the breakdown. They are either corrupt or worn out or politically stultified or fanatical, but one thing is in their favor: their great love of the arts... I am convinced that the Austrians' only chance lies in their huge talent for all the arts, their exceptionally good taste and their artistic sensibility. If they learn to restrain themselves and leave politics to others, they have a future in Europe."

Arrogant, presumptuous, indeed even embarrassing to read now! But at the time I am writing this, over forty years later, not without a few grains of truth. Certainly, in the field of foreign affairs, as in many areas of internal politics, Austria was soon to prove itself in a way that gave the lie to my assessment. The State Treaty, achieved by means of peasant cunning as well as by the exceedingly skillful use of favorable circumstances. The Parity Commission for regular agreements between employers and employees. The long truce between the two camps which had been so hatefully divided between the wars. A sometimes questionable first coalition, which nevertheless did work, while the industrial upturn began. Then, for so many years, a comparatively calm and prudent Socialist regime. During this period, too, came the referendum against Zwentendorf and atomic power. All excellent proof of a healthy democracy. Only in the 1980s – although for me at least since the early 1970s – have some of the tendencies which I believed I had detected among the Viennese, and described so mercilessly in 1946, seemed to become virulent.

And so it was to the milieu of the *Salmschlössl* that I clung in the days before my flight home, to the tough, seasoned, hard-drinking war and foreign correspondents who lived in or frequented the press quarters, to my officer friends from Sammy to "Chalky," a former reporter for the *Windsor and Slough Gazette*. With my most faithful escort, Sam, an intimate little drama came about, for he was no ladies' man and was now at the mercy of contradictory feelings. And then one evening, "Popski" blew in – Lieutenant-Colonel Vladimir Peniakoff, DSO, MC, the greatest swashbuckler in the British Army, who had first commanded a Libyan Arab force of Senussis, then submitted to the authority of the British Near East HQ, and finally set up his own force, "Popski's Private Army," which, mounted on camels and with heavily armed jeeps, fought for the Allies behind the enemy lines of the Africa Corps.

Popski, the one-armed daredevil, a cosmopolitan adventurer who surpassed even T. E. Lawrence in courage and effectiveness, was part of the last experience of this, my first return to Vienna. At one end of the spectrum were the icy winter nights, leaning on a military vehicle parked in front of the *Salmschlössl*, its hood laden with bottles and glasses, listening to Popski recounting one story after another of his desert campaign. At the other was a visit with Viennese friends to Hengl, a *Heurigen* inn, to try to persuade the Grinzing parish priest to find a last resting place for my father's ashes in his cemetery. Easier said than done. For still – although no more than a little bag of dust had been sent to the bereaved families of concentration camp victims or resistance fighters – the church persisted in its ban on cremation.

A game of darts in the cellar bar at the *Salmschlössl*, known as the "Honky-Tonk"; lunch with my uncle Leo Siebert at the press quarters; a last visit to Schöffler; a last evening with David, Gwenol, John,

Robin and Nigel – "we laughed all the time"; then, on the morning of the seventh of March, the flight home to London. On the flight, I wondered what I should write to Torberg in New York about my Viennese encounters. Before I left, he had instructed me – his letter has not survived, unless he made a copy of it at the time for posterity – to inform him "whom one can still shake hands with there." The touchstone, I thought, could be what would have happened to someone and how that person would have behaved if Hitler had been victorious and Austria forever incorporated in a German-dominated Europe. This was how I decided to present it to him. But not everyone with whom Torberg shook hands on his return in 1951, or indeed whom he embraced, would meet this criterion.

In London, Peter met me at the airport; he looked pale and under strain, and was in a bad mood. The weather was dull and grey, and I found everything ugly and depressing. Despite a joyful reunion with my children, I was still restless. I wanted to dash off again immediately. Peter and I quarreled. A few days later, on the eleventh of March, he flew to Berlin to start his new job. For better or worse, I settled down again to running the household in Wimbledon, which I had to do single-handed for some time because my dear Beate went on a long holiday after the weeks of my absence, and in between I wrote my articles for the *Statesman*. Flesch turned up and invited me to the theater, to the premiere of Sean O'Casey's *Red Roses for Me*. Apart from him and my mother there were no visitors to our suburb. At the end of the month, Peter wrote that he was having a very jolly time in Berlin and that he had fallen in love with a "petite, very pretty girl" who was "delightfully silly." I wept with rage.

Letters cheered me up. Like doves of peace after the flood, they came flying in from all directions during those months. Toward the end of the past year, Fritz Thorn had made contact from Nice: "some time ago I heard from someone that you had come safely out of the hurly-burly, and were in London, but it was only yesterday that I found among some old papers a piece of blue paper torn from a letter with your 1939 address. As the post may for once be unreliable in the good sense, I am therefore writing to let you know that I am still around, and I think you will be pleased. I got back six months ago after twenty months in the Piedmont mountains – disguised as an Italian partisan, with a long, old-fashioned shotgun and altogether frightful to behold – I'm married to a Viennese Frenchwoman, or Frenchified Viennese, and for the time being am working for UNRRA as an interpreter." Pleased I certainly was.

The musician Erich Zeisl had earlier written to me, on paper with a Metro-Goldwyn-Mayer letterhead, in his touchingly awkward English, that he was now a "movie composer – how awful," and was composing the musical soundtracks to various films and "Fitzpatrick's Travelogues." The Monte Carlo Ballet wanted to commission a work from him, but he could not think of anything; could we suggest any ideas? The drudgery for the film studio anyway hardly left him enough time, or any spark of energy, for compositions of his own. Nevertheless, he had written a requiem – later he called it a "Requiem Ebraico" – that "strangely enough has already been performed in two of the largest churches for 3,000 people. I think it is very beautiful. Stravinsky rang me up and said 'I am deeply touched, it is a wonderful work.' As you know, I lost my father over there."

Ida Schreiber, the former head of the editorial department at the Zsolnay publishing house, who had looked after my first book, had been disowned by her first husband, a member of the Vienna Philharmonic, after the Anschluss, and now wrote to me from Jerusalem that she had been "saved by a divine miracle" after much suffering and terror, together with her second husband, an optician called Landau, and had ended up in Palestine. Her little son, who had been born in Europe, was going to school there and speaking Hebrew – "and I don't understand him." From Prague, I heard from Dr Lotka Elsnerová-Reiterová, my former fellow-student Lotte Reiter, who had been in the Theresienstadt concentration camp, found a partner there, and survived with him. She had found me by way of the *New Statesman*.

My old Magus – after seven years as a monk in a Belgian Trappist monastery – was back in Vienna and permitted by the Russian occupying forces to return to the rooms where he had lived as a child, on the top floor of his parents' house in the fourth district. The painter Lisel Salzer was now living near San Francisco with her husband, a laryngologist. And finally, my dearest school friend, Maria, wrote to me from Werfen in the province of Salzburg, of her experiences as a conscientious opponent of the regime in that "terrible time": "When I looked out of my window to see the first Allied soldiers below, I thought my heart was going to burst with joy."

Spring came, the grey bell of haze over London lifted, and life itself became brighter, although, ungratefully and impatiently, I constantly complained in my pocket calendar about this "damned housewife's life." Dodo again invited us to Mousehall Mill, where the children went horseback riding for the first time. Flesch took me out to Sheekey's, the Irish fish and seafood restaurant, where we ate oysters. During those weeks, I met some of the great or at least significant figures of our exile: Ernst Polak, who asked me about my stay in Vienna, and Oskar Kokoschka, whom I had seen from time to time during the war and visited at his Park Lane studio, and who now, behind his wife Olda's back, gave me an original lithograph of his image of Christ on the cross comforting the starving children of Vienna, prints of which were to be seen at the time in a number of underground stations. He inscribed a dedication to "Fräulein Spiel" and, when I reminded him that I had children, he exclaimed in his usual dialect: "*Des is do net möglich, so a jungs Madl!* [But that's just not possible, a young lass like you!]"

Once Elias Canetti came to tea in Wimbledon and brought me one of his favorite books, a picaresque novel by Diego de Torres Villarroel, and the English edition of his *Die Blendung, Auto da Fé.* Another day, on the sixth of July – "a big cultural day," I noted – I lunched with Canetti and we then visited his lover, the painter Marie-Louise von Motesitzky, whom he called "Floritzl," and then went to Kokoschka's again. In between, Sammy, who was on leave in London, asked me to tea with his mother at Harrods.

One other episode, before the summer, seems worth relating. Smollett had by now transported his family to Vienna, but our mutual friend Litzy Philby was still here, now married to Georg Honigmann, whom we knew from his previous marriage and as a former colleague at the Exchange Telegraph. During the internments, he had absurdly been shipped to Australia, which probably shattered his loyalty to the land of his exile. At Georg's request, when he returned to England, Peter got him a job with the military government in Germany, but as Georg had no British passport, he had to travel by the land and sea route to Hamburg. Honigmann failed to arrive. Peter sent desperate telegrams, the London authorities rang me up asking me to find out from Litzy what had happened, but she seemed not to have a clue. Then one day she contacted me and said in tones of relief that I was not to worry, nothing had happened to Georg. Soon afterward, it emerged that, instead of going to Hamburg, Honigmann had somehow reached Berlin and gone over into the Russian sector. Peter was beside himself; he had vouched for him. My friendship with Litzy was unaffected by the event.

The week after the "cultural day" with Canetti and Kokoschka, I was granted a second leap to the mainland. With a single-mindedness which was distasteful even to myself, perhaps even heartless toward my daughter, beloved nevertheless, I put her into a summer school, where indeed I imagined her to be well looked after, left my little boy with Beate, under the supervision of my mother, who could be called upon at any time, and once again plunged into the adventure of postwar Europe. First, a day in Paris, where Denise immediately took me to the Café Flore and introduced me to Colette. And I was so dazzled by my reunion with this "supernaturally beautiful city" – as I called it in my journal – that my meeting with that supernaturally great writer, a caustic old lady with a shock of frizzy hair, hardly made the impression on me that it should have. Then, in a sleeping car on the Orient Express, to Linz, where the elegant train was diverted and I experienced a nightmare journey through the Soviet zone: at Enns, the zone border, we stopped for three and a half hours. In Vienna, I was welcomed at the press quarters by my friends, old friends by now, including my sweet, blonde Gwennie, whose husband David was about to be transferred to Carinthia.

A blazing July. We went to the races in the Prater, accompanied by the *Times* correspondent Michael Burn and an elegant Arab journalist who was working in Vienna for the newspaper *Fat-el-Arab* and whom the British therefore called "the fatal Arab." He was to stick close to my heels during my stay. But first, with an easily obtained movement order, I flew to Budapest, stayed in a small hotel run by Margit Schlachta, the head of a lay order which, together with Cardinal Mindszenty, was conducting a political struggle against the Soviet occupiers, and visited my mother's cousins, whom I loved. Aunt Stella, the Klimt figure, who had grown up in the spirit of the German classics, was mourning her son, who had succumbed to the German enemy. Hans, my cousin, who used to declaim Petöfi and Ady to me, could not be replaced by his little sister, but she did her best to comfort her mother for her loss.

It was the week of the change of currency from the pengö to the forint. No one had any cash. Every day Uncle Paul brought home from his office a string bag full of fruit, vegetables, or poultry in lieu of pay. I was to give my report to the American periodical *The Nation* the title "Hungarian Holocaust" – in those days, the word "holocaust," now restricted to the murder of the Jews, was used far more loosely. A Russian soldier, a naive child, tried to take my wristwatch; I shook my head, pointed to my uniform and said "Britannski!" upon which he left me alone. In the evenings, I sat, almost alone, in the Allied Officers' Park Club ("A Szövetéyes Tisztek Park Clubjának Alapszabályai" in this impossible language) listening to the best Gypsy violinist in Hungary, who played close to my ear for hours because no one else appreciated his art. And before flying back to Vienna, I sought out Béla Balázs, the great film theorist – I had quoted from his book in my dissertation.

The things I experienced that hot summer! At the end of July, I flew to Carinthia to visit Gwenol, who was comfortably settled in Dellach, and we went to Udine together for two days, where she knew several Italians in the surrounding villas. There was a party at the Porsche house, given by the Red Cross, with much lively dancing and high spirits. And then Peter suddenly turned up in Vienna and shocked me with the dreadful news of Henrietta Leslie's death. I could not take it in. But the circumstances were known in detail. Henrietta had become ill during a visit to Berne and soon afterward died in a hospital there. In his desperation, her husband, the gentle, soft-hearted scholar who clung to her as to a mother, plunged to his death from a bridge; yet another friend we were not to see again. London without these two, without the comforting haven of Glebe House, was unimaginable for me. Later we learned that Henrietta had bequeathed to our daughter, her goddaughter, the sum of a thousand pounds, invested in gilt-edged securities. How well she knew our irresponsible attitude to money.

Peter's entry into my Viennese circle, in a double room in the *Salmschlössl*, was not without its problems. But soon we drove to Salzburg, to the second Festival after the war. Staying in the American-occupied Hotel Gablerbräu, ourselves in uniform, intensified the schizophrenia. But just as Gwenol had once lent me an evening dress and fur coat in February so that I could attend Brigadier

Verney's party in "civvies," a friend of Hans Weigel's – "Bobbie" Löcker, from Frankfurt, who had married an Austrian – lent me one of her dirndls, and I slipped back into the old familiar skin. Salzburg was unusual and exciting in every way. At the Café Posthof, which managed to serve astonishingly good meals, the prominent Festival guests used to meet, at their center Oscar Fritz Schuh, the director-in-chief of the Vienna Opera, here directing *The Marriage of Figaro* with Maria Cebotari, Irmgard Seefried, Erich Kunz. The conductor, Felix Prohaska, we learned, was only a straw man; in fact, it was Herbert von Karajan, not yet denazified, who had been in charge of the production right up to the premiere.

We reveled in operas, plays and concerts, attending eight performances in the space of ten days. There was a wonderful *Don Giovanni* with Hotter, Dermota, Ljuba Welitsch, and Hilde Güden, and a *Rosenkavalier* with Hans Swarovsky conducting; as ever, my tearful oneness with Hofmannsthal's Vienna was renewed. There was his *Jedermann* and Goldoni's *Servant of Two Masters*, both in the old Max Reinhardt productions. His widow, Helene Thimig, had returned and was now once again to be seen in the role of Faith in *Jedermann*; soon we were introduced to her at the Hotel Österreichischer Hof, together with her brother Hermann, who played a charming Truffaldino, and the unchangingly self-confident writer and man of the theater Ernst Lothar. We heard Edwin Fischer ceremonially performing two Mozart piano concertos with the Vienna Philharmonic, we heard the same glorious orchestra playing Haydn, Beethoven, Brahms and Bruckner, and on one unique Sunday, the eleventh of August, we actually made three visits to the Festspielhaus, the final evening performance being a recital by the newly discovered Grace Moore. She sang Debussy, Tchaikovsky, a Negro spiritual, and the Scottish folksong "Annie Laurie," which finally provoked nostalgia in us for the British Isles. How many hundreds of such artistic experiences we already had behind us and how many were still to come! But only a few are as deeply engraved in my memory as these first renewed encounters with music and the theater in the heart of Europe hardly a year after our seven-year exile, after the dark winter of our world.

With the Salzburg festival still only half completed, we drove, both in summer uniform, to Mattsee, where a decade earlier we had decided to marry. And then, soon afterward, our ways parted again.

Peter had to return to Berlin, but I, once again ardently interested in politics after so much culture, went off to Innsbruck and the Brenner, where I wanted to research the current state of South Tyrol for the *New Statesman*. I had not seen my children for nearly two months, but I could not get enough of this roving life, these expeditions through a realm whose boundaries were blurring and were defined for me at the time only through the "movement orders" of the British Army.

At the press quarters in Igls, high above Innsbruck, there began and ended that inexpressibly moving week, in which, lovingly looked after by the Heiss family at their Hotel Elefant in Brixen, the center of efforts to regain the region for Austria, I came to know all the patriotic conspirators and their helpers. An unusual partisan was the Irishwoman Vera Dockrell, who had made the cause of the South Tyroleans her own and was a zealous co-conspirator. She became attached to me too during those few days and we had a tearful farewell when I left to write my report in Igls. Even the clergy powerfully strengthened my resolve to appeal in England for a reunification of the two Tyrols. I was received by the Bishop of Brixen, who gave his blessing to my plan. At his summer residence high in the mountains, the Prince-Archbishop – yes, this was his title among the archaic Tyroleans – Johannes Geisler graciously granted me an audience. His close friend, a wonderfully old-style Austrian, Baron Sternbach, explained to me, both on the spot and later in a long letter, which I preserved, the complete history of the freedom movement. In this letter, by now a historic document, he also recommended me to our former ambassador Franckenstein, with whom he used to spend time "in the old days in Saint Germain" and whom of course I had known for years. Sternbach stressed that "the intervention of an important publication such as the *New Statesman* would be an enormous advantage to us." For security reasons, he sent his letter from North Tyrol by the former chief officer of Innsbruck, Ernst Mumelter, to me in London, where it arrived on the eleventh of September at the *Statesman*'s editorial office and I received it a few days later.

By this time it was all over. And it was nearly all over with me. On the twenty-fifth of August I had begun to write up my research in Igls. At the press quarters, I bumped into Michael Burn and his beautiful wife Mary, by that time already fifty years old – during the Battle of

Britain she had been the lover of the legendary aviator Richard Hillary, England's counterpart to Antoine de Saint-Exupéry. The three of us fell in love with a tiny fox that had been found in the woods and reared by the landlord of a requisitioned luxury hotel. At home, the Burns, "upper-class radicals," would presumably not have thought of rescuing a little fox from the hunt. Two clear, calm days in the Tyrolean mountain air. I wrote four pages and departed, my manuscript in my kitbag. I could not dispatch it to England until I reached Munich. At the office of the *Neue Zeitung* I was cordially welcomed, met Hans Wallenberg, and was introduced to Ali Ghito, the German actress, for whose sake Hans Habe wanted to separate from his American wife Eleanor. On the twenty-ninth of August, I was to fly to Berlin, where Peter wanted to introduce me to our future home, his friends and his work. The travel order came too late. The next day it was raining. After a certain amount of pressure, I was granted a seat on a Dakota, which left at half past three in the afternoon.

At half past four we got into a turbulent area between two layers of cloud and fell from a height of 4,000 feet to a hundred – about thirty meters. The pilot had lost consciousness as a result of the drop in pressure, which we all felt as a constriction of the chest. After a split second, when we could already see the tops of the trees of Nuremberg, the co-pilot at the last moment pulled the aircraft up again. Soon after that, although one wing was half ripped off, he achieved a safe landing. Apart from myself, the passengers consisted of an American woman army helper, seven U.S. officers and three Jewish gentlemen from Palestine. I, the rationalist philosopher, had prayed during the crisis: "Oh God, get me out of this!" After the landing, we sat, still in a state of shock, on the bucket seats along the sides of the DC3 – our seatbelts fastened, fortunately, with our luggage, which had been thrown all over the aircraft, scattered in confusion around us – and an American major joked that he had expected to be holding a harp. I replied with British sangfroid: "It's all in the game."

We were asked whether we would prefer to continue our journey next morning in another aircraft or travel by train to Berlin. Every one of the US officers chose the safety of the train, whereas the two women and the three Jewish Palestinians opted for another flight. In

Nuremberg, the war crimes trials were still in session and not a bed was to be had, so we were driven for two hours in a cold, drafty transporter to the small town of Rückertsdorf, where we spent the night. Next day, a shattered Peter met me at Tempelhof airport and took me to the city of his youth, to the Hotel am Zoo. For five days we drove the length and breadth of Berlin in the Volkswagen he had been assigned, through the endless ruined wastes as well as the hardly touched suburbs of Dahlem, Zehlendorf, and Grunewald.

I met Peter's superiors and colleagues, I saw his office in Lancaster House – there were also a York House and a Cumberland House – on the Fehrbelliner Platz, and the editorial office of the British-licensed *Telegraf*, which he had succeeded in transforming into a daily paper and for which he continued to be responsible; I went to the opera and the clubs, the Embassy and the Blue and White. It was a continuous giddy whirl in which I managed for the time being to keep a cool head. I left on the Nord-Express, changed trains at Hanover and traveled by sleeping car to Calais. It was a tempestuous crossing. In the late afternoon of the fifth of September I arrived in Wimbledon. On that day the Austrian foreign minister Karl Gruber and the Italian prime minister De Gasperi had signed an agreement in Paris under which South Tyrol was once again denied reunification with Austria, although the Italian state granted the region a very limited autonomy.

My wonderful, exciting week at the Brenner had been in vain, my authoritative report for the *New Statesman* was outdated – of course, it could not be printed now. Two desperate letters reached me from Brixen, apart from that of Baron Sternbach. Vera Dockrell, in words as indignant as they were enigmatic, described her blind fury: "Rage at the folly of man – to throw away a game as good as won!" And my charming old landlord Wolfgang Heiss complained in equally metaphorical language: "The little bride is in love, she'd probably like to travel North." Now she would bow to the inevitable: "But, she says, she would never, never give up this marriage!" And finally: "Don't forget us in Brixen completely! This is our request to the *gnädige Frau*, who was so kind and good to us." Touching words! They reached me at a difficult moment. For even the cool-headedness with which I had believed myself to have got over the life-threatening incident in the Dakota had proved to be treacherous. After collecting

Hilde with Christine and Peter

On the terrace, St. Wolfgang

my little daughter from East Grinstead the day after my arrival and spending the evening with my mother, I woke in the night with a feeling of wild vertigo and a racing heart. The cosmos was spinning around me. I thought – not till then did I think – that my last hour had come. The vertigo lasted for many days, I lay in bed and had to leave the running of the household to Mimi. "Delayed shock," our family doctor, Dr. Walker, called it. It was not until the middle of the month that the attacks gradually stopped.

In Vienna with (left to right) critic Franz Endler, Leonard
Bernstein, Hans Flesch-Brunningen, and actor Heinz
Reincke, 1971

With Herbert von Karajan and Burgtheater director Ernst
Haeusserman

My last weeks in England. Peter reported from Berlin that he had found a wonderful apartment on two floors in the suburb of Grunewald. Preparations began for our move. I wrote articles for *La France libre* and the German weekly *sie*, which was still licensed by Peter for the Americans, published in partnership with Heinz Ullstein and edited by Helmut Kindler. I met my English friends from Vienna, Sammy and the Henekers, who were on leave in London. I had another "cultural day" when I first visited the Canettis with Elias's disciple Anna Sebastian (formerly Friedl Benedikt) and in the evening of the same day was invited to the fabulous house of the painter Isepp, as was Kokoschka, who once again described his levitation on the Stephansplatz in Vienna. I had lunch with Flesch at Santo Romano, dinner with Kingsley Martin, and in between I went to a cocktail party given by Lajos Lederer, the delightful, flamboyant *Observer* journalist; I accompanied the sculptor Georg Ehrlich and his wife Bettina to a performance by Benjamin Britten and Peter Pears at Chelsea Town Hall. On my birthday, the nineteenth of October, I cried, but cannot now remember why.

And then, one foggy November day, the children and I said goodbye to our friends Hans and Tetta Flesch-Brunningen at Liverpool Street station, where we were taking the boat train to Tilbury. Our beloved cat Ha'penny had been left in the care of our cleaning lady, Mrs. Stenhouse. I have never forgiven myself for abandoning him, for soon he ran away from Mrs. Stenhouse, probably trying to get back to Wimbledon, and was never seen again. Even in my old age I mourn for him as for a lost human friend.

The project of the British Army on the Rhine to unite their own personnel as well as that of the Control Commission in Germany with their families was given the name "Operation Henpeck." Perhaps it was only called by that name in the casinos and canteens, not in official announcements. When I boarded the boat for Cuxhaven with my daughter and son, I was entering the world of the "BAOR wives," to which, for better or worse, I was to belong for two years. But another world soon superimposed itself on the first, the world of German journalism, German literature, German theater, and German music, from which it became ever more clearly impossible to extricate myself in order to return to English culture, politics, and society.

With W. H. Auden, 1971

With performing artist and author André Heller in
Salzburg, 1977. "Hilde, du lieber Mensch…"

178

A trio of Austrian writers: Franz Theodor Csokor (top), Alexander
Lernet-Holenia (bottom, l.), Heimito von Doderer (bottom, r.)

Part Two

1946 –1989

For powerless and weak is the
kingdom of a single language
and custom.

St. Stephen, King of Hungary
1000-1038

Nos désirs vont s'interférant, et
dans la confusion de l'existence il
est rare qu'un bonheur vienne
justement se poser sur le désir qui
l'avait réclamé.

Marcel Proust

Garnet jewellery, 'the only collector's passion to which I
allowed myself to give way in Berlin' (c. 1947)

10

The Days of the Satraps

It is easy enough to describe the days of one's youth, with all the changing moods that still linger in the memory. But when events in the wider world begin to impinge on personal feelings, these fall by the wayside. Then one seems to lose what was learned in an early school of sensibility – the sharpened perceptions, the readiness to record the most delicate vibrations of that membrane which protects us from the violent impressions of the world around us, though itself touched by them.

So far in my account I have positively raced through the course of our lives since the outbreak of war, without however admitting how greatly the gloom of those days inwardly affected my husband and myself. The truth is that we had to deny ourselves the luxury of inner emotions. In the face of the appalling daily aerial murder and the latent threat of German invasion, long before the abysses of human devilishness, the "Final Solution," had come to light, we armored ourselves with apathy, almost to the point of numbness, even lethargy.

The equanimity with which the English accepted all the blows of fate made this attitude easier for us to adopt. In Naples, even in Vienna, we would probably have been swept along by the unrestrained terror and despair of those around us. We learned to be stoic, even phlegmatic, in the London of that time, constantly and mercilessly exposed to destruction, to which were added our own personal trials: illness, surgery, the loss of a child, my parents' wretchedness, my father's death. A long time earlier I had seen a film in which the great actor Raimu played a circus manager. When his daughter fell to her death from the trapeze, he tore himself out of his sorrow, murmuring: *"La tenue!"* This admonition to dignity was one I had often given myself in less oppressive situations. Now I repeated it daily.

Even at the end of that long winter of 1945, when doors and windows burst open and we rushed out of doors into the reality of peace, it was at first difficult to give way to our emotions without restraint. Once I broke down, on my first return to Vienna – on the parish square of Heiligenstadt; I had almost expected it. But my ambivalent position among the occupiers of my former home, the wavering between confidence and doubt as to whether we had really put down roots among our new British compatriots and become unconditionally accepted by them, was as yet too disturbing to be fully faced. And so everything penetrated to our consciousness as if through a veil. And even though we constantly confronted the present, with all its absurdities, its pleasures and denials and its continual challenges, we were as unwilling to look forward into the future as to look back into the past.

My husband, Peter, had been active in the service of the Western Allies in Germany since the end of the war. Now, during the second autumn after that date, I had followed him to Berlin with our son and daughter, like so many other families of the British military and civilian personnel. A housing estate in the Berlin suburb of Grunewald, built in 1930 in the functional modern style, surrounded by a great rectangular area whose original stand of trees had been almost entirely preserved, was to be our home until the end of August 1948. Karlsbader Strasse 13a. Our bedrooms, nurseries, music, and reception rooms, together with accommodation for our domestic staff, occupied two floors. It was a grand residence, where for two years – later mockingly dubbed our "satrap days" by Hans Flesch-Brunningen – we were to lead the life of high colonial officials. To our English counterparts, after centuries of imperial administration, this was a familiar lifestyle. It was new to us. And while to some extent we hardened ourselves to the situation, in its remoteness from the heartrending cares and trials of the native Berliners it continually aroused in us feelings, if not of guilt, at least of helpless perplexity.

The first stage was the expressionistic nightmare of the journey over a wildly raging North Sea. A ship tightly packed with people, all, apart from the crew, civilian women, children and WAAFs in their dark green uniform, an unstable cargo, for the most part on slanting surfaces and with crooked perspectives, adults' sighs alternating with children's screams, little ones tumbling about and seasick mothers. My own daughter, Christine, was weeping bitterly, because, just seven years old, she was not admitted to the enclosed play area with its milling mass of babies into which her two-year-old brother Anthony had disappeared. At Cuxhaven, where we went ashore, I noticed that my son was feverish. In the train to Berlin he seemed apathetic, and his skin became ever paler and more transparent. The day after our arrival we summoned the army doctor. But the British Army on the Rhine was ill-equipped to deal with this tiny creature's severe gastric influenza. Peter, still on good terms with his American colleagues of the previous year, sought their advice and as a result appealed for help to the chief health officer for Zehlendorf, Dr. Käthe Hussels. This wonderful woman promptly appeared, accompanied by a venerable, wrinkled little old man, who turned out to be an expert from the children's infirmary. Without any medication apart from a diet of curd cheese this doctor completely cured our child, who had seemed on the point of extinction.

During those first days I walked around the streets of the elegant suburb of Grunewald, already dusted with snow in that wintry late November, breathing the clean, sharp air of Berlin, invigorating, yet utterly strange to me, accustomed as I had become to the warm, damp, fog-laden climate of England, and I felt fear – yes, deep fear – at the sight of the pine and fir trees in all the gardens. When, revisiting Austria, I had again seen the forests of giant conifers on the Arlberg, they had reminded me of the skiing trips of my youth; it was quite a different sensation, in this tamed residential district, to find these prickly monsters standing around all the houses like guards. What Englishman would think of planting conifers in his garden, rather than flowering shrubs, variegated hedges, rose bushes and, if space allowed, protective chestnuts and gentle willows hanging over a little pond? Defensive and aggressive at the same time, even defiant, these trees seemed to me, and particularly obnoxious were the spruce pines and firs in which, quite irrationally, all the Germanic arrogance under which we had suffered so much seemed to be embodied.

What lay ahead for us was the "hungry winter," the "winter battle," as it was called later, of 1946. Daily consumption in Berlin sank to below one thousand calories. Emaciated figures, haggard faces, wherever one looked, and it was only because we were driving from place to place in Peter's little official car that we were not continually confronted with their misery. We ourselves, although living above subsistence level, could obtain better-quality food only on the black market, just like the more prosperous Germans, and our budget did not stretch to luxuries. If Peter had not meanwhile been promoted to the equivalent of a lieutenant colonel, we would have been in even worse straits. We lived on NAAFI goods, paid for with British occupation money – powdered eggs, dehydrated potatoes, oatmeal, canned fish, occasionally meat. The Americans were better off, as we soon found out when they invited us to meals. But even the monotonous and barely nutritious food available to the Western Allies was enough to make a position in their households highly desirable. We had a domestic staff consisting of a cook, a housemaid, and a chauffeur, with occasional help from the cook's husband. They led their own, almost cozy existence in their separate quarters, rather as in a traditional English country house, a lifestyle which was depicted decades later, with as much affection as social criticism, in the television series *Upstairs, Downstairs*.

Frau Kuhn was a buxom middle-class woman from Hesse, who, like any wife of a Viennese businessman or merchant in exile in England, could never have foreseen that she would one day go into domestic service. Before long she had not only proved her worth in the kitchen but also turned out to be a prudent housekeeper, who capably organized the work of the other staff. She supervised the housemaid, Hedwig – a simple, good-humored creature, whose husband Brodkorb, a serving soldier, was at the time a prisoner of war – in her constant cleaning and serving duties; sent her own equally portly husband to take my little son for healthy walks by the Grunewaldsee; and gave the chauffeur Gruehn a hearty bowl of soup whenever he came back, half frozen, after a long wait in front of some military building. Herr Gruehn was the quintessential Berliner, whom I loved at first sight, as I did that whole oppressed city, whole areas of which seemed to have collapsed in on themselves; small, slight, bony, slightly deformed, dry, a man of few words, but when he did speak, always precisely to the point. He took me to the British Families' Shop, waited patiently while I stood in line (just as I had done in London), sometimes for hours, with the other "BAOR wives," for our daily fare, and then helped me heave the cardboard boxes into the Volkswagen, of which he was immensely proud, and in which, as a sideline, he gave me driving lessons. He seemed to be constantly thanking his lucky stars that he had landed a job not only with Allies, but with employers who did not, like so many petty British officers or officials, behave toward their subordinates as though they were in Poona and not in Berlin.

At Christmas, in the midst of the winter battle, all our domestic helpers sat together in front of well-filled dishes. They were among the hardest-working people I have ever met, which did not necessarily have anything to do with the good relationship between us. We received daily confirmation of Germanic conscientiousness, even blind devotion to a task, once it had been accepted. Once, at the publishing house of Heinz Ullstein and Helmut Kindler, as I waited in the severely damaged anteroom with its makeshift repairs, I watched a cleaning lady reverently scrubbing the few remaining wooden door frames, which had been partly replaced with cardboard. As if mortar were not constantly crumbling from the exposed brick wall, she was working away to bring a high sheen to the small area of undamaged wood which now bore only traces of its original white varnish. This scene often came to my mind in later years and helped me to see the eventual reconstruction of Germany as by no means a miracle.

Just as unremitting were the swiftly moving, sensitive fingers of Frau Sibylle, the hairdresser at the Roseneck, as was her fluent tongue. This shrewd blonde lady, whom I visited several times a week, soon became my confidante; twenty months earlier she had been tinting, braiding and back-combing the crowning glories of the "high ladies," the prominent German women. She knew many a secret of the leading echelon under Hitler, for example that most of the gentlemen of the Third Reich had discarded their original wives and acquired younger and prettier ones. After his first Mercedes, the petit-bourgeois parvenu's prime need was for a spouse to match, one who could be shown off more effectively than the previous one.

This continuity of life was no isolated phenomenon. Thus, seemingly without transition, and without any noticeable distress to the various functionaries involved, the ladies of the Allied occupation were now laying claim to the comforts and amenities of the "high ladies" of the Nazi elite, who had vanished from the scene along with their executed or imprisoned husbands. The hairdressers, manicurists, pedicurists, fashionable dressmakers, furriers, maids, and servants were the same people as before. Even in the theater – right through the twelve years of Nazism, and in some cases going back as far as Weimar days – the same actors were performing in front of a totally different audience, which however acclaimed them with the same warmth – and that, after all, was what mattered. When I was still a schoolgirl, Otto Schneider, a visitor from the fascinating capital of the first German republic, had painted these scenes for me in tempting colors. Now they were before my eyes, mere remnants, but still totally recognizable.

Just as I had fallen for the slight figure of Herr Gruehn, I now became enamored of the quintessential smart young Berlin woman – slim, lithe, often affecting a charming lisp, her hair often dyed in shades ranging from demonic copper to erotic tomato red; not malicious, but never at a loss for a waspish comment. These women ranged from my Frau Sibylle and stage beauties such as Nina Raven to the highly intelligent young women, mostly connected with the *Kurier* newspaper, published under French license, and its arts editor, Carl Linfert, who were here developing into the best women journalists of western Germany: Christa Rotzoll, Kyra Stromberg, Karena Niehoff, Sabina Lietzmann, Barbara Klie. This prototype, too, must always have existed, along with that of the stalwart Berlin housewife and mother, and it was difficult for me to imagine either as supporters of that terrible regime. While at that time in Vienna the occasional caretaker or shopkeeper might betray signs of her rapid conversion to a more acceptable way of thinking, here in Berlin such personalities were not to be found. Fir or pine trees in the front gardens might make me nervous, but most people's faces betokened a character in which I could place my trust.

One of the first German homes I entered was that of "Miss Gerda," who had looked after our little daughter in Cambridge and had, with Peter's help, now returned home with all haste from England. For eight long years her fiancé had waited, honestly and faithfully, for Fräulein Gerda Stettiner, who had had to leave her home, although there was nothing to distinguish her outwardly from the other young women of Berlin. The eternally engaged couple, now married at last, lived modestly, though surrounded by books and phonograph records, in belated happiness. Herr Löffler gave me a present, Eduard Kremser's edition in two volumes of *Wiener Lieder und Tänze*, that beloved collection of the words and music of old Viennese songs and dances, with the delightful traditional illustrations. Unknown to the giver, it was an unexpected replacement for our own copies, which had been lost in the course of my parents' "lift" to England. His wife, also in gratitude for their swift reunion, pressed upon me a darkly sparkling little garnet brooch, thus awaking in me the only collector's passion to which I allowed myself to give way in Berlin.

The second German family to welcome us into their home was that of the health officer Dr. Hussels, who had saved our sick son. An unscathed villa in Zehlendorf, with elegant interiors. The couple, both doctors and both musicians, had two daughters, both beautiful and also musically gifted. There was to be a private concert. We found assembled a large throng of cultured people, gathered respectfully around a string quartet; Helga, the talented daughter of the house, was the first violin. The music was – of course – by Beethoven. During the third movement the door opened, and the mayor of Zehlendorf entered. The concert was immediately interrupted; the guests rose to their feet, the mayor approached and shook hands in turn with some twenty ladies and gentlemen, including ourselves. Then he took his seat with great ceremony, and the concert continued. This ritual took our breath away.

"Good Germans," without a doubt. How remote we felt from them! But did we feel more at home with the communal drinking ceremony at which the British residents of the Karlsbaderstrasse took turns playing host? It was the ritual of the English pub, in London as in the country, where at the usual opening times, but above all after a generous Sunday breakfast, perhaps after a church service, a cheerful "booze-up" would take place from twelve until two-thirty, when one would return home for a second substantial meal. Yes, certainly, we belonged there as well, but in both cases not entirely, not in our hearts and souls. Meanwhile, apart from the army and administrative personnel, foreign correspondents had also been given accommodation on the estate. And so, one day, John Peet, whom I had known in the *Salmschlössl* in Vienna, turned up and moved into the house opposite. This tall, gangling man, lovably eccentric, an adventurer in the old tradition of the splenetic "Milord," had, in one of his early phases as a member of the Palestine police, married an Israeli girl. While working in postwar Vienna for Reuters news agency, he succumbed to the charm of attractive women from noble houses and married Countess Christl Gudenus, who brought her young daughter into the marriage. Until his next, even more surprising volte-face, John was to become one of the most reliable of our friends in this multicolored tumult that emerged from the extraordinary social interlinking during the occupation of Berlin by the four Allied powers and which lasted until its dissolution in March 1948.

During my short stay in September 1946, I had had a premonition of how varied and dynamic our existence was to be over the years that followed. Now, almost as soon as my suitcases were unpacked and our little boy was out of danger, my life set off at a gallop. Countless friends, superiors, and co-workers of Peter's from his first, American period of work in this city, as well as his present one in the service of the British, streamed into our house or invited us to theirs, and in addition gathered almost daily in one of the clubs requisitioned by the occupying powers. One of Peter's colleagues from U.S. Information Services Control was Mike Josselson, a quiet, kind, somewhat melancholy man, a Russian by birth, a naturalized American for years, and now responsible for cultural links with the Germans. A passionate lover of music, he had immediately succeeded in ensuring that the Berlin Philharmonic stayed on in the American sector. This had not been unproblematic: apparently Brigadier McClure and Major General Bishop had a row about the question of which sector the orchestra was to belong to. Finally, it was said, McClure said to Bishop: "Say, Alec, why should you and I quarrel over a German band?" And the British officer, disarmed, instantly gave in with a smile.

The British, though not all from the southern part of England familiar to us, were a homogeneous bunch, united by the Army. Michael Balfour, director of Information Services, was a historian, a member of that social and intellectual elite which has always, despite its frequently condescending arrogance, seemed to me the most impressive manifestation of the civilized European. It was thanks to him that *Der Spiegel* was granted its license. But we had far more contact with his assistant, Major Nick Huysman. He was from South Africa, but wore the uniform of the Royal Welch Fusiliers, with a long black ribbon dangling from his cap. This, like the kilts worn by Steel

McRitchie, the controller of *Die Welt*, and another Scot, The McLaren of McLaren, made the Russian colonel Koltypin shake his head with the half-suppressed exclamation, "Ridiculous!" However, we refrained from making a comparison with Koltypin's own staff officers, who went around showing off their profusion of medals in a much more ridiculous fashion.

Peter, who had renewed the license for the *Telegraf* newspaper the previous May and arranged for its daily publication, continued to be responsible for it within PRISC (Public Relations and Information Services Control). The German press people and licensees with whom he dealt first under the Americans, then under the British, were now part of our regular circle. The editors of *Der Tagesspiegel*, about whom he had told me in his first letters from Berlin, Walther Karsch, Erik Reger and the impressive Professor Redslob, linked with Goethe through family connections and decades of research, were our guests at Karlsbaderstrasse as often as the massive Arno Scholz, the first founder of the *Telegraf*, an upright, honest German of the best sort, who, although a journalist by profession and inclination, refrained from newspaper work of any kind after the Nazis' seizure of power and, with the help of a little printing bureau, managed to survive the worst years. The former president of the Reichstag, Paul Löbe, and Frau Annedore Leber, the widow of Julius Leber, a conspirator in the July 20 plot to assassinate Hitler (Leber had been executed), had both been brought under the editorial aegis of the *Telegraf* by Peter, and were among our first German visitors. So was the young, very vital Helmut Kindler, who had been in Gestapo custody for some time, accused of three offenses which carried the death sentence. As well as founding a book publishing house, Kindler was also the publisher of the women's magazine *sie*, among other periodicals, together with Heinz Ullstein (a grandson of the founder of the Ullstein publishing dynasty, whose miraculous survival of the Hitler epoch in Berlin was due to his courageous wife Änne), and for some time after that with another former victim of persecution, Gerhard Grindel. We got to know the writer Günther Weisenborn, a sincere Communist who was imprisoned for years because of his political views. On New Year's Eve Peter Suhrkamp – friendly, but thin-lipped and inscrutable – and his wife Annemarie, or "Mirl," came into our lives, and over the next few months Friedrich and Heide Luft became close friends.

Many of these relationships had been initiated by Peter before my arrival, but now that we were "running a household" they became intensified. At the end of January I reported to Mimi, my mother in London – who received at least one letter a week from me throughout my time in Vienna – on the first social occasion at our apartment: "Forty to fifty people came to our party. Apart from the British, we had a lot of Americans here and two Russian officers, which counts as a triumph. They hardly ever accept private invitations, and it made a great impression on everyone that they accepted ours. I am fascinated by them, as is Peter, and very pleased that they are not shy with us. They drank quite a lot and must have had a good time, or they would not have stayed the whole evening." A week later I wrote to Mimi: "A Catholic priest visited us recently and blessed our house, which will please Lonny particularly. He was a nice, naive little Irishman with a charming Dublin accent."

Now, at last, it is possible to discuss our relationship with the Soviet Russians, our encounters and conversations with them. All the slander and false accusations to which we were subjected in later years went back to our Berlin years and referred to our contacts with representatives of our then Eastern allies. The fact that these contacts were actually encouraged, if not actually prescribed, by Peter's British superiors, up to the dissolution of the mutual Control Commission in the spring of 1948, was of course not common knowledge during the Cold War of the 1950s. But certainly, if we had felt that fundamental detestation of all things Russian that made no distinction between Stalin and his tools and the rest of the Soviet people, then we would not have made the effort we did to maintain a good understanding with the "cultural officers" in Berlin. But we felt no such detestation. After all, it was a Russian, Tsar Alexander II, who had bestowed on Peter's grandfather the order of St. Anne, to which was attached a hereditary title; and his Baltic grandmother, like Moura Budberg, had spoken Russian and French as naturally as German. As far as I was concerned, some of the romantic attachment I had felt for the Russians during my early days still remained, and had transferred itself from Dostoevsky and Tolstoy to Lunacharsky and Kollontai.

Before my move to Berlin, in June 1946, I had written to Peter about a dramatized version of *Crime and Punishment* with John Gielgud and Edith Evans, which I had seen:

and, darling, I was so shaken that I felt like the
fourteen-year-old schoolchild again, who used to
run home crying after seeing Russian plays. Nothing
goes to one's heart so much, nothing moves one
more in one's inner being than the Russians. And if
one reads their great masters with care, everything
explains itself, their politics at all times, the Moscow
trials – it's all in *Crime and Punishment*, when the
house painter suddenly starts shouting that he
murdered the pawnbroker, and the police chief
(wonderfully played by Ustinov) says: 'I know he is
lying, but I can't prove it.' 'Why is he lying?' 'He has
a bad conscience, St. Petersburg has corrupted him,
you know, wine, women. Now he wants to do
penance for it.' And everybody respects that. Well,
what explanation is there for the behavior of the
Russian defendants, except that they and everyone
else in Russia accept unquestioningly that one must
pay for one sin by confessing to another.

Even the shameful verdicts of the Moscow show trials, even the
much earlier horrors of the kulak murders, even the outrageous pact
between Stalin and Hitler, which disturbed us so deeply just before
the beginning of the war, had not destroyed my love of the Russians.
After the Wehrmacht's invasion of the Soviet Union an attempt had
been made to interpret that pact as a crafty means of playing for time.
We were still not aware of the terrible extent of the destruction of the
kulaks, the peasant landowners, in the early 1930s, or of Soviet
involvement in the Katyn massacre. At that time we were not ready
to see Stalin as an inhuman monster, such as Hitler was to us. In a
novel written long after the war had ended, I still referred to Fascism
as the incarnation of evil, but to Communism as only a fallen angel.
Fallen nevertheless, plunged into the abyss. When the emigré Nicolas
Nabokov, later executive secretary of the Congress for Cultural
Freedom, was in Berlin and for the first time encountered a Soviet
individual, a former compatriot, he went up to him, embraced him,
and then stepped back slightly and spat on the ground before him.
Who could have understood this better than we?

But the English too, as their American allies hardly understood at that time, and later even less, were by no means hostile in their feelings toward the Soviets. The relief felt by my father and all other exiles on Hitler's invasion of Russia was shared by most other people in the country. Winston Churchill, from the outset one of the bitterest opponents of the Russian revolution, said at that time, in 1941: "Russia's danger is our danger." And soon he let it be known that he would have made an alliance with the Devil himself against Hitler. The noticeable decrease in bomb attacks on England, the realization that by far the largest and most dangerous proportion of the Wehrmacht were now in action in the East, had aroused in Britain not only gratitude but also feelings of guilt. It was understandable that Stalin reproached President Roosevelt, when the latter repeatedly postponed the invasion of France: "Your decision leaves it to the Soviet Army... to conduct the war alone." This indeed was a highly exaggerated remark, for the Western Allies had long been active on other European and African fronts. But in England one remembered only too well the time after Dunkirk and David Low's cartoon of the British Tommy standing on the chalk cliffs of Dover, raising his fist defiantly toward the mainland: "Very well then – alone!"

Across the Atlantic, the then still neutral Americans meanwhile did not grasp that not even Arthur Koestler's highly regarded book about the Moscow trials, *Darkness at Noon*, or Orwell's *Animal Farm* had been able to shake those feelings of guilty gratitude toward the Soviet Union. But indeed, however much those feelings still linger, even today, among the older English, their great wartime leader Churchill was one of the first, after the war, to face up to the grim consequences of Stalinism and to terminate the pact with the Devil that had been forced upon them by Hitler. In his famous speech at Fulton, Missouri, in 1946, horrified by the rigid regime that the Soviets were constructing in their new satellite states, he coined the term "iron curtain," which was picked up and repudiated as a metaphor in our own times by Gorbachev's foreign minister. But as long as the Allies were still sitting around a table together, which was still decidedly the case in the Berlin of those days, the fair-minded and peaceful British made at least a minimal effort toward mutual understanding.

We, who were known as cosmopolitans, seemed particularly well suited to this pursuit. Our meetings from time to time in an informal context with the high-ranking and powerful Colonel Tulpanov; Colonel Koltypin; the leader of the "House of Culture of the Soviet Union" Major Mossiakov; the editor of the *Tägliche Rundschau*, Colonel Kirsanov; and the rather disagreeable Major Dymshitz, who was responsible for the Eastern Zone writers, were strictly in accordance with the wishes of the equivalent functionaries of the Western Allies. Such meetings occasionally took place at the parties at our house, attended by a wide variety of guests, both occupiers and occupied, and were relaxed in mood and atmosphere. We did, however, have to respect the Russians' provisos. They never explicitly accepted or refused invitations. Whether they came or not depended on unexplained or unexplainable circumstances, probably usually on the prevailing feeling at the Allied Command headquarters. They always arrived together and left together, formed a closed group, and hardly ever talked one-to-one with any other guest.

There was never any question of open conversation with the Russians. It was simply the fact of their presence that seemed helpful or useful to relations between the Allies, as they still were then. How little inclined we were to abandon our mistrust or even our inner reservations about the Soviet officers is illustrated by a little episode which I remember well. In November 1947 Kingsley Martin, the editor of the *New Statesman*, came to Berlin and we, or sometimes I alone, looked after him and introduced him to various people. At Kingsley's request we went together to Mossiakov's House of Culture, where he carefully inspected all the exhibits representing the glorious Soviet people since the Revolution. Mossiakov led him through the rooms. And then Kingsley Martin, who at that time was suspected of excessive sympathy with Communism, pointed to an indistinct mark on a copy of that gigantic painting which portrays the first assembly of the great Soviet after 1917. It was not so much a mark as a gap, a place which had clearly been overpainted on the original. And Kingsley said to Mossiakov: "I wonder who that was?" Mossiakov smiled enigmatically. But we all knew who it was.

The only Russian officer with whom we achieved an open, human relationship was – perhaps not surprisingly – a Lieutenant Feldman, a subordinate of Kirsanov's, who had turned up at a party of Heinz Ullstein's during the March after my arrival. He told us about the siege of Berlin, and how he and his comrades had spent bitterly cold nights under their tank on the icy ground, and had been among of the first of the invading forces to enter the Reich Chancellery. There was no need to discuss with him the brutal acts of violence committed by his soldiers here as in Vienna; that he deeply condemned and regretted them was clear without his having to say a word. Equally, he refrained from laying counter charges, such as were sometimes brought into the attack by those who would defend such acts, which however must remain forever inexcusable: the scorched earth traversed by the Red Army on their day's marches to the cities of the pan-German Reich, the more than 1,700 towns razed to the ground and the 70,000 extinguished villages, the 20 to 25 million Russians killed by Germans, of whom Molotov spoke in 1947. Neither did he refer to the frequently Asiatic origin of these first fighting troops, to whom Western customs were totally strange, and who had arrived as conquerors in a starved and dehumanized condition.

No, Lieutenant Feldman talked to us about the blessings of democracy, which he was fully prepared to recognize. Only one thing was mysterious to him: the way the British clung to their monarchy, this entirely archaic form of government. It was even more difficult for him to understand how we, originally republicans, could defend the royal house, the decent, shy King George VI and his friendly consort Elizabeth, who had stuck it out so bravely through the worst showers of bombs over London, and the morning after particularly bloody attacks had visited the worst-hit districts of London to give courage to the poor bombed-out or injured people among the ruins of their houses. How little influence the King had in matters of government or specifically in the conduct of the war, Lieutenant Feldman could not quite believe, and we argued in the friendliest manner on the subject until well after midnight.

A figure who was even then considered extraordinary, but whose ambivalent character had not yet by any means been recognized, was that of Captain Robert Maxwell, who up to March 1947 was also active in PRISC as an official of the third rank; he was subordinate to Peter in the latter's capacity as the person responsible for the British-licensed press. His picturesque, striking appearance, slim, dark, wiry, and swashbuckling, and not without a certain theatrical quality, seemed better fitted to some Hollywood film, rather than a real arena of war – a judgment which was wide of the mark. The young Maxwell, whose origins were vaguely known to us, but whose real name we had never learned, had in fact proved himself a hero in France during the invasion and received a Military Cross, an honor bestowed only in recognition of exceptional courage in battle. There too he had met his charming wife Elisabeth, or Betty, who for her part seemed in every way to embody the brave Resistance heroine portrayed in the postwar French cinema. During the few months we spent in the same city, we frequently spent time with Bob and Betty. We were highly amused by all the stories that were circulating about him – for example that he had sold half a million British army surplus boots to Turkey. Among all the British officers of comparable rank and type, the Ecclestons, Lynches, and Bells, the Maxwells seemed exciting and original. In March, shortly before they left Berlin, we were invited to the christening of their son Michael. Despite all the anger that Bob Maxwell later aroused in us as well as so many others, we were distressed at the news of Michael's early death.

In retrospect, it seems inevitable that Peter, some time earlier, and now I myself, should have become initiated into, if not embroiled in the political trench warfare, the complicated party formations in Germany under the rule of the four Allied powers. I had sent reports to the *New Statesman* about the conflict between the Communists and the Social Democrats, the latter being unwilling to cooperate with the former, while the British and Americans supported the independent SPD, and the Russians the new Socialist Unity Party, the SED. Neither party could be recognized by all four city commandants, and the whole business was referred to the higher authority, the Control Commission. "Thus a political tug-of-war is taking place over the semi-corpse of Germany, rather than between the Western allies and the representatives of the Soviet Union." Nevertheless, my notes remind me that at the end of February 1947 I was talking to Colonel Kirsanov and Wilhelm Pieck at a reception held by the Russians in the Jägerstrasse in the Eastern sector, and was also drawn into service as interpreter between them and Peter's former employer, the American Colonel Leonard. During those years I was sooner or later to come into contact with many individuals who at that time dominated the political scene, with the marvelous Mayor of Berlin Ernst Reuter, so modest in appearance wearing his usual beret, with Pieck as well as with Otto Grotewohl, Kurt Schumacher, and Jakob Kaiser. How recently Peter, newly arrived in Berlin, had wavered between hostile mockery, even disdain for the Germans and his still surviving sense of belonging to them! And how much more recently – in December 1946 – I had spent a day at the Ravensbrück trial in Hamburg, and glimpsed with horror in the faces of the female concentration camp guards in the dock the abyss into which Germany had for so long been plunged. Now we were engaged in friendly cooperation with the same country's struggle toward a new democratic form of government. Nevertheless, Peter, in his rigorous attitude toward former collaborators, was not universally popular. His occasionally brusque manner, sometimes used toward me as well, and his intransigence, for many people concealed the fundamental Germanness of his soul, which had been so deeply damaged by the Nazis.

But how great, at the same time, were the temptations then for people in our situation to obtain advantages, or even enrich themselves in the chaos of currencies and of trade by barter on an immensely wide-ranging black market. Without a doubt, countless officials and officers of the occupation, not excluding the British, with the help of cartons of cigarettes and alcohol were making off with valuable goods, sometimes whole consignments of Oriental carpets. Others, among the British in particular, wanted nothing to do with the few luxury items still in the possession of Berliners, no matter how pleadingly the latter offered them in exchange for cigarettes, in order to exchange these in turn for foodstuffs – sugar, bread, flour. Peter strictly forbade me to engage in any trade with the tobacco products and alcoholic drinks allocated to us. I desperately longed for a painting by Carl Hofer, an artist whom I admired and who, as I heard, was more than ready to enter into such transactions. But I dared not defy Peter, and also had to deny myself a Leica camera I hankered after, which I could easily have acquired for a couple of cartons of cigarettes. We had hardly any German money, and to juggle with the occupation currency, the BAAFS, outside the NAAFI was considered positively criminal.

Together with my new friend Heide Luft, however, I did give way to the passion we shared for junk shops. Around the Kurfürsten-damm, half destroyed but still bearing traces of its former big-city glory, we tracked down painted porcelain cups, little boxes, vases and faded miniatures, old brass candlesticks, or useless trinkets like little glass slippers. But when I saw anything that was scarlet in color, a little brooch or pendant of Bohemian garnets, all my scruples vanished, and I would buy it behind Peter's back with the ridiculous tobacco currency. No diamonds or other valuable jewels had ever tempted me; it was the dusky sparkle that enchanted me as much on my own finger as it did on the costume of a ballerina, in the role of Odile or the Firebird, who would wear glass imitations of such glowing dark red garnets as a clasp on her turban or on her deep décolleté. As one familiar with Freudian interpretations, I have never allowed myself to examine more precisely my lifelong obsession with this color. "I always think of cherry-red draperies, of something delicate and soft to the touch." This speech of Oswald, as he succumbs to paralysis, in Ibsen's *Ghosts*, spoken in the melodious tones of Alexander Moissi, has never quite left me and arouses in me feelings similar to those produced by the sight of garnet jewelry.

Although, now that I try to describe it, I look back on that time in Berlin as the richest, most diverse, most exciting and closest to reality of my nearly eight decades, a daily life full of impressions and experiences entirely at first hand, not transmitted through art or literature, there is still something dreamlike and unreal that remains associated with it. This presumably derives from the nature of that, for me still ungraspable, untidy city, whole areas of which still lay in ruins, in which a series of incessantly unwinding, breathlessly experienced events took place – a city whose structure differed from all other metropolises known to me, and which I simply did not understand. Certainly, the sectors and their boundaries had something to do with it. It was, after all, in the Soviet-occupied part of Berlin, which we visited only occasionally, that its old heart lay, its palace, still not demolished, the government buildings and theaters, the former newspaper offices, the famous Hotel Adlon, Heine's Unter den Linden, the ruins of the Reich Chancellery and of the Reichstag. The Western occupiers had made do with the business and entertainment districts, the memorial church, now destroyed, and the site of the legendary, likewise vanished Romanisches Café as far as the Nollenplatz. This much was clear to me. Then, on the edge, the villa suburbs, where the social circle was centered. Somewhere, too, was

Tempelhof, where the Berlin edition of *Die Welt* was printed and where there was soon a desk for me as well. But to this day, I admit, I have never mastered the topography of the countless other districts, which still seem to me like islands in a sea of rubble, between which we cruised back and forth, guided by Herr Gruehn in our little Volkswagen boat. I am well aware that a glance at a modern map of the city would reveal what is still missing in my picture. But I am reluctant to extinguish from my memory the only element of a certain trancelike, legendary quality that clung to my existence at that time.

During those two years, as I wrote to my mother in July 1948, we were living "the high life." Never, Peter prophesied toward the end, and he was right, would we again enjoy such secure prosperity, such carefree activity. The days of the satraps indeed, lording it over the German people who were still, for the most part, living in misery. How to come to terms with this? We did not stop to think. The hectic pace of events swept us along, and not only us. "The hairdresser told me that the British and Americans were fresh and cheerful when they first arrived in Berlin, but after a few weeks they became pale and listless, because they spent so much time painting the town red and drinking." We at least had the satisfaction of being able to contribute something to the understanding of the Allies among themselves as well as between themselves and the Germans, and perhaps even to the cultural revival of the city. I too was able to help, to the extent of my powers, once I had taken over the drama review section of *Die Welt*, and by writing articles on English themes in German newspapers and finally long essays in the magazine *Der Monat*.

With the help of my notes and the many letters I wrote to my widowed mother who had been left behind, alone in London, I can recall, almost without a gap, the significant moments of those twenty months. An afternoon in March, for example, at Mike Josselson's, who had invited, apart from ourselves, Jürgen Fehling, Joana Maria Gorvin, and Hilde Körber. The last-named, we were told, had been the wife of Veit Harlan before he married Kristina Söderbaum and made the infamous anti-Semitic propaganda film of *Jew Süss*. We had never, so it seemed to me at the time, come so close to the orbit of evil, and although Frau Körber was a friendly creature, blonde, quiet and a little careworn, I could not combat an inner resistance against sitting and chatting with her naturally at the tea table. In addition to this, in the conversation among the German actors there was some violent criticism of the Russians, and this in the house of Mike Josselson, who was after all of Russian origin, and whom we respected, indeed loved. This disturbed me, I must confess. "A dreadful afternoon. I had to leave early," I noted in my journal. Here too there were mixed feelings, for we felt deep respect for Fehling and for Frau Gorvin, and having seen Lil Dagover and Otto Gebühr a few days earlier in *The Cherry Orchard* we were moved by these great survivors from the early days of the great film company UFA (Universum-Film AG).

My only attempt to promote the career of a friend from Vienna in Berlin seems rather feeble in retrospect. I had brought Franz Reichert the manuscript of Hans Weigel's *Barabbas*, and he staged it the same March at the Theater am Schiffbauerdamm. It was well received by the public, less so by the critics, but Weigel and his wife at the time, Udi, had come to Berlin for the premiere and were happy. Zuckmayer and Roma Bahn were in the theater, and afterward we celebrated until half-past two in the morning at the Karlsbaderstrasse. I believe this was Weigel's first and only success in a larger German theater. The characteristics of Vienna and Berlin never really blended, in spite of the transient triumphs of the Austrians in literature and journalism during the Weimar years, in spite of the later, occasionally successful attempts of Oscar Fritz Schuh, who presented Nestroy and Hofmannsthal at the Theater am Kurfürstendamm. *Barabbas* was soon forgotten. The great event of this spring of 1947 in Berlin was the return of Furtwängler.

Josselson, the passionate music lover, had personally seen to the denazification of the *Herr Staatsrat*. His concert with the Berlin Philharmonic at the Steglitz Titaniapalast on the morning of May 25 was, for this reason, exclusively dedicated to Beethoven. H. H. Stuckenschmidt wrote in the program notes: "As Wilhelm Furtwängler, after two years dedicated to composition, appears again before a Berlin audience, he is greeted by the confidence of those who see in him the most important exponent of a great musical tradition. At this time of threatened stylistic degeneracy and a loss of standards, his task becomes something more than the interpretation of musical works and the direction of musicians. For the more convincingly music speaks to us, the more strongly will it fulfill its moral function:

to be the language of humanity and to reconcile in images of sound, which stand above all logic, what seems irreconcilable in the realm of logic." Might one not be somewhat surprised at these words, which would have been more to the point during the era of the recent past, when stylistic degeneracy was by no means a threat but a fact of life, and when standards were not so much lost as totally misguided?

But the reviews, two of which I preserved, were also couched in strange terms. A Herr Fritz Brust was of the opinion that "as an interpreter of Beethoven" Furtwängler was "a representative of the German soul, of inflexible loyalty to the work," and expressed his pleasure that the Philharmonic under Celibidache had been "well looked after during a time when Furtwängler too would have been oppressed by extreme difficulties in the training of his orchestra" – from which the latter, thank God, had evidently been rescued by his long wait for a favorable response from the denazification court. "As in January 1945," according to Herr Brust, "the gladdening experience was now repeated of a quite incomprehensibly mysterious musician-ship." And in the intermission he was ready "to say with Pogner in *Die Meistersinger*, 'Methinks the old times are renewed.'" A Herr Edwin Kroll, meanwhile, in his musical observations, praised Furtwängler's "sacred-sober re-creation" – alas, poor Hölderlin! – and was grateful for the conductor's interpretation of Beethoven's Fifth, which transposed "that fateful journey through battle and victory" into the realm of pure ideas. This was really quite fortunate; otherwise the four drumbeats at the beginning of the symphony could easily have reminded one of the BBC's German broadcasts during the war.

It is a source of regret to me, and many will take it amiss, that for me the identification of Furtwängler with the "German soul" is hardly to his credit. While I admired the "celestial bandleader" Toscanini and the ascetic Otto Klemperer, a man of still more inflexible loyalty to the work, neither then nor later could I feel any warmth toward Wilhelm Furtwängler's "images of sound," which stood "above all logic." Even the fond memory of my friend Stuckenschmidt cannot prevent me from seeing in the figure of the great conductor, as in his interpretation of music, the incorporation of just that arrogant claim to the hereafter and to eternity which places itself not only above all logic, but simply above all reason: the German character, which, in Wagner's words, was to cure the diseases of the world.

In an article for the *New Statesman*, I wrote that "Furtwängler's return" had been reminiscent in an oppressive manner of a tribal ritual to celebrate the rebirth of a myth. As if to welcome a martyred prophet, who had taken upon himself all their guilt and done penance on their behalf, the whole audience had risen from their seats as he entered. Certainly the way in which the conductor, despite his constantly vibrating baton and trancelike gestures, had brought about an unprecedented power and unity of performance on the part of the orchestra had been miraculous. But the mass hysteria that he induced in his audience was fraught with danger signals. "These poor people," said a bystander after the concert, "they haven't had a gathering like this since the last party conference in Nuremberg."

Later I met Furtwängler several times at Josselson's; privately he was a quiet, scrupulously polite man, always slightly absent-minded, as if floating in higher spheres. Only once did he pay concerned attention, when I, his dinner partner for the evening, mentioned the memoirs of "W. Th. Andermann," a pseudonym for Walter Thomas, the former cultural adviser to Baldur von Schirach in Vienna. This book contained an observation that at the Vienna State Opera "nothing is done without [the involvement of] the Furtwängler office." I confess that it gave me a brief moment of satisfaction to notice that the venerated musician had lost his sublime composure for the same short space of time. And even if he had always clutched his baton while others in the concert hall were giving the Hitler salute, and if he had during the dark years been the indispensable comfort of all Germans, even those who had in all innocence become caught up in events – the fact that after the departure of Toscanini, Walter, Klemperer, Kleiber, and Busch he had been the only one to fill all their empty places and not to withdraw his labor from the infamous rulers of the land, was something I might forgive, but could never forget.

The resentment of the exile – certainly this is what it was. Not only in the rejection of some individuals, but also in the enthusiasm with which I encountered others, there lay prejudices, as well as presentiments from the past. After all, during those years most of the important figures of the present day visited Berlin at some time, people whom I already knew, but many others whom till then I had admired only from afar. Thus, for example, Alfred Döblin and Anna

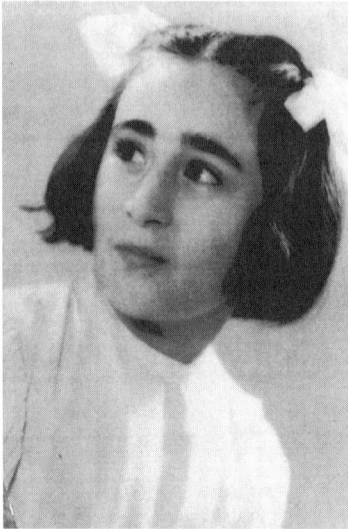

Christine and Anthony Felix as children in Berlin

Seghers were invited to Peter Suhrkamp's one July evening, and I was able to measure my admiration for *Berlin Alexanderplatz* and *Die Gefährten* (*The Companions*) by meeting the authors of these novels in person. I wrote very simply to Mimi: "I didn't like Döblin very much, but Seghers is fascinating – a woman of about fifty, with a sweet face, grey-white hair brushed back smoothly, tremendous wisdom and humor and an enchanting Mainz accent in her voice, just like Zuckmayer's. I was delighted by this meeting, and just making the acquaintance of Anna Seghers has almost made the whole stay in Germany worth while."

11

Interludes – On the Road

There are so many wonderful sayings about mobility, from the classical "*navigare necesse est*," through the assumption "*si Dieu existe, il est toujours en mouvement*," to the mock-indignant exclamation of a patriarch: "Am I a bird, to be in two places at once?" In those days we would have liked to be not in two, but in several places at once, in all the places where we had been before, until they were closed off from us by the waters around the island, and in all those we had never seen and wanted to see now that the world once again lay open to us. Every few weeks I felt an urgent need to make my escape from Berlin, an island, as it were, in the middle of the Russian zone.

In his novel *All That Matters* (its German title was *Das zweite Leben*) Peter, already in exile, described with infinite affection the German landscape, as it had been before Hitler's arrival, when he had traveled from the Italian border into the Hanover area. "It was like holding, for one brief moment, the whole of it in one's two hands, plains and mountains, woods and lakes, towns and hamlets, rivers and roads. I felt that my hands trembled no more... there was now only quiet and peace, rest and endless time ahead of us and no more throbbing of a troubled heart flying homeward in fear and haste. I am coming home, I thought." But it was not then that he came home; not until the spring of 1945. And since then, as if possessed, he had been traveling the length and breadth of that Germany which he had never succeeded in tearing from his tortured heart, for all his early acquired cosmopolitanism.

I often accompanied him, getting to know the only country in central Europe which had until then been unfamiliar to me. We traveled in the opposite direction to that taken by the narrator of Peter's book: in Hamburg, which we reached by the inter-zone train, we took charge of a roomy official car put at our disposal by the military government, and drove all day, with frequent stops, southeast as far as Munich and almost as far as the Austrian border. We saw the towns that had suffered the greatest destruction, Jülich and Düren; we saw the little country roads off Hitler's *Autobahnen*, the river banks and the hills, the castles and convents, and I began to feel almost at home when we reached Franconia, let alone Bavaria. As we had never done before or since, we stayed at luxury hotels, which had been requisitioned by the Allies, always at the Atlantik when in Hamburg, at an Exzelsior here, a Carlton there, and in Nuremberg at the Grand Hotel. But the comfort of these establishments was limited: on the beds, more often than not, we found the rock-hard pillows and rough army blankets supplied by the British and US occupiers; and in the restaurants the food was no better than in the canteens, only served more elegantly. It was just as well. Otherwise the contrast between our way of life and that of the emaciated inhabitants of the ruined towns would have been too painful.

In Nuremberg, once the scene of bombastic Nazi pomp and pageantry, but now of the cruelest humiliation of German hubris, we spent a morning at the trials of war criminals, which were still in progress. Werner Milch was in the dock. As we knew, he was a distant cousin of Georg Honigmann's, and not in fact of totally "Nordic" origin, and now bitterly regretted the blindness which had induced him to throw in his lot with the regime of horror. A few old craftsmen's cottages still left intact in the town reminded me – as I had constantly been reminded on our journey along the Rhine – of Wagner, so well beloved by me since early childhood, and I could not remain unmoved by the power of that mighty German myth, and was well aware along the Rhine and in Nuremberg of those seductive, destructive forces he aroused in the German people.

That it was in Munich that these forces were first called into life was difficult to accept at first, for the Bavarian capital seemed to have returned to a countrified *Gemütlichkeit* which still allowed room for artistic extravagance and excess. Thus, after twelve dark years, we hoped to recapture there the spirit of Thomas Mann and his high-spirited children, the spirit of Frank Wedekind, and of the satirical magazine *Simplizissimus*, blinding ourselves to the sinister oppressiveness of the beer cellars from which, even as I write, an evil phantom seems once more to have arisen, whose influence extends even as far as Berlin. We were moving in the circle of the *Neue Zeitung* with its talents old and new, we renewed our friendship with Carl Zuckmayer, who had meanwhile paid a tearful visit to his old home in Henndorf, and spent a long evening with Erich Kästner and his wife. What did we talk about? Anyone who, after forty years, can reconstruct the gist, let alone the details, of such conversations must be an inventor. I only know that we discussed at great length all the great writers whose inner resistance against the regime resulted in empty desk-drawers at the end of the war – and I remember the unspoken question we would have liked to address to our revered Erich.

Hubert Löwenstein turned up in Munich, declaring his intention of once more taking an active part in German politics. We drove to Chiemsee, where Peter sought out the poet Rudolf Alexander Schröder and discussed seriously and for the first time whether we could not buy a little piece of land to build on in this part of the country, so similar to my beloved Salzkammergut. The thought of creating a summer home in Austria was still far from our minds. Then I left Peter to travel back to the British zone with his chauffeur, and took the Mozart Express to Vienna. We had been away from Berlin for nearly two weeks, and I stayed away another two weeks, unmindful of our children, our household, of all the dizzying bustle of the Karlsbaderstrasse; once again I took up my quarters in the *Salmschlössl*, giving way as ever to my yearning for my native city. I wrote to Mimi: "Vienna is absolutely enchanting, and sometimes I can't imagine that I can bear not to be here."

In what follows, I do not intend to report in detail on my many visits to Vienna up to the time of my final return home. But I do want to record, for my readers and for myself, the broad outlines of what happened during those two central years of my life. It was on this occasion that, in a British officer's house, I met my old friend Willi the architect, with his Elsa, whom for seven years he had been able to protect from deportation, though not from ordeals of all kinds. It was a melancholy, nostalgic meeting; he gave me a long and questioning look, and I felt an indefinable shame in encountering, in my comparatively unscathed state, this man who appeared so wasted, so robbed of his proud masculinity. The couple had remained faithful to each other, but they had not been happy. It almost seemed a relief to me when I found them again four decades later, visiting the now totally desolate Neuhaus in the Triestingtal – the noble Hotel d'Orange was now a refugee camp. They lay at rest side by side, peacefully united in the cemetery. They must after all have enjoyed the time spent in between, in their house at the forest's edge.

In late March 1947, the exiled pianist Peter Stadlen, whose life was to end all too soon, played Schubert in the Vienna Konzerthaus, incomparably and unforgettably. And now old Baron Eichhoff, a courteously tolerated tenant of just one room of a small *palais* whose first floor he had once occupied, told me of the murder of the six other occupants on the day the Russians marched in; the crime was committed not by the victors or "liberators," but by the concierge, his mind disturbed by the horror of events. According to Eichhoff, the dead bodies, not yet exhumed, still lay beneath the lawn of the front garden through which we passed daily. With Hans Weigel I went to the Redoutensaal, to a performance of the Offenbach operetta *Madame l'Archiduc* in the adaptation by his master Karl Kraus, with Käthe Dorsch and Rudolf Forster. I entrusted to the Wiener Verlag a German version of my Italian novel which had been published in England. I was invited to lunch at the Kinsky by the Henekers, along with Charles Beauclerk, the future Duke of St. Albans – a cheerful, unaffected young man whose ancestors were Charles II and the orange-girl Nell Gwyn. And on the first of April, his name day, I had my father's ashes laid to rest at the Ottakring cemetery. As I wrote to Mimi: "Despite emigration, back among his fellow Viennese, where he belonged." Marie and Anna were at the ceremony, held according to the ritual of the Old Catholic church, for the Church of Rome, despite the years of exile and the deaths in concentration camps, still refused to consecrate and allow funeral rites to those who had been cremated.

In mid-May I spent twelve days in London – "home at last," I noted in my pocket calendar – staying with Mimi in her little bachelor apartment in Broadwalk Court, and met all my old friends, as well as the new ones acquired on the mainland since the end of the war. I visited Flesch and his wife Tetta, to whom I had never been close, not knowing that it was the last time I was to see her; I found him "delightful." "London is so beautiful, it breaks my heart to have to leave again." And after hardly more than a week in Berlin, during which that ecstatic return of Furtwängler took place, Peter and I departed for Zurich, for the second Congress of International PEN since the war. Our little daughter accompanied us. With her mother away and her father seldom at home, she had been left too often and for too long in the care of the staff, and she too had been leading a double life; in the mornings she attended the English school with other children of the occupation – during playtime they would give performances of *Winnie the Pooh* and *The Wizard of Oz* – and in the afternoons she played with two skinny German girls in the "*Wäldchen*," the little wood, where they roasted potatoes on an open fire. She had become bilingual, while our little son, toddling through the suburban streets holding the hand of Frau Kuhn's husband, had learnt the German of Berlin as his first language.

And so to Zurich and PEN. To give so much prominence in my memoirs to this association of writers may seem ridiculous to some. But I cannot repeat often enough how elated and lively I have felt time and time again in its circle. Hermann Kesten once remarked that leaving one of its meetings was like leaving one's family. The feeling of belonging to a worldwide, often cordial, often intolerable family, for better or worse always stimulating and exciting, has stayed with me for almost half a century. After all, Arthur Miller in his autobiography devoted a great deal of space to his own activity in PEN. And even if he perhaps slightly overestimates his own significance as "savior" of this organization, whose presidency he agreed after some hesitation to take over in 1965, he did undoubtedly lend to it for a while the luster of his name, like John Galsworthy, H. G. Wells, Benedetto Croce, and Alberto Moravia before him, and Heinrich Böll, V. S. Pritchett, and Mario Vargas Llosa after him.

I myself, like Peter, gave faithful service to International PEN for more than half my life, frequently filling high posts in one center or another, though never occupying the chair, yet I received little recognition for this. In German PEN's documentary report of 1986 our names are not once mentioned, nor is that of Flesch, who was for a long time president of the center for German exiles. My many years of work for the international Writers in Prison committee, during which I sometimes awoke with a start from a nightmare about the Korean writer Kim Chi Ha or one of the many other problem children about whom we were constantly writing letters, telegrams and appeals, all the wide-ranging correspondence collected in the file

I handed over to Kathleen von Simson when she took over my place on the committee in 1976 – it was all done for love, not for the sake of a mention in the PEN report. After all, I have so much more to thank the association for, despite the fact that in many countries it was run in such an inglorious fashion and was justifiably mocked as a result: wonderful encounters, good, even close friendships, from Henrietta Leslie to Heinrich Böll and Mira Mihelič, my beloved Slovenian Mira, who was like a sister to me, with our common heritage, the Austria that had long passed away.

In Zurich, we checked into the Hotel Eden au Lac, and on the evening of the thirty-first of May, before our daughter went to bed and we departed for the first event of the Congress, we strolled around this city which had remained unscathed by the war, filled to the brim with all the blessings of a lasting peace, a sparklingly clean toy town, inhabited by citizens as ingenuous as they were self-righteous: a source of comfort as well as irritation for all of us who had gone through purgatory and limbo, and could admire a paradise such as this only with mixed feelings. It was, to be sure, a neutral place, intact and innocent, where debates about the re-admission of a German or an Austrian PEN could take place calmly and dispassionately. The occasion did not, however, pass off without emotional scenes. From Vienna, Franz Theodor Csokor, Alexander Sacher-Masoch, Carry Hauser, and a few other, perhaps less untarnished gentlemen came to found a new Austrian center, and Robert Neumann, president of the writers in exile, restored to the favorite children of Europe the position he had held for nine long years in London, without a word of objection being raised. The Germans fared differently. Thomas Mann urgently pleaded their cause, but the Belgians protested, and Vercors was for allowing them to return only on condition that they should be subject for a time to international control.

After the initial business of the Congress came the uplifting moments and the little pleasures. Thomas Mann spoke on Nietzsche, and Peter and I lunched with Klaus Mann and his old teacher Paul Geheeb. On another day we ate with Dolf Sternberger and an American we had not met before, Melvin J. Lasky. Now and then I spent some time with the Austrians, who had already been befriended by Fritz Hochwälder, exiled to Zurich. One afternoon the whole

Congress went on an excursion to the island of Au, where Stephen
Spender began to flirt with Darina, the Irish wife of the Italian writer
Ignazio Silone, and our daughter suddenly found herself on a swing
with them. At the closing banquet, Erich Kästner vouched for the
decency and morality of the German center that was to be newly
formed. In a German-speaking city the sting must in any case be taken
out of the resistance. The following year we were to meet in
Copenhagen, where on the insistent pleas of the local German
émigrés the vote was taken in favor of an all-German center, and this
was set up in the autumn in Göttingen, under the direction of
Hermann Friedmann, Erich Kästner, and Johannes R. Becher.

All this said and done, we once again departed in different
directions – Peter with Christine to his father's house in Nice, where
der Rabe – the Raven, as he was known to his family – was living with
his third wife, a Frenchwoman called Claude, and I to Rome. Hansi,
the beautiful Hansi, the friend of my girlhood, after years of bizarre
experiences, was living there with a Triestine called Vittorio in
circumstances which were not yet clear to me, and cordially invited
me to stay with her, as there was plenty of room in her apartment. On
the eighth of June I arrived in Via Pietro Tacchini in the fashionable
Parioli district and found Hansi in more brilliant form than ever,
living in great prosperity. After her escape from Switzerland she lived
in Rome under the name Maria Passalacqua – such an unappealing
name that no one could be suspected of adopting it voluntarily,
making it all the more plausible – and enjoyed the protection not only
of generous lovers, but even, as she told me, of Pope Pacelli, later
such a controversial figure. Although Pius XII at one time was said to
have encouraged the escape of incriminated Germans to South
America, he certainly helped to conceal or support many a refugee
from Hitler's *Grossdeutschland* before the end of the war. Hansi told me
that she had become so reckless in the course of time that she once
went to Gestapo headquarters to plead for her housekeeper's son,
who had been held as a hostage. Whether she succeeded in securing
his release, I cannot remember.

I stayed for ten days in Hansi's spacious top-floor apartment, with
its terrace adorned with oleander and hibiscus in huge terracotta pots.
To Mimi: "Hansi's friend moves in the best circles here. A world of
decadent sophistication. The women look wonderful, the chic-est in

Europe." But Vittorio was also a friend of Alberto Moravia's – the two families were connected in Trieste – and so we arranged to meet him in the Hotel de Russie one evening. Alberto arrived without Elsa Morante, whom he had married and with whom he had spent the last eight months of the Fascist regime hidden in a stable, near the small town of Fondi. The first news I had had of him had reached me before the end of the war, in January 1945, when the brilliant though sharp-tongued writer Edouard Roditi had written to me from New York. He had heard from Rome that all was well with Moravia, "that is to say, his health is much worse, but illness was always one of his social advantages, as it was for Proust. He is once again *la coqueluche des princesses gâteuses* and sees only the cream of society and the art world, writes a great deal and publishes quite a lot."

Alberto, now restored to health, was now somewhat more portly than the slim young man I had met in Capri eleven years earlier, but still fascinating in his gloomy way, indeed very much more so. He was known here as "l'Orso," the Bear, because of his grumpy manner, but it was just that which made him irresistible to women when his grouchiness gave way to erotic delight. It had been by the side of the already somewhat irritable Magus, staying in frugal accommodation, that I had made my first investigation of Rome. During this June the whole city seemed to exude a shimmering eroticism which hung in the air and emanated not only from Hansi's perennially enchanting presence. Even among the fabulous Roman women she created a sensation wherever she went.

She and I wandered through the shops of the Via Condotti and the Via Sistina, spooned up ice cream in the cafés of the Via Veneto or, for a change, visited her German friends, *bohémiens*, survivors like her, who were as far removed from Vittorio's circle and lifestyle as they were from the moon. They were the Berlin writer Dinah Nelken, her burly Socialist partner Ohlemacher, and Rolly Gero, comrade to them both. In between I was invited alone to the ancient *palazzo* of Cecil Sprigge, a British diplomat who had been transferred here from Berlin, and with my hosts to the home of the journalist Luigi Barzini, already well known then and later much more famous; he had not yet written his great books about America, the Italians, and the Germans. Meanwhile there was only one thing I wanted – although I was oppressed by the thought of the fleeting and futile nature of our meeting – and that was to see Moravia again. And I actually succeeded in conjuring him up – I still had the power to do so. As I strolled around Parioli, the district where he too lived, thinking intensively of him, it was not long before he appeared around a corner.

It was a pleasure for both of us – I was now certain, despite his dry greeting, that it was so for him – and we arranged to meet two days later: a harmless enough appointment, in the afternoon at Babington's Tea Room on the Piazza di Spagna. At first he talked in general terms, about fascism and, with contempt, about the bourgeoisie which had put up with this form of government for so long. "The ordinary people and the intellectuals are the only ones worth talking to." Then we began to tell each other what had happened in our lives since we had last met. But presumably I did most of the talking, for Moravia, who wrote so much, was taciturn, preferring to retreat into a meaningful silence, more appropriate to a philosopher than a writer who had adopted the detailed description of human and above all erotic relationships as his constant theme. Why? He admitted four decades later in a conversation with François Bondy: "Every novelist has his key that unlocks the gates of reality. For Balzac it was money, for Proust it was snobbery, for Conrad the sea, for Dostoevsky murder. My key is that ordinary and yet mysterious thing, sex."

On the evening of the same day, my last in Rome, Hansi and Vittorio's guests were drawn from the *jeunesse dorée* – by now somewhat more mature. To Mimi: "There is to be a garden party over the roofs of Rome, and all sorts of *marchesi* and *conti* are coming." Languid gentlemen from the papal or Neapolitan nobility, supple ladies in tulle dresses, in flower-like poses, coiffured, made up and bejeweled as if for a film part, gradually began to fill the rooms. Moravia made his appearance, again without Elsa. He immediately came toward me, but his affected air of distant reserve, which had something provocative about it, as was no doubt his intention, missed its purpose. I turned away from him and toward a young count, Luciano della P., who had begun to pay court to me. People were drinking too much; everyone seemed to be streaming and gliding about in confusion, out onto the roof terrace, from which the lights of the city below could be seen, and back again to the buffet, laden with delicacies acquired on the black market by Hansi's Sicilian maid and displayed in huge bowls, and with innumerable carafes of Frascati and Valpolicella. Long after midnight the guests slowly began to drift away. Moravia too departed, and the last to remain was the *Contino*. By this time I had completely lost my head, and Hansi would not have been Hansi if she had not slyly and gladly enabled me to make use of the occasion. The following day Moravia telephoned and wished me a good journey in a tone of sullen irony. I traveled by sleeper to Zurich and from there back to Berlin.

What a difference, what poles apart, from a brief autumnal expedition deep into the Russian zone, to Leipzig for the *Messe*. In the exhibition halls, displays of carefully produced books, prettily turned wooden toys, elegant porcelain and glass. At the street checkpoint on entering the city we saw an English-language advertisement inviting us to visit Auerbach's *Keller*: "Prices in foreign currency. Intourist Administration." In the evening we followed up this suggestion. This was how I described the modern "devilment": "Apart from a few Swiss, Dutch, and Scandinavians, there was not an honest face in the place. Green dollar bills, not allowed to be exported from the United States, blue pound notes whose possession by the occupying forces was strictly forbidden, Danish kroner, and Dutch guilders were being passed from hand to hand. An American, his shirt drenched with sweat, reeled around with a bandy-legged prostitute. Dubious characters stamped and shuffled about on the dance floor to the strains of German folk tunes played at enormous volume and in the rhythm of military marches. Unexpectedly, the band suddenly struck up the popular song 'Under the Spreading Chestnut Tree.'"

We drank "champagne" – sweetened white wine with a shot of soda water – and ate red caviar which tasted of dyed sago. "Where once the Devil corrupted the souls of Dr. Faustus' students, a disreputable bunch of crafty businessmen were now being fleeced. Glancing from the drunken mass of spectral figures to the solitary Russian officer who was observing all this with contemptuous amusement, one could easily guess what was going through his mind. For him, what was going on before his eyes was the dissolution of Western civilization, whose befuddled representatives were being taken for a ride, and with every justification." My article was published in the *Tagesspiegel* and the *New Statesman* under the title "Intourist Keller." But appearances were deceptive. The West was not in the process of dissolution, but was about to extend its civilization even further and higher in a most unexpected way. The Breughelesque scene, in such blunt contrast to the Roman Mannerism of the spring, soon turned out to be a transitional phenomenon of the early years of the Occupation.

In the zones of the other Allied powers, civilization had apparently already set in by October 1947. We took off once again on a long journey. Peter showed me Rothenburg and the delightful little towns on the Neckar and the Tauber, Wertheim and Tauber-bischofsheim, where the Löwensteins came from, and Tübingen, and the monastery of Maulbronn which Hermann Hesse described in *Narziss und Goldmund*. In Stuttgart we visited Peter's childhood friend Heinrich Ledig, who had transferred the Rowohlt publishing house there for the time being, and in Munich we stayed with Hans Wallenberg in the requisitioned house of the publisher Heinrich Beck, where the beds once again were equipped with the rock-hard pillows issued to the US forces. At the Press Club, where we met the *Times* correspondent Michael Burn, there had just been a row between him and a sergeant from the Middle West, who had repeated to him the catchphrase of the Cold War, which had already broken out: "We fought the wrong war, buddy!" whereupon Michael exploded. Soon after that, he was not to be found. We asked his wife, the majestic Mary, where he was. "He went and had an angry bath." Phrases like these, rather than profound conversations, have stuck in my mind until today. And then back to Berlin, but first to Baden-Baden, that most distinguished and cosmopolitan of German towns, which I was to visit often in later years. Peter visited Otto Flake, a grumpy German writer – it was said locally that if one passed Flake's house carrying a bowl of milk, it would go sour. But one of the books I had found on my father's bookshelves in my youth was his *Horns Ring*, and I had very much admired his *Monthivermädchen*. Then to Göttingen, Goslar, the Harz Mountains. My first encounter with Gothic architecture in brick. For me this was a precious opportunity to comprehend Germany in all its characteristics.

Before we finally left Berlin, I made three more trips to Austria. At the end of October I went with Gwenol for a few days to Udine, a town we both loved deeply. Unfortunately, it was the custom at that time of year in the Friuli area to serve for dinner small birds which had been shot locally. It was only with difficulty that I could bring myself to consume those little creatures with their fragile bones, though accompanied by succulent polenta, as the Dalmontes at Trecesimo expected me to do. My gentle Gwenol, accustomed to the barbaric customs of the hunting aristocracies, and now of the *nouveaux riches*, of all countries, munched them without a qualm. Meanwhile, my Italian novel had been published in Vienna, and the publishers wanted to see my manuscript *The Fruits of Prosperity*. There was talk of currency reform, but nothing had changed as yet. Cultural pleasures were still to be enjoyed in spite of the lack of consumer goods. On my birthday I made a trip to the Kahlenberg and the Wildgrube, "deliriously happy." A few days later I found myself at a celebration of the fiftieth birthday of Alexander Lernet-Holenia, but without actually meeting him. There were concerts given by Knappertsbusch, and the return of Karajan, who conducted Bruckner's Eighth with closed eyes and without a baton. The occasion was comparable with that ritual in the Titaniapalast in Berlin. But the audience for the Vienna Philharmonic, instead of succumbing to excessive transports, greeted Karajan with the intense enthusiasm of true music lovers, rather than that which verged on the ideological or even transcendental. And in my report to *Die Welt* I was carried away into daring prophecy. The orchestra, "flourishing as of yore, but for years robbed of a regular master conductor," was now under Karajan in a position to conquer the heights of universal fame: "For the sake of this hope," I wrote, "we may forgive and forget the errors of this youthful genius."

In January 1948 we went skiing at Ehrwald, at the Drei Mohren hotel; the children were with us. I cannot express what it meant to me to see them tramping in my footsteps, and even sliding down the slopes on their little skis and attempting hesitant stem turns at the decidedly gruff commands of the instructors. While Peter went for walks, I too sped down the pistes – it was like a brief embrace more than a decade after the end of a long and happy love affair. But my love of Austria was somewhat shaken in June, in Vienna. Currency reform had been introduced, the value of money was now stable, goods were to be had in plenty, but periodicals such as the *Plan* and a number of small publishing firms went out of business. Intellectual fare had given way to the material comforts which were now available. "Vienna has become a little Zurich," I noted: not exactly wholehearted praise. During this time Alfred Ibach died, and the whole intellectual world of Vienna attended his funeral at the cemetery of Neustift am Walde. I stood to one side and wept. I have never again been capable of abandoning myself to the questionable consolation of such emotional ceremonies.

There were problems at the Wiener Verlag. Only fifty copies of my Italian book had been sold. A Professor Kurz, the chief editor, adopted an aggressive tone toward me. He had no intention of publishing my Viennese novel, set in the 1870s, in which a Croat peasant's son married into a Jewish family. "It is too early for that" were his exact words. Nevertheless, I saw Peter's *The Nuremberg Documents*, published in German under the unfortunate title *Sein Kampf*, in all the bookshop windows, even if my poor heroine Sandra's journey from the Swiss border to Naples and the Abyssinian war had now ground to a halt in Vienna. Here as in Berlin the nightclubs resounded to the song with the Yiddish lyric, "Bei Mir Bist Du Schoen," which I found embarrassing because I perceived it as a token gesture. The *Blumenkorso*, the flower fair in the Prater, which had been a dream of opulence in the thirties, now seemed to me "shabby." More flamboyant was the phenomenon of Father Diego Götz, a priest of impressive handsomeness, gesture, and presence, whose sermons filled the Dominican church with crowds of his elegant devotees. His soutanes were designed by the leading couturier Kniže, his rhetoric rehearsed with Raoul Aslan, an actor formerly of heroic and now of "heavy father" roles, and currently director of the Burgtheater. An impression of greater wisdom, spirituality and progressiveness was conveyed by a second preacher, who had even skeptics and agnostics under his spell on Sundays in the Peterskirche. Otto Mauer, a lay priest, carried conviction with the deep, even fanatical solemnity with which he addressed the consciences of his community.

As I was to report to *Die Welt*: "While standards are falling here in all walks of life, the sermons of this priest stand on an amazingly high plane. Speaking to enormous congregations from splendid baroque pulpits, he is not afraid to cite authors such as Bossuet, Pascal, and Péguy, or to handle theological concepts in a way which often goes over the heads of his listeners." And I explained why this was so: "The church could never achieve such a position of

216

intellectual power if it had had equally matched antagonists to deal with in the fields of science, journalists and politics. But during the years of Austro-fascism and National Socialism the Austrian intelligentsia was for the most part destroyed or driven out. Within the right wing, allowances had always been made for the level of the agrarian population. But even in the Socialist Party, which had given inestimable service to the workers' movement during the years of the First Republic, that holy enthusiasm has so far not reawakened. And the few intellectuals of the extreme left, having returned from emigration, are all so obsessed with their narrow-minded and intransigent doctrine that they do more harm than good."

I was seeing everything more clearly, more mercilessly on this stay in my native city. The article, which I was to write from the Karlsbaderstrasse in July, ended with bitter words. One could only, I wrote, "follow with astonishment, even with sorrow, a development which, squandering the inheritance of a highly refined culture, threatens to lead from true knowledge to smug superiority, from cosmopolitanism to *petite bourgeoisie*." Today it almost seems to me as if, shortly before we were to turn our backs "finally" on the mainland and return to England, I was already trying to break my emotional bonds with this Vienna, this Austria of mine. And if one makes up one's mind to do this, one can always find good reasons.

That point had not yet been reached. Still comparatively cheerful, unaware of what awaited me in Berlin, I was still sitting at the *Heurigen* with Hans Weigel, Ilse Aichinger, and my friends Zeno and Bobby, I was still visiting the loyal Anna and Marie, Csokor, the Magus. I was to leave at the end of the month. But on June 23 a telephone call from Peter summoned me back as a matter of urgency. The last interlude was brought abruptly to an end. The next act in the tragicomedy of world history was about to begin. It brought with it the division of the world into two camps: East and West.

12

The End of the High Life

During the past year we had desperately clung to the illusion that after a long, devastating war, we would have calm for a while and that no new conflict, let alone an armed one, menaced humanity. The "peaceful coexistence" hoped for by some seemed to others – particularly to those who had never been exposed to the daily reality of bomb attacks or of the battle fronts, but had observed all this from across the Atlantic – an impossibility. They would rather put European countries and cities at risk of deadly destruction once again in order to deprive the unquestionably evil Stalin regime of power, as long as the West still retained the advantage of nuclear power. More and more clearly, everything came down to these two basic positions. We who were at the center of activity, at the exact point of intersection of two opposing forms of government and ideologies, still believed that the worst could be prevented simply by means of human contact between representatives of these two systems. Until shortly before the split between the Western and Eastern powers, we held fast to our official tasks and to our own inclination in favor of such encounters with the potential future enemy.

But since we lived, as Koestler had put it so incisively, not only on the heroic – in this case, historic – plane, but at the same time on the trivial, everyday one, we abandoned ourselves again and again with gusto to the excitements and distractions of this heterogeneous, polyglot society to which, for the time being, we belonged. In May 1947, the highly gifted publisher and newspaperman Helmut Kindler and the beautiful and clever Nina Raven celebrated their marriage with a party where everything except an unbridgeable opposition to the convictions or dogmas personified in Berlin found its expression. Kindler, after all, had been summoned immediately after the end of the war by some former comrades in the Resistance, Herrnstadt and

Erpenbeck, who had emigrated to the Soviet Union, to the editorial offices of the *Berliner*, the first Russian-licensed newspaper in Berlin, although in fact he left it after a few weeks to become editor-in-chief of the *Tagesspiegel*. His links with these old companions certainly still existed, and presumably they too were invited to his wedding.

Not long before that, Edouard Roditi and his mother had installed themselves in Berlin "with all the comforts of Manhattan," as I noted, and began to give big parties. A brilliant essay of Roditi's on Italo Svevo in Cyril Connolly's journal *Horizon* and his connections with the old Austria had prompted me to write to him in New York. At the beginning of January 1945 I received a lengthy reply in which he, for his part, praised my essay on Alain-Fournier's *Le grand Meaulnes* and incidentally gave me that first news of Moravia which I have already quoted. "I hope," he ended, "to hear from you from time to time, in the manner of the eighteenth century, as though there were no war, or rather as though all that only existed as an excuse for intelligent reflections (and if we had handled things in that way for the last fifteen years, instead of pondering over them à la D. H. Lawrence or à la Ernest Hemingway, we could have brought them under control in an intelligent way, of that I am certain)." From this correspondence there had resulted a friendship with one of the most cosmopolitan and original of all spirits, a friendship which was constantly renewed in several European cities and has lasted until today.

At the end of May, we often met Gottfried Bermann-Fischer at Peter Suhrkamp's house in the Zehlendorfer Forststrasse. He had come to Berlin from America for the first time in order to redefine his business relationship with his friend Suhrkamp, who had faithfully looked after the S. Fischer publishing house for him during the dark years. I found "Goffi," as I too was to call him later, to be a man of great charisma, very calm, composed, and pleasant in his demeanor, who even in his outward appearance movingly reminded me of my father in his best years. I had no idea then of the regrettable circumstances in which Samuel Fischer's heirs – his daughter Brigitte or "Tutti" and her husband Gottfried – would later sever their connections with Suhrkamp, or of how much I would have to do in later years with Goffi and Tutti.

Our encounters with Peter Suhrkamp, before he left Berlin toward the end of 1947 in order to establish S. Fischer Verlag in

Frankfurt by agreement with Bermann-Fischer, were revealing in many ways. A man of indubitable importance, who was never quite able to conceal the obstinate self-righteousness behind his often humorous manner, he struck us as a creature of strange contradictions. He had not simply hated but deeply despised the Nazis. He had made a point of attending Samuel Fischer's funeral, and had spent a long time in a concentration camp. At the same time, there were flaws in his character. Flesch, who had been living in Berlin when Hitler seized power, once told us how quickly Suhrkamp had split up with his Jewish mistress at that time, in marked contrast to the wonderful behavior of Änne Ullstein. She had been going through the process of divorce from her husband at the time and had immediately cancelled the proceedings in order to bring him through the evil years safe and sound, if not preserved from humiliation. Her friendship with Mirl Suhrkamp – the latter's sister incidentally was Ina Seidel, who for her part had adopted a far from negative attitude to the regime – seemed to us close and cordial. Often, to the embarrassment of their husbands, we saw the two women laughing and tippling together until late into the night, and more than once, Mirl, her stamina in the end not quite equal to her friend's, would collapse under the table and have to be taken home, not without difficulty.

It was becoming clearer to us every day how many shades and gradations of thought and behavior there had been toward the Nazi regime on the part of the intellectuals who had remained in Germany. Even after long imprisonment or persecution of one kind or another, it was possible to be infected by some of the mental clichés adopted by that diabolical ideology. The "quiet ones in the country," for example, Ernst Wiechert with his radiant halo of hair, and Hans Carossa, the solitary country doctor, despite their well-established abhorrence of the Nazis, were surrounded by the aura of the sublime, unworldly loner which the regime, otherwise so rigid, liked to bestow upon its creative artists. Once and for all, we got out of the habit of generalizing. We learned to judge, and if possible not to condemn, each person by his or her individual inclinations toward resolution, steadfastness, or quite simply a sense of morality. Very soon after my arrival in Berlin, Sebastian Haffner and Eckart Peterich had come to visit us together. Haffner lived very near us in Wimbledon, and his daughter, like ours, attended the local Ursuline convent school, yet we

220

had not visited him more than once or twice when in London. It was typical of the unifying climate of Berlin, however, that he came to see us as soon as he arrived there. In 1938, he had finally succeeded in taking the plunge into lasting exile in England which he had long planned. There he soon gained high esteem as a contributor to the *Observer* and as editor, with Koestler and Orwell, of a highly regarded series of militant publications.

"Ecki" Peterich had been Peter's friend from his youth in Hellerau. We learned that he had spent the war in Florence with his Italian wife and children, but had had to make certain concessions to the German comrades in arms – once, out of dire necessity and in order to protect his family, he had marched in their self-glorifying processions. Never, never did we hold this against him. There were families in Germany, clans of scholars or artists, among them the Peterichs, whose revulsion from their brutal and soul-destroying rulers was so ineradicable, so deep-rooted, that despite occasional concessions, forced from them under the greatest duress, their moral status could never be called into question.

At the beginning of August there came from London the distressing news of Tetta Flesch-Brunningen's death at the early age of fifty. I wrote a long letter of condolence to Flesch and asked my mother to get in touch with him and see if she could be of any help to him. We soon learned that he had gone to Italy, to Forte dei Marmi, at the invitation of the Peterichs, whom he also had known for many years. I wrote to Mimi: "Flesch has always been a faun; Italy suits him, and he will rediscover something there that perhaps he has lost in the meantime." For all his grief for the wife he had lost, he managed to recover his spirits, encouraged by the admiring affection of the Peterichs' youngest daughter, who accompanied him on mountain walks through the marble quarries and the Pania. After this, the correspondence between him in London and myself in Berlin continued uninterrupted.

This was a decisive time for me. I was all set to take up a new career. From August 1947 *Die Welt*, the newspaper founded four months earlier in Hamburg, began to produce a separate Berlin edition. Peter became its editor-in-chief and asked me to take the post of theater critic. I had already done a great deal of writing in Berlin: reports for the *New Statesman* and other English periodicals, articles in

German for magazines and newspapers in Berlin and the Viennese *Turm* and *Neues Österreich*. I had turned my journal notes for 1946 into a little book in English, which was now to be called *Return after the Flood*, but had not yet found a publisher for it, and had translated part of my *Fruits of Prosperity* into German. I had not written any theater reviews since October 1933, when I had sent an article on Erika Mann's cabaret "Die Pfeffermühle" to the *Neue Freie Presse* in Vienna. Now this exercise was to become a regular activity which was to continue for almost forty years.

What had I let myself in for? How had I presumed to adopt the dubious office of judge? Much later, Thomas Bernhard referred to the characteristic and conscious intention of the critic as "walking over corpses." Two anecdotes Flesch had told me much earlier illustrate this. One was about a critic who used to introduce himself in the coffee house with the words: "My name is Holzbock, I can do you great harm." And an actor Flesch knew had once looked through the peephole in the curtain at a first night and, seeing the critic Alfred Kerr sitting in one of the front rows, had promptly thrown up in the wings. This same Kerr, I later learned, had attributed to the critic the qualities of objectivity and arbitrary judgment in equal measure. His own verdicts were said to be influenced by both hate and love, and the tools of his trade were the catapult and the harp. If I doubted the dignity of this profession, I could at least refer to the list of my predecessors such as Lessing, Kleist, Schlegel, and Fontane, not to speak of the equally merciless and mutually antagonistic Alfred Kerr and Karl Kraus.

None of this troubled me in mid-1947. I undertook the task with pleasure, going to first nights sometimes up to five times a week in both the western and eastern sectors of Berlin. Afterward, untiring in the fresh Brandenburg air, I would often write my reviews well into the small hours. I was excited by the opportunity to express opinions of all sorts within the framework of a theater review, but certainly also by the consciousness of precipitately acquired power. Dressed by the Berlin couturiers Noecker und Lutz – with fabrics bought by Mimi in London with her own coupons, although they were always trying to persuade me to buy excessively glittery creations – and my hair piled up in stylish constructions by Sibylle, I would make my appearance in the Berlin playhouses with a foolish self-confidence which was constantly reignited by this city's obsession with its theater and the obsequious reverence it accorded to the authority of critics.

This theater, however, was not to be sneered at. In an almanac published the following year by Herbert Ihering entitled *Theaterstadt Berlin* – "Berlin, City of Theaters" – I was to praise this obsession: "In the midst of the most desolate metropolis in the world, among grey and bleached skeletons of houses, theaters of a splendor such as a Londoner might seek in vain at home still rise, and are rising again. What is he to think? Are these deceptive façades, Potemkin villages intended to simulate a healthy bourgeois life? No, they are not. They are reality itself, the only one that remains. The scenery of the theater has replaced life... Here alone there is still eating and drinking, carefree love and needless death, strutting and warbling, cajoling, laughing... And the theater has not been slow to recognize its own power. Only consider: who owns this city? Actors are the tribunes of the people here, and critics are the magistrates, holding sway through terror."

The same almanac reminds me today who replaced reality for Berliners during those years: all the great actors who, as I have said, had towered above the rest since the Weimar days, or those who, more or less untouched by the infamous occupants of the government boxes at the theater who heaped praise upon them after the performance, had gained fame in more recent years. Paul Wegener and Aribert Wäscher, Elsa Wagner and Käthe Dorsch, Gustaf Gründgens and Ernst Busch – they were all still there, joined by Siegmar Schneider, Wolfgang Lukschy, Antje Weisgerber, and Horst Caspar. These actors were to be seen in the Eastern sector. On the Western stages one could still see Roma Bahn, Axel von Ambesser, Walter Franck, and now there were Joana Maria Gorvin, Ernst Schröder, Hildegard Knef, Michael Tellering – oh, so many! Occasionally they would change places – this was still perfectly possible. But how spellbinding were the productions in which I saw them, how I trembled with emotion at a staging of *Woyzeck* produced by Wolfgang Langhoff, which took me by storm and drew me back again to the heights of German drama from those of the English stage which I had so long believed unsurpassable! I wept, I could not sleep that night. At the same theater, the Kammerspiele, I was stirred in a gentler fashion by Yevgeny Schwarz's Hans Christian Andersen adaptation, *Der Schatten*, directed by Gründgens – I can see the lead players, Lukschy and Schneider, before me to this day.

My memoirs are threatening to degenerate. Only one more remark: if anything legitimizes the despicable office of critic, it is his own passion for the art, literature, or theater which he presumes to judge. And this is a passion I have possessed all my life since, at eight years old, I was taken to the Vienna Volksoper to see the fairytale musical show *Schneewittchen im Donautal* (Snow White in the Danube Valley). But my hubris grew. As early as June, even before *Die Welt* was founded, I wrote to Mimi: "I am once again enjoying some private fame here. They say that if I were a theater critic everyone would be dreadfully afraid of me... The theater is the state religion in Berlin." Soon afterward, I noted in puzzlement: "Serious men are taking notice of what I have to say about Shakespeare." And then, boasting once more: "At the moment I am one of the stars of theater criticism here, and since the theater constitutes the whole of Berlin's intellectual life and is dominated by a small coterie, I have become one of the foremost highbrows and am read everywhere and complimented by all." Four months later, I was blowing my own trumpet even more loudly: "I don't want to brag, but I must tell you what Peter told me yesterday; his cultural editor said to him, 'I must tell you that your wife is the most famous woman in Berlin, everywhere one hears that she is the wittiest woman we have ever had in journalism, and that her reviews are by far the best.'" Earlier I had also reported to Mimi in a slightly embarrassed tone: *"Tout vient à qui sait attendre* – now they are even calling me beautiful. They must have a strange idea of beauty here."

How flimsy all this was, I am well aware and do not need to be told. Peter's arts editor had every reason to want to flatter him. And to give the palm to me in preference to Friedrich Luft, whose reviews were appearing in the *Neue Zeitung* at the same time, was sheer nonsense. But whose head would not have been turned by such compliments? At any rate, for Mimi, who had stayed behind alone in London – Lonny was still in the country – it was a comfort to know that, far away from her, I was at least successful in my career. We all, in any case, knew that this period in our lives that I was describing to her would be brief and limited, and that even my splendid wardrobe would not last. Once, asking Mimi to send me new fabrics, I assured her: "Later, *'in Kuchl,'* I will not need or want to wear any special clothes." This referred to a saying of an old Bohemian cook in Vienna, who was asked by her mistress whether she had been aware of an earth tremor that had just taken place, and replied reproachfully: *"Bei uns in Kuchl wird ma was hör'n!"* ("Us lot in the kitchen aren't likely to hear anything!") And we wanted at any price to go back into the *"Kuchl"*; we had made the firm decision that the children were to grow up in England. Even if we were to live on the fringes of English society, of English literature and journalism, we were not prepared to settle down again in the midst of a community that had so recently driven out or destroyed the likes of us. And we would not be ready to do so for a very long time.

For indeed, now and then, a shiver would run down our backs when highly respected Germans, unintentionally and even unconsciously, betrayed that archaic fundamental attitude which was still deeply rooted in them. One December evening we saw the actor and director Fritz Kortner sitting with Paul Wegener in a front row at the Theater am Kurfürstendamm, at a performance of *A Midsummer Night's Dream*. I believe it was during his first stay in Berlin since the Nazi time. And soon afterward he told us, himself shuddering at the memory, how Jürgen Fehling, meeting him again for the first time, had implored him to return to the Berlin stage under his direction: "You must come back to us, Kortner, we need your black seed." Even today the implications of that remark horrify me. And in quite a different way I am now retrospectively disturbed at the realization of how shaky all our standards had already become. We had of course read *Mephisto*, Klaus Mann's *roman à clef*, when it came out. Nevertheless, we not only admired without reservation Gustaf Gründgens' new and indeed fascinating work at the Deutsches Theater, but we even had a very pleasant chat with him at a party given in his honor by the conciliatory Mike Josselson – no doubt as pleasant as the conversations he had had with his protector, Hermann Goering. "This evening," I wrote to Mimi, "we are having dinner with Käthe Dorsch," the same Dorsch who had had a good relationship with the same Goering and occasionally asked him for clemency toward a Jew under threat. What were we really to think of our own characters when, after Georg Honigmann had attacked Peter in the most vicious way for some time in his Eastern-sector newspaper *Berlin am Mittag*, we were now on friendly terms with him again as if this and his betrayal of us and the British had never happened?

Was it conciliation, tolerance, insight, resignation – or a throwback to those blurred, smudged last few years of the first republic in Austria? Just as we had then, we felt it to be necessary, indeed certain and therefore reassuring, that we would escape from these circumstances in order to live in an England where we would not be oppressed by such dilemmas. After these Berlin years, however, we were not to be able to return free from reproach to our second home; this was clear to us at, for example, the First German Writers' Congress in October 1947, which had been approved by all four occupying powers, and which had probably been initiated by the unlikable Major Dymshits, but whose first session took place in the Hebbeltheater, in the British sector.

The Russians had sent three of their most noted authors as observers: Valentin Katayev, Vselovod Vishnevski, and Boris Gorbatov. Among the German authors under their aegis were Anna Seghers, whom I still fervently revered, and Johannes R. Becher, Günther Weisenborn, Friedrich Wolf, and the young Stephan Hermlin. The representatives of the West included the grand old lady Ricarda Huch, Elisabeth Langgässer, and Axel Eggebrecht. But neither the French, the Americans, nor our English colleagues had brought over any distinguished literary figures. From London, there was our dear friend Hermon Ould, the general secretary of International PEN, but none of his literary lights had accompanied him, only the political writer H. N. Brailsford and the stalwart German émigré Wilhelm Unger. What a missed opportunity to document the wealth of outstanding English authors, which then seemed to us more impressive than that of any other nation! Much has already been written about the appearance of Melvin J. Lasky at this congress, which at a stroke catapulted the young, previously unknown American into a blaze of international attention, and he will probably have reported on it himself by the time this book appears. Katayev's furious polemics against him, as well as against André Gide, who, after initial praise of the Soviet Union, had radically altered his opinion, is still vivid in my memory – as are Edwin Redslob's movingly old-fashioned plea for a new world literature in the spirit of Goethe, and Peter's denunciation of the "technically inadequate standard" of the new German "*Schrifttum*" (literature – a term which had meanwhile become taboo), which once again cost him the sympathy of his Berlin audience. He had, in his well-meaning but didactic way, really intended his words to act as an incentive.

With good reason I will desist from recounting in detail the discussions at this conference, or of those at the dozens of writers' congresses which I was to attend in the course of my later life. I must however report on the totally incredible banquet given by the Russians for all the participants at this congress, a dinner which had a particularly surreal effect in the Berlin of that time, still one of comparative hardship. The enormous table groaned under the weight of bowls of caviar and seafood salad, of the most luxurious dishes and wines, the mountains of butter from which, on the advice of the initiated, we took spoonfuls to line our stomachs in defense against the innumerable little glasses of vodka that had to be drained in an endless series of toasts, which caused one famished German author after another to end up under the table, like Suhrkamp's Mirl. Meanwhile the tones of a balalaika orchestra were drowned by the hum of conversation and the ever more fervent invitations of our hosts to yet another toast to the glorious Red Army, to the King of England, to – I can remember no more. It took us several days to recover from this gargantuan feast.

At the end of November Kingsley Martin returned to Berlin for five days, during which he had discussions with several prominent German politicians as well as with leading representatives of the occupying forces. One evening, from nine until midnight, we held a political salon at which Jakob Kaiser, Ernst Reuter, Arno Scholz, and a man called Buschmann, an *éminence grise* of the new German administration, were present. I wrote to Mimi: "We had to translate everything, in between serving gin and fruit juice and sandwiches and cakes and coffee." But Kingsley also conferred with Kurt Schuhmacher and Ferdinand Friedensburg. He came to Josselson's party for Gründgens, and several times visited the Press Club to obtain further information from the *Observer* correspondent Robert Stephens and the British press officer Betty Morgan. Heinz Ullstein invited us to the "Greif" bar, and Kingsley accompanied us, to watch a rather pitiful strip-tease which for him probably had overtones of Christopher Isherwood's *Goodbye to Berlin*. I was his constant escort, taken as ever with his charm and vitality and the bold outline of his extraordinary profile. "Let's be sensible," said Kingsley with a sigh, when I collected him from his hotel for the last time, to take him to the airport in pouring rain. His visit was soon forgotten. A party to which The McLaren of McLaren invited all the British on the occasion of the wedding of a British friend, Susan Heald, and Susan's reception for hundreds of people after the church ceremony, which we all attended, obliterated the days with Kingsley.

Looking back, it seems to me that at that time the festive activities, the whole social merry-go-round which turned unceasingly, were taking on an even more hectic pace, if that were possible – in a kind of last-minute panic which was decidedly premature. I was to spend another eight months in Berlin, but before the end of 1947 many Germans, Peter Suhrkamp among the first, sensing a definite deterioration in relations among the Allies, were turning their backs on the city, and many familiar faces among the British and Americans were also disappearing overnight. Christmas came, and Peter invited the entire staff of *Die Welt*, from the chief editors to the typesetters and printers, to a party in the Karlsbaderstrasse. The string section of the city's opera company orchestra played Haydn and Mozart, then the carpets were rolled back and a dancing party in true Berlin style began and continued into the early hours of the morning. Peter, who was certainly popular with his immediate colleagues, although frequently condemned by others not on close terms with him as a "ruthless re-educator," gave himself the air of "a real newspaper tycoon," as I wrote to Mimi.

Just before New Year's Eve, Hedwig's husband suddenly appeared at the door. He had been released from captivity by the British and looked plump and well fed. A week earlier, Frau Kuhn had burst into tears because her stepson, formerly a sturdy young man, who had likewise been sent home by the Russians, had died of exhaustion after his return. At the time, I complained to my mother: "It is very difficult to keep up one's hopes of reaching an understanding with the Russians because, although war is to be avoided at all costs, we can see here that the Russians are really doing everything possible to forfeit the goodwill of their patrons. This is really very sad. But at least we can't reproach ourselves with having promoted a break with them if we now keep out of the worst of the hate campaign."

At the Press Club, just before New Year's Eve, Betty Morgan, of whom we had recently grown fond, took out her pendulum and demonstrated her occult arts to us. She was a pretty, robust woman, of mixed Welsh and Cornish origin, which, she told us, gave her authority as a witch. She let her pendulum spin over photographs or personal possessions of people about whom we wanted information, and not only did it take different directions for men and women, but it behaved in an uncanny way in cases about which Betty could not have known any details. A few weeks after the writers' congress the great Ricarda Huch, who had opened it with such an impassioned speech, died in the Taunus. When we showed Betty a photograph of Ricarda Huch with Peter, the pendulum stopped moving, and Betty said that this person was no longer alive. Held over a photograph of my mother it moved restlessly and irregularly. Betty said that this woman was threatened by illness. If only we had taken notice of her magical insight! It may well be that the pendulum was indicating a physical process in Mimi which was to take her from us within a little more than three years.

We spent New Year's Eve at the Komische Oper, now restored; indescribable splendor in the midst of the ruins. Walter Felsenstein had put on *Die Fledermaus*, and had succeeded in creating a production of such intoxicating charm that everyone – not just one Viennese woman in the audience – forgot time and place and was transported triumphantly into the *belle époque* of the Austrian Empire. Hülgert, the bearded buffo tenor who played Eisenstein, won my heart, as years later Cesare Siepi was to do as Don Giovanni – these were relapses into my childish infatuation with a stage presence. Afterward, for a change, we did not go to the Möwe, the Seagull, the East Berlin actors' bar, where we had often ended the evening on our visits to this sector, but to the Western Bühnenklub, the Stage Club. We were already cautiously retreating into our own reserves.

It was by no means certain, I warned my mother at the beginning of the new year, that the Allies would not have to withdraw from Berlin. This possibility may have been under consideration at that time at the highest level and have seeped through to the lower ranks of the administration and the press. In that case the inhabitants of the Western sectors would for some time have had good cause to fear the definitive departure of their protectors. All the more reason for us to preserve for the time being an unaltered attitude to the Soviet occupiers and the Berliners who were subordinate to them, in order to stress that there was no immediate danger. Just as we had gone to the glittering opening at the Komische Oper, we continued to attend the premieres in the Eastern sector: at the Deutsches Theater, the Kammerspiele, the Theater am Schiffbauerdamm. We also visited writers on the other side. When we drove to see Johannes R. Becher at Pankow, we had to pass through a strictly guarded cordon, because not only Becher's villa but also the residences of the prominent Soviet officials were in this district.

To me Becher, now a committee member designate of a new German PEN, was known as one of the legendary figures from the early days of Expressionism, who had then, like Brecht and Gottfried Benn, gone in separate ideological directions: for me a logical consequence of their extremism in literature. I also knew about the tragedy of his youth, the attempted suicide pact in which the girl died and Becher survived. Now he seemed to me anything but a tragic figure, rather a robust, self-confident man, full of Bavarian joviality. It was said that, when Becher went to Aarenshoop on the North Sea, as he often did for relaxation, he would stand on the beach and look out at the sea like the "King of the Baltic." He and his wife Lilly used to entertain us with good and plentiful food. We never discussed our ideological opinions, let alone differences; I believe our main topic of conversation was the first stirrings of German postwar literature. Rather than his ideas about how the latter might best be guided into the channels of a Socialist realism, my main memory of Becher, who later became Minister of Culture in the German Democratic Republic, is of his great partiality to stuffed cabbage. This was prepared by Frau Kuhn and me with great care and plenty of tomato sauce, and he would order it in advance and consume it with the greatest relish whenever he visited us in the Karlsbaderstrasse.

Those who left Berlin during those months before the great breakup were promptly replaced by new arrivals. A few Swiss friends had recently joined our circle, Manuel Gasser and the couple Gody and Alex Suter, who soon became regular guests of ours at home, usually together with the Lufts. Among the British we often saw Bob Stephens and his wife Taqui – who came from Aleppo, but had spent her childhood in England and was the model for Arthur Ransome's

Nancy in *Swallows and Amazons* – as well as Betty Morgan and the faithful John Peet. It seemed, however, as though we had always moved in exclusively German-speaking circles, especially when, after major first nights at the West Berlin theaters, we invited the entire company to a celebration in our apartment, and also asked, for preference, the polyglots among the British and Americans, such as Edouard Roditi and Mike Josselson. And then a close and intimate friendship, which was to last less than half a year, developed between us and one of London's most outstanding writers. But first, on the seventh of January, at the Hebbeltheater, which was licensed by the Americans, an artistic event took place which, in its theme as well as its accompanying circumstances, signaled the disintegration, approaching ever more closely, into a Western and an Eastern world.

This time the impetus came from the French. During all this time, despite their grandiose presence, which Peter had gently mocked, at the Allies' first victory parade, they had played a rather restrained role. The newspaper *Der Kurier*, which was licensed by their cultural officer Bourdain, was well thought of; we visited their sector and repeatedly watched the wonderful films they presented, including *La Symphonie pastorale* and, again and again, *Les Enfants du paradis*, which I must have seen at least three times in Berlin, and about ten times since then. But now the French produced an ace from their sleeve. Jürgen Fehling was to direct a production of Jean-Paul Sartre's *Les Mouches*, with the beautiful, highly gifted actress Joana Maria Gorvin as Electra, and the author was expected to visit Berlin during the run of the play. And so, after the German premiere of the piece in Düsseldorf, Existentialism, which had come into being during the years of German occupation of Paris, out of a strange fusion of French *clarté* and Heidegger's mysticism of "being," made its spectacular entry into Berlin.

I have never experienced an evening at the theater which aroused such violent dissension, which created such an exceptional sensation, which polarized opinions in such a pronounced way, even at Thomas Bernhard's last premiere at the Burgtheater in Vienna, his *Heldenplatz*. For weeks, tickets had been offered and sold on the black market for 500 marks. In the Soviet-controlled press a hate campaign against the "anti-humanism" of the play had likewise already begun. In the "East–West war of nerves," as I called it in an article for the *New Statesman*, feelings were becoming heated about a conflict which was to be played out on the stage, but had its counterpart in bitter reality. Although my review in *Die Welt* brought me particular praise from German readers, what I wrote for the *Statesman* under the heading "Sartre among the Germans" gives a clearer picture of what took place.

The first and most important thesis of the play, according to the organ of the unity party, the SED, a week before the first night, consisted of deep contempt for humanity in general. Here existentialism encountered the "life rules" of Hitler and Alfred Rosenberg (a leading exponent of Nazi doctrine). In its core, *Les Mouches*, like all Sartre's philosophy, exposed "the rottenness of social conditions." It was "a cynical and desperate attempt, in accordance with the great crisis of our age, which is nothing but the fatal crisis of a declining system, to create a myth of death and terror." Existentialism, according to this periodical, was destined to persuade the bourgeois intelligentsia to remain on the sinking ship and go down with it. The play did no service to the democratic reform of Germany – and the argument that art must be apolitical could no longer be accepted in this context.

The *Kurier* promptly responded. "In a page and a half of rather sketchy argument," as I described it to the *Statesman*, "which calls upon the support of Aeschylus, Montaigne, Machiavelli, Schiller, Kant, Hegel, Marx, Heidegger and Camus, the attempt is made to proclaim Sartre a moralist and existentialism as a new form of ethics. 'Existentialism is humanism' is the formula. And finally it is provocatively stressed that those who maintain that Sartre's teachings represent despair, nihilism, barricades against existence, and he himself decadence and annihilation, must be reminded how often he has announced his intention to help modern Europeans to 'rebuild their life in freedom and labor.'"

"Prepared in this contradictory and not altogether enlightening fashion," I wrote, "Berlin theatergoers arrived for a dramatized lesson in philosophy." Future Isherwoods, I suggested, would have more to say about this and other Berlin first nights, which were imbued with a strange, vital tension, as though the counter-currents of European thinking were meeting exactly at this point in time and space.

Moreover, I commented, the director, Fehling, was an extravagant genius, who, like Furtwängler, exercised a magnetic and somewhat irrational power over a large segment of the German public and who had been entrusted with a production here after an absence of eighteen months. As a rationalist, however, the showpiece of new French thought did not do much for me. Following Giraudoux, Anouilh, O'Neill, and Gerhart Hauptmann the author had "hung his patchwork of theory on the coat-hanger of classical tragedy." The "fundamental-ontological guilt" symbolized by the plague of flies could, according to Sartre, be eliminated from the world only by Orestes' cheerful act of murder. "The most cowardly murderer is the one who repents." To present such dangerous ideas at this time on a German stage did seem after all rather a dubious undertaking.

The success of the play, whose message was by no means acceptable to all who saw it, had been due to the intensive efforts of the director, and his attempt to present it as a gigantic Greek Grand Guignol. The critics had not failed to acknowledge this on the following day, but they had unanimously rejected the existentialism that it exemplified. *Die Welt*, as I, quite improperly quoting my own words, told the *New Statesman*, had called this way of thinking an eclectic philosophy which had in common with Christianity – which condemned it – the concept of original sin, but not that of absolute morality, and in common with materialism – which disapproved of it – an atheism which was as antiquated as its metaphysical antithesis. *Les Mouches*, I wrote, had been written to propagate a teaching which appeared neither true or useful as an explanation of the world or as an ethical doctrine, but in its ambivalence and its contempt for life threatened to confuse those spirits which had until recently been corrupted.

Yes, I had the gall to cast doubt on Sartre and Existentialism at a time when the triumphant career of this author and this philosophy, which was to span many decades, had only just begun. I did not agree with Peter, who felt that I exaggerated the danger of these intellectual pastimes for the Germans: after all, the play had been performed for the first time in 1943 in the Théâtre de la Cité in Paris, with the permission of the occupying forces and in a way which left it open to a wide range of interpretations. And when Sartre himself came to Berlin with Simone de Beauvoir and took part in discussions with his adherents and opponents alike on various platforms, I did not alter my opinion: "In the course of discussion he soon lured his

Communist and Catholic antagonists into his own sphere, in which, with remarkable casuistry, he entangled them in new definitions in the context of a purely existentialist philosophy. Before anyone had grasped that he was avoiding the fundamental argument, he had disappeared, leaving behind only the vague memory of his rhetorical brilliance... Whatever other opportunities Sartre may have elsewhere to be regarded as a modern prophet, he has not asserted his authority in the cockpit of Europe. Between the East and the West, the Germans succeeded in misunderstanding him to such an extent that nothing was left of him." And this, I concluded in the *Statesman*, was in its way a welcome result. Presumably my refusal to recognize Sartre as a convincing opponent to Soviet cultural politics was seen as yet another sign of weakness toward communism by my later detractors. But "standing [not sitting] between two stools" – a maxim of Ernst Fischer's, which he himself followed only belatedly – clearly seemed, even then, the only possible position for me.

In February, my journal relates, Rex Warner and his wife and a couple called Clark came to dinner with us. Later Roditi joined us – "altogether a stimulating, delightful party." Rex was known as the man "who had introduced Kafka to the British novel." He was a member of the "Auden generation" – that group of young, mostly leftist writers who gained fame in the Thirties, which also included Stephen Spender, Cecil Day Lewis, and Louis MacNeice – and the only British writer to devote himself to an abstract, allegorical, parabolic prose in the manner of Franz Kafka; he was highly regarded among his contemporaries for his novels *The Professor*, *The Aerodrome* and *The Wild Goose Chase*, but also for his extremely sensitive lyrical verse. He was a tall but by no means bulky man, attractive in that serious, if not actually somber way, yet always tending toward bursts of cheerfulness, that has always entranced me, and with a furrowed brow despite his comparative youth – he was then in his early forties. Frances, his wife, was very gentle and a little sad, which we attributed at first to the incurable disease of her only daughter. With this girl and their two sons, the Warners had left Athens, where Rex was director of the British Council after the war, to take up the same post in Berlin. And a relationship soon developed between them and us that led to almost daily meetings. "More and more," I noted, "I am impressed by his modesty, his wisdom, his wit."

Rex, with or without Frances, now joined in all our visits and enterprises. On Sundays we went to the nearby lake, Wannsee, for picnics with our children, and we brought all our British, American and English-speaking friends to his first lecture on T. S. Eliot. In our long three- or four-way conversations we felt we were entering belatedly into that community of illustrious young spirits which we had seen, as it were from the front stalls, at play in the literary-political arena of London of the "pink decade." We had met Day Lewis and Spender, I had recently introduced John Lehmann at a meeting in Vienna where he was to speak, and many years later I was to enjoy a respectful acquaintance with the master himself, W. H. Auden. But here, in close contact with Rex, we were catching up with part of the development of English intellectuals, just as with our children we were catching up with the early stages of an English life. These months in Berlin, so rich in external events, also brought with them for me such a mass of exceptional human contacts – above all with Rex – that, looking back on my life, I regard them as the most important period of all.

That spring and summer of 1948, the most varied visitors seemed magnetically attracted to the already deeply split, if not yet irreconcilably divided city. "Lunch at the Press Club with the Stephens and Lufts and a man called Hildesheimer." The last-named, a shy young man who had just returned from English exile, turned out to be a schoolfriend of Peter's youngest brother Felix at the Oden-waldschule, and soon made his appearance in the Karlsbaderstrasse. Berthold Viertel appeared and brightened our meetings with his verbal fire.

Just before the arrival of Klaus Mann, I succeeded in bringing my mother over for fifteen days in April. She had now finally secured British citizenship, had a British passport and, as a relative of an official of the Control Commission, was granted permission for a flight to Berlin, otherwise practically impossible to obtain. Although the Russians had introduced new, irksome restrictions on travel toward the end of March, she arrived safely. My instructions to her before she left London had their ludicrous side: "Give the porter a tip of about one cigarette per suitcase, but at least three. In the buffet car some people discreetly leave a cigarette under the plate." And also: "You can have your hair done every day here if you like." Lastly, encouraging my childishly anxious Mimi to behave like an adult: "Now show that you are a *Weltbürgerin*, a cosmopolitan, and worthy of your new nationality."

She enormously enjoyed those few days, accompanying us on the rounds of our duties and pleasures. We showed her the tragic sights of the city, beginning, as with every new arrival, with the ruins of the Reich Chancellery; we sat in the warm spring weather in the gardens of the clubs and the cafés on the Kurfürstendamm, which particularly appealed to her; we took her to a Gorky play at the Theater am Schiffbauerdamm and to the enchanting *Fledermaus* at the Komische Oper, to the Ulenspiegel cabaret, and to *Eugene Onegin* at the State Opera, once again in East Berlin. The Warners too soon made friends with Mimi, who was still pretty and charming, and were pleased when we brought her along to our picnics. Our staff spoiled her; we had a party for fifty people while she was with us; and when, at the end of the month, we took her to Cumberland House and the bus for Helmstedt, our farewell was the more carefree because we assured her that within the year we would quite definitely be back in London. A few days before Mimi left, there came the first significant warning in our immediate circle of the process of crumbling away that had already begun: Taqui Stephens was breaking up her household and going home with the children. I felt it was "the beginning of the end" and so described it in my journal.

The "games on the edge of the abyss," to quote the title of a book by Paoletta Masino that was one of my early favorites, continued. For Klaus Mann, who soon afterward arrived in Berlin, we arranged the same outings, but also a number of more high-powered gatherings and discussions. Once, at the beginning of his stay, he spent an evening alone with us, and on another occasion we also invited his friend Fritz Landshoff and the Bechers. One afternoon he gave a lecture on André Gide, with Peter, the French cultural official Lusset, Roditi, and Melvin Lasky on the platform. Afterward we went to lunch at the Amerikahaus in Zehlendorf, where we met Suhrkamp and a number of other leading intellectuals. This close contact with Klaus Mann, weary, melancholy, endlessly endearing, conjured up, this time for me alone, a piece of the past, a fragment of Peter's youth of which I had heard so much. Flesch later remarked ironically that I had only married Peter because he had been a friend of Thomas Mann's children. There was in fact some truth in that – for the aura of the Berlin of the twenties, which had impressed me so much in Peter's early novel *Fertig mit Berlin* really was bound up with the circle of Klaus and Erika Mann, of Gründgens and Pamela Wedekind, and had still surrounded Peter when he came to Vienna for the first time as an émigré from Paris.

The most ambivalent memory of this visit by Klaus Mann is of an evening at Manuel Gasser's apartment in the Helmstedter Strasse, at a very mixed gathering of about forty people, as usual a cross section of all nations, which included an episode that embarrassed everyone present. Gasser, that most cultured of all Swiss, for many years arts editor of the *Weltwoche* and later editor of the art magazine *Du*, was an imposing, vigorous figure, with a little moustache as worn by gentlemen riders, and for me he was the model of a socially elevated William Tell. But it was always rather disturbing for us – not out of prudery, but as a matter of taste – that he never came to dinner alone, but always in the company of an often grubby youth, a child of the Berlin slums, whom he described as his chauffeur and who sat with him among all the other guests. This time Manuel, in an astonishing misjudgment of his friend Klaus, had prepared a surprise for him which totally misfired. In the middle of the animated conversation he interrupted with a request for silence to hear a boys' choir. About ten somewhat charmless brats burst into the room, lined up in rows and began to sing – mostly crude popular songs in barely comprehensible local dialect. Klaus Mann, who was sitting next to us, gave us a startled glance and muttered: "This really is quite dreadful!" We could only hope that Gasser himself did not realize how inappropriate his tribute had been.

In May we were still visiting the East Berlin artists' club, the Möwe, and as I noted, we "talked to Langhoff and Harich about Soviet Russia" – my journal gives no further details. On the other hand, in my vanity I noted that the actor Siegmar Schneider and the opera singer A. Hülgert, who were also there, addressed me with profound respect. Meanwhile, there is no doubt as to the subject of the conversation. Four days later I wrote a lengthy polemic against Socialist realism, which was published in *Die Welt* on May 29 under the title "The Price of a Mess of Pottage." This article alone should have disabused those who later attacked me for alleged Communist sympathies during the Cold War, if they had ever read it or been willing to admit that I was at no time a henchwoman of the Third Internationale.

At the beginning of May 1948 the *Tägliche Rundschau* had reported on a discussion between "leading members of the Soviet writers' association in Moscow with some of the German intellectuals staying there as guests." These leading Russians had been Aleksandr Fadeyev and Oleksander Korniychuk, and the German intellectuals had included Stephan Hermlin, the worthy Günther Weisenborn, my revered Anna Seghers, and the same Langhoff with whom their visit had probably been discussed that evening in the Möwe. Obviously the Germans had been invited to Moscow in an attempt to make Socialist realism more palatable to them, and even the *Tägliche Rundschau* did not conceal the hesitant and cautious objections they brought forward. Hermlin, for example, while deferentially confirming to Fadeyev that his novel *The Nineteen* was a masterpiece, mildly protested at the removal of certain passages about "physiological love" in the first version of that book, which had later been cut by Fadeyev – but the author insisted on his right to carry out such "cleansing." Anna Seghers pleaded in favor of Flaubert, whose *Madame Bovary* had been condemned by Fadeyev from the standpoint of his own artistic direction, but which, as she pointed out, had helped thousands of women to avoid Emma Bovary's fate. It was no good – Fadeyev proclaimed his theses of "art as a duty," of its duty to "reform life," to "educate the reader for the morrow."

I would like to repeat at this point a few of the arguments contained in my long-forgotten polemic against the spokesmen of the theory of art which for so long exercised its all-powerful and all-destructive influence in the Soviet Union. Art in the sense of a thousand-year-old European tradition, I wrote, was not predictable *a priori* or *a posteriori*. It was not an equation to be worked out, because it was not of a purely formal nature. Anyone who wanted to force the telling of stories into one direction or another, to dam or obstruct the associative flow of the sentences, to rationalize the intuitive formulation, the metaphor which sprang to the mind as if by chance, the cross-fertilization of word and visual image, in so doing was replacing living art with a dead and empty structure. Lenin, who leapt up at a Beethoven concert and fled the scene, frightened by the sensuous magic of the music, had been more honest than his disciples.

"No – one would like to cry – be honest, and say openly that there is no room for art as we know it in your political experiment. Make a virtue of necessity. And revise your terminology. 'Art as a duty' for us is a contradiction in terms. 'Reforming life by means of art' is somewhat nearer the truth. So mint your own coins; define literature, if you will, from now on as 'aesthetic studies,' music as 'heroic harmony,' the visual arts as 'educational design.'.. But do not demand of us that we do the same... What separates the Western European from the Soviet citizen is more than his stubborn refusal to allow simplifications to be imposed upon him in the name of progress – it is the difference between skepticism and faith... The artist as priest and representative of the people, popular taste as the standard of their art – these are concepts which we in Western Europe cannot and will not share."

We were, I said, too disappointed by a series of failed experiments to be anything but skeptical toward ready-made solutions. The artists and thinkers of the West saw their duty not in service to the people, but in service to the truth – in their intellectual and artistic independence. "The only concepts which have proved unshakeable throughout changing times and ideologies are those which the Soviets have thrown overboard for the sake of a ready-made solution. Freedom of thought, objective science, inalienable human rights are the last monuments left standing in the devastated pantheons of Europe. What is rejected over there by deluded materialists is recognized here by idealistic skeptics, who are not prepared to sell their birthright, the European cultural tradition, even for a mess of pottage which satisfies all their hunger."

Read today, these words seem neither challenging nor particularly original. At that time they were a gauntlet thrown down in front of those Soviet suppressors of freedom of thought, objective science, and inalienable human rights, who were battling in their mouthpiece, the *Tägliche Rundschau*, for the souls of Berliners, of Germans, for adherents in the entire Western world. It was possible to oppose their theories. It was harder to shut oneself off from the sentimental testimony of that left-wing resistance of all shades which for years – above all at the time of "appeasement" – had been the only bulwark against fascism and National Socialism. It was one thing to defend oneself against the horrible cultural dictatorship of Fadeyev and the other sinister arbiters of art in the Soviet Union, but another to restrain oneself from emotional surrender to the battle songs of Bertolt Brecht and Hanns Eisler, so movingly sung by Kate Kühl and Ernst Busch at a celebration of Brecht, who had not yet returned home – songs like "Solidarity," which in the despairing weeks after the twelfth of February 1934 in Vienna had signified for me the only consolation, the only hope for the eventual conquest of a murderous regime.

On the day my polemic was published Peter and I, accompanied by Melvin Lasky, drove via Hamburg to Copenhagen for the annual International Congress of PEN. I have not so far mentioned this interlude because in many respects it fell outside the context of the others. We had taken Lasky with us to Copenhagen in order to introduce him to our friends in PEN – authors whom he promptly recruited as contributors to his periodical *Der Monat*, which was now in preparation. But I went off in search of lost time, to Willemoesgade 23, where I had spent half a year as a child, in the care of the generous Lundsteens. The family had not lived there for a long time; my foster parents were dead, their children had moved away. But the noble Scandinavians who were now living in the Lundsteens' apartment invited me in without ceremony to see once again the rooms where I had stirred my cocoa and, most precociously, devoured the novels of Hanns Heinz Ewers. I still have a postcard that my schoolteacher Helene Nüring had sent me in Copenhagen in 1920. I remember now that this good woman, a Gentile like her husband, in order to avoid any suspicion of Jewish origin had changed her original name of Neumann to a more Nordic-sounding Nüring. "Are you fatter yet?" she wrote, and also told me that her son Hardo was nearly ten months old – "and a kiss from Hardolein." I wonder, just by the way, whatever became of "Hardolein" Nüring.

The PEN conference in Copenhagen, the town of reddish houses and green onion-shaped church towers, of fountains and flowers, of brisk girls and dawdling waiters, proceeded fairly uneventfully. Under the influence of the little mermaid in the harbor, a mild, optimistic climate prevailed. The "German question" was solved. The center for writers in exile suggested a list which included Kästner, Langgässer, and Sternberger as well as Seghers, Becher, Friedrich Wolf, and

Ludwig Renn. Peter vouched for these "outstanding writers and upright freedom fighters." They were elected new members by acclamation. Apart from this, an abstract problem was under consideration: *langue morte* and *langue vivante*. The Frenchman Jean Schlumberger deplored the disappearance of the "intellectual, disciplined language" of Pascal, Flaubert, and Gide and the rise of a "hurried, direct language, burdened by unpurified feelings" as used by a Sartre or a Céline. What interested me was the equation of these two, which at that time and place went unchallenged. Moral differences were clearly of no consequence, but a fiery appeal by the Austrian Franz Theodor Csokor for humanity and reconciliation among the nations at the end of the congress supplied the missing dimension.

I attended few of the sessions, preferring to pursue the traces of my earlier stay in Copenhagen, in the Tivoli, where after nearly thirty years a *commedia dell'arte* company, white-faced and white-clothed, were still performing. We made trips together to Klampenborg, Fredericksborg, Elsinore, and celebrated Peter's fortieth birthday in the Frascati restaurant. Melvin Lasky, meanwhile, was getting his money's worth, signing up a number of writers for his magazine. By the fifth of June we were back in Hamburg, and I traveled straight on to Vienna, where, on the twenty-third, I received a message from Peter summoning me to return immediately. The following day I went by train to Frankfurt and tried to book a flight to Berlin. But all the flights were full, for that morning the Soviets had closed all the land and water routes between West Berlin and West Germany. It was only then that we discovered that, since the conference of foreign ministers in London had been cut short in December, the policy of shared occupation by the four victorious powers was already considered to have failed. Now the introduction of currency reform in the three Western zones had provoked open conflict.

I finally managed to book myself onto a military aircraft with the usual bucket seats, but like all the passengers I had to wear a parachute, which was a problem for me: I had no trousers in my luggage. An American woman soldier gave me a pair of bright red pajama trousers, and wearing these surmounted by a khaki army jacket, which created a somewhat clownish impression, I boarded the plane. No one gave me a glance or seemed to find my appearance ridiculous. There was an atmosphere like that of a state of emergency, if not a state of war; we braced ourselves for interference by Soviet bomber planes – in fact, seventy British and American passengers did lose their lives in the course of the airlift. In the low air corridor our plane was violently shaken, and hardly anyone on board escaped air sickness. In Berlin, the first signs of siege hysteria were noticeable, although the Western Allies did everything to prevent panic among the population. Things were not going too well in the Karlsbader-strasse either. Our little son was ill; he had spent the whole four weeks of my absence in bed and had to be operated on for adenoidal growths. On the twenty-eighth of June, the Soviets put the screws on even more tightly. In the Western sectors the electricity supply was throttled, and rations were reduced. And yet on the evening of the same day Yehudi Menuhin played for the first time again in Germany, at the Titaniapalast with Furtwängler and the Berlin Philharmonic. The Warners visited us almost daily. Sometimes we sang together to calm our nerves, Rex with a wonderful, warm baritone. He also introduced our nightly playing of Ludo, a board game whose repulsive German name is "Mensch ärgere dich nicht" (Man, don't get angry). In this atmosphere of nervous irritability, Ludo became our drug. With the help of this children's board game, we managed to rise above the situation, which was daily becoming gloomier.

I was to describe it in a report to the *New Statesman*, entitled "Victories": "If this is a siege, where is the front? If this is a war, who is our enemy? Could it be our old acquaintances Polkovnik (Colonel) K. and Podpolkovnik (Lieutenant Colonel) M., who greeted us with their usual polite smiles at a theater premiere only last week? Only a short time ago, at one of the receptions where it was not *de rigueur* to invite our former enemies, the Germans, our allies the officers of the Red Army appeared and were treated as guests of honor. Now we are on the other side of the fence together with the Berliners." In fact our "old acquaintances" had not smiled at us at the first night of Zuckmayer's *The Devil's General* at the Schlossparktheater. Sergei Tulpanov had pointedly ignored us, Dymshitz had "bowed coldly," and Mossiakov, the playboy and ladies' man, had glanced flirtatiously in my direction, but, as I noted in my journal, "between us and the Russians it is all over."

The tension affected our personal relationships. Our marriage, which had always been difficult, sometimes seemed close to breaking up. "You are the cause of all my misery," Peter said once, "because you can't think straight." What answer was there to that? When Rex's time in Berlin was nearly at an end, he revealed to us that after returning home he was planning to leave Frances. This, we now discovered, was the deeper cause of her melancholy, not merely the illness of her sweet, good-hearted daughter Anna, whose epileptic attacks we had sometimes observed with horrified pity. This too was the reason for the many calls to London which Rex had made from our apartment to his new love Barbara, at the time still Lady Rothschild. We loved him, but we could not understand the heartlessness with which he proposed to leave Frances, Anna, and their two sons. "Sometimes," I noted, "I think humans are savage beasts." Even so, Peter introduced Rex's last reading from *The Aerodrome* at Suhrkamp's in Zehlendorf. And then, in mid-July, after their farewell party – the first of so many – they came to "kiss us goodbye." A painful moment.

I began to struggle for breath at night and suffered from palpitations. The "raisin bombs" constantly passed overhead, with a roar that reminded us distressingly of the last months of the war. My mother wrote agitated letters from London, which for the first and only time I felt obliged to answer with some harshness: "If it should come to war, which no one really hopes for or expects to happen, there is no way of knowing where and on what scale it would take place... I can only repeat that His Majesty's Government would take the necessary precautions if we had to be evacuated... if the entire population of Berlin is not losing control, I don't see why I should panic... As long as I keep my head, everything will be all right. I am doing so, but it would be a help, Mimi, if you could be a little bit grown-up now."

I described our relations with the Russians to her too, but in a gentler light, edited, as it were, for "those of a nervous disposition": "The atmosphere is unfriendly. My old friend Mossiakov smiles at me occasionally, and Colonel Dymshitz bows, but our relationship with the Russians is over, on our part rather than theirs, for with their hypocrisy they would probably go on making conversation indefinitely. I am dreadfully sorry that they are behaving so badly, I really liked them as individuals. We held different views, but our contact with them was enormously interesting. We really live in idiotic times, and the twentieth century constantly jangles one's nerves."

The farewell parties accumulated. We held one ourselves, for we had now decided that I should leave Berlin with the children while Peter stayed behind. The journey was eventually postponed, but for now it was planned for the end of July. Fifteen of our closest friends came to our party, including the Roditis, Mike Josselson, and Franz Graf Treuberg, known as "Bubi," a brother-in-law of Löwenstein's who was at the time a guest director at the Hebbeltheater. From this much-traveled man I learned that Hansi and Vittorio in Rome had separated – it fitted into the picture of general breakup and dissolution. Our son was now in good health, but two days before our planned departure our daughter suffered severe appendicitis and had to have an emergency operation the same night. Dr. Hussels, once more our savior, arranged the hospital and surgeon. Instead of Peter, John Peet came with us and waited for two hours with me outside the operating room until our child was brought out, still under the anesthetic. I have never forgotten this act of kindness by a man who later became so terrifyingly disloyal. And so my daily life in Berlin continued for a month during the airlift, until our daughter's recovery was complete. It was thus that I experienced in August two last surges of British and Russian culture which in their disparateness and their significance impressed themselves on my mind forever.

The Soviets, conscious of their own unpopularity, brought to the city their pride and joy, the Alexandrov Orchestra. There were no tickets to be had for their first concert on August 13, but it was broadcast on the radio, and so we heard that voice which immediately enchanted the whole of Berlin, the voice of the tenor Nikitin singing the song "Kalinka." Five days later everyone, from the West and East sectors alike, rushed to congregate at the Gendarmenmarkt, where the orchestra was performing in the open air and the small, dark singer poured out the magic of this song which seemed to exercise as inexplicable an effect on friend and foe as only "Lili Marlene" had done before. Thousands of people packed the square; we were right in the middle, listening to the orchestra and its singers to the point of total exhaustion. "A fantastic image." Surrounded by ruins, we gave ourselves up totally to the "unbearably beautiful melody" of "Kalinka" and other Russian songs, and felt irritated, even angry, when now and again a British or American aircraft, bringing essential provisions into the city, drowned out the music as it circled above one of the three airports before landing. A whole city had lost its head and surrendered to the Slavic melancholy of its Slavic oppressors, as I had done in my youthful days of Russian romanticism.

A few days later an Elizabethan Festival Week began in Berlin. The evening before we had been invited by Brigadier Brownjohn to meet the members of the Cambridge University Madrigal Society and the Marlowe Society, also from Cambridge, who had come to Berlin for the occasion. Among them were Professor G. H. (George) Rylands, known as "Dadie," who was a friend of John Gielgud and of the late Virginia Woolf; the somewhat younger Noel Annan, a highly gifted and already highly regarded lecturer, who until recently had played an important part in Germany as a lieutenant colonel in the political division of the British military government; and the charming Gabriele Ullstein, Heinz's cousin, and a child of exile who had already given evidence of her exceptional intellect and wit as a student at Cambridge. And all at once our beloved England swirled up around us - Cambridge, for which I had a lifelong love, Bloomsbury in the person of Dadie Rylands – until then known to me, who had long been a devoted admirer of Virginia Woolf, only by hearsay. Add to all this the performance by the guests, a Purcell concert by the wonderful *a cappella* choir from Cambridge, amateur productions of Marlowe's *White Devil* and Shakespeare's *Measure for Measure*, in which Rylands himself played Angelo; all these heartrending, quietly wistful or passionate reminders of the riches of the Elizabethan age. No, "Kalinka," the fascinating Russian girl, could not compete with such splendor, and faded into the dusk of a weary, outdated nostalgia.

We formed a friendship at that time with Noel and Gabriele which was to last a long time, and only later petered out in a way which I found very hurtful. Now, in Berlin, they were drawn with us into the last giddy whirl of revelry. The day before my departure with the children, which had finally been set for the twenty-sixth of August, we invited them to lunch with us at the Press Club and in the evening to our last – for the time being – farewell party at the Karlsbaderstrasse, to which "all the Cambridge people" came, as well as John Peet, the Suters, the Lufts, Freda Utley, and Melvin Lasky with his mentor Sidney Hook – about twenty-five people, all "hand-

picked," as I noted in my journal. The following afternoon Peter
drove us to Gatow airport. A wild storm in the air. On our flight,
which left at six, we suffered more intense vibration than ever before
in the low air corridor above Hamburg. Both children were violently
sick. In Hamburg we fled to the comfort of the Hotel Atlantik, where
we recovered overnight. Next day we continued in glorious high flight
to Frankfurt and Zurich. This time we felt unconditionally "in
paradise" in Switzerland. "Mama von Cube," Peter's mother, met us
and took us to the pension where she lived permanently and where we
stayed for a couple of days. On August 28 I wrote: "Anthony ate four
eggs for breakfast, and two more in the evening."

We – the children and I – were unspeakably exhausted, the little
ones by their operations, I by the tension, the high life, the hard work,
the quarrels with Peter, the nightly palpitations. We had not been
eating well; at parties there were bread rolls with ersatz spread and
wine from Michaelis's general store in Berlin-Schöneberg, which
stocked – but for what currency? – Rhineland and Moselle wine. Our
heavy drinking, not only of wine but of spirits, of which there was an
endless supply in the PX and NAAFI, had adversely affected our
empty stomachs and left them unprepared for the rich abundance of
Swiss food. In the midst of the land of milk and honey, I was
suffering from the privations of recent years. It was time to go farther
south to recuperate, and so the three of us set off at the beginning of
September for Bellagio on Lake Como. It was a postlude, as it were,
during which the transition from the most exciting and eventful to the
loneliest and most monotonous time of my life took place as
painlessly as I could have wished.

Sunshine, late summer warmth, avenues of palms along the
lakeside, the blue water glittering and curling. I was experiencing,
above all during the first few days, a sense of release which I had
hardly ever felt so strongly before, a feeling of limitless freedom,
which at the same time is always a little tedious. In the Hotel
Splendido, with its garden running down to the lake, the children and
I occupied a pretty, spacious room. I had nothing to do all day but
take meals with them, walk, swim, and go to the post office to see if
money had arrived for me. But Peter – impeccably correct in all
business matters – had always had a disturbed relationship with
money, which after all was necessary; he simply did not recognize the

necessity of obtaining it, which often became urgent. "For three days not a sou," I wrote in my journal. There must always be something to spoil that idyll of *luxe, calme et volupté*, which was here fulfilled, at first partially and then completely. For one day a letter arrived from Hansi, to whom I had given my address, and soon afterward I received a telephone call from Milan, from the *Contino*, Luciano della P. Late on Saturday evening he arrived and took a room at the hotel. The children had already gone to bed.

There was a full moon in a clear sky. Luciano hired a motorboat and we crossed the lake to Lermo, where there was an open-air dance floor at the Albergo Roma. We drank wine and Strega and danced and listened to the latest songs on the loudspeakers, "Serenata Celeste" and Piaf's "La Vie en Rose." Then we returned to Bellagio. No hint here of Moravia's gloomy mien and hidden fire, his deceptive coolness and imperceptible advances. The *Contino* was a charming young man, with a certain tendency to stoutness; in a few years' time he would presumably no longer be able to avoid the *embonpoint* which he was still resisting. Irresistible, meanwhile, were his naive *joie de vivre*, his cheerfulness, his love of pleasure. The next day he gave affectionate and good-humored attention to the children – he probably had younger brothers and sisters; we spent the time by the lake and in the hotel park, benevolently observed by the staff, who had pursued me for weeks with sympathetic glances – *"la signora sempre sola?"* – and had now decided that all was well. And in the late afternoon the *Contino* departed once more in his Alfa Romeo. We exchanged letters, and once talked on the telephone in Paris, but never saw each other again.

The rest of the month passed in the gentle light of the September sun and the memory of a moment, perhaps the only one in my life, of Baudelairean perfection. The money had finally arrived at the bank in Como; we paid the bill and left. At Victoria Station we were met by my mother and Beate, who had stayed throughout the past two years in our apartment with the Brewsters, to whom we had sublet it. Back to Wimbledon, to that familiar, rough smell of damp grass. "Happy to be here again." Over the next few weeks I saw all my old and new friends again, my Dodo, the Henekers, the Stentons, the Stephens, Noel and Gabriele in their house in Wilton Road. One evening Flesch came to dinner; he decided that a picture frame containing a portrait

Pastel portrait by Josef Dobrowsky, 1946. "The
Dobrowsky unfortunately was not to appreciate as
astronomically as Schiele's works."

of me by Dobrowsky was too heavily coated with silver paint for his
liking, and he spent hours carefully scratching away fragments of paint
here and there with a penknife, to give it an appearance of antiquity.
Meanwhile, playing on the phonograph was a record of "La Vie en
Rose," which I had brought back from Italy.

Christine in Wimbledon

Statue of Diana the huntress in
Cannizaro Park, Wimbledon

13

A Green Grave

In Wimbledon, where I was to spend the next fifteen years, one grows old before one's time. Time passes so slowly in this green, restful, peaceful place that one pays no attention to it as in the days of youth, while secretly, mercilessly, it takes its course, so that in old age one is amazed to find oneself cheated of a long span of life. In the remote southwest of the capital, on the way to Surrey, a favorite retirement haven from time immemorial of the unimaginative British upper middle classes, Wimbledon seemed to be rather part of that county than a district of London, to which it only just belonged. Here too, not far from the tennis courts which had made its name world-famous, were well-kept streets like those of Esher or Haslemere, where one neo-Georgian structure after another, each bounded by its garden, sheltered the daily life of a highly conventional family. In the social comedies of Noël Coward and Terence Rattigan, Wimbledon has in fact a certain aura of absurdity, as the epitome of suburbia in its most banal and boring manifestation.

Piccadilly lay some seven miles away, and it was more than twice that distance to northwest London, to Hampstead, Golders Green, and Cricklewood, where the Central European émigrés crowded together. Swiss Cottage, on the edge of Hampstead, was for a time so dominated by German-speaking exiles that one bus conductor used to call out "*Schweizer Häuschen!*" on reaching it. It was near here that Sigmund Freud spent his last year, dying in Maresfield Gardens; our friend Smollett, formerly Smolka, lived in Fitzjohn's Avenue; around the corner was the Austrian Centre with its little theater, the Laterndl, and in the café-restaurant Dorice, in the Finchley Road, there were daily sessions, over imitation *Tafelspitz* and apple strudel, of the circle around the Viennese book dealer Suschitzky, who bought up the libraries of deceased dentists from Vienna or musicologists from Cologne, and had soon built up a huge stock of literature proscribed in Germany, from Heine to Brecht.

Lured to Wimbledon by Flesch, who meanwhile had long

departed to the edge of Hampstead Heath, Peter and I continued to live in proud isolation, on an island in the middle of the English island, where it was at its most English. We had a spacious apartment on the ground floor of a three-story block. And opposite, on the other side of the quiet street called The Downs, after its steep downward slope, was a vast lawn, bounded by trees and shrubs, where the children of the house played, constantly admonished by Mr. Jupp, the head porter, for throwing balls or riding tricycles. A former sergeant with the build of a buffalo, Mr. Jupp was our tormentor, the only blot on this otherwise so friendly landscape.

At the top of the hill was the Ridgway, the main street with its little single-decker 200 bus, and through a narrow passage, Wright's Alley, alongside the boys' school Wimbledon College, was the way to the Common, our own, widely extending heath, past the little village green called the Crooked Billet, which had been preserved from olden times. Two pubs stood there, the Shakespeare's Head and the Hand in Hand, where on warm days one could sit in the open to drink mild and bitter, and on Bonfire Night every November the straw effigy of Guy Fawkes was burned and fireworks set off on the green. In front of our windows in The Downs there towered a mighty cedar; our apartment was fitted out with chintz and flowered linen in Sanderson prints, as well as the furniture from the Times Furnishing Company, now somewhat increased in number. What more could we ask – even if we were still constantly short of money? And yet, and yet, this was a lifestyle from which, for fifteen years, we vainly dreamed of escaping.

Even before the long episode in Berlin, in February 1946, I had written to Peter that we could not go on like this in Wimbledon. For me, everything smelled of the war here, of "bombs and boredom and bleakness." Perhaps, I wrote, I would lose this feeling again when the shopkeepers wove their friendly nets around me, "and whenever I look out on our garden, I am enchanted with its greenness in the rain, moved by its melancholy beauty. How can one explain this dreadful urge to give up what one likes so much? It is a green grave – that is why."

But we did not give it up. Certainly, we escaped periodically, in the summer and sometimes in the winter. When we came back in September from the Ligurian coast, from the sand, the heat, the scent of thyme on the hills behind Pietrasanta, back to Wimbledon Close, and opened the windows in the dying light – to that English smell, damp, chill, intimately familiar, a smell of fog, wet grass, autumn leaves and smoldering bonfires in the gardens – we felt at home again, and intensely loved this place we yet constantly planned to flee. It was reassuring to feel that we were re-entering our painless everyday life, among people who intended us no harm as long as we did not get too close to them, safeguarded from gossip, suspicion, aggression, in the shadow of that beautiful cedar which grew ever taller and broader, darkening our rooms more and more: the cedar whose slaughter, thank God, was not perpetrated until long after my departure from Wimbledon.

It was a feeling similar to the one we experienced later when, arriving from the west or the south, we entered the *Bauernstube*, the rustic paneled living room of our house in the Salzkammergut: the scent of pine, of the charred firewood in the ceramic stove, of the sharp mountain air that had entered with us. Here too were English linen and chintz, but in the *Bauernstube* were green curtains and sofa covers from Salzburg with a scrolling vine pattern in white, copied from medieval illuminated manuscripts. In the little salon next door the curtains were of strawberry-colored glazed chintz; upstairs in my bedroom they were white, with a pattern of flowers and vases in muted, delicate colors, both from Sanderson but in complete harmony with the local country furniture. Everywhere English motifs mingled with Austrian, while the Florentine stone lions in front of the whitewashed pillars of the terrace, brought from a stonemason's workshop near Udine, and the great terracotta pots of rhododendrons and fuchsias on the balustrades, reminiscent of those that had stood in Hansi's roof garden in Parioli, recalled my beloved Italy, as indeed did the architecture of this house by the Alpine stream. Three homelands. "Only connect," as E. M. Forster says. Only connect, and life and the world itself become richer.

But now it was October 1948, and I was peacefully settled again in my autumnal London suburb, greeting with delight the resurrection of the houses of Chelsea and Kensington, their front doors freshly painted in dazzling green, dark blue, and scarlet, with shining brass door knockers, "the nimble little delivery vans in all the streets and this atmosphere of dignified prosperity; long, silently gliding, chauffeur-driven Austins, so pleasant to see after the showy American vehicles of the lordly Swiss. What a relief to see whistling bus conductors and smiling shopkeepers again, a warm bath of kindliness everywhere." This is what I wrote to Peter, who had stayed for an indefinite period in Berlin as a political reporter for the *Observer* and had found his place in that world which I had meanwhile come to know so well, the cheerful, boozy, lively world of the foreign correspondent. It was more than geographical distance which now separated us. While he, with his companions, the youthful Flora Lewis, the charming Henri de Turenne from the Agence France Presse, and the latter's girlfriend Lynne, under the umbrella of the airlift followed the progress of the disintegration of the wartime Alliance and the fabulous upswing of western Germany, I dug myself ever more deeply into the existence of a British housewife. "Now and then I go to Soho with the faithful Flesch, or to the theater. It is a quiet, pleasant life, apart from inexplicable attacks of depression."

While Peter was not without company in Berlin, the "faithful Flesch" in London had taken over the role of *Hausfreund* – gentleman friend: a character familiar, indeed completely natural, to me from my youth, as were my mother's escorts. But he was more to me than that. He was a male friend, a female friend, a brother; he was a substitute father, only nine years younger than my real father would have been; he was Vienna to me. Through Flesch, who as a schoolboy had taken part in performances of the lyric dramas of Hofmannsthal with classmates such as Hans Kaltneker in his aunt Adele von Skoda's sumptuous villa in the Himmelstrasse in Grinzing; who, soon afterward, had gone top-hatted to the Café Central to meet with writers of his own age, Heinrich Nowak, Georg Kulka, Ernst Angel; whose portrait had been drawn by Egon Schiele for the periodical *Aktion*; and who, a little later, had ridden into war, as had my father, with the imperial-royal army – through him I found myself transported into a time and place, into an Austria, which no longer existed, but to which I still clung with many fibers of my being.

For all my attachment, indeed my love for Peter, for all my respect for his German intellectuality, his humor, which was neither Bavarian nor Saxon but unmistakably that of Berlin, I could still succumb to the lure of Austria, particularly in such an original manifestation – from Flesch's deep knowledge of the classics, which I lacked, to his lifelong avant-gardism, the counterpart of the *character indelebilis* of the eternal Expressionist. Flesch was moreover, like Yorick, "a fellow of infinite jest," although plagued by periodic fits of madness, just as Peter was by his biting Baltic moods, though I found Flesch's less frightening, and usually succeeded in calming him down. One thing that helped was that, until our marriage at very advanced ages, Flesch and I habitually addressed each other with the formal *Sie*. That my friend was also a writer was something I found completely natural. Although I was one day to assure the London biographer Joanna Richardson, to her horror, that I would rather have had relationships with bank managers than with all those neurotic intellectuals, literary circles were after all my element. In August of that year, before leaving Berlin for Bellagio, I had filled half a page of *Die Welt* with a review of Flesch's latest novel, *Perlen und schwarze Tränen* (*Pearls and Black Tears*), under the title "Vincent Brun and the Dissolution of the Novel."

I had called this book a "journey to the end of night," though in fact it stood in contrast to the *Voyage au bout de la nuit* of the celebrated though infamous Céline. "Here the sickness of our time is grasped in the context of a case verging on the clinical... Today nearly everyone suffers from some dilemma or other, some political, social, artistic, or private conflict. The émigré is the prototype of modern man. Freedom from the burden of a double existence, of divided loyalty and split personality... is the wish and hope of us all." This was how I ended my review. But I also quoted some passages from the novel, visions of a wartime exile dreaming of a peaceful Europe amid the fog, in the BBC's vast, dark Bush House – visions in which "time is smashed to pieces," of the entry of the Western Allies into Tiberius's Rome, of the hero's journey by sea with a slave girl he had bought at the market in Naples, past islands of mother-of-pearl and golden islands with marble churches, of a walk through the town of Aix en Provence to the monument of the "bon roi René": "This was the preserver of the world which he possessed. And behold, it all seemed good to him." Such passages are for me among the most beautiful in German prose written in our time.

When Peter returned from Germany for good, our household was more or less secure, and it did not begin to totter, and finally collapse, until deprived of this support. But he had not yet returned. He spent the Christmas of 1948 in Berlin, although in November we had paid a brief visit to Paris together – another city which, if one were in the right mood, had overtones of home. We visited "Papa," Peter's father Georg von Mendelssohn, with his third wife Claude, and Denise van Moppès proudly introduced us to her baby, Rémy. From a distance we saw Sartre at the Café Flore, and we spent two evenings at the theater, to see Louis Jouvet in *Don Juan* and Jean-Louis Barrault and Maria Casarès in Camus' *L'Etat de siège*. From the little Hotel Sèvres-

Vaneau I telephoned Luciano, the *Contino*, who, in accordance with his social standing, was staying at the Plaza Athenée, but despite tender words, a meeting could not be arranged. The day after our return we celebrated our son's birthday in London; on this day too Charles, Prince of Wales, was born. Peter departed immediately afterward, but we had this time been on better terms than ever, and for some time after that I behaved abominably to my "gentleman friend." Here too, a double existence, divided loyalties.

"The Furies were flying through the house," I noted in my calendar on the first evening of the new year. But why? *Les absents ont toujours tort*: in the Karlsbaderstrasse in Berlin there were certainly no guilt feelings. Soon afterward, it was for Berlin that I left London – damp and cold and beset by pea-soupers as it was throughout that winter – for two reasons: on the one hand to dissolve finally the household in which Peter remained with Frau Kuhn, and on the other to attend the German premiere, on January 11, 1949, of *Mother Courage*, whose author had been living in East Berlin for several months. It was a memorable experience. Who could resist this play, this performance, the enormous tension and excitement in the auditorium of the Deutsches Theater, where once again *tout Berlin* had gathered? Finally, Brecht and Dessau emerged in front of the curtain; the composer had imitated the dramatist in a slightly ridiculous way, for they both appeared in mouse-grey collarless Mao suits – "I believe in the revolving male neck," Brecht said to me a few days later, a remark which now seems somewhat eerie in view of the *Wendehälse*, the "neck-turners" or renegades of 1989 – and with their hair cut identically in a fringe, a style which immediately became *de rigueur* for all German intellectuals, like the moustache later worn by Grass and Biermann – the revered Peter Huchel retained it to the end of his life.

But I do not want to belittle ironically what at the time had so many deeply moving moments for me. Angelika Hurwicz as the mute Kattrin on the roof, Werner Hinz as the army chaplain – they were superb. But in my little calendar is the comment: "Fascinating, but false." What was false? For me, Mother Courage herself. With all due respect to Helene Weigel, a pupil of Eugenie Schwarzwald (although I did not know this at the time), she could not play a peasant, a woman of the people hawking provisions to soldiers. And so I infuriated Friedrich Luft by referring to her performance as "*Bast*," raffia-work. What I meant was that for me it was "artsy-craftsy." You cannot fool a Viennese woman: for me, Helene Weigel could not divest herself of her bourgeois origins. I ventured to guess that she came from the ninth district of Vienna, the academic district. Luft shook his head, but next day he questioned the actress. Reluctantly she admitted that she was from the ninth district, "but from the Tandelmarkt" – the flea-market area. Now, unfortunately, this lies, or lay, at the end of the Berggasse, where Sigmund Freud used to live. In fact Brecht's wife, the great thespian, really had no connection with the traditional life of the people, let alone the world of stallholders and peddlers, and was incapable, to my mind, of even portraying it believably, as Therese Giehse in Zurich had certainly succeeded in doing.

I stayed another week in Berlin for one last taste of the high life, which was then over for me forever. We often met Brecht, once in Ruth Berlau's meager room, where a stained cap hung from a hook on the wall. "And he hung his hat on the nail in her room" – the reference was clear. Ruth Berlau gave the impression of being overwrought, then again subdued, and, as she was to write a year later, "completely helpless. You have more pity... on a bird that has flown into your room." Before this, all of us, including Brecht and Budd Schulberg from Hollywood, had visited an American film studio, where we were shown a "Nuremberg" film – probably footage from the concentration camps, for "I was horrified, and wept." In the evening we went to the Lufts', where our old friend Josselson showed up; in Berlin the future Cold War adversaries were still united within a restricted area.

With Frau Kuhn I packed innumerable chests and suitcases, yet the children's favorite toys never arrived in England, neither the huge teddy bear from Harrods, nor the rocking horse from Berlin, nor the little Gothic town of wood turned by Leipzig craftsmen; and all our most important books were lost forever, among them a first edition of Schiller, and Moravia's *Agostino* in French, which he had sent me after our reunion in Rome. Once more I had my hair dressed by Sibylle, and went shopping in the Kurfürstendamm with Heide. And for the very last time, after the premiere of Sartre's *Les mains sales*, from ten in the evening until six in the morning, a farewell party was held in the Karlsbaderstrasse. There were fifty-five guests; Peter "flirted with four girls at the same time," and as a punishment I spent the whole of the next day at Heide's, where Helene Weigel turned up for tea. In the evening, after "the most terrible scene of our whole married life" – it was not to be the last – I made up my quarrel with

Peter, and the following day we left for Salzuflen in a four-engined York bomber with no seats, crouching on our luggage. Until the end of the month we were still buzzing around Germany together, inspecting the Villa Hügel in Essen; seeing Gründgens and Marianne Hoppe in *Torquato Tasso* in Düsseldorf, and performances in both Dortmund and Cologne of Emlyn Williams' play *The Light of Heart* – my first drama translation from the English. In the middle of all this, Peter heard from the *Observer* that his job as correspondent in Germany was to end in April.

Never again in my life did I live at such breakneck speed. Even in Berlin the pace now gradually began to slow down. The following year we went there again, for the foundation of the Congress for Cultural Freedom, the brainchild of our friend Melvin Lasky together with his mentor, the American social philosopher Sidney Hook. Like other participants from England we were a little out of place there, but this became clear only in the course of the congress. Before that, I had begun to earn money seriously, in order to support our costly household, and had become London cultural correspondent to the *Neue Zeitung*, while Peter became its political reporter on his return from Berlin. We both regularly wrote for Lasky's *Monat*; Peter contributed an essay on Jünger to its fourteenth issue, while my first essay, a hymn to Christopher Fry, appeared in the twelfth. Thus, for several years we were almost exclusively dependent on money from the United States, a situation which was to have its dangers.

Our household began to settle down. Further along The Downs was the Ursuline Convent, with its girls' school and kindergarten, where our children were well looked after, lovingly supervised by the nuns and their Reverend Mother, who came from Jersey. A little Polish nun, Mother Adela, took our daughter under her wing. Peter barricaded himself in his room and worked with tireless industry – a "German busy bee," as Mimi once called him. I looked after the household, made pancakes as soon as we could get eggs again, and tossed them on Pancake Day as prescribed; with the children I explored the newly opened Cannizaro Park on the edge of Wimbledon Common, the former property of a Sicilian vegetable importer of that name, which had been acquired by the local council – the house, garden, and stone statues had great charm, and later there was an aviary too; and on weekends the children and I rambled through Kew Gardens, Richmond Park or Hampton Court. In the evenings the adults played Ludo. Flesch, who was still living in

Hampstead, where a half-brother of the Löwensteins was lodging with him, stayed overnight nearly every Saturday and led the expeditions, as Peter did not want to be disturbed in his work. During the week I went into town to see exhibitions and premieres, and gradually set up a syndicate, supplying cultural reports from London to a range of newspapers, weeklies and radio stations. After my first BBC broadcast to be delivered in person, Flesch said I had sounded "tremendously sensitive, melancholy and distinguished, as though I were very slightly hunchbacked."

One of those beautiful Surrey villas I mentioned earlier was now the home of Vaclav Nijinsky, who had ended up there after many years in Swiss clinics, and was now tended by his wife alone. I drove to this house, Whinmead, and asked to be admitted in order to interview him about his great plans which had recently been reported in the press. Apparently funds were available in America for the realization of his idea for an international university of dance, with additional faculties of literature, music, and the visual arts. The main premises were to be built near New York, but Madame Nijinska was also negotiating with the Austrian Schloss Mittersill. Massine, Karsavina, and Nijinsky's sister Bronislava had agreed to participate. His New York doctor Manfred Sakl, to whom his "almost complete recovery" was to be ascribed, was also to help him, as well as his adviser Richard Quandt, the former president of the Hungarian national bank under Horthy, to whom Nijinsky owed his rescue from the wartime German "liquidation," that is murder, of all mentally ill persons.

This was what I was told by Romola Nijinska. But while I examined the display cabinets containing photographs and souvenirs and sheets covered with the dance notation invented by Nijinsky, something mysterious, even uncanny, was going on in this everyday English country house. Footsteps were heard in the next room, there was a knocking sound from the dumb waiter, doors slammed shut, and Madame ran out hastily, called out a few words in Russian, and returned complaining about the dreadful draft. I asked if Nijinsky would now see me. Unfortunately not, he was too busy, buried in plans and designs, had no time to give out information about them; that was what she, Romola, was there for. The truth, which his wife was desperately trying to conceal, was that he was still in a deeply disturbed state. The world of this poor benighted man seemed to fill the house, but he himself was not to be seen. Madame saw me out, said a pleasant goodbye and closed the door. I turned my head once more as I left. And suddenly I saw him, I saw Petroushka, Prince Albrecht, the Specter of the Rose, standing motionless behind the great window by the front door, his pale face with its turned-up peasant nose pressed flat against the glass, his large eyes, confused and beseeching, watching the departure of the visitor. It was a pitiful sight. A year later, in April 1950, still cared for by Romola, he died.

By the first summer after the German years we had already discovered the Ligurian coast, the Tyrrhenian Sea, to which we were to return often and for long periods at a time. It was at Forte dei Marmi, where Eckart and Costanza Peterich had a house, that Peter's father, two years before Peter's birth, had lived with Theodor Däubler and Jakob Hegner in spartan accommodation. Here, while his friends wrote novellas and poems, Georg von Mendelssohn, known as *der Rabe*, drew up a "systematics of ornamentation" and designed necklaces in ironwork. It was not only this that had lured us to the area, to nearby Marina di Pietrasanta. In London I had inquired at a travel agency about a suitable spot, wavered between Lake Garda and Viareggio, and finally booked rooms in Fiumetto, which turned out to be unsatisfactory. Finally we found "Signor Alberto" and his little white Villa Egea with its marble floors in the "*Seconda linea*," on the edge of the pine grove.

Those were joyous weeks. Not only did we seek out the Peterichs, but in Ronchi to the north, among the scattered bungalows of a stately pension in the *pineta*, we found Kasimir and Illy Edschmid, and with them Erna Pinner, his longtime lover until the beginning of the Hitler regime (when he hastily burnt her letters), all of whom were well known to us from London. Not far away were Darina and Ignazio Silone and, some distance away, Clemens Krauss, who had resigned in bitterness from the world of operatic direction, with his wife Viorica Ursuleac. It was the time of the rumba; we spent many long evenings with our friends in all the night clubs along the coast from here to Viareggio, usually called "Capannina," and in the cafés on the sandy beaches under the plane trees. Again and again we were to experience the joy of life here, naive as we were, without a wish or a care in the world. In later years the Kestens were to join us here on this coast, the revolutionary writer Gustav Regler was to offer jokingly to buy me from my husband for a million lire, and two kindred spirits, Flesch and the *Rabe*, were to meet at Signor Alberto's house – long before the daughter of the publisher S. Fischer, together with

Gottfried Bermann, built a feudal mansion on a hill in the hinterland of nearby Camaiore.

Names and more names. They fill my memories, fill this book. I drop them constantly, reprehensible though this is, because in them, in the people to whom they belong, our own awareness of life and what is called our intellectual climate were embodied in a special way; and because for me, though not for the Marxists, the course of history seems determined or at least molded by individuals, rather than by the working masses. It is with irony that Shakespeare's Mark Antony calls the traitors Cassius and Brutus "the choice and master spirits of this age" – erroneously translated by Schlegel and Tieck as "*die ersten Heldengeister unserer Zeit*," "the first heroic spirits of our time." Many important or simply remarkable figures whom I have known or with whom I have been acquainted have been perceived by me as "master spirits." The title *Städte und Menschen*, "Cities and People," which I gave to a volume of essays, probably epitomizes what has remained for me in old age, beside the all too infrequent moments of the heights of art or of love, as the actual reward of a long life.

The names of good and great people adorned the lists of PEN at its annual International Congresses. We took part in many of these congresses, a dozen or more, in Amsterdam and Lausanne, in Dublin and Menton, in Edinburgh and Vienna. The most beautiful of them all was certainly that early one in Venice to which we traveled in 1949 after our first stay in Pietrasanta: a meeting of writers to which the youth of the city paid ample attention, indeed more ample than we could have wished. A sumptuous buffet had been prepared for us in the Ca' Rezzonico, such as could only have been possible in Italy during those still frugal years, but when the writers, after the long speeches of welcome delivered by those who like to hear the sound of their own voices on such occasions, streamed toward the tables prepared in the banquet hall below the Tiepolo frescoes, they found these almost bare, the dishes long since stripped of their contents by the *giovanotti* and *ragazze* who had somehow gained entrance, the boys in snow-white shirts and trousers, the girls in equally white, drifting gauze dresses with gold sashes, and with gold sandals on their otherwise bare feet – a veritable *jeunesse dorée* of such grace and elegance that at the sight of them we almost forgot our disappointment at the loss of our delicacies.

On the evening of this reception we had left our children alone in their room in the Hotel Excelsior on the Lido, where we were staying. When we returned after midnight, we found them in the dark, cowering on the floor, deeply terrified and clinging together. A flock of bats had flown into the room through the tall window and were now whirring around the ceiling. We called the staff, and the *pipistrelli* were chased away with long brooms, but the children's terror remained with them for a long time. On the excursions organized for the congress the children of course accompanied us, for instance on the boat that took us to the villas of Brenta. Here the Viennese, led by Csokor, preened themselves with particular pride on the beauty of the landscape and the houses, just as if the Venetian republic were still under the rule of Austria. On deck we met the Golls, to whom Peter had once prematurely announced his forthcoming marriage to me – Claire with the typical pallor of the redhead, but Yvan pale as a corpse, for he had leukemia, of which he was to die the following year. On the river trip Moravia finally introduced me to Elsa Morante, who inspected me closely; probably he had told her of our past relationship. A small blonde woman with a melancholy catlike face. Now, each of us *en famille*, Alberto and I were already estranged, and in fact we never met again. His fame was then already at its zenith. He was highly esteemed by Count Valmarana, at whose side he received guests in the Count's wonderful Palladio villa.

The family which caused us embarrassment were not just his wife, my husband, and my children, but the whole great clan of PEN, membership of which had for many lonely and uprooted people compensated for the lack of a wide-branching family circle. As long as we remained in England and for quite some time after that, Henrietta Leslie's Glebe House was the venue for our "family" gatherings. She had bequeathed it to PEN in her will, but only for the unexpired term of her lease, which ran out in 1974. The Church of England, which owned the freehold, demanded such an enormous sum for the renewal of the lease that PEN could no longer afford to retain the property. For a few more years it kept its offices and held its meetings as a tolerated tenant in part of the house; then the English Center moved to another site in Chelsea. Until then, however, for many evenings both the celebrities and the ambitious "novel-knitters" of the Club and their guests gathered under the great portrait of Henrietta as a child, around the mahogany dining table – polished, as ever, to a glossy finish by the loyal Dorrit, who continued to work for PEN – with its long-familiar crystal ornaments, including the little glittering weeping willow which now stands in my apartment in

Döbling. The greatest writer of all, Virginia Woolf, was never seen there, but many members of her closest circle did appear, such as Vita Sackville-West and Harold Nicolson; and practically all the most eminent authors and scholars in the land – from Wells and Priestley to E. M. Forster, from Bertrand Russell, Gilbert Murray, G. M. Trevelyan to Osbert Sitwell and Rebecca West – at one time or another took the chair.

Nowhere else – unless it was in the Café Royal in Regent Street, at the turn of the century – had these shy, reclusive British writers met together so often and so informally outside their own houses, or those of such exclusive hostesses as Lady Ottoline Morrell; nowhere else had they positively sought out the company of other, even foreign authors. There were some arrogant members of this family, some who were malicious, such as Rebecca West, but there were others who were more modest and hence more likable; there were problem children and black sheep and fools, who were suffered and humored according to the old rules of English tolerance. This picture was repeated at the international meetings, always in the spirit of the British founders of this now worldwide organization, whose presidents often hailed from its country of origin, as did its general secretaries until much more recent times. For decades the same faces were encountered at the most varied spots in Europe, as well as outside it: the Dutch radical writer and kindly hothead A. den Doolard; the amusing Baron de Radzitzky from Brussels, who represented the French Center of Belgium; the charming little Count and Countess Piovene from Milan; Ivan Boldiszár, the Hungarian *Charakterkopf*, whose brain was better than his character, who had survived five regimes with as much adaptability as Machiavellian intelligence; or the Bulgarian Leda Mileva, an attractive woman, politically loyal to the bone, who brought all the representatives of the Eastern bloc into line at votes in the executive committee, including of course Boldiszár.

For me, each congress site is bound up with certain events or appearances. In Amsterdam for instance, in 1954, we were all surprised by the comet-like arrival of Bertolt Brecht. It was there, too, that I experienced that good fortune of a magnetic power of attraction, not granted to me for a long time, when, gloomily wandering around the foreign town after a quarrel with Peter, I suddenly became aware of the approach of Flesch, who made me laugh again over a glass of Genever in a little blue-tiled bar. The following year in Vienna, the then highly respected novelist Charles Morgan was so overcome by spring fever that he went into continual raptures about his early love, the operetta singer Mizzi Günther, and delightedly repeated the phrase: "A June night and no war!" In 1956, at a reception for the guests of honor at Marlborough House, Queen Elizabeth and her sister Margaret told Erich Kästner that as children they used to have his books on their bedside tables. And in 1951, in Lausanne, Stephan Hermlin issued dark threats against Richard Friedenthal and myself because at the last moment we managed to prevent the collective participation of PEN in the dubious Stockholm Peace Congress, the tool of a *pax sovietica*. It had not been clear to everyone that Robert Neumann, out of sheer love of intrigue, had been indulging in secret subversive activities in an attempt to further the Communist cause. But David Carver, Hermon Ould's successor as general secretary, laughingly told everyone who wanted to know: "Robert was the snake in the grass."

It was with laughter and forbearance, as was customary in political and social life at the time, that the leadership of the PEN put up with opinions considered false or even dangerous, without however adopting them. Never, in this community which truly brought nations together, were there totally divisive quarrels; every member, however muddle-headed or ideologically stubborn, remained a *cher confrère*. The appointment one day of Stephan Hermlin and Boldiszár as international vice presidents was a token of this liberal-mindedness which was not received with joy by all, certainly not by me. On the other hand, there was no question of the formation of Soviet centers as long as the Soviets refused to sign the PEN charter. Polarization was avoided, but hatred was not sown.

To this day the humane traditions of tolerance hold sway in this institution of English origin, as they had been developed in *Areopagitica,* John Milton's pamphlet on freedom of speech. And it was not by chance that during the foundation of the Congress for Cultural Freedom in Berlin it was Britons, above all the historian Hugh Trevor-Roper, later Lord Dacre, who had harbored and expressed reservations about its martial objectives and fears for the peace which had been so recently and painfully achieved, if not actual resistance against this initiative, in the context of the Cold War which was now so powerfully in progress. The iron determination of most of the other participants in the congress to eradicate the "virus of neutralism," as Sidney Hook later formulated it, "which robbed the

West of its weapons," was not shared by them.

It was difficult then, as it remained for many years, to distance oneself from the militancy of these anti-Communists and frequently ex-Communists – Arthur Koestler immediately addressed them in Berlin as "comrades in battle" – without coming under suspicion of sympathizing with the Stalin regime. Arthur Miller wrote about this problem in detail in his account of his own life. We, if to a lesser degree, were occasionally tarred with the same brush. Nevertheless, looking back, our position seems crystal clear to me. In the meantime, before our congress broke up on June 24, 1950, something surprising happened: John Peet, our good friend, in whom we saw no more than an eccentric idealist, had overnight left his job with the Reuters agency, his wife Christl, and little stepdaughter, and placed himself at the disposal of the authorities in the Eastern sector – not without announcing his intentions to Reuters in accordance with regulations. As we were soon credibly informed, he took only two books in a small suitcase: the pornographic novel *Josephine Mutzenbacher* and Koestler's *Darkness at Noon*. I knew that he owned a copy of *Mutzenbacher*, for he had lent it to all of us, and when I thoughtlessly left it lying around, Frau Kuhn complained vehemently, alleging that Hedwig, whose husband Brodkorb had not yet returned from captivity, had secretly read the book and thereupon attempted to seduce the bald, portly little Herr Kuhn.

So much for the lighthearted side of John Peet's defection. That he had found it necessary to leave the West, to betray it, offended us deeply, for we liked him very much. Rumors that the Americans were planning to arm their part of Germany, a noticeable lull in the process of denazification, and the return of party comrades to the government service and the judiciary were reasons he gave later for his apostasy. He must soon have realized that he had leapt from the frying pan into the fire, but he had no thought of returning, although for the rest of his life he retained his British passport. During the congress, after he had already crossed over, we were to meet him, dreadfully changed. For the time being we were in West Berlin, confronted with an overwhelming force of European and American intellectuals in a climate of political rigor and heat.

A word about the originator of the cultural congress, Melvin J. Lasky. *De vivis nil nisi bonum* has been my resolve, wherever possible. The dead can more easily bear critical observation. But if I can say nothing kind about living contemporaries, then at least I can make an effort to be silent "about them," as Wittgenstein teaches us. This is unnecessary in Melvin's case because, although to this day we represent different if not opposite points of view on crucial questions, he has always been and still is a loyal friend. Never did he take part in the furtive or overt smear campaign during which Peter and, to a far greater extent, I myself were labeled "fellow travelers." And certainly he was one of the few who perceived Peter's speech to the Congress not as totally erroneous, because it was not helpful to the "matter in hand," but as an honest contribution to the problem of the writer who is unable to resist the lure of totalitarian ideologies.

After all, it was Lasky who had published in his *Monat* Peter's debate with Ernst Jünger and in more general terms with *Der Geist in der Despotie* (The Intellectual under Despotism), which was the title of his collection of essays published in 1952, including this article as well as others on Gottfried Benn, Kurt Hamsun and Jean Giono. In Austria the original essay, published in the Christmas 1949 edition of the *Salzburger Nachrichten*, provoked a wild attack by the Jünger admirer René Marcic, in which he suggested to Peter that he should not be surprised that "the likes of him" had gone to the gas chambers. Four years after the war had ended, it was still possible to say such things in a newspaper which for years offered a platform to talented journalists whose record was not the cleanest. Then, in Berlin, Peter spoke in the second working session on the seducibility of the intellectual, such as had already been observed by Julien Benda in 1927 in his book *La trahison des clercs*. As he stressed, this meant that he had temporarily to assume the role of devil's advocate. But when he described the "magic power of attraction" of closed systems on wavering minds, as a result of which "the wisest and most sophisticated persons" suddenly felt drawn "toward the most obtuse and stupid," he left no doubt as to his own powers of resistance. Nevertheless this was not an acceptable admission to make at a conference held in order to represent Western intellectuals as a determined, incorruptible vanguard in the battle – if necessary, in an armed conflict – against the danger of "world communism."

That such a program, moreover, could not be discussed in a calm and reflective manner, but repeatedly, in an atmosphere of heightened tension, was certainly not the intention of the organizer, but the result of a fatal coincidence. Shortly before the first session in the Titaniapalast it became known that the North Korean troops of the Communist leader Kim Il Sung had entered U.S.-protected South

Korea. Stalin was on the advance toward world domination: this was the Congress's immediate reaction. Arthur Koestler, who was to dominate the proceedings from then on – with, and occasionally against, Silone – leapt onto the platform and called in impassioned tones for the formation of an international brigade of writers similar to that in the Spanish Civil War – an event not recorded in the annals of the Congress. The analogy was a weak one, but this disturbed no one except a few "delegates from Oxbridge, who heartily detested Koestler," as Sidney Hook wrote after the event. The English delegates, some of whom did not arrive until the conference was nearing its end, were to conduct their arguments not only against Koestler, who called the governing Labour Party "more insular than the Conservatives," but chiefly against James Burnham and Franz Borkenau on account of their radical theories. A. J. Ayer, the eminent philosopher and British spokesman for the Vienna Circle of logical positivists, had understanding for "honest liberals with their lovable inefficiency" – "we would rather be seen as 'inefficient' than as 'intolerant'." And Hugh Trevor-Roper later conducted the only fundamental attack on the spirit and work of the Congress in the *Manchester Guardian* and the *Economist*.

So many years later, it has been instructive for me to reread extracts from Trevor-Roper's reports. With reference to the applause which Borkenau received for his plan for a "life-and-death battle against the totalitarian threat," he wrote: "This fanatical speech was less terrifying than the hysterical German applause which greeted it. It was an echo of Hitler's Nuremberg... The German nationalists in the audience were anti-Russian, perhaps once National Socialist and *hysterical* with a *borderline hysteria.*" This not only reminds me of the cheering that had broken out in 1947 over the return of Furtwängler – especially since the Congress also began and ended with the Beethoven music so widely promoted on all sides – but it has a certain historical irony even today. When "Gorby-mania" broke out in June 1989 in Bonn, Stuttgart, and Dortmund, when the reception given by the citizens of these towns to the Russian political reformer provoked the French, above all, to criticize the "over-emotional Germans," one could be forgiven for thinking of Napoleon's comment on the Viennese: as they enthusiastically celebrated the birthday of the *Empereur*, who had occupied Vienna for the second time in 1809 and taken up residence in Schönbrunn, he said contemptuously: "*Ils crient toujours!*" The welcoming cheers for Gorbachev, however, had sprung from a deeply felt desire for peace – that peace with the enemy of so many decades which at last, at last, appeared to be within reach.

At the Congress Peter at any rate, unlike Trevor-Roper in this respect, rather like the more moderate delegates from England, was pleading for a less categorical, a more differentiated attitude in the defense of the Western concept of freedom against the rigid dogmatism of the East. Melvin, in his retrospective summing-up of the debate in the *Monat*, was to confirm that Peter had been "almost convincing as a devil's advocate." He did not, it is true, fulfill the goal expected of everyone at this Congress. He did not, like the great physicist and pacifist Hans Thirring, in view of the outbreak of war in Korea, withdraw a paper that was to condemn "warmongers" of the East and West alike. He did not, like Nicolas Nabokov, abandon an original intention to denounce the weakness and vacillation of artists under a totalitarian regime – in Nabokov's case the Shostakoviches – and instead demand of the Congress an "active, constant and obstinate readiness for war" as well as "investigation of all combatants, combat organizations and means of combat, in order to mobilize them." In response to these proposals, the charming, witty, sophisticated aesthete and musician Nabokov was nominated as future congress secretary. And Peter was presumably tagged as a "neither-nor thinker" in Koestler's sense, who was not prepared to sacrifice his critical intelligence to some general demand, in this case the unqualified opposition to Communism, and who as before carried within himself the "virus of neutralism."

I myself did not take part in the debates, as I was not one of the listed delegates, and was by no means constantly in the conference hall, but often escaped with Heide to my little shops and my other favorite spots in Berlin. But I attended all the informal gatherings, such as the one at the radio station, where we met acquaintances from England – "Freddie" Ayer was one of these at that time – or from America, such as Hermann Kesten or Walter Mehring, or Edouard Roditi, then still living in Berlin. Twice, with Peter and a few other visitors to the Congress, I went to the Eastern sector: to a performance of Brecht's adaptation of *Der Hofmeister* by J. M. R. Lenz at the Berliner Ensemble, and on Tuesday June 27 to the Friedrichstadt Palast, the home of the Kulturbund or cultural association, where a peace rally of the Communist intelligentsia was to take place.

It was a grisly experience, not unlike many of my wartime nightmares. On the platform, next to the cold-faced functionaries of the East Berlin regime, sat Anna Seghers, so revered by me until such a short time ago, and our former friend John Peet, with venom spouting from their mouths. I have forgotten whether Johannes R. Becher, our easy-going eater of stuffed cabbage, was also sitting up there, but it must have been so, for he was in Berlin at the time, and later, in his *Tagebuch 1950* (*Journal 1950*), he cursed that "'Cultural Congress,' arranged by a party spy," made the absurd assertion that a fire in the cultural writers' club on June 22 had been started by the organizers of the Congress, and accused Renée Sintenis of having gone "into the camp of the most evil agitators for war." So I presume that he was one of those in the Friedrichstadt Palast who called for a hate campaign against the "agitators." In the enormous hall the atmosphere became increasingly uncomfortable, and it was beginning to oppress the little group from the Western sector in the gallery: ourselves, the Swiss Gody Suter and his wife, Gottfried Bermann-Fischer, and a small group of British journalists. It became clear to us that we were in enemy territory, and that the shouts from the crowd of "*Schweinehunde*" and "Criminals!" were being aimed directly at us, the representatives of western democracy. Finally, when Ernst Reuter, the mayor of West Berlin, a decent, upright man, was described on the platform as a friend of the atomic bomb, the cry "*Vergasen!*" ("Gas him!") rang out. It was no thanks to John that a vestige of common sense prevented the crowd of three thousand frenzied Berliners from lynching us on the spot, for it was his speeches which contributed to the mass hysteria constantly fanned into flame from above.

We finally escaped from the meeting safe and sound, but deeply alarmed, and to shouts of mockery and abuse. Three days later, still in Berlin, I wrote an open letter to John Peet, "Repudiation of a Former Colleague," which was promptly published in the *Neue Zeitung*. Perhaps some extracts from this letter will once and for all refute the accusations which for many years continued to brand me a sympathizer and satellite of the Soviet regime. And even though Torberg, my friend–enemy, wrote a potentially fateful letter of denunciation to Melvin Lasky in which he attempted to devalue my attacks on Fadeyev and Peet as an "ethical alibi," I still believe that I left no doubt in these attacks as to my total rejection of the Communist system. That this so-called "peace rally," supervised by countless men in uniform, by "whole battalions of policemen and policewomen," resembled nothing so much as the warmongering speeches of Joseph Goebbels and the echo they found in his listeners, was something I stressed in my letter to Peet as much as I did our horror over the transformation that had taken place in him personally.

"We saw you," I wrote, "but you did not see us, for only a few days earlier you had left the 'depths of the jungle,' which we had shared with you, for the 'clearing' of the East German republic. Your defection was carried out with all the outward signs of suicide. You disappeared after writing letters of farewell, distributing your property and erecting a wall between yourself and us which now seemed even more unbridgeable than the threshold which leads from life to death. Well, one cannot follow a friend into death. But we followed you to the Friedrichstadt Palast, to see how you had settled into your new surroundings." I then described, as I have done here, the atmosphere in the hall and the horrifying shouts. "*Vergasen!* We had no great desire to applaud at this point, although we had already begun to feel threatened, since another voice had called out to you that the entire British press club was present in the hall. All around us people were already thirsting for scapegoats to attack. And then someone uttered the name of Korea."

It had not been the Communist government of North Korea, I reminded Peet, but the armies of the South which, according to the statements from the platform, had initiated the conflict. "And you nodded, John, nodded at a lie which was no less blatant than that report of the fall of Madrid, soon exposed as false, in an English newspaper in November 1936, which made you so angry then – and rightly so... 'Now they have their war!' you cried. Who? The entire non-Communist world, from the leaders of a few dozen governments right down to us, your friends in the hall? That was how it sounded to us. No wonder that the feeling in the hall, heated to boiling point, suddenly directed itself against your former colleagues, all the more so when you began to address them by name in the face of that unbridled crowd. Now all the rage of the audience was turned upon them, a small group of English journalists who were sitting defenseless, not even in total command of the German language, facing the barrage of fury. Now they were even being commended in loud and clear tones to the care of the executioner... And now even you, as we were able to observe, realized at that moment that you were not at an English Quaker meeting... And so, after a moment of hesitation, of blushing confusion in which we recognized you again, you refrained from 'tormenting' your colleagues any further. You closed with the words: 'Now you must decide for war or peace.' Oh

God, we had decided long ago, not for the East or for the West, no, simply for peace."

Then I announced what I called my "political legitimation." I mentioned my youthful Socialism, my leanings toward the Labour Party in my English exile: "I have left out nothing of importance. If I had been a member of the British policing force in Palestine, I would have mentioned it, for the sake of decency. You did not do so in the autobiography which you have begun to publish in *Neues Deutschland*. Not that it was detrimental to your honor to have belonged to a policing force or, before that, to a regiment of guards. But in order to be able to explain an antithetical and individual course of development to the readers of *Neues Deutschland*, one should be able to admit that life is not conducted in clichés." What John had written in his articles for the Eastern zone newspaper about the gormandizing of the western occupying powers struck me as ridiculous. "As far as I remember, you yourself have never taken a pledge of abstinence. After all, we were expected to forgive the far greater excesses of the soldiers of that occupying power whose mouthpiece you are now. And even that attraction supposed to have been exercised upon the members of the British press club [in Vienna] by countesses who were hungry but not without charm is difficult to understand... The only countess I met in that circle was your wife."

And then I made it clear – in the *Neue Zeitung*, the organ of the American occupying power, whose mouthpiece I by no means considered myself to be – how little personal guilt I felt over the shipwreck of the alliance of West and East: "During the years that my husband and I spent in postwar Berlin, our house was open to all who wished to express their opinions there. Even more, we courted them. And the case of a Soviet Russian officer whom we last saw in our own home is worthy of a brief mention." This officer had been Feldman, and I reported our conversations with him: "His arguments in general followed the traditional rules of Western logic, and no Jesuitical or pragmatic elements had rechanneled or blocked his thought processes. Nevertheless we were not of the same opinion. But we debated. We took pleasure in our differences and in the fact that they did not cloud our conversation. Our friend, however, became ever unhappier and more despairing over the course of the years. What we had succeeded in doing seemed ever more manifestly to have proved impossible on a higher level. 'When one day we are no longer able to greet each other,' he said, 'then everything is over.' And, that last time we saw him: 'The gulf has grown so wide that not even my dead body and yours could fill it.'"

And now, I wrote to Peet, Feldman had disappeared. "Disappeared like nearly all the officers over there, who sought dialogue with us and found it. I hope that the rumors of their imprisonment are unfounded, but I fear they are not." We were still there, I said, our address in England was easy to find out, we would have liked to continue the dialogue, no, it was not our fault. And then I began to talk of how, at the Friedrichstadt Palast, John had made fun of the cultural congress for which we had this time come to Berlin. "The word 'counterfeiters' had already been mentioned, and you spoke of 'dupes.' Well, I can assure you that we bit hard on every coin, and were quite capable of distinguishing the real from the counterfeit. We were not duped. We accepted only genuine currency, while retaining the right to exchange it for another if it did not suit us. You see, that is still allowed here."

"So many men," I closed, "so many opinions. Nevertheless, in the end a manifesto was produced that it was quite possible to sign. Otherwise one certainly would not have signed it. That is all. It hurts us to say goodbye to you, it hurts me to write to you. But you yourself, typically, burned your bridges behind you. *Lebe wohl* – farewell, John. *Lebe aufrecht* – live honestly – is something I suppose we cannot say any more."

Whether in fact I was requested to add the support of my signature to the manifesto in which the Congress finally formulated its demands, I cannot remember. Certainly I *would* have done so, and Peter certainly *did* do so. It contained nothing with which we could not identify ourselves. We even accepted unresistingly that, in view of the "threat posed by the theory and practice of the totalitarian state," "indifference and neutrality" were equal to "betrayal of the essential values of humanity." What happened after that, what path was taken by the Cultural Congress, who turned out to be its backers and instructors, is another story. I only refer to it as it personally affected me. I have never articulated my political beliefs more clearly than in my open letter, and have never considered it necessary. At the beginning of July, two days before it was published in the *Neue Zeitung*, we returned to London. And here the misfortune which had already befallen us shortly before our departure for Berlin was awaiting our return. Mimi was fatally ill, and all the hopes we had nourished from time to time of her recovery proved to be deceptive.

14

The Far and the Near

Every human being determines the manner and the time of his or her own death. So I was told by the psychosomaticist Alf Lepper, and even if this wise and experienced physician was deliberately exaggerating, if his remark only applies to certain circumstances and certain civilizations, it frequently turns out to be true. It seems that in the Middle Ages the old or sick knew exactly when their hour had come; in fact they sensed it so far ahead that they could calmly summon their heirs, their friends, and, if they were wealthy, their servants, and everyone, even with a day's journey to travel, was present at the moment of death. Even today, people who are unable to get over the loss of their loved ones are able to follow them into death. And anyone searching for psychological reasons why someone succumbs to a fatal illness will find them more often than one might think.

"Your friends will betray you or come to grief themselves," Peter had told my mother a few months before the Anschluss. Now her loneliness was renewed and redoubled, for not only had she lost her husband, but two of his closest friends, who had fled to England like him, had died in middle age; the rest returned to Austria, and those who had stayed behind had not sent any signals that they missed her. While we were in Berlin she had found some work with a solicitor, an émigré German, who had started the whole wearisome study of law all over again, and on his naturalization had exchanged his original name for no less than that of the Lord Protector of England: he was now called Cromwell. But my mother, for whom the old gentleman soon developed a cordial affection, for some not entirely obvious reason called him Spitzweg (the name of a popular Bavarian painter), and he had no objection to this reminder of a German small-town idyll, for he had a sense of humor.

Mimi possessed, on the other hand, a certain poetic imagination full of fanciful associations, as when she said of one of our friends that he was "a violet sprinkled with milk." And yet her prevailing mood of cheerfulness was also clouded by sudden fits of melancholy, which attacked her for often totally unexpected reasons. In the London Underground stations there used to be – perhaps there still is – a poster advertising Start-Rite children's shoes. It showed a little girl in a red jacket, blue skirt, pointed cap, and red shoes, and a boy dressed in green and blue with a tartan cap. The two children were holding hands and seemed to be at the beginning of an apparently endless road down which they were about to run. Above them were the words "Little feet have far to go." My mother always sighed deeply when she saw this poster, because this path of life which the children were about to tread so joyfully in their Start-Rite shoes, was, as she herself well knew, a road full of dangers, of early disappointment, often of sadness, and, in spite of many good and happy experiences, in the end a *via dolorosa.*

It was on the Underground, the same Central Line whose rumbling and grumbling had accompanied my first months in Linden Gardens, that Mimi traveled from Notting Hill Gate to Holborn and back, in the rush hours, squashed between dozens of other working citizens. The lady who used to stroll every morning from the Sirkecke to the Kohlmarkt in Vienna had become a conscientious office worker. For all her friendly intimacy with her employer, could this be a lifestyle that she found rewarding in her advancing years? Certainly she had a daughter, she had grandchildren, whom she loved tenderly, but Mimi was not – even if circumstances had allowed – a woman to lose herself in her child and her child's children. When she visited us in Wimbledon on the weekends she was sometimes a little absent-minded, dreaming of another place, another time, perhaps in the past. In addition, with her lifelong childlike anxiety, she had her worries about our marital situation, which was managed by its participants themselves for the most part with great, if only outward, composure. That she had gone through similar experiences did not occur to her. On her deathbed, these fears fought their way out of her subconscious.

Childlike she was too when the sickness befell her, when she got into the hands of the doctors, when – presumably in error, and disastrously – the decision was made not to operate, but only to treat her with radiotherapy. "Mimi cries all the time. In pain. All the others are ill too." This was the entry in my calendar in March 1950. My son was constantly running a high fever and had throat problems, our black cat Ebony lay listlessly in her basket, and I had for a long time, since our difficulties in Berlin, been waking night after night to battle with attacks of asphyxiation – perhaps a sort of nervous asthma. I got rid of it, at first only gradually, after my return to Vienna, and then, as it were, it disappeared overnight. In May the irresponsible Mr. Davis, a surgeon like my own National Health doctor and, in fact, his son-in-law, declared Mimi completely cured. So we took the risk of taking her with us to Austria in July, to Mallnitz in Carinthia, where we stayed at the Gasthof zu den Drei Gemsen – the Three Chamois inn. Those were carefree family days. In between, Peter and I visited my dear friend Maria at nearby Tenneck bei Werfen, where she lived with her husband and two children, who were close to ours in age. It was the first time we had seen each other since the war. Joy and embraces. In Mallnitz the artist couple Georg and Bettina Ehrlich joined us; Flesch too was allowed to come and even to accompany Peter and me for two days in St. Wolfgang, where we were invited (without Flesch, however) for an evening at the house of the publishers Gottfried and Tutti Bermann-Fischer.

After sixteen years I was revisiting the place where I had experienced events of such a fancifully dramatic nature, the place which was soon to have a fateful resonance for us. The Bermann-Fischers, since April once again in total control of their publishing house, had rented Haus Breitgut, known as the Bernau house, for this and several further summers. In later years it became the residence of Robert and Ruth Jungk, then for a longer period of Hans Habe and his sixth wife Licci, and then, less significantly for us, of Joachim Kulenkampff. It had been owned by the late director of the Vienna Volkstheater and possessed all the charms of a country retreat: splendidly painted peasant furniture, old pictures of saints, historic military paraphernalia. In his day, Habe held a gala party there, to which he invited the film makers and composers from California who at that time used to spend the summer weeks in St. Wolfgang, as well as some of the local nobility, but not Peter and me. We found out why: among those present that evening were journalists and photographers from the glossy magazine *Das Schöne*, to whom Habe, always a brilliant poseur, had represented the peasant baroque furniture as his own collection, and the rented house as his property. If we had been there, we might, even with the best of intentions, have given the game away.

I am digressing in order to delay my account of Mimi's end. There were still many happy experiences to come during that summer of 1950. From our beloved Fiumetto, where we had traveled from Mallnitz, we rushed further south, stayed at the beautiful Albergo Porta Rossa in Florence, and in Rome – not for the last time – at the Inghilterra in the Via Bocca di Leone, so rich in tradition, now totally ruined by marble and costly "styling." And it was Holy Year: in the midst of an endless, and endlessly good-humored, throng we saw Pope Pius XII crossing St. Peter's Square, borne high on an open sedan chair, clad in white from head to foot, a supernatural apparition, a living image of grace which moved our children, then still devout Catholics, to deep religious emotion, as it did all those around us.

What did we know then, years before the première of Hochhuth's *The Representative*, of the ambivalent position of that Eugenio Pacelli who, when still a cardinal in 1933, had brought about the Reich *Concordat* with Hitler, and forced the dogma of the bodily assumption into heaven of the Virgin Mary upon a Catholic community not untouched by modern science? Long afterward, at the Goethe Institute in Milan, whose director was then Eckart Peterich, the respected converts Jakob Hegner and Rudolf Hirsch discussed with concerned countenances this belated *sacrificium intellectus* which was being demanded of them. But I, who knew from Hansi that the Pope had protected the émigrés in Rome – just as he had protected the henchmen of the Third Reich when they were fleeing to South America after the war – was unreservedly moved by this unblemished symbol, as I considered him, of a faith that I could no longer share but have always respected, as I do to this day; and moved also by the magnificent staging of this open-air spectacle.

On the day of my return I had to enter the London Clinic to submit once more to the surgeon's knife. "*Grande ouverture du ventre,*" I wrote with feigned nonchalance in my calendar. And not long afterward I had a grisly dream, in which Peter, Flesch and I were dining with Mimi in a cemetery. Winter came, the periods of darkness lengthened. Mimi was in and out of the hospital. In between she lived at Broadwalk Court, where Flesch visited her almost daily and played rummy with her. At the end of January she left St. Bartholomew's Hospital, where nothing more could be done for her, and moved in with us in Wimbledon. The torment lasted for five weeks. We enlisted the help of day nurses and night nurses so that she should not be left alone for a moment. Myrtle Walker, our staunch friend and doctor for whom the phrase "no nonsense" seemed to have been coined, provided her with ample medication. Nevertheless, it was heartrending to watch the slow extinction of her life. Simone de Beauvoir wrote a whole book about her mother's death. I will spare my readers and myself a great deal, but not everything. If one holds fast to memories to preserve people and encounters, earthly happiness and misfortune during the short span allotted to us before the plunge, the endless fall into the black emptiness of eternity and infinity, one cannot then evade the remembrance of the most hopeless moments of existence.

I sat with her for hours at a time, tried to sketch her in a few lines as she slept, noted down the little phrases she spasmodically uttered between sighs, and her occasional cheerful fantasies. She often mentioned her brother Felix, but as a child, when she called him "Belischi." Once she heard music at a distance: "Who is that splendid person," she murmured, "playing the piano or singing?" Or, this time in English, which she constantly mixed in with her German: "Why don't you introduce the gentleman? There, under the floor." When I offered her food, she said very politely, again in English: "Thank you, I had a complete meal at Mrs. Burleigh's." And her fears: "All the poison they put into my body, yours too?" "My brain has become so small, I can't understand things." And this too: "Does Peter know already that you are mad?" Even worse: "And what if he shoots Peter and Peter shoots him? You'd go mad then, Hilderl!" There were moments of euphoria too: "So much love, how lovely... Tea? Yes, how lovely, lovely." Then her fear again: "I have to stay awake, I mustn't go to sleep, because I have to know what they are doing with me." Five days before the end: "How much longer must we wait here, Hilderl? I'm so tired already." Next morning: "Hilderl... you're the best, the only one, and those others... " Whom did she mean? And finally: "*Servus*... prepare yourself... I'm dying slowly..."

Dr. Walker and the night nurse, Nurse Jenkins, had decided: the time had come. On the morning of the first day of March she fell asleep; I was with her, holding her hand, and Peter was sitting behind me. When it was over I went to my room, sat down, and continued writing the essay on Virginia Woolf that Melvin Lasky had commissioned on the occasion of the tenth anniversary of her death. On the tenth I sent it to Berlin, in time for it to be published in the March issue of *Der Monat*. And at the beginning of April I fled to Vienna, where I wanted to bury my mother's ashes in secret in her birthplace, as I had done with my father's urn – deep in the soil of the Ottakring cemetery, in the midst of the citizens who, though equally well established, had, however, never been driven out. And it was on this emotionally laden journey that I met my friend-enemy Torberg again and had the decisive angry confrontation with him that was to determine the future. It took place one night, up to half-past three in the morning, in the little, somberly cozy Café Hawelka, which had recently become popular and now seemed to suffice as the only venue for all the artists, musicians, literati who before the war had found their spiritual homes in a dozen such establishments in Vienna. Hans Weigel was there, his wife Udi, and the actress Kitty Stengel, who was like me horrified at the idea of a new war with Russia, which Torberg described as inevitable.

Here I must mention Klaus Dohrn's visit to us in London. *"Der dicke Klaus,"* "Fat Klaus," as he was known even in childhood, was a friend of Peter's from his days in Hellerau. Whether it was during the autumn of the previous year or after my fatal encounter with Torberg in Vienna I can no longer establish, for I did not enter the event in my calendar. But I remember very clearly this appearance of his, which made us increasingly indignant. Dohrn, whom I had already met in Vienna in the thirties and immediately perceived as a highly dubious character, had then fled the Nazis with the help of the highest church connections, and finally that of Paul Claudel, and after a longish stay in France had gone via Spain to the United States. There this brilliantly gifted man, who was, however, obsessed with his hatred of Russians, had found a welcome in all possible circles – those of Otto von Habsburg, of the Paneuropa movement, and finally, before his return, the Time-Life organization. Bruno Kreisky, who later met him in Vienna through the good offices of Torberg, reported in his memoirs that Dohrn's activity in America had been characterized by the words (in English) "He is doing a Catholic job."

The occupation of "Fat Klaus," a scion of one of the noblest German Protestant bourgeois families, during the postwar years can only be guessed. When he visited us in Wimbledon he tried all evening to interrogate us about our political opinions, our friends and connections. Slowly we became mistrustful, particularly since he seemed to be trying to pin us down to admitting excessive indulgence toward Communism. "What does Fat Klaus want? Who sent him to us?" asked Peter, after closing the door behind him. "I never want to see him again." And so it was. It was not till much later that I learned that Dohrn had made friends with Torberg in New York, and that the two men had maintained a close connection since then. Even three years before Dohrn's death Torberg requested him by letter "to do everything within your powers" to take action against Robert Jungk, the anti-nuclear campaigner, whom he opposed. "It is high time for a general mobilization. The enemy groups have already crossed all the borders." This was in 1964, and the military metaphor was not as outlandish or simply ironic as it might seem. For thirteen years earlier, immediately on his arrival back in Europe, my friend-enemy had gone upon the – at least verbal – warpath. Even between him and me, after so many more or less light-hearted skirmishes since our youth, things now became serious, bitterly serious.

The reader who wants to skip the next few pages may do so. I have no intention of describing all the disputes in which I was now to become embroiled for many years, a few of which I myself provoked – sometimes out of pure high spirits, more often in self-defense. To sum it up as briefly as possible: my friend-enemy, now an enemy pure and simple, missed the union of the Cold War participants in Berlin, he was not there at Crécy nor at Arques. He was one of those about whom, at the end of the Cultural Congress, Arthur Koestler quoted the words of the French King Henri IV: *"Pends-toi, brave Crillon: nous avons combattu à Arques et tu n'y étais pas."* But now things were moving ahead, brave Crillon was at his post, what had been neglected was being made up for. The task was in hand. In June 1951 Torberg wrote to Koestler that he was already drawing a salary, and "from September I will be working in Vienna with the State Dept. as 'Adviser to the Office of Cultural Affairs.'" The following year – as he wrote to his old friend, the former water-polo player Fritz Thorn – he was invited to the Paris Cultural Congress "as one of five representatives of Austrian intellectuality." And in 1954 he obtained from the Cultural Congress *plein pouvoir* and means, "plushy" means in fact, as his later assistant and successor Günter Nenning admitted, for the foundation of a periodical, the *Forum*, which for ten years enabled him to vent his wrath on all his enemies.

But to return to this night in April, soon after Torberg's return. He himself gave an account of it, in a letter to Koestler, in which he asked him to intervene against me with Melvin Lasky. Here he speaks of a "violent collision" in Vienna, which took place "with the lady de Spiel de Mendelssohn, because she took Thomas Mann (about whom her husband two or three years ago published a reverential brochure) under her protection as a 'naive and misused' prince of writers, and described Berthold Viertel, who has been practicing his propaganda antics at the Burgtheater for years now, as an 'honest seeker after truth.' As early as the day after this collision, threatening telephone calls emanated from the circles of prominent fellow travelers (who had been informed immediately by the lady Spiel)..." and so on. It seems that Koestler took his time before replying or making an approach to Lasky. In the meantime he had, after all, completely withdrawn from the Cultural Congress which he had helped to create with so much enthusiasm. But finally, although apparently still hesitating, he declared himself prepared to accede to Torberg's requests. And this was Torberg's reply, in English, on September 1 of the same year, 1951: "I'm almost as late with my letter as you have been with yours... Thanks for your readiness to take that Spiel thing up with Lasky – but I'd rather you didn't. It would be too much of a *kowed* [honor] for that little *Filzlaus* [crab louse], if you know what I mean, which you do."

This was to suffice for the time being. In May, months after the "collision," Torberg seems to have sent his novel *Die zweite Begegnung* (*The Second Encounter*) to me in London, for his book is in front of me inscribed with that date and the dedication "for Hilde Spiel, as the last contribution to a conversation which must end, presented a quarter of an hour before the decision, and until then." What decision was I to make? In favor of the Cold War and its witch hunts? Never! And yet I despised the Stalinist system, I admired America, for its writers, its music – Dos Passos' *Manhattan Transfer* and Gershwin's *Rhapsody in Blue* had long ago given me a foretaste of New York – and I fell in love with America when I visited the United States with Peter in April of the following year.

Our journey, on the railroads which still covered all parts of the country, in fact introduced us to twenty of these states, even though we saw some of them only from the windows of our trains, and we stayed for longer or shorter periods in fourteen towns, each of which proved to be an impressive or even intoxicating experience. We omitted the Middle West, saving even New England for future visits. But we traversed this mighty land from the East coast to the deepest South to the Californian West, and returned via a northern route to our point of departure. I wonder whether the self-styled spokesmen for America who tried to brand us their political and ideological antagonists had done such thorough research from Manhattan to Hollywood as we did during that hot, glorious spring and early summer of 1952.

So many Europeans, so many German-speaking young people since then have looked around them in the States and found the stimulation for subtle fables and gripping films. It seems tasteless to boast of such travels across the globe, now that every self-respecting person takes holidays in Honolulu. But a journey across the Atlantic in the early fifties, to that country which was developing at such a breathless rate, changing so incessantly, now seems like an expedition into history. When a turn-of-the-century skyscraper such as the Woolworth Building has something of the aura for Americans that a Gothic cathedral has for us; when, on our first visit to the city museum of Salt Lake City, we saw the oil lamps and flatirons of our Alpine country houses, and even a *fin de siècle* piano, exhibited as curious survivors of a far-distant past; when the authentic Dixieland sound was still to be heard in New Orleans, and there was no German summer school yet in Taos, New Mexico, the American fifties may, forty years on, seem like a deeply submerged era – almost nearer to pre-Columbian times than to the jet tourism of the present day.

It began with the five and a half days on the high seas, which give quite a different impression of the distance between the continents from that of a flight, or rather it began at Waterloo Station, at the boat train which took transatlantic passengers to the seaport. The elegant *monde* of London were milling about on the platform, for this lengthy and expensive expedition was then undertaken by members of an exclusive stratum rather than by less well-off citizens – not to speak of youngsters laden with sleeping bags. The large groups of friends and relatives that assembled brought with them orchids which the departing ladies and gentlemen pinned to their shoulders, as did I, for Flesch had presented the obligatory farewell gift, which was meant to symbolize a successful sea journey, before the departure of the train. We were to board the *Liberté* in Southampton. The *Champlain*, on which Peter had made the Atlantic crossing in 1938, had been sunk by the Germans during the war. That this new, beautiful, sleek ocean steamer of the French Line, of some 50,000 metric tons, had been launched under the name *Europa* in Kiel or Hamburg now passed unnoticed, for the boat, awarded in reparation to the co-victors, was now as French, from the captain's bridge to the chef in the kitchen, as one could imagine – and, in the latter case, as one could wish. Its first-class restaurant was recognized as the best to be found on the high seas.

But we were traveling tourist class, and there the first two days on board were anything but a pleasure. In the musty atmosphere of the narrow cabin I lay wretchedly on the rumpled sheet, trying to shut out the whole globe with its stormy waters – longing only to survive in order to set my foot on dry land again, on a surface which would no longer sway and lurch beneath me. Then the sea grew tranquil, the sun came out and we put up deck chairs on our modest, though open deck. Having ascertained from our passports that we were authors, *des auteurs*, the captain, obviously a friend of literature, granted us the privilege of disporting ourselves on all parts of the boat, even entering the first-class area with the help of a specially issued pass, although he tactfully gave us to understand that the invitation did not extend to meals. And so we sometimes spent an afternoon hour in the Palm Court on the luxury deck – where we were allowed to take tea – and there saw T. S. Eliot sitting in a comfortable armchair near the orchestra, his head bowed over a book, listening with one ear to the Viennese songs and gentle swing melodies more attuned to the *beau monde* than harsh jazz. On the final evening we were, at last, invited to dine with the captain in first class, and I entered in my calendar: "Horrid shocking boring menagerie of millionaires."

And then came our arrival in Manhattan. We got up at half-past four in the morning to see the Statue of Liberty in the first glow of dawn, and soon afterward the outline of the skyscrapers on the lower edge of the Bowery rising out of the mist. And how infuriating it must be for those born after us – to whom my descriptions of day-long wanderings on skis in the mountains, at a time when there were no ski lifts, must already have seemed like tiresome, sentimental bragging – if I now declare that landing at Kennedy airport cannot remotely compare with the experience of entering the Hudson River. Just the first glimpse of the mainland – or rather of that little peninsula on which the most exciting part of New York is crammed together in those lofty towers, those gigantic castles in the air such as had never been seen in Europe at that time, a Valhalla from Wagner's *Ring*, looming up before us in the rosy and pale-green early light, at first far, far away, then ever nearer and more tremendous – this alone, and with it the feeling of adventure which one must have after days of isolation on the empty sea, when a new world is reached, is granted to some passengers on cruises, but not to the great mass of present-day air travelers; not to speak of taking possession of a city as one glides past its flanks, to dock in the end at a pier on the Westside Highway. More than ten years later I too was to become one of those jetsetters to whom the runway of a foreign part of the world looks no different from one's own, even if one kneels to greet it with a kiss. But it was worth experiencing what may here be counted an advantage of being born in an earlier era, when, after the horror of so many years we had been forced to endure, we could share the feelings of a Christopher Columbus or a Captain Cook on the discovery of new shores.

In his one-act play *New-Found-Land*, which I had the privilege of translating into German, Tom Stoppard allows an ordinary English ministry official to describe a journey straight across the United States – thrilling in its vitality and its sparse, impressionistic clarity. In my own, much less grandiose manner I had tried something similar many years earlier, in the American novel I wrote after this journey, in which the Baltic first-person narrator left the New York she hated, and traveled by car with her lover along the mighty highways of the land to California, to settle in San Francisco and banish from her thoughts for all time the East Coast with its European immigrants, indeed the whole of wretched Europe. It was not in such a mood of hasty, rhythmic intoxication that we moved through the States at that time, but in much more restful phases, stopping for now longer, now shorter spaces of time in places which seemed worth seeing, or where we had friends, with whom we often felt impelled to stay longer than was strictly called for.

It was Hermann Kesten – that quick-witted key figure, once of the *Neue Sachlichkeit*, now of German exile – who welcomed us after the tedious formalities on board and our eventual, magnanimous admission to the richest country on earth. The famous Riverside Drive, the first street we encountered, already seemed a little oldfashioned to us with its houses of dark brick and moderate height, so dazzled were we by the white skyscrapers that had greeted our arrival. We first went to the Hotel Manhattan Towers on Broadway, which we found in fact rather too dreary, and ended up, with Kesten's help, at the Hotel Colonial on Central Park West. As I got out of the taxi my eye fell on a restaurant nameplate next to the entrance, which bore the name Neugröschl. This had been the name of the most famous Jewish restaurant in Vienna, in the second district. Our little hotel suite with sitting room, bathroom, "closet," and refrigerator cost five dollars a day. From here we began our conquest of New York.

Our first visit to Hansi, the beauty I had last seen in her full splendor on the roof terrace in Parioli, was shattering. She looked thin and pale, her still regular features darkened by bluish shadows. Clearly conscious of the change in her appearance, she had dimmed or turned off the lights in most of the rooms in the apartment where she was living with her latest husband – a blond, Teutonically spruce medical man with an air of restlessness. The closed or half-closed curtains with which she shut out the garish American reality created for her an artificial, unreal world of subdued light in which she found it easier to endure the fading of her charms and powers. A nondescript young woman, of what descent I no longer remember, waited on her in place of the formidable Sicilian woman who had baked such delicious pizzas for her in Rome. The good times were over. Hansi, as she defiantly informed us, had cancer. That she was also a drug addict – had already begun to use drugs in Italy, with Vittorio – we learned next day from Nellie, my dear Nellie from Zurich, who had emigrated to New York with Robert Seidl after the war.

And so our sunny day was already beclouded, although not for very long, in this overpoweringly vital, instantly rejuvenating city, which seemed to spark a zest for life, a hope for the future, a joy in being in this world that we had never before felt so strongly, so thrillingly, which tore us out of all our sorrow and world-weariness, if only we were prepared to surrender to it. And we did surrender, we journeyed through the dead-straight streets, like canyons between the mountainous buildings, and in the evenings joined the throngs in Times Square, where hundreds of hot neon lights vanquished the cool night wind; but we also caught glimpses of the crass contradictions of the American social fabric: the glittering ladies in blue mink jackets in front of the picture palaces, the beggars and drunks, the many black faces and supple bodies – an unaccustomed sight for us, arriving from England, where the influx of West Indians had not yet taken place. We had supposed London to be the hub of a multicolored, turning world, but here, where all the languages of Europe, including Yiddish, were spoken without inhibition or fear of xenophobia, we realized how fundamentally insular, how predominantly Anglo-Saxon was the capital of the British Empire.

Limitless possibilities! On our second day at the hotel the porter gave me a letter, addressed to "Miss Hilde Mendel, Room 703" – the correct number of our suite – which read: "We want to inform you that a person of your experience is needed in a job, and will you apply to this office as soon as possible." An employment agency, without knowing me, was holding out a friendly hand to me. What job could it be that they wished to offer me? I did not dare to imagine. There followed a week in which we raced from museum to museum, from one rendezvous with émigré acquaintances to another, we sought out Harlem, Chinatown, the Brooklyn Bridge, chatted with Manfred George in the office of the *Aufbau* newspaper, lunched with the publisher Mike Bessie in Greenwich Village on the tenderest roast beef of those years – in England that sort of food was still rationed – and returned to Hansi's lamplit living room, dining room, and bedroom to meet with the remaining representatives of German and Austrian intellectuality and dignity, who had by chance been born under the wrong sign and thus had to depart into the *Wildfremde*, into strange foreign parts, as Wilhelm Speyer had once called them.

Then, at Pennsylvania Station, our journey of discovery into the real America began, an undertaking of enormous proportions, the traversing of half the world, a plunge into a gigantic fairground railway which reminded me of the little one of my childhood in the Vienna Prater, where again and again the most astonishing, most entrancing scenes appeared out of nowhere, populated with equally exotic figures. For Tom Stoppard it was a train called Silver Chief which propelled the English civil servant Arthur through a wealth of places and landscapes, whirling together in geographical confusion. There all the New World clichés came to life, from the green horse pastures of Kentucky by way of the abattoirs of Chicago and the burning city of Atlanta to the barges of St. Louis and the sheriffs of the prairie. We too were not to escape the clichés as we took a trip on a Mississippi paddle steamer or saw the sun rising behind the Grand Canyon. But what an ecstatic feeling it was when all the images long familiar to us from the books of Mark Twain, Theodore Dreiser and Thomas Wolfe, and from the great old Western films, all at once became tangible reality.

So first to Philadelphia, and then on to Washington, where we, the dangerous Russian-lovers in the eyes of so many Cold Warriors in Europe, were admitted into the Pentagon – that well-guarded fortress, where we were received by Peter's former superior officer, General McClure. Cities and people: again and again I found myself leaning on the pillars of my memory. Our old friend Ferdy Kuhn, and Jimmy Wreston, another great journalist of the time, took us to the Capitol, the Senate, and the House of Representatives, and showed us the Library of Congress. And finally, in a café, we met the Germanist Heinz Politzer – later so successful and well-known, but at that time, as I noted, "poor and helpless," because he had recently lost his post at the distinguished women's college Bryn Mawr. It was not until our return journey that, once again attracted to Washington, we had an enjoyable lunch with Peter's Colonel Leonard. In the capital of the United States, at least, we were regarded as allies.

And so to Charlottesville, a university town built in Georgian style, where the great historian and political scientist Stringfellow Barr, to whom we had a letter of introduction, invited us to a brilliant dinner party. However, I developed an allergic reaction to the enormous strawberries, which looked as if they had been painted by some Flemish still-life artist; the following day I awoke with a high temperature, swollen cheeks and arms, and an itching rash. And here again we encountered T. S. Eliot, not in the flesh this time, but in a bookshop window, in which, to my horror, I saw a display of his anti-Semitic writings: an illusion, an admiration paled. I have forgotten the real name of the train which, after an hour's lingering in Jefferson's home at Monticello, carried us southwest, but remember that during our journey I was constantly humming the song: "Pardon me, boy, is that the Chattanooga choo-choo? Track twenty-nine, boy, you can gimme a shine," for we were now heading for Tennessee and Alabama. We were astounded by what we heard in Washington: the first white settlers, we were told, had colonized the American South in 1607. Four years later they bought a consignment of African slaves from a Dutch seaman, and these had settled in the area before the Pilgrim Fathers arrived on the *Mayflower* at Cape Cod in 1620.

At the town of Orange, north of Charlottesville, we had already seen from the window of our train the separate waiting rooms on the platform marked "White" and "Colored." "Jim Crow" law was in force here – the absolute separation of races. And now, on the route to Knoxville, all along the railway embankment we saw the wretched shacks of the dark-skinned, long-established inhabitants, as well as the no less dilapidated houses of rotting wood where the "poor whites" lived, with the same sun-bleached porches, on which stood the same shabby wicker rocking chairs, the same household trappings which looked ready for the trash can. After Chattanooga we reached the state of Alabama, which belied the idyll of Brecht's nostalgic song "O moon of Alabama, we now must say goodbye," for in Birmingham, where we stopped briefly for a couple of hours, we already sensed that clenched hopelessness of unemployed blacks which, decades later, was to trigger the first great race riots there. And so straight through Mississippi to wonderful New Orleans, which we reached on the scorchingly, suffocatingly hot evening of the twenty-fourth of May.

The shabby little Hotel St. Charles had no air conditioning, only an enormous fan which relentlessly whirred all night on the ceiling of our room. Next day we were delighted by this 250-year-old capital of the French Louisiana which Napoleon sold in 1803 to the United States, and in whose harbor, according to the Abbé Prévost, Manon Lescaut and Des Grieux had landed – this mixture of French charm, Spanish sense of proportion and ornament, black African gracefulness, all this merging in the Creole language, Creole cuisine, Creole architecture, and the enchanting girls, "quadroons" and "octoroons," whose partly black heritage made them the most beautiful creatures on earth. We walked around all day in the Vieux Carré with its houses painted in delicate ochre or pale pink, the endlessly diverse wrought iron balconies and the shady patios – the Court of Two Sisters and the Patio Royal – where, then as now, one could dine on spicy fish and seafood dishes: oysters Rockefeller, gumbo, soft shell crab, shrimp Creole.

It was in New Orleans, about the turn of the century, that jazz had come into being. Now the jazz venues were lined up one after another in Dauphine Street and Bourbon Street, where connoisseurs, or rather addicts, of the "Dixieland Sound" would spend half the day under the spell of drum and trumpet, saxophone and singer. We too listened as if possessed to "Basin Street Blues" – "Bassin Rue" in Creole – still sung in a cracked voice by the old black singer Lizzie Miles in the Mardi Gras Club in Bourbon Street, tearing ourselves away only to be captivated by Fred Coleman's Band a few doors further down. The end of each hour we spent there was marked by "Sultry Serenade," their number for solo trumpet and percussion, and we emerged dazed and befuddled by the drumming of Coleman himself. We took a river trip on the steamer *President* with its great paddle wheels, and a journey to the terminus and back on the bus called "Desire" – the streetcar of that name had already vanished by that time. A black lawyer, Dr. Thureaud, enlightened us about the situation of the black population, so exceptionally creative, and so exceptionally underprivileged. And, of course, we allowed ourselves to be driven a few miles out to one of the old plantations, with its manor house decked with pillars in the midst of flourishing shrubs and glossy green undergrowth, immortalized by Margaret Mitchell in her magnificent kitsch novel.

What could Texas offer to compare with this? We left Dallas with its oil barons, Houston with its faculty of German studies, later so highly regarded, and crossed the Rio Grande on foot, at the frontier bridge at El Paso, to Juarez, where the whole of Mexico could be experienced in a nutshell: the mission churches, always freshly whitewashed, the peasant weddings with the women's whirling skirts, the souvenir shops with their tragacanth skulls. Another Mexico, the American New Mexico, awaited us in Albuquerque, in Santa Fé and in Taos, that place still forgotten by the world, forgotten by Europe, on the edge of the Sangre de Cristo mountains. And there we met figures long anchored in the English literary consciousness: the widow of D. H. Lawrence and his most faithful follower, the aristocratic Dorothy Brett – the only one of all those present who got up and left with him and Frieda at the legendary Café Royal dinner in late 1923, when Lawrence, in Messianic mood and consciously alluding to the Last Supper at Emmaus, challenged his disciples to give him their allegiance in founding an artistic community called "Rananim" in the mountains of New Mexico. And so "Brett," once a brilliant hostess and a friend of Katherine Mansfield, had remained in the wonderful wilderness, together with Frieda and the American millionairess Mabel Dodge Luhan, whom Lawrence had lured to Taos during the First World War. In an article I wrote for the *New Statesman* called "Three Wise Ladies of Taos," I described these women, who had continued to spin out their petty jealousies long after Lawrence's death and now lived together in peace.

What had induced us to make this expedition? The son of the singer Elisabeth Schumann, who was working for the BBC, had begged us before our departure not to omit it, and had given us an introduction to Frieda Lawrence, née Baroness von Richthofen. Leaving sultry, stuffy Albuquerque behind, we had driven up into the mountains to Santa Fé, which was already welcoming strangers, and into the highlands of Taos, and had rented a room at the Hotel La Fonda, on the plaza of the little town of ranchers, trappers, anglers, and horse breeders. Then we presented ourselves to Frieda. She was seventy-two, married to the former *bersaglieri* lieutenant Angelo Ravagli, "Angelino," whom she, at the age of fifty-four, had lured away from his wife, and was still very attractive with her casual, voluptuous femininity, with her scarcely faded maize-colored hair. A corn goddess, an earth mother, indeed "the mother of orgasm and of the enormous, living mystery of the flesh," as Mabel Dodge had called her. She received us very cordially, for we spoke the German of her youth, kept us there for hours, and showed us those "scandalous" oil paintings of Lawrence's which she had not entrusted to her friend, the Greek owner of La Fonda, for exhibition. I noted what she told us about her life in Taos and further up on the Kiowa Ranch with her Indian servants, Trinidad and Rufina, but neither in the *Statesman* nor the *Monat* did I betray all the details.

Another German called Mendelssohn, as she immediately told us, had visited her recently: a scientist working at nearby Los Alamos, the birthplace of the Hiroshima bomb, where atomic research was still continuing. In fact there were family connections between the Richthofens and the Mendelssohns – her aunt Fanny had been a granddaughter of Felix Mendelssohn-Bartholdy's sister, Fanny Hensel. But she talked not only of her forebears, but also of the three children she had once left behind for Lawrence's sake and now occasionally visited in England, with her grandchildren. She did not want to return to Germany; all her relatives there were so poor and had suffered so much, the whole Silesian family had lost everything. When the Russians were advancing, a neighbor had come to them and asked her to look after his treasures. "And what was their greatest treasure?" asked Frieda with her harsh, throaty laugh. "A lock of Goethe's hair!" To her, the wife of a writer, and the prototype of his Lady Chatterley, in her "wisdom of the blood" – Lawrence, the puritan, in his philosophy of freedom from sexual inhibition came dangerously close to certain "myths of the twentieth century" – such glorification of outworn relics seemed simply comic.

Mabel Dodge had wanted to fix Frieda quite firmly on this level of a purely physical existence. "She was his [Lawrence's] medium, he needed her in order to see, and she could only perceive life from the sexual center." But this woman had more than natural intelligence. She described the Indians among whom she lived to us as very kindly people. Their tribe had not been exterminated because it was basically a peaceful one. They called themselves Christians and were "polite toward that religion," but they celebrated their own pagan rites in August by the sacred blue lake and sternly forbade the whites to approach too closely, indeed they had already killed some inquisitive Anglos who ignored their wishes. Her maid Josephine, down here in Taos, always borrowed her best shawl for these festivals. "It probably has something to do with sex," said Frieda, laughing again. And how charming they were, what true friends! She had announced to Trinidad and Rufina up in San Cristobal: "Listen, this land once belonged to you. When I die, you will get it back." At first they were enthusiastic. But then: "What will the governor say?" And next morning they came and said: "Frieda, you are not rich. Why don't you sell the land and keep the money?" They were openhearted, and taciturn only when it came to their secret religious practices. Even Tony Luhan, Mabel's patient Indian husband, the first and only man to endure the moods of this eccentric woman, had never breathed a single word about them to her.

She did not begin to speak of Lawrence until Peter mentioned that Taos, that high plateau country, that land of light with its fragrant mountain sage and plum blossom with its scent more beautiful than that of cinnamon and carnation, as soon as we arrived at the top of the winding roads, had seemed to us like "the roof of the world." Strange, she cried out, that was what Lawrence had called it; he had used those very words. But before she could go on, the Honorable Dorothy Eugenie Brett, known as "Doll" as a child, then forever as "Brett," appeared, a big weatherproof Englishwoman, with a plainly visible hearing aid in her ear and a beret fixed to her hair with metal barrettes, splashes of paint on her upper lip, a well-filled blouse, and blue jeans tucked into boots. She abducted us to her house opposite in Questa Road, built, like all those in Taos, in the adobe style of the Indian clay buildings, but bearing the coat of arms of her noble family which she had painted over the entrance. In her studio she showed us those great oil paintings in which she had given expression to her forbidden knowledge of the ritual dances on the sacred mountain. Wild, colorful visions of the "sun and moon god" and the girls sacrificed to him – perhaps even accurate, for the Indians took fright when they saw the paintings, and Brett had to explain that she had only dreamed everything.

"See the cobra that killed Grace Wiley!" read an enormous poster on the highway alongside a kilometer-long "cobra garden" near Grants, a few hours west of Albuquerque. We were on our way to Arizona, this time by bus, straight through the Petrified Forest and the Painted Desert to Williams, where we stayed the night, driving to the Grand Canyon at daybreak. I will refrain from describing this wonder of the world, but make a leap to Los Angeles, because it was there, after New York and Taos, that the most significant encounters of our months in the States took place. The film city on the edge of the Pacific was at the time the home not only of Peter's youngest brother Felix and their mother Frau von Cube, now well advanced in years, but still dignified and ladylike, enthroned in shantung silk and matte pearls, but also the composer Erich Zeisl and his wife Trude, whom I called Susi, and after fourteen years it was an indescribable pleasure for me to see them again, together with their pretty little daughter. And here, what was more, most of the leading figures of the German-speaking colony in Californian exile, which has already passed into history, were still living. The Brechts and Eislers had left; Heinrich Mann and his wife, Arnold Schoenberg, and Franz Werfel were all dead. But the lifestyle and the memories of those who remained were intact. And it is not only because that skillful boulevardier Christopher Hampton perpetrated a wicked travesty of them all thirty years later, in his *Tales from Hollywood*, that I would like to linger with them a little. In my description of Bertolt Brecht in Berlin, I have already contradicted Hampton's stage portrayal of that playwright – who, after all, was somewhat the superior craftsman – as an evil little rat.

Certainly there were and are, as in every group, widely differentiated individuals among the émigrés in that city. In my memory they range from the august to the vulgar – from, let us say, Thomas Mann, as distinguished as he was modest, without a trace of Olympian vanity in his behavior to his guests, to Paul Kohner, who had arrived here long before the Hitler days, a former film producer and now agent for many prominent figures. Albert Bassermann, John Huston, Maurice Chevalier, and Charles Boyer, Remarque and, years after our visit, even Ingmar Bergman and Liv Ullmann were among his clients. He was labeled "the magician of Sunset Boulevard" by his more naive and likable brother Frederick in a eulogistic biography. To us, Paul Kohner seemed an embodiment of everything that was dubious about Hollywood, that "market where lies were sold," and Hampton might have done better to turn his attention to such matters. Visiting him at the behest of "Pem" (Paul E. Markus), the former Berliner and chronicler of exile, we sat endlessly in an anteroom of his villa, until he appeared in shirtsleeves, ungracious because we had interrupted a poker party by the side of his swimming pool. What did we want? He clearly expected that two authors could only have come to ask him about making film versions of their books, and was amazed when we expressed no such desires. Then why had we come? Because Pem had asked us to pay him a courtesy visit. He was at a loss, and in his perplexity offered to arrange a tour of Paramount Studios for us. We thanked him and took our leave. All I can remember of the visit to the studios is the shooting, in forty-three takes, of a minute-long scene from a Western.

How different was the tea party in the mansion on Pacific Palisades, reminding us of Lübeck, Munich, or Zurich, where Thomas and Katia Mann received us exactly as they would have in Poschingerstrasse or in Küsnacht. We learned that they were on the brink of their return to Europe, to Switzerland, but there was no hint of haste, of preparation for departure; the conversation was calm and relaxed, without reserve or timidity, and with a natural courtesy on their part which belied Hampton's caricature of an arrogant, cold, intellectual dandy. We had arrived with Salka Viertel, Berthold's wife, who had brought us up from her house in Santa Monica and afterward also came to the Feuchtwangers' with us. The prevailing tone in these undoubtedly well-appointed establishments allowed us to draw conclusions about the manners of the Germans and Austrians during their time together in the city on the Pacific Ocean, so far from Europe, imported patterns of behavior which had degenerated neither into self-satisfied pathos nor, despite all the lively communication, into embarrassing over-familiarity. At the famous birthday party held for Heinrich Mann at Salka's house in the middle of wartime, if he and his brother Thomas made ceremonial speeches about each other, Hampton may have found this ridiculous in retrospect; Salka herself said that "splendid, brilliant ideas" had been expressed that evening, and that many of the refugees present had listened with tears streaming down their cheeks.

It was Marta Feuchtwanger, active and communicative well into her late nineties, who became the source of later distortions. On my frequent visits to Los Angeles I repeatedly listened to her imaginative reminiscences, which had long ago taken on their own reality. She was a witty, brave, energetic woman, committed to an ancillary role during her marriage to a dominating husband and, while living at Sanary, overshadowed, in addition, not only by Feuchtwanger's numerous mistresses, but above all by his secretary Lola Sernau, who was his intellectual companion. In Marta's memoirs her name does not occur. Survivors are always right, as one might say in a reversal of the French maxim referring to the absent. That little episode when Nellie Mann, wearing an excessively revealing negligee, opened the door to Ludwig Marcuse, who was paying an unexpected morning visit, was transformed by Marta into a half-naked appearance by Nellie in front of a dozen evening guests – Marta's account remains unconfirmed by any other. When on that occasion we visited the splendid Villa

Aurora, her flow of words was continually stemmed by her ugly but lovable little husband, Lion Feuchtwanger. His writing methods, involving many versions on differently colored paper, his collection of incunabula and early books built up for the third time after the entire loss of the first and second, and above all the style of furnishing of his home, were certainly not matched by the quality of his books, but corresponded to their financial success.

Later, in Mabery Road, at the home of Salka, Greta Garbo's scriptwriter and best woman friend, there was no evidence of a butler or a cook, as in Hampton's play, but all the more of European culture. A large, stately woman, she had, like Frieda Lawrence, the aura of a venerated mother goddess. Two of her sons were there, Americanized versions of Berthold Viertel. Salka was already divorced from him then, but they kept up an intimate and frequent correspondence. She was not able to visit him in Austria before his premature death: the witch hunters denied her a passport, among other reasons because she had signed a petition for the persecuted Hollywood Ten. He was dead by the time she was finally allowed to leave the States and settle in Klosters near her son Peter. In the seventies, on my repeated trips to California, apart from Erich Zeisl's widow and daughter only two of the great old guard of émigrés remained: Gina Kaus, who had introduced us in 1952 to the sculptor Anna Mahler, then still living in the orphaned Werfel house, and Marta – two fabulous but very different old ladies. It was always Erich whom I missed most bitterly on these occasions; he had died, literally of a broken heart, on a scorchingly hot day, at the age of fifty-three like my father. On this, the first trip, he had played for us on the piano a few deeply moving passages from his opera *Job*, which was to remain unfinished, based on the novel by Joseph Roth, before we traveled on to San Francisco.

In this most beautiful of all cities Peter once more fell into one of his black moods, inexplicable as they so often were. To make things up to me he bought me a little jewelry case, which has been a carefully guarded treasure to this day. In Salt Lake City we bought and studied a Mormon bible, and inspected the temple and the luxury dwellings of this sect, as abstruse as its members were efficient in business matters, and also saw a fashion show, which all the ladies who adhered to the revelatory religion of Joseph Smith and his angel attended in the opulent glow of jewelry. Then came the long drive through the Rockies to Denver, a night in a hotel there where the members of a Republican convention had gathered, a strange bestiary

with their gaudy rosettes, and finally to Chicago: its wonderful
lakeside road along Lake Michigan, Picasso's portrait of Gertrude
Stein in the Art Institute, and an outing into the country, into deep
green Illinois, where we stayed the night in a house called "Acres
Away" with the delightful actress Monica Miller. She was the daughter
of my grandmother Laura's family doctor, who never visited her
without wearing white gloves, and a school friend of Peter Smolka at
the *Gymnasium* in Kundmanngasse, and was now married to a wealthy
father figure.

And finally, a significant experience after arriving back in New
York. Peter had stayed behind in Washington for a few days, and I
took a taxi to the Colonial Hotel. After getting out, I missed my new
red jewelry case, and was frightened out of my wits. Fifteen minutes
later – I was still standing in the hotel reception area – the same taxi
stopped in front of the entrance and the driver came in carrying the
little case. He was a little man with a stubbly beard, of Czech origin,
Julius Kohout, Yellow Cab 5270.785 – he wrote his name and number
down in my notebook. I kissed him on both cheeks, which seemed to
give him more pleasure than the couple of dollars' reward I pressed
into his hand.

Hansi was not in town; she had gone to France to have an
operation. We did not have much time left and spent our last evening
with Heinrich Eduard Jacob and Dora, the former Dora Angel from
Flesch's circle, for Ernst Angel, her brother, was the friend of his
youth. The next day, the twenty-sixth of June, we embarked on the
Queen Mary, in conditions of 100 degrees Fahrenheit and 90 percent
humidity. The half hour during which we stood in a line on the
gangway was more strenuous than the entire remainder of the journey.
We arrived in our cabin soaked in sweat. The American dream was
over, the apotheosis of our lust for travel was complete. Despite some
outbreaks of an unpredictable temperament this was perhaps the
happiest enterprise of our life together.

For now, after attaining the farthest distances of our lives,
something nearer to hand again exercised its attraction, beckoned ever
more forcefully, called ever more loudly: Austria. And in the long run
Peter, with all his changeability, his temporary passion for Oswalt von
Wolkenstein, for the Tyrol, despite old and new enchantment by the
charm of easy-going people, of Alpine landscapes, could not fit in;
where he really felt at home, if not in prewar Berlin, was in the
sunshine of France or Italy, in the lands of the Mediterranean. And so

for years we always spent a few weeks at Marina di Pietrasanta, but St. Wolfgang would not let us go, wrapped us in its perhaps deceptive, but yet so comforting homelike atmosphere, a security in the midst of – perhaps only apparently – like-minded, like-thinking people. Here, watching the flashing, curling waves of the lake – *pimpant*, as the Belgians once called it – with the bold peak of the Schafberg behind us, the hollow of the Vormauer to the left, the distinctive curve between the Sparber and the Bleckwand on the opposite shore, we were drawn in ever more deeply to a community, a summer lifestyle which for so long had made this whole region into a beloved habitation of writers and artists and musicians, which later so many of them could only yearn after with nostalgia.

This community and this lifestyle had continued in the same course since the thirties, though its numbers were reduced between times by those who were driven out or sent to their deaths, and had been preserved to this day. Even in wartime, almost completely unaffected by air attacks, let alone the din of firearms or the rumbling of tanks, the urban nobility spent all year or at least several months of each year in their country seats alongside the local people, and gathered together sociably. The Grand Hotel had become a military hospital, and in the beautiful Auhof high above the lake, at the end of the war, the rulers had accommodated King Leopold III of the Belgians, who had been dethroned by them, with his morganatic wife Liliane de Réthy, and the idyllic peace of the spot had been sought not only by a whole series of Viennese writers, who were to become our intimate friends, but even by the SS General Wolff. Just one lady of Jewish origin had survived in the village, protected by her husband's family, whose allegiance was entirely to the Nazis. But now the outcasts were rushing back, not only from London but from the environs of the deserts of California and Israel; they were intoxicated with the Salzkammergut as they had been so much earlier, and had thirsted for so long in vain for fresh mountain air, for the smell of pinewood and cyclamen, but above all for rain, that spicy rain which washes the landscape so clean that on the next sunny morning it sparkles more gloriously than all the pine-covered hills, all the silver-grey olive groves, sleepy seas, and eternally blue skies of Italy.

And so here they were again, in these and other villages and towns in the mountain and lake district, after long absences, endured with not too much difficulty by those left behind, compensated to some extent by occasional nostalgic recounting of their jokes and witty sayings – Leo Perutz and Ralph Benatzky, Fritz Kortner and Ernst Deutsch, Mischa Spoliansky and Adolf Wohlbrück (Anton Walbrook), Ferdinand Bruckner, Berthold Viertel and Friedrich Torberg; in St. Wolfgang moreover, for a few summers, there were some of the best film makers, composers and lyricists from Hollywood such as Robert Siodmak, Fritz Rotter, and Hans Jacoby, not to speak of successive tenants of Haus Breitgut, the Bermann-Fischers, Habes, and Jungks. And they were given a warm welcome, not, as the disillusioned Rahel Varnhagen complained after the newly kindled "Judensturm" of 1819 at the German universities, subjected to "torture and contempt, to kicking and throwing down stairs," but rather to love, even to embraces, to renewed attention to their jokes, now related at first hand (although they no longer had much heart to tell them), to the revival of dialogue and above all to the realization that the Nazi regime that had been fundamentally hated by all, but endured by necessity, with its disgusting intrusions into the comfortable daily routine and finally with all the sacrifices that had been demanded in the course of the reconquest of Europe, was now finally at an end. Anti-semitism with its fatal consequences was finished; at worst it had become a trifling offense, off the record, as in the good old days.

And all of them, all the homecomers, for that was what at least the Austrians among them were, rejoiced beyond measure, forgave everyone for everything, made no enquiries as to which of their old or newly acquired friends had shared the guilt, and to what extent, for the misfortune that had now come to an end. Only Elias Canetti, who spent a few days in St. Wolfgang in the fifties with his young traveling companion Nassauer, claimed to have overheard evil talk over the beer and wine in bars such as the "Wiesbauer" which were not frequented by those homecomers, and departed with the observation that Hitler was still alive everywhere here. But Canetti had made himself so unpopular by his arrogant and aggressive behavior toward the other writers that it was easy to disregard this embarrassing voice of warning. And after all, whatever traces still remained latent of the old erroneous beliefs and evil deeds, they no longer had the power to hurt. Leo Perutz, unlike us, accepted medical treatment from the former *Ortsgruppenleiter* Dr. Reiss, magnanimously forgave Mirko Jelusich and Weinheber for their histories, and had repeated meetings with Bruno Brehm here and in Bad Aussee.

That August, staying for the second time at the Villa Tyrol by the

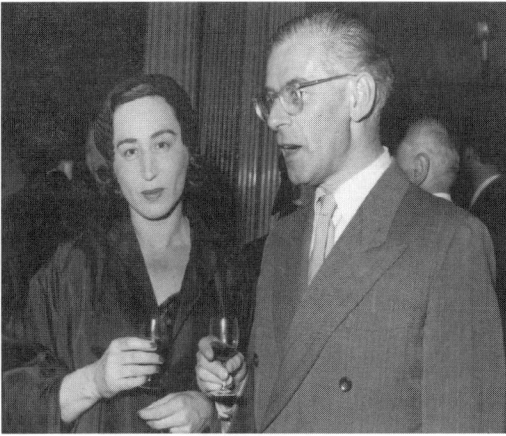

Hilde and Peter in Dublin, 1950

lake, we met Perutz at the house of Alexander Lernet-Holenia. Like him, not long back from the United States, we plunged into the pleasures and the encounters of the Salzkammergut, met in the mornings at Furian's café, dined with the varied throng in the evening at the Weisses Rössl, or nibbled at *Zwetschkenfleck* – plum dumplings – and raspberry ice cream late into the night at Wallner's cake shop. In Salzburg we sat at the Café Bazar with Ingeborg Bachmann and at the Tomaselli with Theodor Csokor and his friend Bruckner, and at the Hotel Tyrol we were visited by Melvin Lasky, Golo Mann, and the latter's former fellow student, Countess Lichnowsky, who all arrived together in a battered old jeep. We met Thomas Mann again in Strobl, and the Hermann Kestens in St. Gilgen – for everyone, every single person we knew, sooner or later turned up at the height of summer in this neighborhood. Meanwhile, on a short trip to Vienna we just had time to strike up a friendship with the author of *Die Strudlhofstiege*, Heimito von Doderer, who had attained a late but all the more substantial fame.

The entry in my calendar for the twelfth of December in London read: "Fog every day. This evening Dodo and her husband, Anna Kallin and Freddie Ayer came to dinner." A few years later the philosopher, the representative of the Vienna Circle of Logical Positivists in Oxford, whom we saw frequently in those days, had completely forgotten our existence, and in 1983, when Melvin Lasky gave a welcoming party for me in Chelsea, he hardly recognized me.

Peter

Hilde and Peter in St. Wolfgang

15

The Agony of Decision

From time to time a word or expression needs to be fetched out of the attic, dusted off, and polished to its former brilliance. So it is with the phrase, or cliché, "the agony of decision." Every statement, one might say, is either untrue or a cliché. But I have experienced the truth of this phrase. For what dominated my life and continually made it hell for the next eleven or twelve years, until I had made my choice, for good or evil, of my final place of residence, was an inner uncertainty, a turmoil, a sense of divided allegiances – of a choice between countries, partners, or lifestyles.

The advantages and disadvantages, the enticements and deterrents on both sides were great. And yet the direction I was to take should have been clear enough to me, and I repressed it for many years only because of a still steadfast loyalty, a deep and ineradicable love of my second home, and consideration for my children, who had been born there. While the English world slipped away from us more and more, however much we refused to acknowledge it, the world of our origins, above all that of my own origin, was stretching out countless feelers toward us, feelers which became tentacles, which finally brought me, although not Peter, back to my beginnings. St. Wolfgang, which we had not sought out, which had confronted us out of pure chance, or through some inexplicable stroke of fate, when we visited the Bermann-Fischers at Haus Breitgut, proved the strongest magnet. After spending several summers in the lakeside Villa Tyrol, we were able to buy a little house there, and become residents at least for several months of the year; but this was the result of a piece of good luck which, at the decisive moment, increased our chronically inadequate funds by the amount we needed.

One of Peter's finest books, which appeared as his third, but originated from the first short story he had written, *Krieg und Liebe der Kinder* (*War and Love among Children*) – the story was published by his friend Klaus Mann – was entitled *Schmerzliches Arkadien*, "Sorrowful Arcadia." It sounded even more melodious in the French translation

Denise van Moppès had made before the war: *Douloureuse Arcadie*. For a long time Julien Duvivier, France's most noted film director after René Clair and Marcel Carné, who had become famous in the thirties with *Pépé le Moko* and *Un Carnet de Bal* and later made his mark with *Sous le Ciel de Paris* and the Don Camillo films, had been trying to acquire the rights to his favorite book. It was *Le grand Meaulnes*, and was a favorite of ours, of mine as well; it had been the subject of my first article for the *New Statesman*. But Isabelle Rivière, the author's sister and heir, would not give permission for a film version. And so Duvivier discovered Peter's early novel, published in France by Plon, which like Alain-Fournier's book is set in a country boarding school, among sensitive boys and girls, and concerned with tender, unexplicit, and unhappy relationships between them, with early, unconsciously homoerotic attachments and awakening feelings toward the opposite sex.

In March the agent André Bernheim telephoned from Paris to inquire on Duvivier's behalf about the film rights to *Douloureuse Arcadie*. Peter was to name his own price. He was at a loss, and recklessly agreed immediately – for him this was *"de l'argent trouvé dans la rue."* The sum decided upon was one thousand pounds, a large sum to us, but ludicrously small in the context of the total costs of the film. After a few weeks Duvivier himself telephoned to ask Peter to read his screenplay and then to translate it back into the original language, for he planned to make a German version of the film in parallel with the French one. And in August the four of us drove in our "new" (second-hand, of course) car to Hohenschwangau, where Duvivier had settled in with his crew. The assistant director was Marcel Ophüls. For a few days we watched the filming and then, from our base at the Villa Tyrol, began our search for an inexpensive property, with the constant encouragement of Alexander Lernet-Holenia, who showered us both with proofs of his friendship.

Austria was still occupied; this area was under the benevolent rule of the Americans, but the future was uncertain, and prices were not high. Apparently there was a possibility of our acquiring a property on the lower border of the wonderful parkland in which Lernet's house stood. It lay by the Dittelbach, a mountain stream dividing the provinces of Upper Austria and Salzburg, and was not far from the lake. The grounds were small, as was the house, built in an unpretentious Italianate style in 1938 by a Finn, Nils von Nyman. Having parted from his first wife, Herr von Nyman had married a local woman, and now occupied the ground floor with his second wife and small son, while the first wife remained on the upper floor with the addition of a lover, and an old lady was accommodated in a tiny box-room. All these people were crowded into a minimal space in this pretty house, with one bathroom and kitchen between them; but finally their cramped life together under these emergency postwar conditions became unbearable, and must now come to an end. We had agreed on terms with Herr von N.; all we now needed was the consent of the divorced Frau von N. And then we received the news that the sale would go ahead.

Exciting weeks! On the tenth of September Duvivier's crew began shooting in nearby Fuschl, and on the following day Haus am Bach, the house by the stream, as we later called it, became ours. The castle in Fuschl — once a summer residence of the archbishops of Salzburg, in more evil times the vacation home of Ribbentrop, who signed his fatal agreement with Count Ciano there, and today a luxury hotel — this castle was adorned by the French film company with a deceptively authentic-looking side turret, probably because they thought it looked a little too bare and unattractive, particularly after Hohenschwangau. In between negotiations with Herr Brandl, the builder from Bad Ischl, about the construction of a large terrace at the side of the house, we drove out several times to the Fuschler See and mingled with the film crew. Meanwhile the Duvivier ladies had arrived, the director's wife and sister, elegant elderly Parisians who admired my summer dress in shocking pink — the fashionable color of the day — which, I happen to remember, had cost me three pounds at Galeries Lafayette in London.

The Duviviers loved Austria, they loved the Salzkammergut, they ate "Kalbax" every day, as they called *Kalbshaxe*, the country dish of knuckle of veal. The young actors made friends with us too — Pierre Vaneck, who played Vincent, the hero, in the French version, and his German counterpart, Horst Buchholz, in his first major role. Young Jan was played by Peter Vogel, who later tragically took his own life, and a delightful boy, Michael Ande, played little Felix, the child at the country school. Today he is known as the grey-haired detective Heymann in an endless German television series, *Der Alte (The Old Man)*. Peter described a great deal of this the same year in an amusing book, in whose sixth chapter, not for the first time, he made use of passages I had written, these from my essay on *Le grand Meaulnes*.

To see the mirror image of his own youth realized by a master such as Duvivier; to have acquired a house in a place which he then still liked so much; all this should have banished Peter's black moods for a long time. But on the way home there was already an explosion – almost to be expected, for, as so often happened, it followed a magical experience. We had reached Nancy; it was already dark and for the first time in our lives we found ourselves in the brightly lit Place Stanislas. The wonderful houses around us, built in the purest late baroque style about the middle of the eighteenth century under the exiled Polish king Stanislaw Leszcynski, *Stanislas le Magnifique* – town hall, theater, art gallery, fountain, triumphal arch, with a profusion of gilded wrought-iron railings, gates, lanterns – made us all, the children in particular, dizzy with delight. We even stayed the night in the old hotel on the square, with its enormous bathrooms. And then, for some trivial, long-forgotten reason, came an outburst which shocked and distressed the whole family to the point of tears.

What was the origin of this belligerence? "The gentle art of making enemies," as Hans Habe, who for his part had not been left unscathed by Peter, called it. Often there were reasons for it – too much political argument, for example with the friendly German cultural attaché Eugen Gürster, a Bavarian conservative, which led to a violent interchange and an abrupt end to a dinner party I had carefully planned for him and Countess Wydenbruck with their spouses. Too many Austrians – as when Heimito von Doderer, whom Peter in fact held in high regard, on my invitation paid us a visit which, after a quarrel out of the blue, ended in unpleasantness. Too much of Flesch – whom he for the most part tolerated: as a man from the same background and profession, with whom one could converse on equal terms, but also as a support of the household, as a helper in times of need – at least three times, when the bailiff was literally standing at the door ready to seize our possessions, it was Flesch who hurriedly got hold of enough money to defer the worst crisis; and finally as a substitute father, a godfather as he was in any case, who visited the children in the hospital (which Peter, on principle, never entered) – but who, somehow, again and again fell from grace. Generally, however, there was no obvious reason for my husband's surges of anger, so that inevitably I came to see him as an unconscious instrument of poetic justice, that merciless force which prevents happiness on this earth from exceeding a certain measure and from lasting too long.

Sometimes, if rarely, I could understand and even share Peter's anger. In the spring – here I am going back a little in time – we were traveling from Pietrasanta to Zurich in our first car, a ridiculously small Ford, its roof rack piled high with luggage. At Lake Como, where we had meant to stay the night, there were no rooms to be had. Someone advised us to try the Villa d'Este. Unsuspectingly we stopped in front of the palatial hotel and asked for rooms – it was ten o'clock at night. A suite was available. It cost almost more than a whole week at Signor Alberto's, but the children were tired and hungry and we had just enough money in our pockets; the *Weltwoche* in Zurich would surely help us out. Our car registration and passports confirmed us as eccentric British travelers. So we were admitted. As we crossed the hotel lobby in our creased beach clothing, we saw, sitting among the distinguished, elegant guests, no less a personage than King Leopold of the Belgians, who had been deposed two years earlier, with the beautiful Liliane. In the restaurant we ordered scampi, then a great luxury – in for a penny, in for a pound. In Zurich, as was right and proper, we stayed at the Urban, the hotel of the literati. Manuel Gasser, now the arts editor of the *Weltwoche*, explained to us with many apologies that we were to go with him that evening to see an affluent Viennese-born hostess, who had heard of our arrival and, as it were, commanded our presence.

And now for the source of the anger which burst out at "Evchen" Röder's – she was the daughter of Lilli Kann, a friend of Karl Kraus, whose portrait in lithograph by Kokoschka greeted us in the entrance hall. The guests were illustrious; only one of them, whom I will not name, is still alive. At the dinner table our hostess took center stage in the conversation. She dropped heavy hints about her munificence toward other, less prosperous foreigners in Switzerland, and Alfred Polgar, the great writer and critic, whom we met here for the first and last time, seemed to find this equally gratifying, for he flattered her in an embarrassing way. He brought the conversation round to her contributions to the *Weltwoche*, occasional book reviews which he praised with sycophantic servility.

Peter was becoming more and more restless; I sensed this and inwardly agreed with him. Then, when Evchen Röder stressed how often she had given a helping hand to his aunt Anja – the sister of Peter's father, the *Rabe*, and for a time a follower of C. G. Jung in Switzerland – came his explosion. Everyone rose from the table. The hostess gathered all the guests of honor in the nearest adjoining room, and banished us, together with her husband and Polgar's wife, to an otherwise empty room. Here, for some fifteen minutes or more, we listened to the bragging of these two about their traveling experiences and the hotels where they had stayed. We trumped them effortlessly with our ace, the Villa d'Este. Then I got up and went to take our leave of Frau Röder. The intention had presumably been that in the course of a long evening we would be reprieved and fetched back. It was not to be.

On the second occasion, to which I have already referred, when I was totally on Peter's side, it was Elias Canetti who aroused his wrath. The vanity of this outstanding writer – whom I will spare here as little as he spares himself in his own memoirs – is well known. When, in 1952, I was giving a talk on contemporary Austrian literature at an exhibition of books held by the Anglo-Austrian Society in London, I noticed that Canetti had joined the audience and was waiting to see whether I would mention his name. After hearing what I had to say about him, he immediately slipped away while I was still speaking. Now, if I recall correctly, during the first year of our ownership of Haus am Bach, he was paying us an after-dinner visit, and causing increasing offense to our other guests – Alexander Lernet-Holenia, Franz Theodor Csokor, and Leo Perutz – by declaring that no one who wrote for money could ever achieve anything worthwhile.

Peter was trembling with rage and finally flared up: he said he had not a penny of inherited fortune or savings, but he had a family whom he had to support by commissioned work, even by the journalism that Canetti despised so much. Then Leo Perutz intervened. He said quietly and with great dignity: "I have never read a line by Herr von Mendelssohn which was not excellent." Canetti fell silent. He was to take his revenge on us in London by spreading malicious gossip. Recently, however, I came across the second volume of his memoirs, in which he relates an encounter with Bertolt Brecht in Berlin when, aged twenty, he had expressed the same views. Brecht had replied: "I only write for money. I wrote a poem about Steyr cars and got a Steyr car for it." For Canetti, as he reported in all seriousness, this was "as though it had come out of the mouth of the devil."

After a summer of pleasure, poetic justice took its course in London, and Peter had nothing to do with it. Our tomcat Ebony had vanished, although we had left him in good hands. So much grief over animals! Ha'penny was gone, now Ebony, and the following year our much-loved Lucky, black and silky with deep blue eyes, named in a moment of bravado, was overtaken by disaster on the busy Ridgway – we found him, a heartrending sight, by the side of the road. We had overcome the historic strokes of fate, the great losses, and now it was the turn of the lesser ones, but these blows seemed no less painful; almost more painful, because we experienced them so directly, than the news, a year after our reunion in New York, that Hansi was dead – whether from drugs or her illness, no one could tell us with certainty. This, it is true, was a wound that would not close, which began to heal only when I tried in a novel to conjure up Hansi's image, mingled with features taken from others, even from myself. I realized only very recently that in the figure of her maid I was trying to absolve myself of my betrayal of her twenty-six years earlier. Now, seven months after Hansi's death, I began to write about the émigrés in New York. Meanwhile Herr von Zsolnay – still inflicting stains on a soul which had long been protected by a shield of steel – had again rejected a book of mine, *The Fruits of Prosperity*.

And so to everyday life in England, in Wimbledon, which began to emerge ever more clearly in the fifties as one of three possibilities for existence among which I would have to choose. Until the middle of the decade the children had been accommodated at the nearby Catholic schools, our daughter at the Ursuline Convent, our son at the Jesuit Wimbledon College. Both schools eventually became intolerable. The gentle Reverend Mother from Jersey had been replaced by a merciless Irish nun who would not allow the fourteen-year-old girls to talk in the cloakroom, and nipped all their harmless laughter in the bud. At this time none of the good day schools in London were accepting new girls, but finally we succeeded in sending our daughter to Badminton, a boarding school in Bristol, from which she was to transfer without difficulty to Oxford.

Our son, five years younger, in the care of the Jesuits, was not only disciplined rather too often with the ferula, but was also confused by the totally antiquated, dogmatic view of the world which was presented to him in science lessons. This made us consider a more up-to-date, worldly wise education. The Bursar of Westminster College, an apoplectic ex-military man, apparently a xenophobe, gave us an unfriendly reception. The parents not "British born"? Catholic too? No, dear Mr. de M., it is of no interest to us that you have proved your worth and made a name for yourself as a government official, a writer, even a biographer of Churchill. We got nowhere with him. And we ended up, once again, at a boarding school in the country; Bryanston was one of the best and most progressive in England, and its headmaster was the great pedagogue T. F. Coade. But first our son was to make the transition from one system to another by way of a preparatory school, and we were without him too for several months of the year. Like his sister, he was still a practicing Catholic. At Wells in Somerset, where he went to church, the priest tried to persuade him to take holy orders: "You could be a light of the Church."

So, after 1955, both children were out of the house. This was a turning point which did not improve the atmosphere in the "green grave" during the school year. During the day we were both deep in our work – I sat at a little desk in the dining room, writing cultural reports for newspapers, magazines, and radio stations, working to the point of exhaustion, stealing time from these breadwinning pursuits to make efforts on behalf of my novel, and, in between, writing letters and making telephone calls to London publishers about foreign rights on behalf of S. Fischer, who paid me a small fee for this. In the evenings Peter and I sat together wordlessly, withdrawn and drained, with music our only comfort. We received few guests apart from Flesch, who spent his weekends with us. This was the basic pattern. But certainly we occasionally went into town, from 1953 onward in a battered little car; I usually went on my own to the events on which it was my job to report to readers and listeners in the German-speaking countries, although Peter and I went out together some evenings to visit friends, among whom the Austrians increasingly outnumbered the English.

The friends we saw most often were Nora Wydenbruck, one of those titled Carinthian ladies whom Rilke had chosen as his patronesses, and her husband, the artist Alfons Purtscher. Despising the Nazis, and preferring to live in straitened circumstances in a foreign country than in unresisting submission to the rulers of the time, perhaps even honored by them in their own land, they had left their home and with difficulty built a new life. They had transformed their little terraced house in Addison Gardens, West Kensington, into a miniature palace. Alfons, the tall Tyrolean, had painted the walls with frescoes of landscapes and handsome horses, and furnished the sliding windows with beams painted in red and white horizontal stripes, reminiscent of the Carinthian castle of Hochosterwitz.

Nora, a woman of impressive appearance with a nobly prominent nose – she scorned small noses as a sign of stupidity – received her guests in the midst of furniture acquired in junk shops and efficiently glued together, upholstered, and re-covered by Alfons. Occasionally she devoted herself to parapsychological exercises. She had made a name for herself as a translator of Rilke and T. S. Eliot. Even after the collapse of the hated regime the couple preferred to stay in London, and violently rejected anything which survived or even reminded them of Nazism. When in 1956 Carl Orff and Luise Rinser arrived in London to attend the English premiere of *Carmina Burana*, Nora and Alfons, along with the British philanthropist Sir Robert Mayer, expressed their indignation at the stamping, "terrifyingly Teutonic" rhythms of the work. They wanted nothing to do with Orff, who after all had been prepared to replace the Jewish composer Mendelssohn's incidental music for *A Midsummer Night's Dream* with his own. And when Nora, lying in the Brompton Hospital, felt her death approaching, she summoned a woman friend and sat up in bed to draw up, in all tranquility, her own death announcement and a list of those to whom it was to be sent.

So many, indeed most of the Central European exiles returned home as early as the fifties. There still remained – for a little while longer, until he returned to settle at Lake Geneva – Oskar Kokoschka, there remained Canetti, Erich Fried, Robert Neumann, our dear friends Georg and Bettina Ehrlich, both artists; and Peter Stadlen, once a wonderful pianist, now turned reviewer, with his wife, who had been a student at the Schwarzwald school. They felt they had settled in well in England and did not want to uproot themselves a second time. Others, such as Fritz Thorn, who had lost their nearest relatives in cruel, often unimaginable ways, denied themselves even a visit to their places of origins for a long time, sometimes forever. But even they were unable to banish the places of their childhood, of their youth, entirely from their hearts. Whenever anyone visited us from the Continent, great writers and trustworthy informants such as Paul Celan, Ilse Aichinger, Ingeborg Bachmann, they would rush to meet them, to find out how one could live, in Bachmann's words, "among murderers and lunatics."

The fact that, apart from the embassies, a German and an Austrian cultural institute had now become established and we were tempted by chamber concerts and readings drew us back more and more into the spheres of our origins. At the same time, we at least held fast to our English friends; my close friendship with Dodo lasted until her death; we were, as before, well liked at PEN; we were on more or less intimate terms with the philosopher Kathleen Nott – wise Kate; with the historian Veronica Wedgwood, who during the war translated Canetti's *Auto da Fé* under great difficulties, under the author's strict supervision; with the great critic Philip Hope-Wallace and the good-hearted writer Eleanor Farjeon, the gently whimsical poet and "authority on sadness," as she was called, and Inez Holbrook, from whom she was for a while inseparable. We also occasionally saw Rex Warner with his second wife, in Woodstock or London.

But here and there we were already beginning to notice the other side of English helpfulness, generosity, integrity and stimulating intellectuality: this was a deeply rooted arrogance toward all "Continentals," which came to the surface once again with the end of their consideration for them in their time of need. Lady Cynthia Asquith would graciously draw us into the conversation, but what her father-in-law, the prime minister, had once named as a characteristic of graduates of his own Oxford college, Balliol – "the tranquil consciousness of effortless superiority" – applied to her as well, as it did to many others. Not everyone, of course, possessed the malice of Rebecca West, who asked Peter: "How is it, Mr. de Mendelssohn, that you write so well and yet are so little known?" And the famous "British freeze-up," the blank, chilly, stony look of someone who, out of boredom or sheer caprice, was determined not to recognize us, was something we now came to experience from time to time, from Stephen Spender or John Lehmann, who knew very well who we were.

The *New Statesman*, to which we still occasionally contributed, to whose "crowd" we had once belonged as Arthur Koestler belonged to the "*Horizon* crowd," sometimes invited us, as for example to its jubilee celebration in May 1956 at Londonderry House. We met Elwyn Jones there, and the great cartoonists Vicky, Osbert Lancaster, and David Low. Kingsley Martin too greeted us in a friendly, vague way, as though he had supposed us to have half disappeared from view already. To exaggerate only slightly, we were gradually sinking back to the level of the *métèque*, or alien. A *métèque* was what Flesch, the classical scholar, ironically called himself at the BBC, where the Germans and Austrians who had been naturalized for years were still treated with condescension by the British department heads. But it spoke very much in his favor, and softened the disrespectful tone adopted toward him, when his family, remotely connected by marriage to the British royal house, was tracked down in Debrett by his superior, Christopher Dilke.

Set against this the respect, indeed the love, apparent or genuinely felt, which we now encountered "over there." Over here, as we knew at heart, we would never fully belong to an intellectual world which was as elitist as it was exclusive in its lifestyle, and whose purest manifestation was found in that most distinguished of residences, Albany in Piccadilly, where Byron had lived and to which we were occasionally invited by Edwin Muir, Cecil Sprigge, and J. B. Priestley. Over there, we were accepted, joyfully integrated into others' lives. And there it was the summer weeks in St. Wolfgang, now at Haus am Bach, habitable since 1955, which gave us a feeling of delightful companionship. But with whom? With our so-called comrades in destiny, who like us were finding their way back for longer or shorter periods into their former world. But also with people whom we admired as artists, as writers, but whose recent past should have given us pause, had we been prepared for such reflection.

There was one man who at the age of forty-two had still taken part in the "Polish campaign," in which he received a slight injury, and who now bore a "badge of the wounded" on his loden hat, whose swastika was so carelessly obliterated that the local gardener Putz, still *völkisch* in his allegiance, always greeted this hero of the *Wehrmacht* with particular deference. Another man – or perhaps the same one – after the departure of a "racially non-viable" colleague drew more than ten times the income of a highly paid arms production worker. That a lecherous old aesthete, the editor of a daily paper, tolerated the most shameful attacks in its pages against the scapegoats who had, in any case, been driven out long ago; that the particularly artistic and charming doctor from Vienna had dedicated his services to the SS: these were all things that at the time we did not know, and did not want to know; we did not look under the carpet, or search for snakes in the grass.

It was too pleasurable to sit at those gatherings round a table, to remake friendships in such a strangely optimistic atmosphere, to feel at home once again in a small market town of inexpressible, then still unspoiled charm, with a church containing not only the most beautiful Gothic winged altar by Michael Pacher but another, exuberantly embellished by the Baroque artist Schwanthaler – so much splendor, so much of the past in the smallest space, and round about the idyllic, romantic landscape, just as it could be seen in the old engravings, with its bold, though not too bold, mountain slopes, its gentle, though not too gentle meadows, and the lake, constantly displaying itself in a different light, mirror-smooth, rippling or dramatically surging, all in the purest, most fragrant air we had ever breathed, or would ever breathe. We abandoned ourselves helplessly to all this, and still felt in retrospect that those years, those decades, had been filled over and over again with the most paradisical pleasure possible on earth. And it was only when the pretty farmhouses had become overblown tourist hotels, when the peace of the place had been destroyed and throughout the country, in the wake of a presidential election, the wicked old songs, the long-buried prejudices and feelings of hate had reawakened and were once more ringing out loud and clear – only then did we wonder whether that heavenly existence had perhaps been only an illusion.

We were familiar with such illusions from the magical fairy tales of Raimund, and for me at that time there was something magical too about the reappearance in the Austrian world of great numbers of the higher ranks of the nobility, that positive superabundance of counts and countesses, even of princes and princesses, who resided in the area during the summer and turned up at Alexander Lernet's, until he publicly antagonized them by his defiant attacks, which arose from various instances of offended pride, and drove most of them out of his house. After the left-wing and mainly intellectual circles I had frequented in my youth, in England I had come into contact with members of old and noble families, beginning with the Löwensteins, and learned to appreciate their dignity, their good manners, their genuine courtesy, combined with no lack of intellect. Now, in no time at all, I was befriended by three countesses and one divorced princess, connected by her marriage to the chief family of the land; my dear friend Maria brought a young hereditary prince to tea on the terrace of Haus am Bach; and in Vienna, whenever we visited the Hofburg, where Alexander had been granted one of the ridiculously cheap apartments reserved for public servants or other worthy personalities, the same stream of the "first society" continued – "a covey of counts," as I noted in November 1955, swirled around on all occasions.

But this month of November was only the last shining highlight in a year in which the monotony of our London suburb was interrupted by repeated escapes. As early as February I had had a moving experience: I was received at the Hogarth Press in Bloomsbury by Leonard Woolf – a gaunt figure with a gloomy, embittered charm – with whom I was to negotiate on behalf of S. Fischer Verlag about the German translations of his late wife's works. In March we went to Paris with the children to attend the premiere of *Marianne de ma jeunesse* – this was the film title chosen by the producers, as more commercial than that of the book which had attracted Duvivier's attention, *Douloureuse Arcadie*. In German it sounded even more banal: *Marianne – meine Jugendliebe*. But what did it matter? We celebrated on the Champs Elysées near the cinema where the film had been shown to great acclaim, constantly humming the haunting Argentinian theme tune, and spent the next evening, before our return home, at Dominique, the inexpensive Thirties borscht restaurant which meanwhile had attained a certain *mondanité*. In May we shared the general astonishment and satisfaction at the news of the State Treaty which made Austria a free country and put an end to the occupation. And soon there were new incentives to travel to the Continent. The first was the celebration in Zurich of Thomas Mann's eightieth birthday.

Here, as on most questions of artistic taste, Flesch was in total agreement with Peter; he loved and admired Thomas Mann, had also corresponded with him and was now to accompany us on this journey, particularly since we were going directly on to a PEN congress in Vienna. And so, in our "new" old car, an absurd light-blue monster of a Standard Vanguard, which Manuel Gasser had dubbed the "Easter egg," we went first of all to Switzerland. The public ceremony took place on the evening of the fifth of June at the Zurich Schauspielhaus. Bruno Walter conducted *Eine kleine Nachtmusik*, the great actors Therese Giehse, Maria Becker, Gustav Knuth, and others read from Mann's work, and finally he himself stepped onto the stage, read with quietly smiling gravity from *Felix Krull*, and as an encore gave us the opening words of *Der Erwählte* (*The Chosen One*), in which "the sound of bells, the swell of bells floated *supra urbem*, over the whole city, in its air that was filled with their tones" – that glorious page of prose, one of the finest that Thomas Mann ever wrote, as he well knew and allowed us to realize with visible pleasure, up to the last sentence, when Rome trembled "in swirling universal harmony, as if transformed into bronze," and everything resounded "for the great festival and sublime procession."

To incorporate this, the *deutsche Repräsentanz*, as Peter was later to call it – the representative or exemplary manifestation of "Germanness" in its best sense – , and to enjoy it so much himself, to preside over his own feast, stately and yet not without self-mockery – who would begrudge him this, who would not be moved and honored to be in the company of Thomas Mann? Afterward too at the reception, where the ceremonial guests gathered around him to pay tribute, he accepted it not arrogantly, but with a good grace, not with undue presumption, for it was his due. A final act, a final chord corresponding to his importance and dignity. As for us: we all three felt gratitude for this manifestation, and many years later, when the strange weaknesses in the depths of his soul were unsparingly exposed in his published diaries, we could not recant our love and admiration. And when, in August of the same year, we heard the news of Mann's death on the radio in the little salon of the house in St. Wolfgang, we fell silent in paralyzed sorrow, unable even to shed tears.

In between came the writers' congress in Vienna, where in the plenary session my enemy Torberg directed an attack on the man we admired and he hated, and was equally publicly rebuked by Flesch. Edouard Roditi, the simultaneous interpreter at the congress, had a difficult task explaining to non-German-speaking delegates Flesch's reference to the essay on Frederick the Great, whose author was now being attacked by a "little Friedrich." On the way there and back we inspected the building work at Haus am Bach and began to fill the rooms with furniture, bought partly locally and partly at the Dorotheum, the Viennese auction house. Before we moved in, Mischa Spoliansky, once Berlin's most captivating revue composer, was to rent the little house from us during July. The small piano he hired stayed there for the rest of the summer, and so I, for the last time, practiced what remained of the little skill I had acquired as a child – Beethoven's *Für Elise*, the first movement of his Moonlight Sonata (the other two were too difficult for me), or the two Russian songs from my father's wartime stay in Cracow, which I still knew by heart. Then, on the twenty-eighth of August, came the housewarming party, to which Hans Habe brought his own guest, Fritz Kortner, and all the guests, from the aristocratic Otto Windisch-Graetz and the Thuns from Salzburg to the local physician Dr. Leifer and the pension landlady Grete Vogler, entered their names in the guest book donated by Alexander, as did every subsequent guest up to 1986.

In November I was lucky enough to be present at the apotheosis of Vienna's now total freedom from occupation: the opening of the resurrected Opera House, which was at the same time the first great state ceremony of independent Austria. A miracle which has never been explained up to the present day was the envelope containing press tickets to the three premieres which arrived in the post in Wimbledon. I scraped the last of my money together and left on the same flight as Johannes Schwarzenberg, the new ambassador to the court of St. James's, and Raimund von Hofmannsthal. In Vienna, because I could afford nothing else, I stayed in the "broom cupboard" at the Lernets' apartment in the Hofburg – a windowless storeroom behind the kitchen, into which a little fresh air penetrated at night through the open door, mingled with cozy cooking smells. From here, I proceeded in my evening dress to the "premiere of the century," as this production of *Fidelio* on the fifth of November was already being labeled halfway through the performance. There followed a *Don Giovanni* and a *Frau ohne Schatten*. On the first of these evenings the audience was a truly global one. And it was not the singers on stage who moved me the most, but those I saw in the long intermission, seated side by side on a sofa, in the only foyer to be unscathed by bombs and preserved in the style of the early 1870s. They had returned from America, the Florestan and Leonore of years gone by: Alfred Piccaver and Lotte Lehmann.

All sorts of fringe events grew out of the Opera House reopening: a matinee of Beethoven's Rasumovsky quartets in the palais of the Count who had been his patron, in the presence, moreover, of the entire Rasumovsky family, although it was no longer their home. Heaps of invitations from the nobility. A gala reception at the Musikverein. And I now plainly realized what, in the years to come before and after my final return home – with or without the currently rather over-represented nobility – was to exercise such an irresistible magnetism upon me: the continuing attraction of my native city, as it has affected all who have ever grown up there. It was a sociable life of such density and permanence, with visits to each other's houses, regular gatherings at the same tables, Heurigen parties, communal excursions, and country vacations, that one could never feel alone or exposed in the threatening expanses of the universe, but always surrounded by human warmth and long-standing friendships, however deceptive these might prove to be. I will not speak here of the disadvantages of these constant concentrations in a narrow space – gossip, malice, intrigue, rancor, an incessant minuet of quarrels and reconciliations. But much, much later, after I had taken root once again, I longed from time to time for English discretion, discipline, distance.

312

And so, after this glorious autumn, my visits to Austria became more and more frequent, while the possibility of this alternative existence, temporarily restricted, but often already shared with Flesch, intruded into the intervals of my everyday English life, which meanwhile continued unaltered; ever more often I imagined myself playing rummy evening after evening in the Café Hawelka with a horde of artists and officials headed by Hans Weigel, already a long-standing member of this group and, in Doderer's words, "profoundly bogged down in the old familiar ways." Heimito von Doderer was already a key figure for me in the Vienna which I was to reclaim; after I had given glowing reviews in various publications earlier in the 1950s to his novel *Die Strudlhofstiege*, he had become a good friend, as he had been to Flesch in their youth. Only a year respectively separated these three men, Flesch, Doderer, and Lernet, all born between 1895 and 1897. Each of them, even in the days of the second Republic, carried a little prefix around with him: "*Edler von*," "*Ritter von*" or "*Herr von*," and all of them were characterized by the Slavicized formula for the true "old Austrian," first devised in Zagreb not long ago: "*hercig, wicig, nobl und fes*" (warm-hearted, witty, noble and elegant). With them, one day, there would depart the last great generation of those who still possessed an urbanity, a *concordia discors*, a background derived from many languages and cultures of the Habsburg empire, which was quite naturally their own.

The fact that in this Vienna, which was drawing me in ever more powerfully, or seemed to be doing so, I still had a real enemy, did not frighten me off. Torberg had, thank heavens, been unsuccessful in his attempt soon after our return from the United States to cut off, as it were, the thread of income for Peter and myself. He had written two letters at the end of 1952 to the editors of *Der Monat* and of the *Neue Zeitung*, the two periodicals from which we earned our living. These letters were intended to present me as a Communist fellow traveler and therefore unworthy to contribute to American publications. It was for a ridiculous reason that, after the approach he had attempted in the spring with the help of Arthur Koestler, he was now taking action against me in person. That summer, as adviser to the U.S. Office of Cultural Affairs, he had succeeded in preventing the actor Karl Paryla, identified as a Communist, from obtaining a part in *Jedermann* in Salzburg, which was then still under American occupation. In my report for the *Monat* on the 1952 Salzburg Festival, under the heading "Cabal and Art," I had mentioned in one sentence that Paryla, "because in private life he was too Red even to play the Devil," had been replaced at the last minute by Peer Schmidt. Torberg, witty though he was, could not take a joke. In eight single-spaced pages written to the publisher of *Der Monat* he accused me of being a fellow traveler.

At the height of the Cold War, when Senator McCarthy sent his wretched emissaries Cohn and Schine to Europe to guard the interests of the Right (Roy Cohn died of AIDS in 1986), this accusation could have meant the end of our activity for the German-language American press. Torberg's letter to *Der Monat* came to light among his effects after his death. If it was correct – the letter ended – that the aim of this periodical was to contribute to the unmasking of Bolshevism and totalitarianism, "then Miss Spiel is out of place among its contributors. Miss Spiel is not one of those who unmask Bolshevism. She is one of those who camouflage it. And the point of my polemic is not whether Miss Spiel wrote something contentious in one issue or another of *Der Monat*, but whether Miss Spiel should be allowed to write for *Der Monat* at all."

However, my enemy was barking up the wrong tree. The editor-in-chief of the *Neue Zeitung* was still our old friend Hans Wallenberg, and the publisher of the *Monat* was, as before, Melvin Lasky, who was no less well disposed toward us. Both, loyal citizens and servants of the United States, although they did not show us the letters, let us know that they existed, and they did not pass on Torberg's denunciations as he had intended. I cannot express how much it was to Lasky's credit that he protected us at that time. For Melvin had committed himself totally to the Cold War – as recently as the eleventh of November, 1989, he declared that it "had been worth fighting," as though it had not been above all the example of peaceful and tolerant democracy which was needed. For the rest, Torberg's continued malicious gossip cut no ice; he informed my kindly friend Kate Nott, when she visited Vienna, that "your friend Hilde Spiel may be quite a nice person, but politically she is a louse." Well, everyone needs an enemy, as the wise Pole Andrzej Szczypiorski declared many years later. I had had one for a long time, but this would prove troublesome only when I returned and was exposed to repeated mockery in the magazine *Forum*. Meanwhile, this was still far ahead. The Fifties were not yet over.

What filled those years? Since Christmas 1955 a new Ferguson radio-phonograph had stood in the apartment in Wimbledon Close, huge and mirror smooth, as a counterweight to the fabulous Viennese opera premieres. Up to the end of the decade – when it was replaced by a television set which was despised by Peter and installed in my room – the music on the radio and on phonograph records formed our evening entertainment, to which we listened in silence. As a result of the burdensome school fees, our mania for traveling, and the maintenance of the house in St. Wolfgang, we were, despite our considerable work output, never free from financial problems. The word "overdraft" kept recurring. We were constantly in debt to Stevenson & Rush, the local delicatessen; when our bill rose to £100, there would be an admonitory letter or an embarrassing telephone call. The eccentrics and unusual characters in Wimbledon included Henry Carr, the heir to the old biscuit factory, infinitely well bred, harmless though mentally disturbed; the nameless, unwashed, shabby lady who talked in supercilious Queen's English on the 200 bus; the meteorologist Sir Henry Brunt, who lived in our apartment building and whose weather forecasts were always colossally inaccurate - we encountered all these with polite greetings, but without any attempts at rapprochement.

Once a month I would drive to Godalming to see Rex Warner's daughter Anna, the poor epileptic girl who was very fond of me, and each time I was deeply upset; these visits were invariably followed by a nocturnal asthma attack. Often on a Sunday Theodor Kramer would appear from Guildford, eat with us, drink a great deal of cider, and toward evening proceed into town to visit pubs and girls. Later it became my task, and that of a few others, to visit him in a psychiatric clinic in Virginia Water, to empty and repack the locker by his bed according to his imperious instructions, to collect and return his laundry, until, in 1957, with the help of all of us, he was able to return to his own country for the sadly short time that remained before his death. It was not every evening, in fact, that I sat by the radio-phonograph; after all, it was part of my job to go to the theater from time to time. But even the finest performances were, even then, slightly spoiled for me because I had to give an impression of them to people unknown to me, a faceless throng of newspaper readers far away, with whom I had no sort of relationship.

Then there were telephone calls, correspondence, visits to publishers and authors on behalf of S. Fischer, with little result. One single book, the first one I had recommended to them, William Golding's *Lord of the Flies*, was published through my mediation by that firm, but no more throughout all those years. When "Tutti" Bermann-Fischer came to London I was constantly on duty, even driving her to Oxford to meet the Pasternak sisters. At least this interrupted the monotony. An autumnal life, during which old age drew imperceptibly nearer. Walks with Flesch in the fog-damp, melancholically beautiful Cannizaro Park on the edge of Wimbledon Common, where there was a little statue of the goddess Diana sadly gazing at the deer she had slain, brought from his Sicilian home by the former owner of the property (the words "Villa Reale, Palermo 1813" were engraved on its base); poeticizing her grief, we always stroked her slim, finely chiseled back of porous stone. The school vacations were brightened by the brief visits of our son and daughter.

In 1958, Flesch was pensioned off by the BBC and decided to return to Austria. My escapes there were becoming ever more frequent; a reason, not just an excuse, was my extensive research into all the archives of Vienna and among all the noble descendants of my heroine, Fanny von Arnstein from Berlin, the epitome of emancipation of women and of Jews, whose biography I was now writing. Usually Flesch and I spent a week or more in wintry Lofer, his childhood home, in the comfortable Gasthof Bräu, managed with charming dignity by "Frau Major" Baumgartner, née von Rauchen- bichler. There I sometimes received bad news from London: our cat Domino – he too – run over on the Ridgway, or the illness of our son at Bryanston or our daughter at Oxford; and my immediate return was demanded. And I did not always make the effort; sometimes I lay low, waiting for the crisis to resolve itself. *Mea maxima culpa* – just as during the first year after the war. When I later returned to London, I woke up crying every morning and could find no way out of my misery.

It became more and more difficult to maintain a marriage which so clearly had had its day, but we kept postponing the end, because from time to time we believed that it could after all be saved. But even on one of the last of those journeys together, now journeys of despair, which we undertook less to assuage our wanderlust than as possible therapy for the situation at home, Peter frequently exploded in what seemed to me irrational or even heartless rage. In September 1959 for instance, in the midst of glorious Provence, at night in the Hotel St. Rémy, when I had a severe stomach upset, I crouched sleepless on the floor in order not to disturb his rest, an attempt in which I failed after all. And yet, until then, how exciting had this journey been in a more spacious, this time really new Ford, from Landeck through Switzerland, past the Rhône glacier and Grenoble to Manosque and the town in the hills, forsaken by humankind: Les Baux.

Up there, in the spot Peter had had in mind when he wrote his novel *The Hours and the Centuries*, the book I loved so much and had translated into German, the film *Le retour d'Orphée* had been shot just before our arrival, and on all the dilapidated house doors we found huge chalk drawings by Cocteau, who had already left. But Picasso and his friend the bullfighter Dominguín were still there, and in the afternoon, in a café a little lower down near Les Baux, we saw them both sitting at the next table, with a young female companion – Picasso's mistress Jacqueline Roque? Dominguín's wife? – and two small children. Inhibited as ever in the presence of a true genius, we dared only to cast sidelong glances at the sturdy little old man.

And then, at night, my perhaps partly hysterical attack of illness. And the next day on to Arles, where a bullfight was announced and we bought tickets, because Peter wanted to see it, and I did not know how cruel and sickening was this ballet of death. We sat right at the top, on the highest platform, but the slow torture of the animals did not escape us, nor did we fail to notice that Picasso and Dominguín were seated below in the front row. Recently I read that in the "Dangerous Summer" of 1959 Hemingway had come to Europe to see a bullfight, in order to write a book of that name which was never published, and in which he described the deadly rivalry of his friends Antonio Ordóñez and Luis Miguel Dominguín, Spain's leading matadors. Had he too visited Arles? No, we never saw him; I never met him in my life, a fact perhaps to be noted with satisfaction by those readers who might be tired of my constantly steaming "kitchen of names" – a phrase of Canetti's.

We continued our journey via Aix – which Flesch, as I had not forgotten, had so splendidly praised in his book *Perlen und schwarze Tränen* – to Bandol and Le Lavandou, the destinations of the first German flights from Hitler. Then to St. Tropez, which one then used to pronounce with its final consonant, as it was not yet in fashion. We checked into the Hotel La Pinède, and there I noticed, among other elegant couples, a tall Italian gentleman, no longer young, wearing a hearing aid, by the side of an equally distinguished blonde lady. Five years later I was to meet the couple again in Dubrovnik, in the hotel where I was staying with Flesch, when they spoke to us and we learned that he was a Prince Colonna and she an Austrian baroness, though not his wife. Meanwhile, Peter and I left St. Tropez after a few days and made only one more longish stay, at Cagnes-sur-mer, where Peter had lived in the thirties and had been very happy.

Like Peter, the painter and writer Paris von Gütersloh had settled there, along with a dancer with an equally fanciful name, Primavera Mariagraete, and Gütersloh had taught Peter how to prepare Wiener Schnitzel, beating it paper thin – a debatable matter. Peter had been there with his first wife Tschu, whom he loved, and although she loved him too, she left him in the end, because she did not want to emigrate. If he had changed his name, Peter could have remained unscathed in the Third Reich, as did many a cousin of his who had the same Jewish grandfather in his proof of ancestry, but was after all not called Mendelssohn; indeed, as did his own half-sister, who did not suffer in spite of bearing the same name, although she experienced some injustice. But he was much too proud to rescue his marriage in this way, and he had hated the new rulers too much to want to be a German among them. He was a cosmopolitan, but as German as the Dresden Zwinger, as German as the Gedächtniskirche or the Sendlinger Tor. He should have stayed in Germany after the war, or returned there earlier than he did. He was very unhappy in England, but would not admit it, and made those around him unhappy. Only in the last ten years of his life did he find a way of life that suited him.

As a matter of fact, in the summer of 1958, Peter seriously considered moving to Munich; we both considered it. We received a visit at Haus am Bach from his former friend and later stepfather, Walther von Cube, a sinister figure for me by hearsay, responsible for traumatic injuries to Peter's feelings in his youth. A large, portly figure, he sat on our terrace all day drinking enormous amounts of mineral water, as sinister now for me as formerly in my imagination, endlessly self-confident, always smiling in amusement to himself and generally ironic in his conversation. Peter, at fifty, was only two years younger than him, but Cube treated him arrogantly, as if he were a green youth. A shrewd, evil man, was my impression. Others, even Peter's youngest brother, perceived him as a significant and lovable personality. He decisively dissuaded us from going to Munich: we should get that idea out of our heads. After his departure Peter was totally discouraged, utterly crushed. A few days later, when we were invited to the Starnberger See by the then publisher of the *Süddeutsche Zeitung*, Werner Friedmann, our last hopes were dashed. All that Friedmann wanted from us was information about Torberg's letters of denunciation to Wallenberg and Lasky. It was a ghastly evening. In the Munich hotel afterward I was "sick literally and at heart," as I entered in my calendar. Then Cube decided on a consolation prize: he gave Peter a contract to supply political reports from London to the Bayerischer Rundfunk, the Bavarian state radio station, which at least offered us a small safety net for our financial tightrope act.

We made two more attempts to rescue our marriage. They consisted in my fetching Flesch back from Vienna and a plan, which reached a very advanced stage, to give up Wimbledon and move into central London. Flesch had already made himself very much at home in a house belonging to friends in Döbling, and was on the point of obtaining a small apartment in a local housing project, but he did not turn a deaf ear to my plea to return to London in the autumn of 1960. He too disliked the separation from me. There had been too many tearful farewells. I had found a bachelor apartment for him in Broadwalk Court, where my aunt Lonny was still living in my parents' old apartment. He was now banned from Wimbledon, but now I often saw him elsewhere, and that helped me to endure the last two years in the "green grave," from which Peter had resolved last New Year's Day to free us. He took a permanent – as we thought – job at the publishers Thames and Hudson, which suggested to us the idea of buying a little town house. I found one, newly built and pretty, in Sussex Square, north of Kensington Gardens. We paid a deposit. I went there several times with a tape measure and a carpenter, with whom I discussed the building of cupboards and shelves; I worked out the layout of the rooms in my mind, imagining us already living there. But as early as July, Peter fell out with the publishers, and we had to withdraw from the purchase, losing our deposit of £400.

What would have happened if we had begun a new life together in Sussex Square? And what might not have happened? Idle questions. After this failure, this regression to the everyday life of Wimbledon, which even the children now often avoided in their vacations – at Easter they preferred to go on the Aldermaston march organized by the Campaign for Nuclear Disarmament – Peter succumbed to resignation. He did not even raise an objection when I went off to Greece for five weeks with my daughter, who had successfully taken her final examinations at Oxford, and Flesch, in an old Renault Dauphine bought in Vienna. I drove the little car from St. Wolfgang over the Grossglockner to Brindisi and from Patras to Sparta and Mistra, then in a circle around the whole Peloponnese. This is not a travel book, even if it appears to be so for long stretches, and is not intended as one. But it would be difficult to say nothing of the halcyon days in Epidaurus.

In the early sixties this was still a place of great peace, as were all the other classical locations. Coaches daily arrived at the amphitheater, but the people were swallowed up by the vast arena and were soon gone again. Not far away, yet out of sight and hearing, were some little apartments which could be rented. As usual, I took one room with my daughter and Flesch the other. There were a kitchen and sanitary facilities. Round about there were only fields and meadows with grazing sheep. Total stillness. A warm sun, not too hot, for it was now September. A balsamic breath of wind, in which our wet laundry was dry within an hour. And the feeling, the utterly archaic feeling, that in this place, once dedicated to Aesculapius, all suffering was healed. Years later I told a Greek at his embassy about our stay at this numinous site, and he stared at me in disbelief, shaking his head. I was obviously a foreigner with an overdeveloped imagination. Clearly, I realized, miracles happen from within.

The consciousness of being equally at home in Alpine regions presented itself on the journey back, on the Brenner, overnight in Gossensass. The keen mountain air through the window, the proudly swelling feather beds, under which one was protected from the unaccustomed cold, the pine trees and the dense high forests – after all the bare mountain ridges of the south, lying like bleached bones under the merciless blue sky – brought us back to our native climate. In London, Peter gave us a boisterous welcome. But his good mood did not last long. He did not want to travel to Austria any more. St. Wolfgang was spoiled for him, it rained all the time and he didn't like the people any more. Indeed, much had changed there. Leo Perutz had been dead for years.

At the end of August 1957, I had been on my way back from Salzburg just before midnight when my car was stopped in front of the Villa Seerose, where Perutz lived. He was lying in bed struggling for breath. His wife and Eva Lernet were with him. I stayed with them until four in the morning. Soon after I had gone home, he was taken to the hospital in Bad Ischl, where he died the following morning. We and the Lernets drove together to the funeral. At the Grüner Baum restaurant Alexander and Peter refused to go up to the room where the mourners were gathering, but waited downstairs in the bar. Eva and I went up. There we found some ten relatives of the writer, all dressed in black, mostly women, who had come from

London or Israel, and among them, in a traditional Styrian suit with a black armband and tie, was Bruno Brehm. Only that summer Perutz had offered to introduce him to me at Wallner's pastry shop, and I agreed as a favor to him. I exchanged only a few words with Brehm – I respected Perutz's generous attitude toward so many supporters of the past regime, whom I found disagreeable, but was for the most part unable to adopt such an attitude myself. At the grave in the beautiful cemetery in Ischl, Lernet gave an address, and Brehm, the nationalistic writer, also spoke with genuine feeling.

Since then, one after the other, the visitors from Los Angeles had migrated elsewhere, among the first of them the great Robert Siodmak, whose early film *Abschied* (*Farewell*), with the young Brigitte Horney, I had found unforgettable; most of them had moved to Ticino, which was more sophisticated and where, in Ascona or Locarno, the French fashion designers and perfumers had their boutiques. As soon as the first autumn breeze blew, the ladies from Hollywood would put on their minks and hurry to the Café Verbano. In the meantime it had become quieter in St. Wolfgang: a lull before the renewed rise, for me the decline, of the "Pearl of the Salzkammergut" – a phrase which says everything. But in Vienna, in the early spring of 1962, there had been warning signals which should have made me think more carefully about the final return which I planned to make the following year. Again on a research trip, this time for a book I was writing on Vienna, I decided after an evening with Peter's former host that the Viennese were after all "either malicious or boring."

I recorded a visit to the venerable writer and retired president of the senate Kurt Friedburger as a "tea party in the morgue." And at a "carnival celebration" at the Lernets," where the noble visitors had by now for the most part dispersed, I met, in addition to Hans Weigel and the brilliant cabaret artist Helmut Qualtinger, the theater historian Kindermann, whose past was entirely unknown to me. Indeed, soon afterward it was at his request that I gave a talk on the English theater at the Theater Institute of the University of Vienna, which was not far from the Lernets' apartment. And it was not until I discovered Kindermann's book *Das Burgtheater*, published in 1939 at the Austrian Cultural Institute in London – not in a poison cabinet, but on open display in their library – and read it, that I was horrified by the trap I had fallen into, by the traps which still threatened me. In this book the success of Schnitzler's *Liebelei*, so many years before the Anschluss, was regretted with the statement that "the conscious ability to distinguish between German feeling and Jewish sentimentality" had been "given only to few in those days." "Jews and Freemasons," the author alleged, had acted as Schnitzler's "frontmen and the men behind him." And in his introduction Kindermann unequivocally declared that his new history of the theater was based on the "basic values of race, *Volk* and *Reich.*"

What was the danger that loomed here? A new age of blurs and compromise, as the years after 1934 had appeared to me, when one constantly found oneself facing crises of conscience. Certainly, I still had the choice. But for a long time I had been inclining toward a decision in favor of Austria. Much was working in its favor, including the ever-growing insight that there were very discreet but unbridgeable boundaries to our life among the British. Just before these weeks in Vienna I had flown to Berlin with the novelist Angus Wilson. I had translated a volume of his short stories and had been invited by Walter Höllerer to appear with Wilson at his "literary colloquium." These were entertaining days; I spent a great deal of time with the Lufts and often saw Günter Grass. Neither then nor at any other time did I find the Berliners "malicious or boring." But on the flight with Wilson I became aware, through many examples, of English malice, quite the equal of the Viennese variety, and, moreover, laced with arrogance. My new compatriots were after all just as amusing and gossip-ridden as the old ones.

Among the stories my companion told me was one about the Duchess of Devonshire and the German-born wife of a noted Cambridge professor, who was reputed to be highly intelligent and above all anglicized to the highest possible degree. According to Angus Wilson, the Duchess, a daughter of Lord Redesdale and thus one of the Mitford sisters, who included Unity, the admirer of Hitler, and Diana Mosley, had said of this lady: "We asked her to see if she was somebody but she wasn't anybody so we didn't ask her again." Funny, yes. But cruel. And as offensive, as deeply wounding as the three words with which the publisher Peter Calvocoressi had rejected my American novel: "Well, not quite." Not quite up to the high standards of Chatto & Windus, not quite satisfactory as a British subject, not quite as refined, as well educated or subtle as "our sort," "the British-born."

The Darkened Room was soon afterward accepted by the equally discriminating firm of Methuen, and immediately on its publication in

June 1961 it was praised at the head of the list of novels in the *Sunday Times*. This, my second novel in English, was pronounced beautifully written and fascinatingly unusual in its subject matter. I was appeased by such remarks as these. It fell to a young Trinidadian Indian writer, in the *New Statesman*, with which I had close links, and in which his first book had had an unfavorable review three years earlier, to publish a review, as brief as it was smug, of my novel, of whose subject matter – Central Europeans in exile in America – he could have understood little. This incidentally was V. S. Naipaul, who will one day probably receive the Nobel Prize.

The realization that my contributions to the *Statesman* over many years, which admittedly had ceased some time earlier, had already been forgotten, and an outsider allowed to review my book in such an offhand manner, no longer caused me much pain. A few months earlier I had completed my biography of Fanny von Arnstein, which I had written in German, and was as satisfied with the manuscript as I have never been before or since. The research for this book alone had again and again brought with it moments of true happiness – not only the many hours under the reading lamp at the British Museum and the Nationalbibliothek, as well as the archives of the Austrian state, the city, the court and the nobility of Vienna, but more, when, searching through old chests in Vienna or in a Carinthian castle, I found handwritten testimony of my heroine's life, her wills and notebooks, of whose significance, indeed existence, her descendants themselves had not until then been aware.

And so to the last year in England. After graduating successfully from Oxford my daughter had taken a job at Robert Maxwell's Pergamon Press, but after a short time Maxwell's boorish behavior and the wretched working conditions at Pergamon drove her out of the firm and into a nervous breakdown. My son, after the completion of his time at Bryanston School, had been awarded a scholarship at Oriel College, Oxford. At the beginning of April the publishers S. Fischer gave a launch party for *Fanny von Arnstein*, and Peter wrote me a beautiful, moving letter, saying that he admired the book so much that he was prepared to give me my freedom. It was an upsurge of feeling which he was soon to regret. From Frankfurt I had driven once more to Austria, and together with Flesch I undertook a little journey to research into his and my past. We crossed the border into Moravia at Nikolsburg, the town of my maternal ancestor Markus Benedict and his family, a pretty little place at the foot of low hills.

"They must have found life very comfortable there," I entered in my calendar.

In Brünn we discovered the Palais Flesch on the glacis, where Bismarck had once been a guest; now it looked rather rundown and its famous blue windows had probably disappeared long ago. Olmütz still bore many traces of the old Austro-Hungarian army, as I had experienced it in my childhood with its imperial-yellow buildings – but nothing was yellow any more, it was all dirty grey, although the sun was shining. We even found the little town of Krönau, a little higher up, where we had been quartered with my father in 1916. In those days we had driven for half an hour in a one-horse carriage to reach the chief town of the district; now I covered the same distance by car in a few minutes. All the road signs were in Czech, but the old German names, Leitomischl, Podiebrad, the targets of old Austrian farces, were still visible. We spent a few days in Prague and drove back to St. Wolfgang via Budweis – nowhere in the world was there such beer!

Peter telephoned from London and took back everything he had said in his letter. He told me that I had missed the last opportunity to put everything right. Now he wanted to break things off; he had already told the children. Of course I cried endlessly, as so often before, incessantly tugged back and forth by conflicting loyalties. Then Flesch and I drove to Ischl and ate trout for lunch at the Hotel Post. "This is the life I would like to lead from now on," I wrote. In the evening – it was Good Friday – we watched the people of St. Wolfgang carrying lights in procession up the Kalvarienberg. Two days later I was in Wimbledon. Everything was in blossom. "I relish the comfort at home." I went back to my work as though nothing had happened, and at the request of S. Fischer Verlag I visited the poet Yevtushenko at a hotel in Oxford Street. I found him a self-important young puppy, who never took his long cigarette holder out of his mouth while speaking – then, although probably no longer, he was called "the court poet of the Kremlin in all its forms, equipped with an opportunistic early-warning system." His political fluctuations, two steps forward and one back, or sometimes the other way around, have always reminded me of Stephan Hermlin's.

A visit to Coventry, half rebuilt after the war damage, for the premiere of Britten's *War Requiem* with Fischer-Dieskau, which only now, in 1962, seemed to set the seal on England's reconciliation with Germany. In Oxford, long after the final examinations, the BA degree ceremony for my daughter's year took place. And then, in mid-June, I was off again for the whole summer. Peter, as I had hoped, did not spend it alone, for he had already struck out on his own, for Pietrasanta. In St. Wolfgang I had a stream of house-guests; the Doderers spent a night in the "gentleman's bedroom" upstairs, and good-hearted "Minze" (Maria von Doderer) rushed into the kitchen after every meal to wash the dishes, although Frau Hutterer always put things to rights in the morning. My favorite guests were always my children, especially, however brief his visits, my son, whose life was soon to become so unstable.

Lonny moved into the little room usually occupied by my daughter, for she had also gone off to the Mediterranean. But my aunt, my only surviving close relative, had been in poor health for some time, and as her heart was deteriorating, I had to take her to the hospital at Bad Ischl. At the beginning of September the most extraordinary encounter of that year took place. Peter had telephoned from Italy and asked me to meet him in Lienz in East Tyrol. Tanned and cheerful, he arrived from the south in the big Ford Zephyr we had bought together, and I from the north, over the Isel mountain, in the little Dauphine. We checked into the Hotel Zur Traube and got on better than we had done for an eternity. Next morning we looked out of the window together to watch the colorful Tyrolean shooting competition. It was Wimbledon, the monotony of the green grave, which had wrecked this marriage.

I promised to return in October. I had to leave Lonny behind in Ischl, but Flesch continued to stay at Haus am Bach and took the bus every day to the hospital, where Lonny was sharing a double room with another lady. This lady assumed that Flesch – who was after all only five years younger than my aunt – was Lonny's husband, and it did not occur to anyone to correct her. It was the last joy of her life for my spinster aunt, who had been disappointed in her only great love, that at the end of her days she was thought to be married to a gentleman of such stately appearance. I telephoned Flesch on the fifth of October from Lonny's London apartment to ask how she was. "No change." He said he had been with her an hour earlier. I told him that I was about to go on to Sadler's Wells. At the time of our conversation Lonny had already died. He was informed of her death a moment later, but did not call me back, deciding to give me the news in the morning, so as not to spoil my evening at the opera. Lonny, who had received the last sacraments much earlier and was at peace with herself, had passed on as quietly and unobtrusively as that good, pure soul deserved. We buried her not far from Leo Perutz, in the cemetery at Ischl, one of the most beautiful resting places in the world.

I returned to Wimbledon. I drove my son to Oxford, where he was given a quiet room in the quad at the rear of Oriel College; I had to clear out Lonny's apartment – only Flesch still remained, for a short time, at Broadwalk Court, that block of apartments in Notting Hill Gate which was so fateful for us all. For it was becoming ever clearer, although Peter and I mostly stayed politely at arm's length from each other, with only the occasional flaring up of rage and discord, that we must soon go our separate ways. In December London was once again wrapped in a thick pea-souper fog, for what was to be the last time: later the Clean Air Act was to drive away forever this affliction of the city, which, according to Virginia Woolf in *Orlando*, had been visited upon it only since the Victorian era.

After all this, it took another six months before our separation became final. I spent most of my evenings in front of the rented television set in my room; a new satirical program, *That Was The Week That Was*, among other portents announced the dawn of the "Swinging London" of the sixties. I sensed what was in the air and reported on it to my newspapers, but the decision as to whether I should remain in England or return to Austria did not depend on this. Even then, I continually considered staying here and managing on my own, with the help of S. Fischer Verlag and my work as cultural correspondent. On the twelfth of June, after an almost unbearably emotional parting from Peter, I traveled by train and boat to the Continent. Only when negotiations with the *Frankfurter Allgemeine*, which had begun started some time earlier, led to a firm agreement did I finally decide on Vienna. Here too I once again put my trust in the expectation that the course would be set for me, that I would be spared the agony of decision. And so it happened.

Then I spent a few days with Flesch in Baden-Baden with his close relatives, at the "country house," an annex of their vineyard on the Fremersberg. A family idyll. In the little private chapel his parents had been married more than seventy years ago. A growing consciousness of my newly won freedom lifted me above the pangs of conscience, the feelings of guilt, the tormenting indecision which I had suppressed for years but which had still continued to nag at me. It reached its height at a jeweler's in the inner city of Vienna, where

326

Peter lecturing at the Bavarian
Academy of Fine Arts in Munich,
March 1972

my wedding ring, which had become a little tight, was sawn through.
The symbolism had one small flaw: the ring had been given to me not
by Peter, but by my father. Seeing that I was still going around
wearing the brass curtain-ring that had been placed on my finger at
the register office in Marloes Road – Peter had long since abandoned
his – my father had given me the money for a gold ring. That had
been just before the Anschluss, on my last visit to Vienna before the
war.

16

An Awfully Nice Nursery

In one of the Grimms' fairy tales a young man is punished for his lack of hospitality by having his wishes granted by God. May he make three wishes like his neighbor? he asks. Yes, says the Lord, he may, but it would not be good for him and it would be better if he did not wish for anything. It turns out badly for him. And at times when I regretted returning to Austria, although I never rescinded my decision, this story came into my mind. Everything I have longed for has been granted to me, at least for a time, in such generous measure that it has deprived me of necessary leisure and time for inward reflection, if not of the urge toward true creative work.

A heavy sentence. Ludwig Wittgenstein once said he could not work without England and could not live without Vienna. If great things may be compared with small, this applied to me too. Those of my books which were most important to me – the biography of Fanny von Arnstein and the novel about exiles in America – came into being in the dreary yet fruitful solitude of Wimbledon. Articles, prefaces, talks and translations, some weightier essays, a journal written much earlier but recast, a film script, a story, and a handful of poems were the result of many hundreds of thousands of words, of an activity as unceasing as it was in the main ephemeral. "Twenty years largely wasted," T. S. Eliot's phrase about the years between the wars, could describe the next two decades of my literary existence.

Had I stayed in my English suburb, moreover, I could have experienced for myself a phase of great and exciting changes in the land. In the early sixties there was an upheaval in the capital, it began to vibrate, to dance and swirl. "Swinging London," miraculously rejuvenated under an arch-Conservative government, enticed not only the young people from every nook and cranny of the island but also adolescents from the Continent, now freed from the burden of war. It began with irreverent revue and television programs, with a magazine that was even more daring, aggressive, tactless, and disrespectful than France's old *Canard enchaîné*. Disregarding traditions of civility and distance, the satirical revue *Beyond the Fringe* was performed nightly on a tiny stage by four Oxbridge graduates. From Oxford and Cambridge too, still the source of more intelligence than the more recent red-brick universities in the industrial cities, came the mocking spirits who in 1961 founded the fortnightly magazine *Private Eye*, today still as lethally witty as ever. The most impudent and stylish television commentary on the week's events that had ever been shown, *That Was The Week That Was*, also included challenging voices from non-academic circles, and this too was a sign of the times. For now, alongside and in concert with the elite groups of the past, indeed even more effectively than these, the provinces were gaining the attention of the British public.

The Beatles appeared from Liverpool, and threw the whole of England, soon the whole world, into a state of rapture and rebellion. From the North of the "dark satanic mills," as William Blake had called the factories already springing up in his day, came writers such as John Braine, whose love stories unfolded among chimney smoke and the fog of exhaust fumes, in the grey slums of Manchester and Sheffield; while in the middle-class suburbs such as Clapham or Croydon, just as dreary in their own way, or in the East End of London, the kitchen-sink drama came into being, whose characters no longer spoke in the accents of Jane Austen or of Ivy Compton-Burnett.

A gloriously vulgar subculture took up the reins of fashion. For no obvious reason Carnaby Street, a stone's throw from Piccadilly Circus, became a center for the new, cheap casual clothes. Hair and beards, meanwhile, were being grown unprecedentedly long. The flower children and gentle hippies, cradled by the rhythms of John Lennon and Bob Dylan, were followed onto the scene by leather-clad Hell's Angels, and by the mid-seventies the first spiky-haired and peacock-bright punks were parading in the King's Road in Chelsea. There was change, too, in high fashion, previously the preserve of the *haute bourgeoisie*. Mary Quant popularized the miniskirt; and at the remodeled Derry and Toms store in Kensington High Street, once the haunt of ladies in tweed skirts and twin sets worn with a double row of pearls, the Biba boutique established itself not only in all the realms of apparel, but also in household goods and interior decoration; everything they sold, predominantly in black and all shades of purple, had a macabre elegance.

The year in which I left England, 1963, later became known as the most significant of its postwar history, a watershed between a public morality which was still almost Victorian in its strictness – or at least trapped in an Edwardian hypocritical conventionality – and one which had now become openly unbridled. The Secretary of State for War, John Profumo, was forced to resign after his affair with the demimondaine Christine Keeler had become public knowledge, and almost dragged the prime minister, Harold Macmillan, and the whole cabinet with him. A twilight world emerged from below the respectable surface of English society. Keeler had also conducted a liaison with the Soviet attaché Ivanov, and after revelations of the deep involvement of a whole generation of Cambridge students of the thirties in espionage services for their former allies, the scandal was further heightened by the possibility of a new betrayal of British state secrets to the now potential enemy.

Everything had begun to totter. But life in London was all the more lively. I, however, not yet fully aware of the far-reaching nature of the step I was taking, had decamped at a moment that seemed more pregnant, more full of promise for the future, for the loosening of all the rigid forms of life on the island, than ever before. I had fled blinkered into a new existence. It had been easy to say goodbye, but my departure proved heavy with consequences. Again and again over the years that followed, above all whenever I returned to Vienna after one of my frequent visits to England, I was plunged into misery. In my memory, Wimbledon, which I had found so boring, even paralyzing, turned into a lost idyll. The little path through the turnstile on the Ridgway through Wright's Alley to the Crooked Billet, the old village green on the edge of the Common, where recently I had so often met Flesch for a glass of Guinness between shopping and lunch – illicitly, since he was banned from the house; the bonfire and fireworks there every fifth of November; the rain-damp, earthy fragrance of Cannizaro Park and my beloved Sicilian Diana – all this gradually took on the numinous aura which the parish square of Heiligenstadt had possessed for me during my English years. Only the distant, the unattainable, has such power over us.

In Vienna I was instantly embraced by the warmth, the close, if not always deeply rooted, cordiality of my friends, those who had stayed behind and others more recently acquired. Certainly I sensed, indeed I knew, however much I buried this knowledge in the depths of my soul, that this return had also been a relapse, indeed a fall. But from where, and into what? This is difficult to explain without distressing those still living today in my homeland. Perhaps I can do so by means of an image. In a novel by Nigel Balchin, which I had translated, the narrator describes meeting some British compatriots again after spending weeks with American cronies in Paris. These compatriots happened to be his estranged wife and her lover, for whose sake she had callously left him. The Americans had been kind and helpful to him. "But with them I always felt as if I were in some awfully nice nursery. With these two here I felt, at least that evening, as though I were among children of the same age."

It was as persons of the same age, or rather, as adults, often superior to me, that I had experienced the English, even those who did not wish to know me or whose presence I enjoyed only indirectly: in books, on the stage, in political commentaries, or in the arts section of the *Times*. Now I found myself in a nursery, though one that was, at least for the time, "awfully nice." I felt I could not hope to learn anything from anyone here. I was not, as I had been in England, constantly intellectually challenged – either by the newspapers or the conversations in our circle. All those well-brought-up, charming people who made up my social life when they met together in groups talked almost exclusively about the latest opera or theater productions, and particularly about the actors and their private lives, or discussed their summer vacations, the little follies of absent friends or the malicious gossip of others, which they themselves disowned; they never discussed the real problems of life, and rarely spoke of politics. In Austria at this time, of course, things were relatively quiet on the political front, at least until the invasion of neighboring Czechoslovakia by Russian tanks; and if people were breaking each other's heads far off in Turkey, according to old custom one did not worry too much about it.

But how cozy, how restful and undemanding were these gatherings, whose cast of characters hardly varied, at the habitual lunchtime tables, the same year in, year out, with infallible regularity; then again, late at night after the theater, in one of those inner-city restaurants that were in full swing during those hours; or on otherwise unoccupied evenings, farther out of town at a *Heurigen* inn known only to native Viennese, where there was no music and which was closed to strangers. And I was anything but a stranger in Vienna; this had been my home and was now my home again, and at last I felt comfortably ensconced once again in a community into which, after all, I had been born. A euphoric condition. Among presumably benevolent fellow citizens I felt protected, and walked cheerfully "through the rustling leaves of the past," as Heimito von Doderer had said. But here I must turn my attention to a few great figures who towered above the closely woven, though hardly shimmering web of this social fabric, and with whom, in the narrowest circle, we came together in admiration or in conflict, as coevals, sometimes as inferiors; yet whether united or at variance, at the same eye level, at least with the same eye for artistic quality.

Heimito was one of these, and so, certainly, was Alexander Lernet-Holenia, who had won our utmost respect with his finest poems and the choicest of his variable prose: his character and conduct demanded our love, because otherwise they could not have been tolerated. I remained capable of this love under the most difficult of circumstances and to the bitter end. And how rarely, beneath his mask of a nobleman far removed from any intellectual, let alone literary activity – never did one see a manuscript, a letter from a publisher on his desk, never a book in his house, unless it stood bashfully on a little shelf in his wife's bedroom – how rarely Alexander betrayed what really went on in his mind. Occasionally he did confide in me. In the springtime of our friendship, in the fifties in St. Wolfgang, we were often alone together, in his boathouse, among the reeds on the lake when he, not a keen swimmer, would row me and his little dog to the opposite shore, on walks over the Falkenstein, to the Auerriese or the Schwarzensee. In the course of one stroll around that dark, high-lying lake he related to me the story of his last important novel, *Count Luna*.

An *amitié amoureuse*, conducted with calmness and composure – for we were no longer young, and were becoming visibly older – which, despite all the associated perils, passed smoothly into a cordial attachment. I was generally unscathed by Alexander's fits of bad temper. Even during the last months of his life, when he was consumed by fatal illness, usually confused, like Don Quixote in his final shattered state, he would twist his mouth into a forced smile when I entered his room. Meanwhile I suffered again and again, as did everyone around him, from the baffling chess moves of his thoughts and actions, sometimes from his underhandedness or even treachery. But so strong were my feelings for him, so deep and honest my delight in his poems such as the "Prophecy of Tiresias" or the "Journey of the Three Kings," in stories of Kleist-like flawlessness such as "Baron Bagge," or a novel like *The Two Sicilies*, which contained in its core so much of what was dear to me in Austria, that I forgave him everything, overlooked everything, as I did later with only one other friend, with whom Alexander had more in common than either suspected: Thomas Bernhard. Flesch, in his posthumously published memoirs, called Alexander "the reverse side of the gold ducat of Austria," and he certainly did not mean this only in a derogatory sense. For Flesch's friends Lernet and Doderer were each as eccentric as he was himself, and all three manifested those distortions which in certain individual cases underlie the image of the light-hearted, easy-going, effortlessly artistic and knightly Habsburg subject of the old school.

In his own extreme old age, constantly threatened by the clouding of his own consciousness, Flesch had profound insight into the complex essence of both Lernet and Doderer, and described them, including their outward appearance, with such wonderful verbal power that I can add little to these portraits. He had known both of them, to a greater or lesser extent, in their youth, and had presumably taken a more critical attitude to them after the experiences of the intervening time of separation than did I, in my all but blind passion for every incorporation of the old Austria, in however rudimentary and illusory form it still survived. Only in more recent years did I become implacable in my opposition to the darker ideological and moral side of my compatriots, when, in the wake of an ominous presidential election, all that was evil, malevolent, and intolerant in the national character, long submerged and believed dead, once again rose to the surface.

But at that time, and for a long time afterward, I could live with the mischievous contrariness with which Alexander continued to wear on his hat a military badge bearing the inadequately effaced emblem of a regime he still hated; and with the fact that in Heimito's Vienna apartment there were fixed to the side of a bookshelf – if I remember rightly – two photographs in crass contrast to each other: one of Pope Pius XII in the angelically white soutane I had seen him wear in 1950 in St. Peter's Square, and below this a repulsive picture of the East German minister of justice, Hilde Benjamin, whose husband had been killed by the Nazis and who now knew no mercy in the courtroom when confronting the henchmen of the Third Reich.

Doderer's *Die Strudlhofstiege* had enchanted me. That the mighty novel whose predecessor this book had been, *Die Dämonen*, was originally to have been called *The Demons of the Ostmark* and bore clear traces of anti-Semitism, that the events of July 15, 1927, were portrayed in it in a questionable way – what did it matter to me? I was defenseless against this quintessence of Viennese awareness of life, this language as precise as it was absurd, this power of construction combined with a vividness of detail which was continually astonishing. I accepted everything: that Heimito had confused the Third Reich with the Holy Roman Empire, a claim which he himself never made, although his friends made it on his behalf – a confusion which can really hardly be believed of an illegal party member, who ought by rights to have read that party's bible, *Mein Kampf.* And I accepted, since they did not concern me personally, the more or less secret sexual excesses of this great man, the unbridled pleasure in acts of violence of every kind which he described in *Die Merowinger,* as well as the verbal coarseness which seems to represent an antidote to complex, perhaps even melancholic refinements of the spirit – as with Mozart's notorious letters to his cousin.

Unforgettable for me is a visit to Landshut, to the home of his "Minze," where Doderer had invited us to dinner, before our final return to Austria. On arrival we took rooms at the inn Zur Sonne and entered the good housewife's rooms, furnished in sensible pine wood. There we were greeted by a huge steaming bowl filled with *Weisswürste* – countless pairs of this pale veal sausage formed of meat and intestine, which became more revolting, the more one ate of them. They were served up with a great deal of beer, but without side-dishes of any kind, neither mustard nor cabbage nor potatoes. And it was with positively impish delight that Heimito urged us to consume this "real Bavarian meal" (as he called it) to the point of surfeit. It was probably in Bavaria that he found his escape from the Viennese decadence to which he had fallen prey in his youth. He liked to point out that his Minze was the niece of Ludwig Thoma, a popular humorous Bavarian writer. I wonder whether he knew of her uncle's offensive utterances in the *Miesbacher Anzeiger,* to which attention has recently been drawn again. I doubt it. Elsewhere, in the foreword to a volume by H. C. Artmann and Gerhard Rühm, whom he esteemed and encouraged, he dismissed Thoma rather contemptuously, placing him at the end of a list of earlier writers in dialect.

When speaking of those who enlivened the climate of the "nursery," I must not omit the name of Ernst Fischer. He too was a child of the old monarchy, although born at the turn of the century and an exact opposite, if not of Flesch, certainly of Lernet and

Doderer. Nevertheless he was linked to Alexander by a strange respect and fondness, which was, however, not so inexplicable, for both were dreamers and poets. It was only after some time that Fischer entered our lives, as probably the most notable of our group of newly acquired friends – a true superabundance of more or less faithful friends, or so it seemed to us after our long English isolation. I will refrain from naming them all, not only because of that danger of a "kitchen of names" to which I have so often succumbed, but because it would be impossible to please all those among them who are still living, no matter what I said about them. Only where it is unavoidable will they appear in my account of the next few years. In his work *La Vie de Henri Brulard*, Stendhal asks: *"Où se trouvera le lecteur qui, après quatre ou cinq volumes de je et de moi, ne désirera pas qu'on me jette non plus une verre d'eau sale mais une bouteille d'encre?"* Even at this point in the second part of my memoirs, I am afraid that the eternal "I" and "me" may make my readers reach for an inkpot.

I had, therefore, better dash through the next few decades as quickly as possible – although much that affected me happened during that time. However, I must at least explain what I mean by the fatality of wishes that have been fulfilled, and why the euphoria to which I had given myself up for so long could not last. Is there, incidentally, any such thing as a lasting euphoria? Now (we had thought when we left England) the peaceful evening of our lives was about to begin. But it was nothing of the sort. It was still only the afternoon; storms were raging, even if only in a teacup, and sometimes the heat of the sun was too strong for us. Although Flesch and I were not yet married, and would not be for some time, we managed to move into a little apartment together, in one of the housing projects despised by Viennese society, although this one stood in the exclusive Cottage district, and had trees, which I found quite simply indispensable, in front of all the windows. A *pied à terre* in town: this was how we saw it, although in fact we spent the greater part of the year there.

Our real home was St. Wolfgang. And whenever we drove there – which was at every possible opportunity – I was "happy to be here"; this was invariably the first phrase, never omitted, of every entry in my calendar after arriving. The unpretentious apartment in Vienna, surrounded by *Jugendstil* villas, certainly had its good points: it protected us from snobbish society, as well as from the necessity of conducting a costly and time-consuming salon. In the country, at least for a few weeks in the summer, what a friendly man from St. Wolfgang was to call the "green salon by the Dittelbach" began to take shape as if of its own accord. Here we had house guests, dinner guests, guests at all times of day and by the dozen.

To be able to flee from the cultural activity of Vienna, whose hectic pace had surpassed all our expectations, even our fears, to the quiet of the little house, surrounded on three sides by a backdrop of trees and bushes, always struck me as an undeserved gift of fate. Yes, I was always mindful of the privilege, in this ever more populous and shrinking world, of having this pretty house and bit of garden just for myself and those close to me, and when in the end it was torn away from me again, I was shattered, but not fundamentally surprised. Every penny I earned went into this modest property; I took out loans in order to buy, tract by tract, the adjoining meadow, to have a two-room annex built, and to install central heating; with Alexander's permission I planted fruit trees on the remaining part of the lawn which still belonged to him; at his request I protected a common entrance with a gate, and added a dozen birch trees as a living fence along the drive, and two magnolias, my favorite of all shrubs. No luxury, just necessary comfort. I had the bathroom and showers inexpensively tiled. The next owner, in an as yet unimaginable future, was to substitute more decorative tiles as his first improvement.

The course of my day was exhausting. To write for a German-speaking readership from a German-speaking viewpoint turned out to be a highly arduous task. In England it was I who had the power to decide what artistic events, what intellectual and social tendencies should be communicated to readers and listeners on the Continent. Here in Austria I was an instrument of the editorial office, which was fully informed about activities in the neighboring country and would telephone me with a reminder to file my copy if I occasionally missed an event or did not feel inclined to attend. This applied mainly to theatrical events, the most newsworthy here as in London, with the exception of the rarer operatic first nights. New movements in politics and society did not originate in Vienna. Nevertheless there was an accumulation of activities of all sorts, of which it was my duty to be aware. Thus, when I was once asked how I spent my day, I replied that in this city there was never time to think, because there was "always something boring going on." Admittedly each of my contributions immediately evoked some response on publication, whether approving or critical. But later, when the praise turned out to be hollow, the criticism to arise from concealed resentment, the great mass of those into whom I had so willingly and joyfully integrated myself to be vacillating and insincere, the delight vanished, and my bread-and-butter work, as I found myself thinking of it, became more and more of a burden.

Add to this the actual root of all evil, my own hyperactivity, which today strikes me as embarrassing, to say the least. The urge to be everywhere, to exert an influence – certainly it was understandable, but it was also, after all, ridiculous. After standing on the sidelines for so long, I was now trying to compensate by leaping straight into the center of things and staying there. And where was there a better opportunity to do this than in the community of writers, Austrian PEN? It was inevitable that I should join it; but to serve it for nearly seven years in a voluntary capacity proved. equally inevitably, to be an error of judgment. My excuse is like that of Heimito and others like him, who claimed to have confused the Third Reich with the Holy Roman Empire: I confused the PEN of Vienna with the PEN of London. The analogy is not as eccentric as it may seem. At the head of the association were blameless people such as Franz Theodor Csokor, the painter and poet Carry Hauser, the prose writer Alexander Sacher-Masoch, all former exiles. But with the remaining members of the executive committee, even those who had been awarded state prizes, one could not be so sure. Some had not managed to avoid writing poems in praise of Hitler. Yet Heimito von Doderer had been the only one to be refused membership for a long period, because he was the only one to admit his transgression.

I did not apply for office. But when, in 1966, the selfless soul of this PEN center, the journalist and managing secretary Erika Hanel, died prematurely, a reshuffle took place and I was persuaded to take over as general secretary in place of Carry Hauser. A fatal decision. It was made on April 20 (Hitler's birthday), and I noted that it was accompanied by "a sharp little pain in my heart." These were evil omens. Nevertheless it is to this decision, which in the end brought me deep disappointment, that I owe many new friends in this international association, frequent meetings with my London PEN colleagues, and also kindred spirits in the most various of countries, the feeling of global unity which came into being spontaneously, although it could evaporate just as rapidly. It is also to this decision that I owe the truly meaningful task to which I devoted many hours of my life: my work for the International Writers in Prison Committee on behalf of writers throughout the world who were imprisoned, sometimes tortured. Certainly there were some good-for-nothings, indeed rascals, and even idiots in this family of PEN, but at the same time there were wonderful, good, and enchanting people, from Heinrich Böll to my Slovenian "sister," Mira Mihelič.

The position had changed; the schizophrenia continued. Now our field of vision encompassed more and more of what remained of the old Habsburg links and soon reappeared as a dream of a new "Mitteleuropa" – a dream which soon faded, however, in the face of the most recent, far-reaching changes in this part of the world. In the very first summers after our return Flesch and I visited Opatija, Portoroz, and Dubrovnik – formerly the vacation resorts Abbazia, Portorose, and Ragusa under the dual monarchy. Now the Slovenian writers were being joined by annual visitors, first in Portoroz and Piran, and then in Bled, which was familiar to me from my childhood. Mira, the president of the Yugoslav center, led the conferences that took place every May; she was a dark, strikingly attractive woman, the daughter of a bourgeois citizen of Ljubljana, who had joined the partisans during the war, suffered deprivation and danger, but emerged as the subtle novelist and true cosmopolitan that her origins and education had always destined her to be. She spoke English and French without difficulty, but preferred to speak German, for her forebears had regarded Vienna as their capital and often visited the city. When she tenderly called me "Childerl," with the slightly aspirated "H" that she added to my name, I was totally disarmed. Everyone who had anything to do with her loved her and her gentle rule over the Slovenian *pisatelji* – with such absent-mindedness sometimes, with "Pannonian" unconcern, in her own phrase. And when she had fears about the weather for the outing that took place at the end of each conference, or when disputes broke out between the Yugoslav factions, she would dash off to light a candle to St. Anthony, who came to her aid again and again.

Venice was not far from Portoroz, and we traveled there often, via Trieste if not direct from Vienna. Over many years we stayed for a few weeks in late spring, always at the same artists' pension, Alla Salute da Cici, in the quiet Dorsoduro district, I in Room 38, Flesch in Room 8. My room had a weathered little iron balcony above the vine-covered awning of the restaurant, from which there was a view of the cupolas of the Salute church; often, after drinking tea there in the afternoons, we would go to Gino's café around the corner, to gaze through the narrow *calle* at the end of which it lay, where every so often we could see a ship gliding past along a section of the Canale della Giudecca. Gradually we became familiar with all the churches and museums and made a point of regularly visiting a selected few of these. Our first destination was always the room in the Accademia with the Bellinis and Giorgione's *Tempesta*. Even more than by Bellini's charming Madonnas, I was enchanted by the five panels of his *Allegory*, and most of all the *Fortuna Incostante* – the goddess of fortune with eyelids lowered in melancholy, her garment blown about by the wind, on a rocking boat, holding on her knee a blue globe which a putto helped to support, and three other little boys with her in the boat, two others beside it in the shallow ocean, one of these blissfully floating in the waves. This one particularly appealed to me, and when my grandson was born, I thought I detected a resemblance.

In the evenings, Peggy Guggenheim sometimes came to Da Cici with her three silly little Pekinese, as did Ezra Pound, for both lived nearby, and Signor Manin's cuisine was good. Once, when no other tables were free because it was raining and everyone had to sit indoors, Pound, with his companion Olga Rudge, joined us at ours, where he sat in silence for two hours, while she, equally mute, saw to his needs. I contemplated the bearded old man full of reverence and without any disgust, although I knew of his odious wartime broadcasts: a blind genius, now extinguished and fossilized in his old age – a sacred awe was all I could summon up before him. Year after year we would follow all the rituals of these visits to "our" Venice – for all who fall prey to her believe themselves her only true possessors. After the first reunion with the *Allegory* came the long ramble to the church of SS Giovanni e Paolo, known as "Zanipolo," where I sought out my favorite baroque statue of Belluna, and then to the Tiepolos on the top floor of the Ca' Rezzonico; the mornings on the piazza, sipping a sweet liqueur called Aurum to the foolish melodies of the musicians at Quadri or Lavena; the shopping sprees at the *merceria*, at the end of which there was always the homage to Goldoni, high on his plinth in the midst of his *veneziani*; the lunches in the leafy shade of the garden of the Trattoria Montin; in the afternoons, sometimes the café in San Stefano, frequented by students and housewives; toward evening, an hour of gossip in her little palazzo (next to Peggy Guggenheim's) with Doxie Brunetta, a woman of extraordinary charm, from whom we learned many stories and anecdotes of Venetian society. It was only after Flesch's death, and after the artificial and disastrous revival of the old carnival, that I gave up my claim to this illusory possession.

All the old links were now being forged anew. We looked around in Prague, once the "golden," now grey, before the suppression of its "spring." In Budapest, in a dismal foggy autumn in the seventies, we visited Stella and Oszkar Udvarós, my mother's relatives of whom I was so fond, in their house which was now even more dilapidated – their daughter and all the rest of the family had fled Hungary in 1956; and not far from them in Buda, in his well-kept villa, we saw the "rehabilitated" Tibor Déry, on the occasion of his eightieth birthday. A *grand seigneur* of a man, as familiar to me as if he too had been one of my uncles. Soon after that I discovered Cracow, where I had not been since my early youth. And here, summoned in the winter of 1976 by the Austrian Cultural Institute, I almost came to believe that all my life I had been clinging to a false image – the onion-shaped domes of Cracow with their greenish patina, which I could not find at first. Then I discovered them after all on the Wawel, the old royal palace, which in the meantime had been deconsecrated because it had been the "residence" of the German governor general and mass murderer, Hans Frank. In the cafe at the Cloth Halls on the Rynek Glówny, the main square, I felt that I must be in the same place where, as a five-year-old, I had sat with my mother drinking hot chocolate and eating bonbons.

The following year a symposium on Thomas Bernhard brought me to Trieste, which until then we had only driven around, and from then on I returned frequently and met many survivors from the time when this was the most important trading port of the dual empire: admirals' daughters, already advanced in years; Baron Banfield, the last surviving knight of the Order of the Empress Maria Theresa; sons of Viennese officials and doctors, and, in this city once again submerged in nostalgia for Franz Joseph, formerly mocked as "Cecco Beppe," I met Claudio Magris, the young reawakener of the "Habsburg myth" who at the same time was anything but a conservative. I also made another woman friend there, Hansi Cominotti, sweet and clever, a somewhat plumper counterpart to Mira; she was comfortably settled in a house high above the town, in Opicina. Later she became the inspiration for the character of a gallery owner in a film script, *Mirko und Franca*, which I set in Trieste. When her husband Nino died, she pined away, and finally took her own life in her grief and illness, and I mourned and wept for her as I had done for that other Hansi, and one day too was to mourn for my Mira.

All this belonged to the world which I had re-entered, and, as gradually became clear to me, it contained more wishful dreams of the past than present temptations. The present was still more powerful for me in England, where I had left my children behind, where Peter continued to live in Wimbledon, still cared for by the same household help. As early as the autumn of 1963, while I was still temporarily staying in Berthold Viertel's Vienna apartment near St. Stephen's Cathedral, which I had rented from his widow, I was summoned back to London because of a small family tragedy. My heart rent in two, I moved back into my old room, now however stripped of certain pictures and pieces of furniture which had already been shipped overseas, and stayed a week until the problem had been sorted out. After that, I did not stay in Wimbledon again, though I occasionally spent an evening there, when the children, who lived in various places at various times, had birthdays which were to be celebrated in their old home. Then I would arrive with full shopping bags and prepare a festive meal as I had done in the old days. Peter mainly stayed out of sight. Every year, up to the time when I once again became a resident in England for a short time, I would visit London two or three times – in the end, mainly because of my daughter, the only one who did not give up the land of her birth, but also for any other reason that presented itself: the children's weddings, PEN meetings, lectures, broadcasts – when I was asked to take part in the BBC's Round Europe Quiz. Never did I have the feeling that I was no longer at home there.

In London too the present had its rituals. In the seventies the Portobello Road market every Saturday was a center of youthful subculture. The "scene" took place in the many pubs, particularly at Henekey's, at lunchtime over beer and sandwiches; the long-haired, the bearded, the bejeaned, the miniskirted, from market stallholders to dukes' daughters who had chosen the slumming of the Twenties as a permanent lifestyle – interspersed with foreign buyers, mostly Americans, for whom at that time there was still an immeasurable range of antiques, furniture, silver, netsuke, Buddhas, Indian wood carvings and art nouveau lamps on offer, in a country which no foreign power had occupied and ransacked since the eleventh century.

In Lonsdale Road, just off the market, I made the acquaintance of a commune, where "spades" (black "brothers" from the Black House), peaceful hippies, harmless junkies and flipped-out characters of all kinds went in and out, where joss sticks were constantly burning and somewhat awkward attempts were made to produce a psychedelic effect by means of lighting. In the basement lived a good-looking, fair-haired Hell's Angel with the poetic name of Bob Wild Child, by night perhaps a terror to the local citizens on his roaring motorcycle, by day friendly and willing to provide information to the visitor. I asked him why his black leather jacket was adorned with so many swastikas among all the other emblems. His face became serious, he frowned and thought about it. "I suppose," he said hesitantly, "they mean something like power."

Some of the inhabitants of this commune had difficulty in coming to terms with problems from their childhood and adolescence. Two understanding psychiatrists were at hand to lend assistance. One, Ronald D. Laing, a dark, nervous man, in his book *The Divided Self* explained "ontological uncertainty" as quite natural, for fundamentally it was society which was sick, and the neurotic, in possession of true recognition of reality, who was healthy. Laing's friend David Cooper, a huge man with red hair and beard and a reassuringly cheerful manner, had in his main work, *The Death of the Family*, discovered the root of all evil to be the inadequacy and superior strength of parents. In the case of mothers who were prepared to write checks for £50 for therapy sessions, he would overlook their misdemeanors and recognize them as exceptions.

Once, squatting in a circle with the inhabitants of the commune and their visitors, I tried to smoke hashish in a pipe, but my unimaginative brain refused to give way to intoxication. However, toward the end of the sixties I was captivated by a rock concert in Hyde Park, before an audience of half a million. Surrounded by my children, their partners, and friends, I sat on the grass, listening blissfully to the throbbing, rhythmically beguiling sounds from the stage far, far away, where figures in skintight clothes with handheld microphones were wandering vaguely about, sounds that reached the immense, thoroughly good-natured throng by means of loudspeakers. An experience I would not have wished to miss, even if it seemed diametrically opposed to a concert by the Vienna Philharmonic on a Sunday morning in the Goldener Saal of the Vienna Musikverein. But I was equally devoted to the more bourgeois pleasures of London and Oxford.

Now, when in London I would stay in the environment of which I was fondest: at Dodo's pretty little house in Fulham, where she had been living since her separation from her husband and departure from Pembroke Square in Kensington; at the bachelor apartment in Holland Park of Dodo's old friend Patrick, Lord Barrington; at the now widowed Bettina Ehrlich's apartment in Palace Gardens Terrace, near our Broadwalk Court, in Notting Hill; or in one of the little hotels in Lexham Gardens, near Marloes Road, where Peter and I had married more than thirty years earlier. Patrick sometimes invited me to lunch or tea at the House of Lords, and I was able to sit in the visitors' gallery to hear some of the speeches. In Oxford I visited Dodo's daughter, who was married to a Germanist lecturer and researcher on Kafka, and strolled with them both along the bluebell-edged river bank by Magdalen College. Here tradition was still intact, perhaps because students who were enticed by the teachings of that false prophet William S. Burroughs, or by the spirit of the 1968 uprisings on the Continent, preferred to depart quietly from the university rather than attempt to revolutionize it. I had no intention of taking sides in this matter. And finally I returned again and again to the comforting atmosphere of Glebe House, where, among mahogany furniture and crystal ornaments, surrounded by the portraits of venerable departed members such as Henry Nevinson and Hermon Ould, and watched over at all times by the great portrait of Henrietta Leslie, the representatives of the International PEN centers would meet and dine – loyal Communists from Bulgaria and East Germany, waverers and hypocrites from Hungary, liberal hotheads from Holland, elegant rhetoricians and lovably greedy novelists from France – until in 1977 an acute lack of funds forced their London hosts to abandon their beautiful premises, which Henrietta had been able to bequeath to them only for the term of her lease.

It was this atmosphere, this feeling of community that I tried to rediscover at the Viennese PEN, and thought I had found in the charmingly untidy apartment of Erika Hanel, where at that time one could meet informally, casually and cheerfully, for official or private purposes. Here too *confrères* from other countries would turn up, as James Baldwin did one day when his play *Blues for Mr. Charlie* was premiered at the Volkstheater. At Erika's request I took him and his Turkish friend up the Kahlenberg to show them the Vienna woods and the view of the city on the Danube, explaining to their amusement that it was from this point in 1683 that the counter-attack took place on Kara Mustapha, which drove the wild Ottomans forever out of Central Europe. I will never forget Baldwin's face lighting up when I embraced him in saying goodbye. Since 1956 Erika had been living with György Sebestyén, a Hungarian emigré, who soon set out to conquer literary Vienna with her help, and many years later actually achieved the office of president of Austrian PEN. But when Erika herself died before her time, it was left to me – with the support of her assistant Mimi, who not only bore my mother's name, but was as loyal to me as she had been to Erika – to take charge of the center for the next seven years, in premises which we ourselves found and equipped as an office.

In 1966 I flew with the PEN president, Franz Theodor Csokor, to a congress in New York – partly as a delegate and partly to look after the eighty-one-year-old writer. Csokor, the eternal wandering scholar – a humanist with some little faults such as all humanists have, if they are truly human – was more stimulating, more worldly wise and even more tireless than many a prematurely old member of his association. We stopped off in Paris on our journey, and he insisted on strolling with me through the *quartier latin*, stayed the night with his friends the Zuckerkandls and then cheerfully trotted off to catch the flight to America. "Old wolf, trot, trot along!" was his best poem, and the one that described him best. In New York, which he was visiting for the first time, he immediately felt at home, and teased me with nonsensical comparisons, such as one between Eighth Avenue and the Praterstrasse in Vienna. He gathered all his friends around him: Otto Weininger's brother Richard, who, in direct contrast to that brilliant neurotic, had become a prosperous businessman and ship owner with offices on Madison Avenue; Hertha Pauli, the companion of Ödön von Horváth, a reddish-blonde, sprightly, warm-hearted woman; and finally Friederike Maria Zweig, Stefan's first wife, a little fussy and lacking in taste, but utterly goodhearted, though it was said of her that soon after her arrival in New York, giving a dinner party for some illustrious guests, she had cleverly decorated the table with wreaths of poison ivy.

And so I was back in New York after such a long time, with no Hansi – indeed, most of the émigrés I had met there fourteen years earlier had either died or left town. Yet the city's atmosphere was even more refreshing, more invigorating, and despite all the dire poverty in the slums it inspired the will to live, the epitome of defiant, unshakable idealism. Arthur Miller presided at the PEN Congress, and many of the great Latin American writers such as Pablo Neruda attended. I too made a brief appearance with a plea for the writer as the "daring young man on the flying trapeze," who "carried out the *salto mortale* of thinking things through to the end – even to the point of absurdity." Sartre and Koestler, I said, had brilliantly undertaken this task and so spared us all from many dangerous or even false trains of thought. Today I am, and have been for some time, rather in favor of an end to such *Narrenfreiheit*, the license granted to jesters. At that time my words received a benevolent hearing, and the periodical *Aufbau* reprinted the text, otherwise I would long have forgotten about it. I was also reluctantly forced to approach John Updike and Saul Bellow in the role of interviewer, for the head of the literary department of the Hessischer Rundfunk, who was supposed to interview them, suddenly lost his courage, and as I happened to be standing nearby, he simply pressed the microphone into my hand and propelled me toward these giants.

The Congress was over, the "family" had scattered, I left the Fifth Avenue Hotel and found a hideout in a little room at the Austrian Cultural Institute, which served as a base from which I could explore the island of Nantucket, New England, Boston, and the little university town of Cambridge. Thus I managed to catch up on some of the experiences denied to me in 1952. In Cambridge Hertha Pauli picked me up from the house of a Harvard professor and his wife, who had been my hosts, and drove me back to New York. We had been invited to stop for tea on the way at Arthur Miller's, at his farm in Roxbury. He was now married to the wonderful photographer Inge Morath, whom I had known well in Vienna just after the war; they had a delightful little girl. No one mentioned Marilyn Monroe. Miller showed us mementoes of his family, who came from the eastern provinces of the Austro-Hungarian empire: group pictures of his forebears and their siblings, portraits and documents of all kinds, all lovingly guarded treasures whose preservation filled him with pride and delight. How sad it was to learn later that his house had burned down and all his relics had been lost in the fire.

In Vienna, among my friends, one generation was gradually succeeding another. Soon after our return, we became practically inseparable from Heimito von Doderer – returning one day from a party given by his and my publisher at Schloss Schleissheim, the three of us, with Dorothea Zeemann, took a kind of oath of eternal friendship. Heimito celebrated his seventieth birthday in the autumn of 1966, with great ceremony, and died soon afterward. We buried him in January. And there, at the end of the funeral procession, in which Torberg had also taken part, Alexander Lernet approached us, in an attempt to reconcile Torberg and me in view of the vanity of earthly quarrels. A kind of truce followed, although six years later there was a renewed and final rupture between us. In the preceding year Torberg, having gradually lost his former financial backers, had handed over the magazine *Forum* to Günther Nenning. It was then that the little kicks in the teeth and pinpricks finally ceased, the barbed remarks to which I was constantly exposed under the name of "Hulda Spitz," which he had coined for me in the unmannerly style of Karl Kraus. Now the polemicist turned his attention to his intended masterpiece, the novel *Süsskind von Trimberg*, and if he continued to fight out his feuds, they were directed elsewhere. An uncertain peace, which was constantly threatened. At any rate, my enemy-friend, as he had now once more become, for a time allowed me to follow my own path in peace in PEN – particularly since, in accordance with my own inner convictions, I always defended the viewpoint of the West at all international meetings, and vehemently opposed the resolutely Stalinist Bulgarian Leda Mileva and her companions, whether fanatical or merely cowardly, from the People's Republics, whenever a question of freedom of speech or of support for threatened or imprisoned dissidents arose.

As a result of my conspicuous enthusiasm for such activity, I was asked to take part in all sorts of panels, including the one which awarded the *Förderungspreis*, the education department's prize for novelists, at the beginning of 1968. The choice among the hundred prose works which had been submitted was not easy, but finally the supporters of Thomas Bernhard, with the backing of two conservative but artistically open-minded ministry officials, succeeded in securing this first Austrian honor for this author, still comparatively unknown at that time, and his book *Frost*. The award was presented to him the following March, but he angered the minister of the time so much by an existential funeral oration that the latter, red-faced with fury, called out: "All the same, we are proud Austrians!" and left the hall, banging the door behind him, in the direction of the buffet in the adjoining room. He was followed by the entire fraternity of Viennese writers and thinkers, all in an equal state of outrage. Only a small handful of people including, to his credit, a section head from the education department, hurried toward the prizewinner, who was feeling like a leper, to declare their loyalty to him. I later reproached Bernhard for stating in his book *Wittgenstein's Nephew* that he had seen only Paul

Wittgenstein (the nephew in question) and his life-partner Hede by his side on that occasion. I had of course been one of the others. Literature and life, he said unrepentantly, were not the same. I had also written a letter to the minister to explain Bernhard's speech, but received no reply. This, at any rate, was the beginning of my friendship with Thomas Bernhard, and a few weeks later, at my request, he gave a reading from his works at PEN.

Mediocre or not, the association had its uses. When the Russian tanks had rolled into Prague in August 1968, the embassy of a friendly neighboring country had approached us with the request that we accept a substantial sum of money from them, to be distributed among writers who had fled to Vienna. It had to be done so secretly that the origin and purpose of the payment should not appear anywhere, nor was any account to be given to the donor of the uses to which it had been put. Mimi and I opened a special account which enabled us to give immediate and appropriate aid to any person in need who could give proof of being a writer. When I was thrown out in 1972, we were accused of having spent PEN money without keeping proper records and perhaps even embezzling it. Before that, however, in the autumn of 1968, exiles began to arrive from Poland, where Gomulka had begun his persecution of the Jews. With the help of another Western embassy they had at least been able to send on to us their documents, academic school-leaving and graduation certificates, which the authorities had officially forbidden them to take out of the country. They too benefited from what little was left of that donation.

In my thirst to get things done, I had set up an action committee of about seven or eight members in their forties or thereabouts, in order to bring a little fresh blood into the organization, which was dominated by somewhat fossilized individuals. Nearly all of these were to stab me in the back as soon as the cue was given to do so. One of them said at the time that of all the serpents I had nourished in my bosom, he had been the only one not to bite me. But not so fast: one day he too was to sink his teeth in. With another member I initiated what was probably the most useful action ever taken in the context of the Austrian PEN. But when the witch hunt against me began, he also broke with me, although under duress. As long as my euphoria lasted, I was happy to have joined forces with a young group that included, quite in the imperial tradition, an emigré Southern Slav who had settled in Vienna, a Hungarian, and a German-Bohemian.

Nevertheless it was the older members, the great and the nearly great, as long as they lived, with whom Flesch and I preferred to spend our time. We had made friends with Arthur Schnitzler's son Heini, a quiet, distinguished man, who produced his father's plays just as the latter had envisaged them. We often saw Fritz Kortner, who confided in us about problems with colleagues at the Burgtheater. On Saturday mornings, year in, year out, we would go to Lernet's levee, followed by lunch together at the Michaeler-Beisl, where some notable guest would always appear – Julien Green with his adoptive son Jourdan; Gregor von Rezzori, the skillful inventor of himself; or figures from the past such as Eckart von Naso. Sundays on the other hand were devoted to Ernst Fischer and his wife Lou, who had been married for twenty years to Hanns Eisler; we would meet them and other friends and acquaintances for lunch at the restaurant Zur schönen Aussicht on my parish square in Heiligenstadt, for decades a meeting place for the most congenial people in Vienna.

I will be as brief as possible in describing – sometimes only in snapshots – the events of the next few years. How I went to Israel only a few months before the Six Days' War and so first encountered that country in its original meager borders, in its age of innocence, as it were. And how, when the war had broken out, at the request of one of their diplomats I went to the Israeli embassy early every morning to translate the English-language reports from the scene into German, and even had them duplicated so that they should reach the Austrian press and the agencies as quickly as possible – all this, while the pompous champions of Zionism were still lolling in their beds, night-workers for their own cause as they were in imitation of their idol, Kraus. Finally how, this time through the intervention of Ernst Fischer, I agreed to be reconciled with Canetti, and he joined us one day at our Sunday lunch table, where Theodor W. Adorno was already installed. We were sitting in the restaurant garden under a chestnut tree. When, the following night, a storm raged over Vienna, the tree was directly struck by lightning, which split it from crown to root. We came to the conclusion that the combined and concentrated vanity of the two intellectual heroes had lingered in the air, thus inviting this eruption from the heavens.

In Ernst Fischer we admired an aesthete and interpreter, a skillful translator of Virgil and Baudelaire, a wise and enthusiastic friend, quietly benevolent within his small circle. Long before he became a leading figure of the Kafka renaissance in Liblice and then of the

Prague Spring, before he conferred on the latter the designation – promptly picked up by Dubcek – of "Communism with a human face," and in his disgust at the Russian invasion coined the term *Panzerkommunismus*, the communism of tanks, we knew of his rupture with the ideology which by then had totally degenerated. We never spoke of his earlier aberrations; he himself confessed them and attempted to explain them in his memoirs.

We had a taste of the rhetorical pathos that, as a politician, Fischer knew so well how to kindle, when we traveled with him and Lou to one of the spring festivals in Slovenia. Near Hradinje, where an incomparable fresco of a medieval *danse macabre* is preserved in a little church, in the middle of a peaceful picnic on the slope of a hill, on the last day of the trip, Ernst Fischer suddenly arose and gave a rousing speech, unexpected, perhaps even inappropriate, but impressive in the extreme, and indeed wildly applauded by adherents of the left, who thought just as little of state Communism as he did.

Another snapshot: one afternoon the Austrian chancellor Klaus had invited all the Austrian writers that could be reached to the Palais Dietrichstein. Never before nor since has there been such an attempt to bring politics and literature into closer contact with each other. Even the young rebels Wolfgang Bauer and Alfred Kolleritsch had been summoned from Graz and arrived in a rented car. We were standing in the anteroom of the magnificent hall when the heavy door opened slowly. Through it, with all the signs of extreme embarrassment, there entered a page wearing black knee-breeches, white stockings and buckled shoes, and a loose white shirt. It could have been Hamlet, just arrived from Wittenberg. But it was Ingeborg Bachmann, who a few days earlier, fashionably dressed and adorned with Roman gold jewelry, had been presented with the Great State Prize for Literature, and had now chosen this disguise, but lost her nerve at the last moment. She stood around irresolutely until she was called into the great hall, to sit at the table of honor with the Bundeskanzler, where, with a no less tormented visage, Thomas Bernhard was already sitting, not far from Franz Nabl, and opposite him, now shaking hands with the page, was the poet Christine Lavant in an ankle-length dress of heavy printed cotton, her head wrapped in a scarf of the same fabric, which pointedly emphasized her peasant origins. Two years later she too was to receive the Great State Prize, but Thomas Bernhard never did.

During the year after his "insult" to the minister, Bernhard, as was his habit, came to visit me in St. Wolfgang for the day from his farmhouse in Obernathal. He would usually arrive about eleven, we would go for a walk, have lunch together on the terrace, have an afternoon rest and then a cup of tea, and he would leave toward evening. This time, as we were having tea, Alexander Lernet, whom I had thought to be abroad, approached through the little iron gate to his park. He had been one of those lights of Austrian literature who had stormed out of the hall to leave the prizewinner alone in his shame. Lernet-Holenia was a writer of the old school, continually moved to wild outbursts against the new generation by fears of the possible waning of his creative and virile powers, and of being superseded by his juniors. Why indeed should he have taken the part of this young man, whom he found somewhat sinister, although his talent had been fostered by Lernet's friend Zuckmayer, and whose speech he had found disturbing, because he did not know the man himself?

And now, at my house, he was meeting a cultured man, wearing country clothes, whom he did not – or pretended not to – recognize as Thomas Bernhard. He asked me who my visitor was. We began to laugh. "Let's just call him Rumpelstiltskin," I said, and Lernet, suspicious, but whimsical enough himself to be satisfied with this answer, began a polite conversation with Bernhard. The talk revolved around the joys and sorrows of owning property in the country, malicious or quarrelsome neighbors, the advantages of cross-country vehicles, above all in winter, in this mountainous terrain, and so on. And the two got on so well that neither gave any sign of leaving, and both gladly accepted a hurried invitation to dinner, over which there was further discussion: of cider presses, of the stubborn character of the Upper Austrians, and of the astonishing skills of the local joiners and smiths, handed down in their families. After Bernhard had taken his leave, Lernet asked me who my agreeable guest had really been. I told him. He smiled incredulously. Or was it mischievously?

Splinters of memory that cannot be extracted. Like the occasion at Weidlingau near Vienna, a few years after Doderer's death, when a housing development was ceremoniously named after him in the presence of his friends and relatives, and the local worthy in charge of the proceedings who came up to me with the words: "I greet you as a pioneer of European literature and similar endeavors." Or, more seriously, the memory of Efim Etkind, who then still lived in Leningrad and had come to Vienna for a symposium, and who accompanied us to the Salzkammergut, to stay with us for a few days over Easter. He asked me to stop for a moment on the hill above the Traunsee. "I have never forgotten this view." We asked him when he had seen it for the first time. He had come here in 1945 with the Red Army, at about the same time of year, and had experienced the beauty of the landscape with almost painful intensity. Then, with his comrades, he had liberated the camp at Ebensee, and this too was something he could never forget. At his request we stopped at the camp, which we had never cared to visit before, and went in with Etkind. He commented dryly that among the memorial stones for the French, Dutch, and Greeks there was not one for the Russian inmates of Ebensee. But this was to be explained by Stalin's decree that the existence of Russian prisoners was simply to be denied, by expunging all references to them. What was the saying? "The Guards die, but do not surrender." The heroes of our time were those who perished unsung in the quarries of Ebensee.

Finally my experience – unknown until now to his English friends and his biographers – with W. H. Auden. Auden had bought an old farmhouse in Kirchstetten, in an area which had little charm for me, and there, up to the time of his death, he spent every spring and summer with Chester Kallman. Since 1966, when he too was presented with a literary prize in Vienna and I made the speech in his honor, we had met from time to time, most notably during the time when I was translating a selection of his poems for a bilingual edition, or when he needed my help in his battles with the Austrian tax office. In May 1971 we were invited by a Count Colloredo to his little *Schloss* near Auden's house, with Auden and Kallman and various other couples, such as the Viennese forensic expert Wilhelm Holczabek and his wife. Lunch was over and the guests proceeded into the salon to chat in comfort for an hour or two. But Professor Holczabek, monomaniacally obsessed with his subject like so many eminent authorities of his kind, immediately monopolized the conversation and bored the other guests with his complaints that he and his anatomy students suffered from a lack of corpses to examine. People were not bequeathing their bodies to science any more, and the families of deceased persons were possessively protecting the remains of their loved ones from the grasp of the hospitals.

Auden became more and more restless, his feet in their famous felt slippers began to scrape impatiently, and suddenly he leapt up and commanded: "Chester, we must go." The host and all the rest of us were dismayed, but the pair had already left. Two years later, after an evening at the lecture hall of the Palais Palffy, where he had been reading his own text, and others read the German translations of his poems, Auden died during the night at the Hotel Altenburgerhof. Chester Kallman claimed to have found him dead next morning – this was what he told the English friends who came to the funeral. But Kallman had not attended the reading that evening; he had been at the opera, and had spent the night in his own little apartment in Vienna. The account I heard at the time seems much more plausible: Auden's death was discovered by the hotel staff; the hotel had only his American passport and therefore notified the United States Embassy. The Embassy staff knew nothing about him, and so, the cause of death being uncertain – as Kallman confirmed – his body was subjected to an autopsy. And who should it be but Professor Holczabek who conducted the examination?

And so to the end of my euphoria – the first one; for a second, truly existential one was destroyed even more cruelly at the end of these decades. I had truly believed that it was worthwhile taking part in public activities in Vienna, that one could do this unscathed, whether out of sheer self-importance or also because of an urge to contribute a little to the common good. After the death of our dear Csokor at the beginning of 1969 my name had been mentioned as a possible successor to him at PEN, but I immediately recommended Lernet, despite his unaccountable temperament: at that time he was, after all, the most important living representative of Austrian literature. He was content to let me go on managing things as I pleased; the business and duties of the organization were of little interest to him, and when it was not a question of talking him out of accepting the application for membership of Gustl Kernmayr, a writer who had formerly supported the Nazi regime, things in general went smoothly.

In January 1970 I invited a group of German writers to Vienna to discuss amicably the highly controversial question of an Austrian literature separate from that of Germany, to which I was committed. This group included Erich Kästner and Hermann Kesten, Peter Härtling and Horst Krüger, Ingeborg Drewitz and Thilo Koch. They arrived in glorious wintry weather; were fêted; held several passionate discussions, without, of course, reaching agreement, for and against the individual existence of our literature; tramped cheerfully through the crunchy snow to Döbling to visit Adrienne Thomas, who had invited a large number of uniformed and highly decorated officers of the armed forces, friends of her late husband, Julius Deutsch, the former defense minister and general in the Spanish Civil War, to take tea with the bewildered Germans; and climbed the "emperor's steps" up to Lernet's apartment in the Hofburg, which, with its furniture, still for the most part on loan from the court furnishings management office, seemed to convey to them a sense of the imperial past.

The action committee, my "Young Turks," as I called them, had helped, and one of its members, the Serb from Budapest Milo Dor, in the autumn of 1970 came up with the suggestion that they should concern themselves with the efforts in the Bundesrepublik on behalf of the rights of creative writers, and perhaps even initiate such efforts in our own country. Imaginative but a little indolent, Milo did not in the first instance want to take an active part himself, but persuaded me to take part in the writers' congress in Stuttgart in November, which was to respond to Heinrich Böll's call for an "end to modesty." Fired with enthusiasm by the three days during which Böll's second demand, for "unity among the isolated," was fulfilled, I returned and began preparations for an initial *enquête* or investigation.

In mid-January 1971 it was decided to found an organization, then still designated an action committee, and on the last day of the month, in the presence of the representatives of just about all the writers in Austria, as well as Bruno Kreisky and Christian Broda, a number of politicians gathered to listen to our demands; Reinhard Baumgart came from Germany to support us. In March there was a second *enquête*, conducted with the help of Dieter Lattmann, with an audience of some eighty individuals, as well as representatives of all the media, in our conference hall at the Concordia-Haus. The editor-in-chief of the *Presse* referred to me, chairing the meeting among so many men, as the "Pasionaria of Viennese writers." At the end of June 1971 the *Interessengemeinschaft österreichischer Autoren*, the Syndicate of Austrian Writers, was legally set up, with myself as president and Milo Dor as vice president.

During the next eighteen months my volume of work practically doubled. Visits to the parliament, to the departments of finance, education, and justice, continual sessions to unify all the conflicting groups within the umbrella organization, problems with lawyers, trouble with pedants, obstacles, setbacks of all kinds. In between, there was a move to preserve the house built by Ludwig Wittgenstein for his sister from demolition by a speculative builder, and PEN too was asked to participate in the campaign to save it, which had been initiated by a group of architects led by Bernhard Leitner. One afternoon the responsible minister appeared on the spot; she was too stupid and stubborn for her job, and thus made some disastrous decisions by which the museum and university administrations are still hampered. She planted herself squarely in front of the edifice, which had already been robbed of its backdrop of trees. "Well," she said, "Wittgenstein may have been worth something as a philosopher, but as an architect, no, you can't talk me into believing that." With admirable patience, Gertrude Lipp, the representative of the national office for historic monuments, asked the *Frau Minister* at least to be so kind as to inspect the interior of the building. Still shaking her head as she left the house, with a majestic air that lent something comic to her little frame, she indicated to us, waiting outside in silent fury, that she would look into the matter. In the end it was not the state that bought the Wittgenstein house, but the Bulgarian embassy, which set up its cultural institute there. Another "Wiener Komedi," as Hofmannsthal says in the *Rosenkavalier.*

The Syndicate achieved its first success, the only one in my era, but no mean one: the payment of value-added tax was abolished for freelance writers. Hans Weigel has insisted to this day that this achievement was the *raison d'être* of my whole life. Be this as it may, in December of that year, overworked to the point of physical exhaustion, which manifested itself more and more in nervous heart attacks, I handed over the general secretaryship of PEN to Dorothea Zeemann, although I kept my post on the committee. In Dublin we had elected Heinrich Böll International President of PEN, and since he was to a high degree committed to the Writers in Prison Committee, of whose inner circle I had become a member, I was to spend more and more time in the coming year in the company of that great and good man. However, at home things were coming to a boil. In June, Robert Jungk, the anti-nuclear campaigner and opponent of all war, at that time the war in Vietnam, took part in a demonstration against Richard Nixon, who was making a stopover in Salzburg, and was manhandled by the riot police. At PEN, Carry Hauser, Dora and I tried to organize a declaration of solidarity with Jungk. But my enemy-friend opposed this behind the scenes, and soon one of the Young Turks became his tool and came out against the decision. The elderly committee members also began to grumble about Heinrich Böll, whose call for "mercy for Ulrike Meinhof" had been so fundamentally misunderstood and had branded this most peaceable of men a friend of terrorism and violence, as did the action committee, which had been infiltrated by ditherers and cowards. In September, Torberg in person reopened the Jungk case and reproached me bitterly for the bland compromise statement we had managed to get accepted.

The final act began as a farce. On the nineteenth of October, Böll was awarded the Nobel prize. On the same day my birthday and that of Alexander Lernet were being celebrated at PEN. Later, as we sat together with others at the Michaeler enjoying our dinner, someone brought the news that the same morning, behind everyone's backs, Alexander had resigned from PEN in protest against the honor bestowed on Böll. It was with mischievous defiance that he returned my gaze as I speechlessly looked him in the eye, in despair over such an absurd, insidious action. And now the storm was roaring in the nursery which was not so awfully nice any more, which I had entered, where I had played among the children, to whose rules I had subjected myself. All the deception of those years became clear to me. A guerrilla war, full of low-minded intrigue, of hypocrisy and treachery, was beginning.

Torberg had decided to strike his last blow against me, the defender of Jungk, the supporter of Böll, his irksome adversary since our youth. His strategy was brilliant. I had foolishly agreed to stand as a candidate for the presidency of the Austrian PEN center in the hope of salvaging my long-cherished plans for its rejuvenation. He brought into the arena a candidate who was a member of the same Freemasons' lodge as one of the most enterprising of my Young Turks, as well as the education minister, Sinowatz. All the "brothers" were instructed in their duty. The male society deployed its tactics with its usual skill. Torberg's candidate was elected; the minister sent a congratulatory telegram to the new president, and made a fivefold increase in PEN's annual grant. The day after the election, I resigned from all my honorary posts in the country and, in a manner of speaking, retired from public life.

"You don't know what it is like to want to live intellectually in Vienna and in Austria, to want to make oneself heard! It feels like living in a padded cell. In there you can shout yourself hoarse, you can turn somersaults. Not a sound penetrates to the outer world... This city is drowning in the banality of its popular street songs... In this city there is no alliance of intellects, only bourgeois conformism for the

At an International PEN Congress

benefit of self-expression by the half-men, the inferior, the imprudent." This was written by Anton Wildgans to Kurt Wolff in February 1918, and it may be an appropriate postscript. But he also wrote: "One evening in an Austrian garden is reason enough, evidence enough, for the understanding of the magic and the curse of this country." Everyone has experienced the magic, all have suffered from the curse, if they remained unsatisfied with the one and exposed themselves to the other. Without yet having read this quotation from Wildgans, which Friedrich Heer unearthed a few years later, I made the decision that from now on, as a basis for continuing to live in Austria, I would only cultivate my garden.

With Hans Flesch von Brunningen, in Vienna (top) and St. Wolfgang

17

The Passions of the Old

What after all was the point, especially at an advanced age, of this
dubious desire to serve the *bien public*, which was never quite to be
distinguished from a lust for power? How much more rewarding –
indeed, how delightful, how indispensable it was, whenever I was at
my Haus am Bach in St. Wolfgang, to rest on the balcony after lunch,
while shadows slowly crept across the house. The sun would depart
at about half-past three, and when I awakened I would see it flashing
through the high treetops and slowly sinking in the west, and
sometimes a wonderful glow would spread across the sky.

A sense of happiness without compare. But then there was also
the brief hour, stolen from my tasks, in the Lernet boathouse, solitary
now since Alexander's death in his late seventies, to lie on the grey,
rotting wooden boards of its landing stage, and then swim in the cool
water of the little cove, protected from the motor boats and water
skiers. How comfortable to sit with Herr Hutterer, my *Hausmann* – the
modest property hardly warranted a title such as manager or steward
– over a glass of *Schnaps* in the *Bauernstube*, the rustic living room,
discussing necessary repairs and plantings; how pleasant not to have
to stand at the stove myself at times when, not needed by her own
family, his wife Rosina prepared for us the delicious pancakes called
Palatschinken, with chanterelle mushrooms, or trout bred by her son.

To drive through the Hauptallee, the main thoroughfare of the
Prater in Vienna, when the chestnuts were in blossom – oh, those
banal street songs! To sit outside a quiet *Heurigen* inn in the late
afternoon, with only a few other guests, each with a mug of wine in
front of us – just as I had once sat with a slightly more bulbous glass
of Guinness, on a wooden bench in front of the Hand in Hand pub
in Wimbledon. Surely this was enough; this was the evening of life
which I had promised myself with Flesch. Then there were the few
writers whom we loved and were able to admire, whom we saw from
time to time, such as Ilse Aichinger at Grossgmain in the province of
Salzburg, from whom I always returned enchanted by her gentle,

almost angelic nature, almost in a state of exaltation, as if I had been to church. Or Thomas Bernhard, who at that time, before he became a total recluse, often used to telephone unexpectedly, or appear suddenly on the terrace; who, if I met him by chance in the center of Vienna, would come the same day to spend several hours with me in the Cottagegasse. Or Ingeborg Bachmann, on one of her visits to Vienna when she was trying to decide whether she could live there again, with whom I would sit eating ice cream in the garden of a café on the Ring, as we discussed all the pros and cons, the magic and the curse, fluctuating between jest and earnest, as was her habit. But Inge fell victim to one of the most dreadful of all deaths. And it had been only a few weeks before the night in which her ordeal by fire took place that she had telephoned me and we talked for a whole hour, and she told me how impatient she was to leave Rome, which was now hateful to her, how she was looking forward to the apartment that was waiting for her in Vienna, and then, most importantly, asked me for the address of my tax consultant – so precisely was she planning her return.

It is not for my own glory that I here mention the names of these three writers, but because they represented for me a sort of compensation for the disloyalty of those less talented Young Turks, and, even more, the fulfillment of what I had always hoped for from an Austria of today, not only in talent or even genius, but in equal measure in decency, in moral refusal to compromise. Certainly there were other friends who were not famous, but who were congenial and even artistic in their leanings, and whose company we enjoyed after the disappointments of the past years. Nothing drastic had happened; I had simply fallen out of love with those who determined the cultural, social, and political life of the country. And what was still missing from that evening of life we dreamed of, namely peace and quiet – we could have had it, but we were not able to summon it up.

The main reason for this was that, driven by the furies of duty, of existential fear, but also of an undiminished thirst for activity, I still did not reduce the volume of my work – the reports, the literary articles, the essays, the translations, the contributions to, or even editing of, German or English anthologies. That, despite shrugging off the main burden of my committee-mongering, I continued with my casework on the Writers in Prison committee; That, as a member of both the German and the English PEN centers, I attended international congresses as I had always done, as well as the conferences of the Darmstadt Academy, of which I had become a member, and allowed myself to be nominated to panels such as those of the Berlin *Theatertreffen* or the Klagenfurt Bachmann Prize: all this became more and more strenuous, indeed grueling, for a woman who was, it had to be admitted, no longer young.

I had been fifty-nine, and Flesch just turned seventy-six, when, in the feverish weeks of the first *enquêtes*, in February 1971, we had married in St. Wolfgang. It was not until then that we stopped addressing each other as *Sie*, as we had done throughout all the situations of life. This late marriage, in spite of everything, lasted for a whole decade. How did it come about? After years of refusing even to think about it, Peter had recently asked me for a divorce; he had formed a relationship with a granddaughter of the publisher S. Fischer and wanted to marry her. I was happy for him, and was now free from any feelings of guilt. Now Flesch insisted on the ceremony in St. Wolfgang, which we went through with a certain lighthearted irony, although not quite without some inward emotion. Meanwhile Peter had moved to Munich; he too had made a clean break from his English life and finally attained his destiny, which presumably he had always striven after: the representation of Germanness at its best. And no sooner had he installed himself in a pretty little rented house near the Herzogspark than our relationship began to improve. It was to become ever closer, more intimate even, during the twelve years that still remained to him. But first he would have to overcome one of his life's most dreadful blows of fate. Only a few weeks before he and Gaby Fischer were to marry, she, who could have become the dearest, most stimulating, and above all intellectually equal companion of his old age, died in an automobile accident.

Our children too, both of whom had meanwhile been married and divorced, were at that time giving us cause for concern. It was a great help to me that I now felt able to discuss their problems with Peter. On March 30, 1971, my son was arrested in Northern Ireland. As he later explained in the Zurich *Weltwoche*, he had flown to Belfast at the behest of the German magazine *Twen* "to report on the everyday life of the residents of the poor Catholic districts of the city." But since the majority of these people at least passively supported the IRA, he had soon come into contact with activists among the resistance fighters. "Tempted by over-zealous curiosity," he had been among them when a bomb attack took place on Queen's University at midnight. When the police arrived, and others had already fled the scene, among those arrested, along with the armed and well-known rebel James McCann, were an American photojournalist and the *Twen* reporter – two innocent observers who had not been aware in advance of the intentions of the IRA arsonists. At the police station my son was interrogated for thirty-six hours, with demands for the names and addresses of contacts. "The IRA," he wrote months later in the *Weltwoche*, "has little understanding for informers and tends to render them harmless by shooting them in the back of the head. It was therefore not only out of professional confidentiality but also justified fear of death that I refused to give evidence." Admittedly the police detectives had told him that in any case he would not leave the city alive. If he persisted in his silence, they would denounce him as an informer and release him in a pro-IRA district. He was not physically harmed.

These details were not known to us at first. But we did know that my son would spend a long time on remand awaiting trial, and would be unlikely to escape a lengthy prison sentence without the help of a first-rate defense lawyer. We found a law firm prepared to take on the case, but it was associated with the Catholic community of Belfast, which hardly augured well for success in a Protestant court. And again it was PEN, our extended family, which came to the rescue. At our next gathering in Bled, the international treasurer, Peter Elstob, declared his willingness to attend the trial. But even more decisively, the president of the Belfast center, Jeanne Foster-Cooper, advised us to change lawyers immediately and entrust my son's defense to a Protestant firm. She recommended to us Desmond Boal, QC, who was reputed to be a friend of the Reverend Ian Paisley and moreover the most renowned orator in Northern Ireland. He, and only he, she said, could save my son from a heavy sentence.

Two weeks before the trial date, the new firm took over the case. One day earlier, James McCann had escaped from Crumlin Road Jail in spectacular circumstances – one less hurdle for his co-defendants. On June 30, I flew to Belfast with my daughter. The *Belfast Telegraph* reported, under the headline "Mother flies from Austria for QUB case": "A German woman flew to Belfast today to attend the trial of her son, who is accused of arson at Queen's University. Dr. Hilde Spiel took her seat in the public gallery at the Courthouse after the lunchtime adjournment. She had flown from Australia [*sic*] early this morning." And then one of the great dramas of my life began to unfold.

My son and his American co-defendant, Joe Stevens, were taken through an underground passage from the prison to the court building on the opposite side of the Crumlin Road. There he stood in the elevated dock, surrounded by policemen, above us in the middle of the courtroom, while the trial proceeded. After the questioning of witnesses and the public prosecutor's speech, it was the turn of Boal, whose forensic and verbal brilliance took our breath away. If the fate of our son and brother had not depended on it, we would have been lost in admiration for his skill as in a perfect crime film. The tension was unbearable until, after an hour and a half, the jury returned and gave their verdict to the judge. It was an indescribable moment when a little door was opened in the dock and my son came out, a free man. And the few remaining days we spent in Belfast were unforgettable; it stayed light until midnight and an uncanny silence reigned before the expected storm. "Get him out of here as soon as possible," Boal had said to me after the trial, "it's going to be a hot summer." And in fact there followed a new wave of the civil war between Protestants and Catholics in Ulster, the IRA terror which has still not come to an end.

In Vienna and St. Wolfgang too, however, certain clouds were beginning to form. Flesch was becoming increasingly temperamental and quarrelsome. He drove out one housekeeper after another with his moods. At the same time, I was finding it more and more difficult to carry out my tasks. A new wind was blowing through the newspaper for which I worked; apart from my other cultural reports, I was now being asked to contribute more and longer articles for the literary section, which admittedly gave me much more pleasure. Nevertheless I was still expected to get up at six on the morning after a premiere to write my review and spend a further two to three hours telephoning it through. Preparing lunch after that, when from time to time I had no help in the house, exhausted me almost to the point of a heart attack. Translation work, too, was piling up. In addition, quite in contrast to Charlotte Bühler's theory that many branches of the tree of life die off in old age, during my seventies my tree was increasingly ramifying. Soon after Belfast, my son had gone on a journey to the Near East, from which he now returned with a new wife and a baby son, my first grandchild, and they settled in Vienna. He had sent ahead a "Bedouin desert dog," golden as a lion, which had joined their household in Jerusalem as a stray puppy – our beautiful Dorli, still alive in 1990 and in the object of numerous declarations of love in literary form. A little granddaughter was born. Sometimes, on festive days in St. Wolfgang, there were nine of us in the house, and I was by no means spared kitchen duties when it came to my turn.

Certainly, I was working too hard, traveling too much. But I tried to do everything to ensure that Flesch did not suffer as a result. Whenever possible he accompanied me on my longer journeys by car or by air. He was with me on my second visit to Israel; we drove together through the now more extensive territory, visited the old city of Jerusalem as well as the then less hazardous Jericho, Nablus, the whole of the area conquered in 1967 during the Six-Day War. At the beginning of 1976 I undertook a demanding lecture tour of six American universities, returning after a long interval to Taos, where the aging Dorothy Brett was still living, and venturing into wildest Montana, entertained by academic friends in Rattlesnake Valley; and the following year I took Flesch with me for his first and only visit to the United States.

New York frightened him, but Los Angeles, where he stayed for a month with my friend Susi, the widow of the composer Erich Zeisl, soon became familiar to him. And during two days with me in San Francisco – in the Fairmont Hotel, which was to become famous in all its splendor through the television series *Hotel* – he went into transports of happiness. On the pleasure steamer which took us around the bay in brilliant sunshine, he sang at the top of his voice: "San Francisco, open up your golden gate!" and declared that he owed me the last great experience of his eighty-two years. But more were still to come. In the spring we had visited Bayreuth and seen Chéreau's *Ring*, about which Flesch, an avant-gardist of old, was enthusiastic. We were to make three more visits to see the *Ring* and other productions at this magical place, which, quite in the manner of the master composer, was able to awaken not only the highest musical emotions but also others which were dangerous, indeed evil.

And then, in that very summer of 1977 during which we had visited the States and returned to Bayreuth, Flesch fell in love, with someone half a century younger than himself. His own power of attraction for the generation of those who might have been his grandchildren was indisputable. The *vieillard terrible*, as I began to call him sometimes, impressed the brighter ones among them with his wit and original intellect, his apparently unimpaired vitality – whose breakdowns were not apparent to the outside world – and with his ever more uninhibited outbursts of applause or displeasure at the theater or the opera. At a revival by Wieland Wagner's widow Gertrud of his production of Strauss's *Salome*, whose cesspool-like ambience roused half of Vienna to loud protests, Chester Kallman began to boo, and Flesch called out *"Kusch!"* to him, the word used to silence a barking dog. He himself yelled "Shame!" when a pregnant woman was kicked on stage in Wolfgang Bauer's play *Change*: an understandable reaction from a gentleman born in the nineteenth century. In Vienna these excesses, in which no one else dared to indulge, became expected of him, while I felt obliged to move away from him at least physically on such occasions.

By the end of 1972 Flesch had already experienced his first attack of aphasia. This was not repeated for a long time, but his highly strung nervous system became less and less able to endure such upheavals. "Flesch, you are an excessive man," a saying first uttered by a Berliner during his youth, was now frequently quoted, and overheated reactions to private or political catastrophes were constantly to be expected from him. Now, with almost insane impetuousness, he was plunging into a gulf of newly awakened emotions, while I was overwhelmed by a despair I had not known since the lovesick days of my youth. Let no one underestimate the passions of the old, even the very old! Within a short time Flesch became positively obsessed with his infatuation, manically unable to speak of any other subject, with an ever-increasing lack of consideration for my own suffering over this situation.

If it had not been for the deliberate, cold-hearted coquettishness of the object of his affection, who fanned his emotions without regard to the threat to his over-stimulated nerves, the flame might perhaps have died out after a while. But throughout the remaining years up to his death it was constantly rekindled, and what had been for so long, so very long, a uniquely harmonious life together now became a hell. His blind obsession revealed a demon in him whose presence I would never have suspected, who tortured me daily, spared me no distress. But how could I abandon another human being whose physical state, despite the alertness of his brain, was declining more and more rapidly, and to whom, moreover, I was devoted with every fiber of my being?

It is still impossible to explain how such an attachment could come into being. The fact that in England Flesch had represented for me my home, my late father, the relatives and friends I missed, that in so many ways we were of one mind, does not quite shed enough light on why I was never able to tear myself free of him. It is probably a case of that unknown force discussed in Goethe's *Wahlverwand-schaften* – perhaps even better expressed in the English title *Elective Affinities*. And so I was prepared to weather the torments of this decade which was now nearing its end: attacks of genuine mental derangement, during which Flesch did not shrink even from physical violence, continually alternated with highly lucid phases, and it was only gradually that the former increased and the latter decreased in frequency.

I found a series of Polish ladies, trained as nurses, who were prepared to take over the housework and the care of Flesch for half the day. In Vienna, I rented a bachelor apartment around the corner where I could be undisturbed in my work at least in the mornings. In this way, life was to some extent endurable. And slowly I began to realize that there was a second euphoria that needed to be buried, a lifelong illusion, or perhaps only a truth which had become an untruth. After all, had we not been warned in the songs of the *Threepenny Opera*, which had been constantly in our ears during our youth: "Love will endure or will not endure / regardless of where we are"?

There were consolations during those years. I was helped by the affectionate attentions of a Salzburg art dealer and patron, who gave me presents – Kokoschka lithographs, drawings by Wilhelm Thöny, and a bracelet with a gold coin by Manzù – and referred to me in front of third parties as the "darling of his heart." A very gallant, always distant, always discreet relationship, which had the power to restore my severely shaken self-esteem. I was also cheered by the joking offer of marriage made to me by a bird of paradise among Viennese artists in the event of my separation from Flesch. But above all, I drew strength from my renewed intimacy with Peter; despite his having formed a new relationship, we resumed our old marital ties, as if it were a matter of course, whenever I stayed with him on the occasion of a visit to the theater in Munich on behalf of the *Theatertreffen*. It was only when, informed by others about my situation in Vienna, he persistently pressed me to return to him and finally even presented me with an ultimatum, that things became difficult. And finally I was supported, but at the same time burdened, for reasons not to be discussed too precisely here, by the appearance in our inmost circle of a second younger individual: a person as extraordinary as she was highly talented, and whom, since I cannot avoid mentioning her, I will call the *Jünglingin* or "She-Youth," as the poet Georg Trakl's sister was known.

At a symposium on the same Trakl in March 1978, Flesch had still been a brilliant speaker; the following January, at a reading from his last book *Die Frumm*, he gave the impression of being burned out. Lapses of memory, speech disorders, mental delusions were danger signals of which he himself was probably aware, but could not control. That summer in Bayreuth, where we stayed not at the Schloss Fantaisie, to which we had already become accustomed, but at the Eremitage, equally beautiful but unfamiliar to him, so-called friends avoided us, because the confused old man was disturbing the pleasure of their post-performance supper. Then, to her credit may it be recorded, Joana Maria Gorvin, iridescent as ever, joined us with her husband. She, who had selflessly cared for Jürgen Fehling in a similar predicament, showed understanding for Flesch's shattered spirit. It was not indeed shattered for good. In the autumn, a famous neurologist told us that such things came and went; there was nothing we could do about it. And in fact Flesch pulled himself together, and the following February, at a celebration of his eighty-fifth birthday, he extemporized a speech of thanks to his eulogist which kindled the listeners' admiration.

He was determined to defy death. And he succeeded for a while longer. When his cousin Luiga died in Baden-Baden in her hundredth year, he shouted angrily: "Too soon!" He survived my Salzburg admirer, he survived my enemy-friend Torberg, whose passing, abruptly announced on television, unaccountably reduced me to a flood of tears. During the days after that birthday he began to write his memoirs and sat at the typewriter every morning, until he had committed to paper some nine hundred pages of partly impressive, partly chaotic prose. During that spring of 1980 we had intended to return to Venice, but on the journey, in Trieste, he suffered an attack of pneumonia. He overcame it with the help of an Austrian, Dr. Michelazzi, and two months later we made the journey to Venice after all. The She-Youth and I lifted and pushed him over the steps of countless bridges, he screamed with anxiety when climbing aboard a *vaporetto* by way of a wobbling pier, but he succeeded in visiting all our usual favorite spots as we had done in earlier days. In August, however, we canceled our visit to Bayreuth for the last evening of the Chéreau *Ring* cycle, for which we had tickets, as neither he nor I could muster the energy for it.

The year of sorrows, 1981, began. We celebrated one more birthday; his book was finished, and he now spent hours every day revising it. His beloved object confided a secret to me – she was pregnant; I implored her not to inform him yet, because he would inevitably go into a frenzy. She promised that she would not. I had been to a Schnitzler symposium in Bari the previous month, and was now to attend a panel discussion on Heine in Paris. Ominous forebodings made me hesitate. But our Polish housekeeper Maria and the She-Youth promised that they would take good care of Flesch; there was no need to cancel my arrangements. Paris was in a state of upheaval. Mitterrand had triumphed in the presidential election and was proceeding to the Panthéon, a red rose in his hand, to convey his thanks to the great intellectuals of France. The city was more bewitching than ever. On the day of my departure I wandered around in the vicinity of the Panthéon, in my favorite little square, the Place de la Contrescarpe, and walked back across the Seine to the Louvre. My flight to Vienna arrived at night. Here I entered a scene of devastation. In my absence, Flesch's beloved had betrayed her secret to him, he had flown into a rage and attacked Maria with his stick; Maria had given notice. Long after midnight, Flesch himself, now recovered from his fury, and the She-Youth related the story to me with embarrassed smiles.

The next day I managed to persuade Maria not to abandon us. I assured her that I would no longer leave Flesch's side for a single day. We traveled to St. Wolfgang, where we moved him from his upstairs room to the ground floor. He often lay on the sofabed in the living room, where he scared away visitors. I sometimes refused to allow this, which I later felt to be heartless, reproaching myself bitterly. Theatrical as ever, Flesch extracted the greatest possible enjoyment from his own decline. The house trembled before him. And when, in the evening, he wearily prepared for bed, the wreck of a body to which I had once been so close, I could not bear the sight, and the She-Youth – to whom I remain grateful to this day – looked after him. Just before entering the hospital at Ischl, because we could no longer supply the special care he now needed, he entertained a friend of Eva Lernet's with the most stimulating conversation of which he had ever been capable. At the hospital he immediately won the heart of the ward nurse. And so, two days later, I dared to fulfill my responsibilities and drive to Salzburg for the premiere of Georg Büchner's *Danton's Death*, directed by Rudolf Noelte. Next morning there was the usual torture of the hastily written review and the long telephone call. After my midday rest I drove to Ischl. Flesch lay there, calm and composed, while the doctor told me in an apparently casual manner that "a little operation" was necessary. At half-past five he was taken to the operating room. Before saying goodbye he asked me to come the next morning, as early as possible. Then: "Love me?" "Yes," I replied. He sighed: "Now again."

Next day he was in a coma and did not recognize me any more. Nevertheless I felt that he was aware of what was being said, and cursed the doctors, who were loudly discussing his condition in the room where he lay. How can one know what goes on in someone's mind during the last hours of his life? I sat with him until evening, even though he appeared not to be conscious of my presence. Next morning he passed away. It was the first of August, the day on which his father too had died. The funeral, a week later, was beautiful; the coffin was carried by men wearing the local Ischl costume; the young priest spoke unaffectedly and with wisdom. But there was discord too; friends had come from Vienna, and by early evening a quarrel had sprung up between them and the She-Youth. After their departure she too left the house.

I had three months – for the most part alone in St. Wolfgang with Frau Maria and Dorli, the dog – to come to terms with the sufferings of the last few years. As it turned out, this was not enough. Work, occasional guests, a brief visit by my daughter and her new husband, an expedition to Vienna to move my belongings out of the additional apartment I had rented, all these continually interrupted the time I was trying to reserve for reflection. At the beginning of October, the day before my final return to Vienna, I went up the Schafberg with Maria and Dorli on the rack-and-pinion mountain railway line, returning on foot by the steep downhill path to the *Alm*, "a great strain," I noted, "but worth it."

Soon afterward, in Vienna, after lunch I had an attack of severe stomach cramp; I should have gone to the doctor but could not get around to it. First I had to take some articles of clothing from Flesch's wardrobe to a friend who needed them. Then, when I was already writhing in pain, the She-Youth insisted that I should attend a prize-giving ceremony for herself and some other writers at six o'clock. In a state of semi-consciousness I somehow made by way to the lecture hall. The ceremony dragged on. Finally, almost incapable of walking, I got to the doctor, who immediately arranged an operation. By half-past ten I was in the operating room; there was an abscess, an inflammation, a perforation – I had been rescued at the last moment. But in a week's time I was to travel to Germany, where a whole series of festivities and honors were in preparation for my seventieth birthday. I fought, I summoned all my resources, I forced the hospital to release me prematurely, I drove off, my wound burst open, I lay in state amid masses of flowers, as if I were dead, in the hotel rooms in Frankfurt and Darmstadt, which I left only to have my dressings changed at the clinics, and to receive my prizes. Finally I was taken by Red Cross ambulance to the train for Vienna.

By December my weakened heart had begun to grow steadier, and my wound had healed. There followed a further year in Vienna, a new, great joy, and another shattering loss. In January my third grandchild, my daughter's daughter, was born. And in August, almost exactly a year after Flesch, Peter succumbed to a severe illness which he had tried to ignore, which he had failed to fight with all his might. It is too painful to recall the last stages. But it would not be right to remain silent about the way in which a lifelong relationship came to an end.

It had been in May 1980 that he had presented me with that ultimatum, and because I had not been able to give him the answer he wanted, he had once more severed all relations with me. A year later, after the Schnitzler symposium had ended, we had spent a few days in Bari with Heinrich Schnitzler and his wife. We rented a car in which the four of us toured Apulia – actually I was the only one who drove, for among other things I have always been a Martha – but Peter was depressed, one might say preoccupied; in fact he was gravely ill. He had asked me to come to Würzburg to attend his re-election as president of the Academy there, and as it turned out my vote was urgently needed. But when, in the autumn, I went to receive a prize from the Darmstadt Academy, Peter treated me with polite indifference. After the presentation, when I was about to return to my hotel bed, he did not say goodbye.

For months we did not hear from each other. He had moved and was now living with his partner, and wanted nothing more to do with me. That June I was to return to Taos, where five years earlier, while Flesch was staying in Los Angeles, I had spent two weeks at the German summer school of the University of New Mexico, holding seminars and lectures on Doderer, Bernhard, and Handke. But the heart specialist forbade me to travel to the nearly 10,000 foot high location in Taos Ski Valley. As a consolation, I treated myself to another journey, accepting invitations from three of my women friends. I spent some happy weeks in California, at Susi Zeisl's pretty house on Montana Avenue in Westwood, in the little room I had already come to love, and went with Susi to Palm Springs, where her daughter Barbara, who had married a son of Arnold Schoenberg's, had a small bungalow. Then on to Ottawa, to Erika and her Canadian husband, by car with her to Boston, and on again to Sabina in North Cornwall, Connecticut. In Ottawa I had already received news of Peter's illness, his rapidly deteriorating condition, and the rest of my journey was overshadowed by the threat of his impending death.

During a stopover in Frankfurt, an exciting plan was proposed to me. I was to go to London for a while to send cultural reports to my paper, the *Frankfurter Allgemeine*. My long-cherished wish to give up this activity at last was countermanded by the prospect of a return to England, if only for a limited period. For the time being I deferred the decision. From St. Wolfgang I was finally able to telephone Peter. His voice sounded pitifully weak. We were to be allowed to visit him, my daughter and her baby and I, on the fifth of August. He held his rosy-faced little granddaughter in his arms for the first and last time. I was alone with him for ten minutes and took my leave of him; I will not recount what was said. He died five days later. We drove to Munich once more to attend his memorial service. When Peter's ashes were interred at the cemetery in Bogenhausen, near the grave of his friend Erich Kästner, I was not there.

Now that both the men with whom I had shared my life were gone, I was able to draw up the accounts. And I had to recognize what had become increasingly clear to me over the years: Peter, despite his many terrible outbursts against me, which stemmed from traumatic childhood experiences, had been quite simply the better person. He was whatever you like, but never a *filou* – a villain. It might have been possible to stay with him, though never to return to him. It also became clear that a phase in my life had begun that prompted me to take a new path. And so I soon agreed to move back to England for a year or two. This decision resulted in battles of nerves in Vienna and had other undesirable consequences too. It was wrongly reported that I was leaving Vienna forever; people practically broke down my door in the attempt to secure my apartment for themselves. There were also increasingly numerous signs that my health could now only go downhill. But like Flesch, who wanted to be

370

immortal, I was putting up a fight.

During the last weeks of September in St. Wolfgang, I spent a great deal of time with Thomas Bernhard and his wise, kindly, motherly companion Hede. She was a contemporary of Flesch's and had got on well with him, and now Thomas seemed to want to learn from me how to survive without the person who had been indispensable to him. He reproached me with not having invited him to Flesch's funeral; he insisted on visiting the grave in the cemetery at Bad Ischl, and the old lady too stood thoughtfully gazing at it. We agreed that it was good to know where one would be laid to rest one day, and he praised the cemetery at Grinzing, where he and his companion had already secured a plot for them both. It was an experience of macabre coziness, between lunch in the open air and tea at the Café Ramsauer in Ischl, that spot in the Salzkammergut where time seemed to stand still.

But it did not stand still, and the following January I had to submit once more to the surgeon's scalpel. Meanwhile Eva Lernet had given up the struggle, and soon after Christmas she passed away in the hospital at Ischl, like so many of those close to us before her. In March, after a cool Easter at Haus am Bach, I decided to recuperate once more in the warmth of California before my move to London. I returned to the care of my friend Susi, to the little bedroom on Montana Avenue, to the hot swimming pool in Palm Springs, and again the moving parade of aged exiles took place on Susi's terrace, led by the doyennes "Feuchti" (Marta Feuchtwanger) and Gina Kaus. Gina told me stories of a time eons ago, of her daily telephone conversations with Karl Kraus, and her affair with the bisexual Anton Kuh.

By the last week of March, strengthened above all by the days in the desert air, I was back in Vienna and packing my suitcases. I arrived in London on May 7. I moved first into the Stanhope Court Hotel (since closed) to begin my search for an apartment from there. But two days after my arrival I was in Oxford staying with Dodo's daughter, for a Kafka exhibition which her husband, the critical editor and rescuer of so many manuscripts from the clutches of the chance inheritor of the Kafka estate, had arranged at the Bodleian Library. We dined at Magdalen College. Kafka's niece, the generous donor of the writer's personal possessions to the college, was with us. Back in London, I immediately set out to inspect various properties in Chelsea and my favorite area around Kensington Church Street, but in each case I arrived too late.

Then Miss Sutherland of Chestertons took me to the upper end of Earl's Court Road and through a narrow lane to a little square with a few trees in the middle, surrounded by low-roofed houses painted in various colors. I was reminded of certain squares in Paris, of the Place de la Contrescarpe, which however was somewhat larger. There was a furnished house to let. I glanced through the window and saw a vase in the shape of a green dolphin – it was identical to the English stoneware vase that had stood for years in my living room in St. Wolfgang. The omen was unequivocal. And what was more, in the little bedroom on the upper floor, which Miss Sutherland unlocked for me, there hung prints of Redouté roses, just like the original prints which Peter and I had been given by our friend Madge as a wedding present. The same reproductions, cut out of a calendar, adorned the staircase at Haus am Bach.

I told Chestertons I would like to rent the house, with the agreement of my newspaper. There followed lengthy negotiations. I had not yet been handed the keys. On May 13 Patrick Barrington invited Dodo and me to the House of Lords, as he had so often done before. Then we went in her car to Pembroke Place so that I could show her the little house at least from the outside. She gazed benevolently on my future temporary home and said, with all the naiveté of her "effortless superiority": "Oh yes, this is where our servants used to live." I gave her a hug. Then she left for the country for a while, first to her son in Cambridge, then to her daughter in Oxford. Three weeks later she became ill with meningitis. I never saw her again.

Celebrating her 70th birthday (top, with critic Marcel
Reich-Ranicki)

18

The House in Pembroke Place

All things come to those who know how to wait, as I had written to my mother many years earlier. But what if we pass away too early to reap the benefit of that which we had longed for, that which is still in store for us somewhere up in the clouds? Or, perhaps even worse, if we attain it so late that in the meantime it has already lost much of its value for us? The fact that at the advanced age of seventy-two I should at last have achieved something I had once desired so fervently, which might perhaps have been the saving of my first marriage – the pleasure of living in a house in Kensington – once again leads me to conclude that it is not always a tragic force but sometimes an ironic one that controls our destiny.

While making plans to settle in London once again, I had looked forward with all my heart to sitting by my own fireplace with my dearest English friend, to living so near to her that we could drop in on each other daily. Over the decades she had stayed loyal to me, and had often come for weeks at a time, with or without her companion, to stay with me in St. Wolfgang. And now she had been torn from me, without even having once entered the house in the square where her servants had once lived – modest indeed in size – which she had viewed with a slightly ironic smile, and given it her approval, as she would certainly have done, for she was fundamentally unpretentious and in her mature years had reverted to the ascetic lifestyle of her Wiltshire forebears; she had no time for luxury, but nevertheless, or perhaps for that very reason, set store by good taste. Undoubtedly she would have approved of the little Regency tables that I bought at the Kensington Furniture Mart in the High Street to supplement the pretty but inadequate furniture of the house in Pembroke Place. And in other ways too the furnishings somewhat resembled those of her own cottage in Milborne Grove, where I had often stayed.

But it was not for Dodo alone that I had come too late. Many others whom I would have liked to see and spend time with again, whether old acquaintances or those into whose orbit I had only recently been admitted, had meanwhile died, or were no longer accessible as far as I was concerned. Before my move back to London I had come to know two of the most prominent Viennese residents in England, having been commissioned to interview them. Anna Freud – who had received me on several occasions, in whose house Paula Fichtl still reigned and daily dusted off the numinous couch of the founder of psychoanalysis – had died during the previous October. Karl Popper was someone whose work I had spent months studying, whom I had regarded as second only to Schlick, under whom indeed he had also studied, and admired accordingly; I had been allowed to visit him at his house in High Wycombe, but now the relationship had been broken off. He had been displeased by an expression I had used, with the greatest respect, in my article about him, and perhaps also by my views certainly naively formulated, about his recently developed "Theory of Three Worlds" – in which he conceded the same existential status to a "third world" of human conclusions, theses and critical proofs as to tables and chairs. I had received a wounding letter from him, and had replied that I must now, in disappointment, withdraw from the circle of his adherents. I was to meet him once more, in the company of his friend Ernst Gombrich, in the garden of the Glyndebourne opera house. We shook hands but nothing more was said, and to my sorrow we remained unreconciled.

A few weeks after my arrival Melvin Lasky gave a welcoming reception for me at his home in beautiful Markham Square, where it was intended that old bonds of friendship should be renewed. But not much came of this. Nevertheless, I cannot stress strongly enough how greatly certain sobering experiences to which I was exposed on returning to my second home were counterbalanced by constantly recurring moments of happiness; how well able I was, despite one failure or another, to realize my expectations, to appreciate the gift of a lifestyle I had often dreamed of and now finally attained, and to enjoy it in the knowledge that it was granted to me only for a limited span.

It was an indescribable feeling for me on that day in May 1983, a Sunday, when I moved into Pembroke Place with the crockery, pots and pans, and other household goods that I had bought at Peter Jones in Sloane Square, with a great deal of luggage and many cartons of books, and with my summer clothes, for there was too little storage space for a whole year's wardrobe, and immediately set about furnishing my little study, with its view over the leafy courtyard. This so-called courtyard was in fact a narrow path between the low brick walls of the gardens opposite and the little patios built onto the back of every house in the row, which were walled in, but supplied with tall potted plants, and here and there with trees. To the left was a vine someone had planted a long time ago, whose branches now ran the length of all the patios and formed a bower over mine, a cool retreat where we would sit during the heat of the summer.

My arrival had disturbed the peace of some of the inhabitants of Pembroke Place, and soon a little group of them were standing nearby, casting furtive glances in my direction, just as if we were in some village square, and not a bourgeois area of London. I went out and introduced myself, as was clearly expected of me. The ladies, Penny and Mary, and a youngish man called Barry greeted me as their new neighbor, and all, with the addition of Maggie, whom I met soon afterwards, quickly became my friends and have almost all remained so until today. Warm-hearted, sympathetic, full of loving loyalty from the moment of our first meeting – in all the years in Wimbledon we had not made friends like these. Soon I was on good terms with everyone in the square, and was constantly invited to one house or another. In a very short space of time I was part of the community. The rickety white Mini which I soon bought in order to get more easily into the West End in the evenings, or to more out-of-the-way addresses, could be legitimately parked under the trees or in front of my door, thanks to a resident's permit. I was issued a pensioner's pass to use on the bus or the Underground, and obtained a card for the public library. And I was even put on the voters' register, for I had retained my British nationality alongside the Austrian one which had been restored to me.

That sense of security which I had felt in the first euphoric years of my final return to Vienna – I felt it here again, and was not to regret it. They were goodhearted people, in accordance with the basic English character – these older and younger women, these often unmarried, charming young men with a greyhound on a lead, these childless couples on Pembroke Place. There was no trace of the arrogance, let alone the "calculated rudeness," that one sometimes experiences on the part of the intellectual elite of this country. And Mary, the oldest and most well-read of my neighbors, was some compensation to me for the loss of Dodo, for she came from a similarly cultured and utterly liberal background.

But none of this would have sufficed to make me feel at home again immediately in England, if some of my family had not lived here too; my good and beloved daughter, whose home was nearby and who visited me almost daily, with my little granddaughter in her stroller; her husband, and also my son's first wife and her own son, whom we all considered as a member of the clan, and who in fact bore Peter's surname. All of these, and friends of theirs, soon began to turn up for lunch at weekends. On fine days we would sit on the patio on that white-painted wrought iron garden furniture which reminded me of Brussels lace, and which I had always coveted, although I had never had my own garden in London before. At Rassell's, the garden shop in Pembroke Square, I bought decorated earthenware pots and plants. Around me everything was green.

And so, with a new vitality, I set out on my rounds: to the ballet or the opera in the venerable scarlet-lined auditorium of Covent Garden – in its *belle époque* splendour the right setting for these nineteenth-century arts, as had once been the interior of the Vienna Opera House, now rebuilt in the white and gold style of the Imperial Chancellery; to exhibitions at the Royal Academy; to poetry readings at the Arts Theatre or symposia at one institute or another. I still had enough energy for my exhausting job; the productions at the National Theatre or at the Barbican Centre by the Royal Shakespeare Company still had the power to pluck me out of the lethargy that had recently all too often befallen me in German theaters. The Mini, shabby but nimble, flitted through the London traffic, and I quickly traversed the old familiar routes. I even enjoyed the maneuver of entering and leaving the traffic circles at Marble Arch or Hyde Park Corner, so crowded and yet so carefully negotiated by English motorists.

The city belonged to me again, and I belonged to it. But how much it had changed! I only noticed this when I began to live there again. Even in my immediate surroundings on the Earl's Court Road, I found that the few old junk shops had been supplemented by grocery stores, run by friendly, industrious Pakistanis, mostly called Patel, where one could buy everything one needed until late in the evening, and on Sundays too. The black people, to be seen in all possible contexts, were friendly too; as bus conductors, station guards, sales assistants in the stores they had almost entirely supplanted the whites. But already, as in New York, it had become impossible to enter certain areas of London safely at night, for the young West Indians, often unemployed, including the wild-looking Rastafarians with their hair in terrifying dreadlocks, were becoming lawless to an increasing degree. I had no fear at all of the punks, who were still around, walking the streets in the most imaginative outfits. But it was with some horror that, for instance while shopping in King Street, Hammersmith, on a Saturday, I saw groups of brutal-looking skinheads selling National Front publications.

It was Maggie Thatcher's England, it seemed to me, which had for the first time justified the old, travestied image, not of perfidious but of hardhearted and selfish Albion. The humane attitude of the earlier Tories, whose unshakable class-consciousness and resolute grip on their properties and their privileges was nevertheless accompanied by a latent sense of social justice, or perhaps simply a bad conscience, which provoked them to private charitable activity and, in the spirit of Disraeli, would not allow them to overlook the needs of the underprivileged, the "two nations" of this land – all this had been thrown overboard by the grocer's daughter. The gulf between the two nations, the haves and the have-nots, was growing wider day by day.

The greatest increases were in rents and house prices. Whenever I considered settling permanently in London again after all, at least acquiring a *pied à terre*, it was the cost that immediately frightened me off. My neighbor on the right, a member of the distinguished Cavendish family, implored me to buy my house at number 12, Pembroke Place. But its Scottish owners did not want to sell it, nor would I have been able to raise the horrendous sum required, fifteen times what it would have been only a few years ago. It became clear to me that I could exist here only through the good graces of my newspaper. But how long could I really continue to carry on my trade of cultural reporter? And despite my unceasing activity, here too the editorial office kept telephoning to commission some additional contribution or other. It was not for lack of willingness that I was now slowly becoming tired. When I had first met Anna Freud she had taken me for much younger than my years. "How do you do it?" she asked me. "Work," I said. She nodded: "Yes, that's how I did it too." During this summer and autumn I would still be able to manage the tasks imposed on me. But during the coming winter I would be forced to recognize that I could not extend my stay in London indefinitely.

And yet, how intensely I sometimes longed to cling to the second identity I had won back for myself! At Dodo's funeral in Oxford – an unusual one, because she had become an anthroposophist in her old age and had requested a service in the spirit of Rudolf Steiner's teachings – William Blake's "Jerusalem" was sung. Not until then did I burst into tears. It is with this heartrending hymn that the British have long reaffirmed their noblest aspirations. "I will not cease from mental strife..." It always stirs up my feelings too. How much, after all, we are molded by songs! I can follow all the phases of my life with their help. The Viennese songs from the Kremser collection, which I used to sing as a little girl in the Wollzeile. The songs by Brecht and Eisler, which strengthened us in our solidarity with the poor, our revolt against the Nazi threat. The English nursery rhymes, as naive as they were enigmatic, which we learned along with our own children. The old folk songs of the British Isles, many of them Irish or Scottish. Which do I find more moving now? "Greensleeves," reminiscent of the Elizabethans, of Shakespeare's poetry? Or the simple *Heurigen* song "Steht ein alter Nussbaum drunt in Heiligenstadt"? This dilemma sums up the schizophrenia of my life.

Not long after I had settled into Pembroke Place a television team arrived from Vienna to make a documentary, a film portrait of me. The idea for this was certainly suggested by my decision to turn my back yet again on my native city. The enjoyment of self-criticism, even of self-mockery, is after all a feature which distinguishes the Austrians, or at least the residents of their major cities, from their German neighbors: a virtue, I feel, more rewarding than the undiminished self-confidence later recommended to them by a president of dubious credentials. Since Lasky's invitation happened to fall on the day after their arrival in the middle of June, the film crew asked for permission to shoot at the party for a little while. Whether the viewers at home would recognize those present was irrelevant. Among the guests in fact were Tom Stoppard and James Saunders, whose plays I had been translating for some time, and the philosopher "Freddie" Ayer, my old acquaintance, with whom I had sometimes gone out alone during the postwar years and who now, although he was well aware why he himself had been invited, greeted me in an offhand manner which came pretty close to the "British freeze-up" I have already had cause to mention.

For the rest, apart from my daughter and my old friend Fritz Thorn, Melvin had gathered around him primarily members of his own circle, colleagues of the magazine *Encounter* which he edited; I found them interesting, but we had little in common. My friendship with Melvin and his partner did not suffer as a result of the limited success of this occasion, after which we were to meet often and gladly. Jimmy Saunders, too, often drove from Twickenham to see me. But Tom Stoppard, once such an intimate friend – when Flesch and I once met him and Miriam by chance in Venice, the four of us several times visited our favorite restaurants together – Tom, with his growing success, had more and more assumed the airs and graces of the London intelligentsia and did not once seek out my company in the whole of the year that followed. At the *New Statesman* I had long been forgotten. Some former friends, who had transferred from the academic hierarchy of Cambridge to the highest ranks of the London art and intellectual world, invited me to their house on one occasion, just before I left England again. PEN, now more modestly accommodated in comparison to Glebe House, gave me a friendly welcome, but most of the members of my generation were gone, and the younger ones did not know me. It was politely rather than cordially that they invited me to a glass of sherry at the little bar.

Once, before leaving London for the summer, I drove to Chichester to see a production of John Osborne's *A Patriot for Me*, and to visit Christopher Fry before the performance. He was still grateful to me for having written enthusiastically in *Der Monat* about his early plays. I still admired him, his creative imagination, and his altruism and goodheartedness, inherited from his Quaker forebears and deeply rooted in him since childhood. He had become quieter and more melancholy; the waning of his all too short-lived fame had overshadowed the rest of his life, and moreover his house in Little Venice, on the Regent's Park Canal, where I had once often visited him, had been burgled of all his unpublished youthful poems and letters to his wife, as well as the rest of his possessions – furniture, pictures, books. An enormous furniture van had driven up in front of the house and cleared out the entire contents. Since then, Christopher's only home had been in Chichester. In his living room stood a tree, artificial or perhaps preserved in some way, covered thickly with stuffed birds. I could not have endured the sight, but he took pleasure in it. I met him in London on a few more occasions, but his hermit-like existence did not allow more frequent encounters.

In the summer I had little time to relax. At the beginning of July I flew to Munich and Vienna, and soon afterward I spent a month in St. Wolfgang. My dog Dorli was with me, and the She-Youth. The television crew, which had been shooting at all the locations of my past in London, turned up. My granddaughter Anna was chosen to enact my own childhood: they filmed her in the deserted Lernet boathouse. And soon the Salzburg Festival opened, and of course I had to report on this too. Meanwhile, I suffered a physical crisis, brought on by the strain of a tax investigation, which put me in hospital for eight days. And in the second week of August the Edinburgh Festival was imminent; this was stimulating, but demanding too. As early as September I had to consider how the house in Pembroke Place, which, although small, was cool and drafty, was to be heated. I bought a bottled gas heater to supplement the feeble central heating. Soon I developed symptoms of illness, precipitated by the cold weather. Here was another reason to be aware that I could not prolong this way of life at my age, if only because of the climate. It was all the more defiantly that I threw myself with all my energy into descriptions of English life for my newspaper; I did not restrict myself to the cultural scene, but usurped the realm of the political correspondent, rather to the distress of the latter.

Margaret Thatcher was then at the height of her popularity after the Falklands war, and I could not deny myself a pen-portrait of her as the "British Bellona": "Was it for this that the suffragette Emily Davison threw herself under the hooves of the royal horse at the 1913 Derby, and her companions chained themselves to the railings of the House of Commons? It is no peace-loving friend of the poor, but a belligerent monetarist who has moved into 10 Downing Street." The unexpected way in which the hopes of the feminist movement – which had had its origins in this country – had been fulfilled affected me deeply. I was equally incensed by the Mosley clan and its upper-class connections, for I remembered only too well the Blackshirts' acts of violence before the war, and their declaration of faith in the German Nazi state.

The release by the Home Office of almost the entire dossier on Sir Oswald Mosley and his Union of British Fascists – but also the publication of a biography of that seductive but disastrous man, in which his own son Nicholas ruthlessly described his Jekyll and Hyde nature as a genial paterfamilias, womanizer, and turbulent demagogue – positively forced me to concern myself with his still deadly influence. After all, his widow, a sister of the unfortunate Unity Mitford and herself a former friend of Hitler, was constantly promoting the Mosley legend. And finally, the following March, when I was already preparing for the final farewell to my British way of life, I described with great inward sympathy the volte-face which had for some time been driving intellectuals here into the Tory camp.

Like so many European movements, the change in political attitude among leading spirits first took place in England. Here, as a platform for the "New Right," a "Conservative Philosophical Group" was established, which was joined by some of the most discerning and articulate personalities in public life. Among their founders was the Oxford epistemologist Anthony Quinton, familiar to me as my opponent in numerous amicable contests in the BBC's Round Europe Quiz, as was John Julius Norwich, the son of the splendid statesman Duff Cooper and the famous beauty Diana Cooper. These two men had always seemed to me the epitome of superior and humane open-mindedness. Now Quinton, if not Lord Norwich, had become a leading figure among the Thatcherites, and was indeed soon rewarded with a peerage.

But while he himself had not yet made a clean break between his former "liberal-elitist" attitude and his new stance, his comrade-in-arms Roger Scruton, a young professor of philosophy at Birkbeck College, was a Conservative of the most pitiless stamp. Scruton conceded no validity to the term "social justice"; he rejected feminism, the trade unions, the Campaign for Nuclear Disarmament, he yearned for the return of the gallows, and found the "classism" of the Socialists as bad as the racism of anti-Semites and the color-prejudiced. And soon after the upheavals in Eastern Europe, a few weeks after Vaclav Havel's election as president, Scruton turned up in Prague to spread these views among the disillusioned Marxists.

The new right-wing tendency in British intellectual life was now more than six years old. Hardly anywhere in Europe was the intellectual bias still toward the left, and for many people Socialism had become a dirty word. But even then, when I was raising my weak voice against a world view whose primary concern was no longer a more equitable distribution of goods but the security of industrial growth, even then the terms "left" and "right" had already lost their significance. And because this book is to end with the description of my English year – with only an epilogue to follow – I will here allow myself, as I did earlier in the context of the Cold War, to define my point of view, which remains unchanged by the revolutions in the former "People's Republics."

I would prefer to do this by means of an illustration, for abstract discussions, which I want to avoid as far as possible, seem to me out of place here. So perhaps I should describe what happened on

February 1, 1984, at the Royal Festival Hall in London. Here, at a memorial exhibition and commemoration, organized by the London County Council, of the Viennese civil war and the destruction of social democracy in Austria, three great British witnesses had gathered: Lord Elwyn-Jones, the minister for justice in the last Labour cabinet; the Scottish writer Naomi Mitchison; and Dora Gaitskell, Hugh's widow, now a life peeress and member of the House of Lords. These three, with all of whom I had become friendly after that twelfth of February in Vienna, now reawakened my faith in an unselfish, self-sacrificing, truly philanthropic form of Socialism.

A leading Social Democratic politician had come from Vienna for this event and had presented Elwyn, Dora, and Naomi Mitchison with the Victor Adler medal in gratitude for their help at that time. When he saw me in the hall after the ceremony, he approached me and told me that the television portrait of me, which had been shot the year before and recently aired, had caused some displeasure at home. In a statement which had been recorded in July 1983 and shown in this program, I had lamented the fall of social democracy in Austria, which was regarded as progress. I had discussed certain local scandals, which were already well known to the general public there, and in general made no secret of my aversion to many of the "comrades" of today.

After a meeting of the council of ministers the day before, so I was told by the visiting politician – himself, by the way, a man of total integrity – Chancellor Sinowatz had been asked in the press lobby what on earth could have induced me to attack the SPÖ (Social Democratic Party) so violently. Sinowatz had replied that he did not know; there must have been personal reasons for it. The politician from Vienna now asked me if this was so. "In a certain sense, yes," I said, "because you have betrayed the ideals of my youth." That for at least fourteen years, after the First World War, a "Socialism with a human face" had been made a reality under the aegis of a "Red" city council – this was something I could confirm, for I had experienced it. "Where there are stronger people, always on the side of the weak." And no new slogan about "capitalism with a human face" could convince me of the higher ethics of a social structure oriented purely toward the market economy.

Here too I will repeat something I said in an old novel, a belief on which I have already touched in these memoirs and which is so often disputed today: that the extreme left and the extreme right, at least in their roots, cannot be compared with each other. Thomas, the émigré in my book, who has long abandoned Communism and has himself begun to doubt the efficacy of moderate theories in setting the world to rights, poses a series of questions which he is unable to answer. The last of these are: "If Hitler could be destroyed at the expense of Coventry and Dresden, what was Stalin worth? If Fascism was the incarnation of evil, but Communism only a fallen angel – should the same sacrifices be made for their destruction?" And I still think that, despite the horrific way in which both ideologies were put into practice, it should not be forgotten that the basis of Marxist teaching is a desire for that "social justice" which has been ridiculed by Roger Scruton, while that of the National Socialist movement was an inhumane lust for power. This admittedly does not excuse anything that has been done in the name of either.

Never again, after my final return to Vienna, have I been tempted to indulge in direct criticism of public conditions or events; only once or twice, when my sense of political ethics was outraged to an exceptional degree, have I made a brief comment. Not having been by any means a saint in my own private life, I do not feel qualified to pose as an authority. However, I found the volte-face in English intellectual consciousness even more shattering than the degeneration of the decent *Socialismus militans,* as I knew it under the first Austrian Republic, to the corruption in the ranks of the *Socialismus triumphans* of the seventies. As for the "effortless superiority" (in Lord Asquith's phrase) of the English, of which I have often enough made fun, at heart I did actually believe in it myself. The tradition of democratic and liberal ways of thinking, from Magna Carta via Milton to the British statesmen of the pre-Thatcher era, had been predominant here for so long that I could not but see it as this country's only reliable guardian. And now they were all going over to a heartless money-bag philosophy, even invoking Edmund Burke and Lord Salisbury as their models. Tom Stoppard, likewise, had soon shown his face in the Conservative Philosophical Group, whose meetings were sometimes attended by Margaret Thatcher. And the countermovement, created after my departure from England by Harold Pinter and his wife Lady Antonia Fraser in their salon under the name of the "June 20 Group," had, after the impressive announcement of a "Charter 88," soon lost its impetus.

Nevertheless the memory of an intellectual nobility, in whose circles the lack of charity manifested by the New Right would have been taboo, was still alive. The wonderful Virginia Woolf was a snob among many other things, but she would have given the shirt off her back to alleviate real suffering, even though the smell of poverty was undoubtedly offensive to her. The Thatcherite economists leaned on J. M. Keynes's theory of employment, but their social attitude, much closer to the Italian *sacro egoismo*, was certainly foreign to Keynes. At that time I happened to encounter on more than one occasion a descendant of Bloomsbury, the son of Harold Nicolson and Vita Sackville-West. One evening in November a strange spectacle took place at the Riverside Studios, an exceptionally lively arts center in Hammersmith, run and frequented by the rebellious and the unconventional. Eugène Ionesco, Alain Robbe-Grillet, Nathalie Sarraute and other great figures had come from Paris to perform a forgotten play by Virginia Woolf, *Freshwater*, a satire on the Victorian writers and artists Lord Tennyson, G. F. Watts, Ellen Terry, and a great-aunt of the author's, the photographer Julia Margaret Cameron. This enchanting absurdity had been first performed in 1935 by members of the Woolf and Bell families, and had now been unearthed by these eminent Parisians. The result was an Anglo-French *bizarrerie*.

I will never forget Ionesco as Tennyson, with a luxuriant white beard, laboriously reading his lines from a notebook, or Nathalie Sarraute's flawless portrayal of the maid Mary Magdalen, as well as the breeches part of a kid-gloved butler. Before the performance Nigel Nicolson had stepped up to a lectern and spoken, without notes, about his youthful experiences of Bloomsbury. Afterward there was an informal celebration of Ionesco's birthday; an enormous cake with innumerable flaming candles was brought onto the stage, and the audience – all of us – were given slices of cake and glasses of wine, congratulated Ionesco and fraternized with the cast, the luminaries of the *nouveau roman*. The following January I met Nicolson again at one of the famous receptions given by the Viennese publisher whose business partner he was, and he assured me that this was currently the only literary-artistic-political salon in London, and the only one of its kind since those of Bloomsbury. "Unfortunately I am not always invited," said Nicolson in mock sorrow. I appreciated all the more the fact that during those last months in England, and subsequently on occasional visits, I was repeatedly invited. And if, in the circle of my neighbors in Pembroke Place, I occasionally missed the stimulus of intellectual companionship, this is where I might have found it: at Lord Weidenfeld's salon in Chelsea. But the time remaining to me was too short. I could no longer summon up the patience and persistence one needs in order to acquire new friends in writing, journalistic and publishing circles.

In December I had already begun to feel ill, and spent several days in bed. Nevertheless, at Christmas I flew to Vienna, and on Christmas Eve, before visiting my children, I called on Thomas Bernhard and his Hede at their nearby apartment; it was the last time that I saw her, already very weak and apparently close to death. She died the following April. I also spent a week in St. Wolfgang. On the most beautiful day of snow and sun, I watched my family preparing to go skiing, while I was forced to sit and work on a film script about George Orwell, and I thought of Büchner's Woyzeck, who even in heaven had to help make the thunder. The following day I overcame my sense of duty and accompanied them, but the sky was overcast and I stood shivering while the others enjoyed themselves on the ski runs. In London the air was warmer, but it was icy cold in the little house, and damp penetrated through every pore. Continually driven to my refuge upstairs among the Redouté flower prints, clutching a hot-water bottle to ease my abdominal pain, I finally came to terms with the fact that I must refuse my paper's invitation to continue my work in London. The most difficult part of this was the renewed separation from my daughter, who was as attached to me as I was to her, and who visited me daily, despite her own work and family commitments.

The pattern of minor breakdowns and defiant attempts not to let myself be vanquished by them continued for the rest of the winter. Shooting began on the television film on Orwell; I met the crew in Paris and with them explored the district where Orwell had lived during his years of poverty, the house in the Rue du Pot de Fer, and even my beloved Place de la Contrescarpe; I dined, at the company's expense, at Robespierre's restaurant Chez Procope, and then presented myself at Edouard Roditi's, to interview him in front of the camera about his experiences with Orwell. It had been arranged that I was to stay with him, but through a misunderstanding he was not at home when I arrived, and so I joined the team at a hotel in the Rue de Richelieu, which opened up to me a whole new *quartier* of Paris – and I had thought I knew this city. I can hardly believe that this was when I discovered the Place de la Victoire for the first time.

Roditi, that most lovable and wise of eccentrics, was only too pleased to give us information about Eric Blair (the later George

Orwell), and it never entered his head to give himself airs. In this he was unlike the last representative and chronicler of the "pink decade" in England, himself a legend, like his former companions Auden, Isherwood and MacNeice, and, thank God, still very much a living one. Stephen Spender, a little reluctant at first, had been prepared to make a brief statement, but after doing so, he made his annoyance about the interruption more than clear. While the equipment was still being dismantled, he disappeared and, as we passed the half-open door of his study in leaving, ignored our words of gratitude and farewell. It did not occur to him to rise from his desk and say goodbye at least to me, whom he had often met at PEN meetings or in a private context. "Calculated rudeness" – I have referred to it often enough. We departed crestfallen. "I hate the English intellectual elite," I wrote furiously in my journal.

In March the University of California in Los Angeles had invited me to take part in a conference on exiled writers, and so – for the last time – I headed for Montana Avenue. Tom Stoppard, whom I had met earlier at George Weidenfeld's, expressed his displeasure at the fact that I had chosen to go to the States rather than attend the German premiere of his *Night and Day*, which I had translated, at the Akademietheater in Vienna. It was soon afterward that our collaboration ended. The healing powers of the warm, quiet days on Susi's terrace, gazing at the luxuriant, brilliant green subtropical flora around her blue pool, hours in the deck chair, as we spooned up lime yogurt or refreshed ourselves with mangoes or pomeloes, helped me over the span of time up to the spring in England. There, already mindful of my impending final departure, I undertook expeditions to Kew Gardens just as in the old days, for even my son was present on a short visit to London; an excursion to the Hampstead Heath fair with Fritz Thorn, who encouraged me to go on this outing with my daughter and granddaughter; Saturday mornings at the Portobello Road market, where Henekey's pub was now refurbished as the Lonsdale Arms. And for the remaining time in which I could enjoy it, I bought more plants for my patio, even a magnolia, whose next blossoms I would not see, but which later found a new home on my daughter's balcony in Glazbury Road, West Kensington.

I did not deny myself a short trip to give a reading in Belgium, although when in Brussels I was unable to meet my old friend, the model for Vincent, the Flemish character from one of my early novels – that good, loyal and exceptionally sensitive man. He however

contacted me soon afterwards, after a time lapse of fifty years, and
then began to write me the most poetic letters, which brightened up
my later days. A few weeks before my departure from Pembroke
Place, for it was already May, I traveled with my English family in
their camper van to the Lake District. And here my eyes were opened,
for what I saw before me was a tranquil Salzkammergut, almost
untouched, lakes and mountains of inexpressible beauty, but hardly
disturbed by visitors, for here people moved about full of reverence
for the landscape, without hustle, bustle, or noise.

I was staying at Mrs. Batty's farmhouse near the dark Coniston
Water; my children were camping nearby. Only cows and rosy-
snouted calves wandered on the hillside pastures; further up, by the
roadside, was Ruskin's grandiose Victorian house Brantwood, which
we explored as we did Rydal Mount, Wordsworth's beautiful
Georgian villa, and little Dove Cottage, his first home at Grasmere,
into which he moved in 1799 with his sister Dorothy. So many lakes
– Grasmere, Windermere, Derwentwater, Rydal Water, tiny Tarn
How – and the town of Keswick, where two other Lake poets,
Coleridge and Southey, had settled for a time. We sat for a while
outside the sinister-sounding Dungeon Ghyll Hotel; my daughter's
husband, born in Bolton, had rambled as a child in the Langdale
Pikes, the craggy mountains surrounding the valley. Now I
understood why he felt so much at home in St. Wolfgang, despite the
degree to which it was already spoilt.

On May 17 I completed a report on the London theater, "the last
of its kind, I hope," as I noted. And the following day a review of
Elisir d'amore at Covent Garden – glad to have got this "final exertion"
behind me, and yet full of sadness, because I would miss it very much,
that house of scarlet-lined walls. One more reception at the salon in
Chelsea; Harold Wilson and the widow of Anthony Eden were there,
as were several Austrians: the venerable Ernst Gombrich, Alfred
Brendel, and also, surprisingly, Josef Krainer, the *Landeshauptmann* or
governor of the province of Styria. My first home was drawing me
back. On the last day of the month, number 12 was emptied of my
possessions, some of which were now stored in my neighbors' cellars,
and we loaded countless suitcases and boxes of books into the
ancient, roomy BMW, already when Peter had bought it in Munich,
which the English family had taken over and which I was now driving
back to the Continent, to pass it on to my son. Mary, Maggie, and
Penny waved; the monster was propelled slowly round the corner

through the little lane to the Earl's Court Road; my daughter and granddaughter blew kisses, and I was off. My year in Pembroke Place was over. I thanked my good fortune for this fulfillment of a lifelong dream.

At a Frankfurt Book Fair

With Christine and baby granddaughter
Rebecca (Beckie), 1982

Epilogue: Three wardrobes

They stood in the shop of the gilder and restorer Alois Scherrer in the middle of the village, opposite the castle, in the *Schwesternhaus,* so called after the holy sisters who had long lived on the upper floor, where they cared for little girls. The castle, which shared the façade of the adjoining house, was a former Benedictine priory which until well into the eighteenth century had given refuge to pilgrims, even exalted, indeed imperial ones, to the *Wallfahrtskirche,* the Pilgrimage Church, of St. Wolfgang. After its secularization it had remained in the possession of the bishopric of Mondsee until, in the 1920s, the remainder of these chilly old rooms were acquired by the lay co-owners of the castle from the parish priest in exchange for a comfortable presbytery with an orchard, such as he preferred.

One of the gilder's brothers was a master painter, another an artist and woodcarver, who was addressed as Herr Professor, but this brother had moved away long ago and was now director of the school of carving at Hallein. Little Herr Alois Scherrer in the Schwesternhaus was no less an artist than the Professor, for it was he who preserved the wonderful altars of the church in superb condition, particularly Schwanthaler's baroque altar – a never-ending task, because the gold leaf was always falling off the wings of the many little cherubs. In his shadowy antiques shop he even had a carved Gothic angel on a column, allegedly by the school of Michael Pacher, who had created the high altar of the church in 1481, but Herr Scherrer would not sell his angel, and indeed sold very little of his stock. Many other objects, difficult to identify, lay or hung in the dimly lit room: chests, boxes, shelves, and also pilgrims' flasks, naive pictures of saints, sacred articles of all kinds, in which yet another priest in a nearby parish had seen only old-fashioned and useless junk, and which had been bought from him by the knowledgeable gilder.

The three wardrobes, painted in the traditional peasant style, were not the only ones that stood in the overcrowded gloom of the shop, but they were the least showy and the most beautiful. The first one had an upper and a lower rectangle in whose frames, as in a relief, reddish tulips grew out of a fenced lawn. Between these, two clock dials were depicted on the pale marbled door, and above, to the left and right of the initials of Jesus Christ to which a cross and heart had been added, the numbers 17 and 94 – the year of the Paris Terror. The second was delightfully decorated with flower-filled amphoras in vermilion and sea green; it bore the date 1828 – the middle of the peaceful Biedermeier period – and it was crowned by a noble, if somewhat irregularly curved architrave, as one might call it. The third and largest, adorned only with four little flower drawings, also enclosed in rectangles, had been made in 1841, during the period of unrest preceding the German revolution of March 1848; it bore, above an "eye of God," a majestic ornamental top in the form of a double scroll. The year was now 1955. Herr Scherrer wanted one thousand schillings each for two of the wardrobes, but for the third, the one with the clock faces, he was asking twelve hundred, as it was the oldest.

Soon the three wardrobes were standing in Haus am Bach, in rooms which were still half empty, but before long they had company. The finest pieces were assigned to the same room as the clock wardrobe. Two armchairs in Louis XVI style – not genuine, but presumably nineteenth-century reproductions, for their gilding too had long ago flaked off or faded in many places – had been found in the Dorotheum in Vienna. A sofa with almost the same decoration and the same fluted arms and legs had been awaiting a buyer for a long time in the window of an antique shop in Chepstow Road; the shipping costs were higher than the purchase price. The upholsterer Herr Rechberger of St. Wolfgang had covered sofa and chairs with the same green and white striped silk damask from London; now they looked as if they had always belonged together, and the wardrobe had no need to be ashamed of them. A baroque chandelier from Salzburg with a turned Turkish stem had been added, and on the walls of the little salon hung Hogarth prints, together with a number of little London views of the same period.

The two other wardrobes had been brought upstairs, the scrolled one into the "gentleman's bedroom," and the Biedermeier piece with the amphoras to the "lady's bedroom." The successive occupants of the former room, and finally my grandchildren, complained in turn that there was too little room in the scrolled wardrobe for their clothes and shoes, and would rather have had a modern and more spacious piece. It was surrounded by dark-stained peasant-style furniture, a large bed (later replaced by two smaller ones), and, as long as the room was inhabited by a writer, a huge refectory table with a mighty armchair. Among other pictures on the wall was an old print after the well-known painting of the Mozart family by Johann Nepomuk della Croce, in which the composer's deceased mother is indicated only by her likeness hanging framed on the wall, and Wolfgang Amadeus himself is portrayed as a somewhat unprepossessing young man, seated at the piano. The wardrobe in the lady's bedroom was loved and cherished for more than three decades, above all for the sake of its gentle and inexplicably soothing curves, which could be observed from one's bed, always the first pleasure of a new day. Not only were its patterns, by a happy chance, repeated in the window curtains and bed cover of English chintz, but its colors overflowed into this and later into other rooms of the house, for all the tables, bookshelves, even the beds newly bought for an extension which was built later, after they too had been transformed with the traditional curved lines, had been painted vermilion and sea green.

None of this had altered over thirty years. But with the growth in prosperity of the whole province, the town of St. Wolfgang was beginning to lose its character. The houses of the tradesmen and middle-class citizens in its center, mostly still dating from the fifteenth or sixteenth century, until now beautifully proportioned and framed with ornamentation in muted colors, were given additional stories and supplied with larger windows and more bulbous balconies, while crude frescoes, awkwardly portraying kitsch versions of scenes and figures in traditional costume, appeared on the freshly plastered walls. But first of all, the inn Zum weissen Rössl – the White Horse Inn – was completely rebuilt. Ralph Benatzky, the composer of the operetta of that name, who used to spend his vacations there after his return from exile, was dead, and buried in the local cemetery. Now there appeared on the lakefront a hotel in the urban style of Salzburg. The gabled roof, brown wooden balconies, and green-painted shutters had been ripped off; in their place there appeared a yellowish, bare, flat-roofed structure. The former charm of its location in the narrow, winding street, the view of the church tower were destroyed, totally distorted. But elsewhere, round about, other buildings too were launching themselves upwards, preening and distending themselves in crazy proportions, breaking out in over-ornate, sometimes wrought-iron decoration. Only a few houses, including that of the confectioner and pastrycook Wallner, which was granted a "wax-chandler's license" in 1520 and had stayed essentially the same since

1606, still attested to the ancient architectural tradition of this favored spot.

Then it was the turn of nature. That more and more housing was crowding out the meadows and gardens was part of the modern way of life, and had to be accepted as inexorable. But on the other side of the stream, the Dittelbach, in the district of Ried, which was actually part of the province of Salzburg, but was still provided with all its daily needs by St. Wolfgang, there stretched one last great green space, more beautiful than one could have imagined: a little over ten acres of grass, flanked by tall trees and dense shrubs, in its center a row of trees which stretched from the house called Förster-heim down to the lakeside road. Now, in the early Seventies, this too was declared a site suitable for development, without a murmur of protest from the *Naturschutz*, the conservation department. Seven gigantic apartment houses, containing hundreds of dwellings, were constructed there – with saddle roofs at least, the only traditional feature still specified by the authorities. These non-protectors of nature were concerned only with form, not with proportion; the fact that this lack of proportion, that the whole development with its pseudo-rustic, monotonous architecture, was inconsistent with the character of the landscape, did not worry them. And so for the first time the peace and quiet of Haus am Bach were disturbed when countless noisy activities began on the former "Fritzwiese," and when with merciless regularity the rattle of power lawnmowers interrupted meals on the terrace and the afternoon rest.

So far, the house in this formerly quiet spot had been spared the sight, if not the sounds, of the colony on the other side of the stream by whose banks it stood; bushes and weeping willows edged the mountain torrent, whose rushing sound on rainy days and in the time of the melting of the snow was so wonderful as not to be forgotten for a lifetime. This stream was on the right of the house; to the left, the grounds, somewhat wild and sparsely planted with fruit trees and shrubs, of which, over the years, more and more, finally the whole piece of land, was to become part of the little property, ran down as far as an inoffensive boundary fence. But on the other side of the rusty iron railings which ran the length of the drive to the Margaretenstrasse some hundred yards away, and opposite the main entrance to the house, its terrace, and its first-floor balcony, lay that park of some one and a half acres belonging to Alexander, our neighbor and friend; it was his mother – née Fräulein Sidonie von

Holenia, later a Baroness Beuneburgk, and finally, after being widowed, the wife of the naval lieutenant Lernet, in a marriage which ended on her wedding day – who first began to lay it out as soon as work was completed on the building of her villa in 1902.

What until then had been a dense, unplanned little forest, she planted with beech, ash, maple, lime, pear, chestnut, and fir trees. On the garden side of the house, which received the full strength of the afternoon sun, a gravel-covered area was created, and reserved for white-painted wicker furniture. From here a lawn, always beautifully mown, surrounded by rows of shrubs, stretched to the beginning of a grove, well kept and carefully thinned out, in whose center, on a little mound, stood a log hut, which later fell into disrepair. In this house and garden her sons grew up, the elder a baron, the younger only a commoner, although he had a double-barreled name because he had been adopted by a Holenia uncle. The younger son was more attached to this villa in Upper Austria than to the Carinthian mansion where he had been born, and he assigned his share in the latter to his brother in exchange for the former, after his mother had died there at an advanced age. Since his fifth year it had been his true home and refuge, and even when, having long since attained literary fame, he had been granted the favor of an apartment in the Hofburg in Vienna, he repeatedly escaped from the capital in his battered second-hand Volvo to mow his lawn in St. Wolfgang, and visit his mother's grave at the cemetery. His summers in the Salzkammergut began in June and stretched well into October.

In this epilogue, which is above all a lament for a spot which was once almost a paradise on earth and has now been destroyed, let us forget the earthly transgressions and errors of Alexander Lernet-Holenia. Here we will consider only his love for his house and garden, where there was nothing he wanted to change, where everything had been close to his heart for many years – the ever more densely thickening undergrowth at the lower end near the stream, and the fir trees which had by now attained about 80 feet in height, and none of which he had ever had cut down, even when their needles had become brown for lack of light. In the same way, he never liked to remove from the house anything that had been there since his childhood, such as the wooden curtain rods, or the draperies, which had survived since the turn of the century with hardly a sign of wear, or the paintings of ancestors, or as much as one piece of furniture, with the exception of the Renaissance clock, with its gold and silver decoration, which one day he transferred to his apartment in the Hofburg as being after all too showy for a country house. Everything was still in the old style; this was how he liked it, and it gave him comfort, for the transience of things had always been oppressive to him.

It was during the thirties that he had expressed his fear that he might not remain here always and forever, in one of his most beautiful poems, the "Prophecy of Tiresias," in these words, addressed by the seer to Odysseus:

> And did you dream to yourself
> above the beating of the waves
> how the meadow at home
> ripples in the afternoon sun,
> and that the pear tree hangs high above it,
> ah, but the meadow long since
> has not been the meadow,
> ah, the wood is no longer the wood, ah,
> your house no longer your house!
> Quietly weeps now the stream,
> the wind goes in and out,
> and where you used to belong,
> you are I know not who, –
> always, when a wanderer returns,
> no one knows him any more.

The fear of going and not returning had haunted Lernet-Holenia throughout his life, and with it the premonition that even what was as close to him as he was to himself might one day vanish altogether. "Not you," he wrote later in another poem, "The Departure," "but what you have left behind retreats / from you, changes as the face of the dead / changes, is transformed, disappears. / How silently the landscape is disfigured."

And how true his prophecy turned out to be. He had made provision before his death that his property should remain untouched, and should later be put into the hands of someone who would undertake to preserve it. His widow believed she was acting according to his wishes when she promised his real – though not his literary – estate to a distant great-nephew, but finally she had to recognize that he was unworthy of it and tore up her will, although she had not the strength to make a new one. In an "oral bequest" the whole inheritance, including the literary estate which had been intended for her husband's other nephew, was secured from the sick woman on her death bed, indeed four days before her death. And then the poet's unworthy heir went about his work. Hardly was the widow in her grave when he emptied the house of every single picture, every piece of furniture. Then he had the trees around it felled, so that it stood there lonely and shivering, exposed to the glance of all the curious passers-by from whom the poet had all his life withdrawn. In the following year, when no objection had been voiced or action taken to prevent him, he summoned the local forester and had the gigantic eighty-year-old fir trees cut down, some forty of them in the whole garden. And the year after that, when still no one had intervened, neither the local authority nor the Upper Austrian conservation department, he gave orders to clear the whole property, maple and ash, beech, pear tree, and chestnut tree. The garden, laid out by "Frau Baronin" Sidonie, as she was known to the locals until her death, was now razed to the ground in its entirety. She herself was not even allowed to rest in peace in the earth of the cemetery; the unworthy heir failed to renew the payment for her burial plot, and now the remains of another lie there.

In December 1986 Christmas was celebrated for the last time at Haus am Bach. The families from Vienna and London had gathered together once more, and in the salon, in the corner between the clock wardrobe and the Louis XVI sofa from Chepstow Road stood the Christmas tree, hung with decorations both very old and new, and beneath it, splendidly glittering in the candlelight, the three kings, birds, horse riders, all stamped out of sheets of colored metal, a present from Johanna Hofer, Fritz Kortner's wife. We sang Austrian Christmas songs and English carols. Deep snow lay heaped upon the terrace, so that only the side entrance could be used, and was piled in high mounds on the two iron lanterns to left and right of the steps. Behind them, in the Lernet garden, the beech and ash trees groaned under their load. Everything was taking its course, as it had done for decades. On New Year's Eve, when the snow had subsided a little, rockets were set off on the terrace from empty wine bottles; the great Catherine wheel was fixed to the giant beech in that corner which formed the boundary between our property, Lernet's and the "Kenneweg" plot which stretched farther down by the stream, but which strictly belonged to the Lernet property, so that eventually it too fell victim to the vandals; the Catherine wheel scattered its sparks far and wide, and the children danced in the garden, wildly waving their sparklers, until well past midnight. In the new year we saw the *Glöckler* of St. Wolfgang, the "bell people," who went on their rounds of the local houses with paper images of churches and saints, painted and illuminated from inside, mounted on sticks and fixed on their heads, and loudly ringing their bells; and we also drove to Bad Ischl, where this local custom was even more magnificently observed.

I said farewell to Haus am Bach, not knowing that it was forever. In February the loyal Herr Hutterer telephoned me in Vienna and reported that the woodcutters were in "Herr Baron" Lernet's garden – as he was known in the village – and in the process of clearing the whole area. I begged him to hurry to the town hall and make a complaint; but they knew nothing about it, or were not interested. No one protested against this outrage until it had been completed. I grieved, and still grieve today as one does for a human being, and made the instant decision never to return to St. Wolfgang, and to sell the house. But if, as I have already related, after the devastation in the village and in the context of a darkening of the political landscape throughout Austria, we had considered "whether that heavenly existence had perhaps been only an illusion" – now, after it is over, we must understand it as the truest realization of such an existence that is possible on earth. For whenever we doubted where we belonged, or would prefer to belong, whether London or Vienna, here we, my children and I, were at home in any case. And whatever else might happen in the country, when we sat around the table on the terrace, on the side nearer the stream, or in the Lernet boathouse for as long as we were still allowed to do so, now lying in the sun, now plunging into the water of the lake to return dripping to the hot, brittle floorboards; when on rainy days we played chess or cards in the living room, or scaled the Schafberg as far as Aschinger's farm with its little restaurant, where now and again we could watch the little train puffing by on the mountain railway line, and where there was the most beautiful view of the lake – none of that could touch us.

In the autumn of that year the house was cleared, or rather those possessions were removed from it that we did not want to leave behind for the new owner and occupier. We left him a great deal; for the furniture specially made and painted for these rooms, the curtains and upholstery, the wooden hanging lamp only recently discovered in Bad Ischl in the living room, and the other ceiling lights simply belonged to the house, and we could not have brought ourselves to rip them out. The pictures, however, the Louis XVI sofa and chairs, and the baroque chandelier in the salon, and above all the three wardrobes, were taken away. The cheerful Biedermeier wardrobe with the amphoras of flowers and the beautiful curved lines now stands in my daughter's bedroom in London, and if it misses the English chintz curtains of a similar pattern that were once its companions, it now has by its side a pair of curtains which served their time at Haus am Bach and are somewhat faded, but still intact, made of handwoven Salzburg linen, patterned in white on green with the Gothic vine motifs of old incunabula. And here too, by another happy chance, its curves are repeated in the carving of the head- and footboard of the bed. Downstairs are the Mozart family, with the unhandsome Wolfgang Amadeus playing a piano duet with his sister, between the two Hogarth prints of the "Strolling Players" and the "Beggar's Opera," and in the passage and along the length of the stairs the little views of London have returned to their origins. The scrolled wardrobe has been placed by my son in his large living room in a house at the foot of the Wilhelminenberg in Vienna, together with the baroque chandelier and the furniture from the salon, whose gilding is still flaking off.

The clock wardrobe, however, has now found an unexpected home, by no means appropriate to it, although somehow satisfactory to me: in the only room of a hut, so-called although stoutly built of bricks and wood, at the upper end of a garden between Neuwaldegg and Pötzleinsdorf. I bought this, as well as the garden adjoining it, with part of the proceeds of the sale of the house in St. Wolfgang, and only because both gardens are totally surrounded by wooded slopes. At the front one can see the Schafberg – not the one we used to know, but another mountain which happens to have the same name – and at the back the Michaelerberg; between the two, through a narrow valley, runs a road which is closed halfway along and reserved for residents, and sloping down from this road, stretching down from it as far as a trickle of a stream at the edge of the wood, are a whole series of gardens, ornamental gardens, not allotments, and on nearly every one a little structure, a log cabin or perhaps only a shed for deck-chairs and garden equipment. In my "hut" the clock wardrobe reigns supreme, almost touching the low ceiling, among wicker chairs and a large sofa bed, where, as in the little attic under the pointed roof, connected to the downstairs room by means of a ladder, my

In Salzburg, 1978 or 1979

English family can be accommodated when they visit in the summer. The gardens, the trees, the shrubs, the honeysuckle, the rhododendrons and azaleas, the vines, the roses, the view of nothing but the dense green of the hilly Vienna woods: all this is a blessing, belatedly granted to me, that has lent a last, unforeseen brightness to my life.

Recently Flesch appeared to me in a dream, cheerful and self-confident as he was in his best days, and accompanied by the ending of the last of Richard Strauss's "Four Last Songs." What music would one like to hear while passing into eternity, or into nothingness? I had always wished for a melody by Schubert. Or perhaps Telemann's sonata for oboe and harpsichord in C minor. And now I am haunted by these closing notes of the Strauss song – "*wie sind wir wandermüde*" ("how weary we are of traveling") – in which the motif of *Death and Transfiguration* is repeated. Very well, I say to myself, if this is a hint from the world beyond, then I will take it. After all, I have always tended to fall in with a suggestion from elsewhere, as long as it made sense to me.

Afterword

by Felix de Mendelssohn

I am particularly happy that these memoirs can now appear in my sister's English translation, since English was a language my mother felt had become in her years of exile as much her own as German. Her most mature and successful novel was originally written and published in English. To admirers of her spare but sparkling German style she would occasionally say that it was her command of English that gave her German prose its clarity and concision, saving her from those academically baroque excesses of thought and description which mar so much of the work of her Austrian contemporaries. However, this belies the fact that her earliest *Jugendromane* were already written in a lean and direct manner, under the influence of the early 1930s school of the *Neue Sachlichkeit*.

I do not remember growing up as a very small child or speaking my first words of German in Berlin, as my sister does. For me the memories start later, in the exile/home of my two writer parents in postwar suburban London. There, language was *the* issue. One of my most disconcerting reminiscences from the early 1950s is of certain friends and acquaintances of my parents – émigré authors, journalists, theater people – who in their years of estrangement had no longer retained fluent German nor yet managed to attain fluent English.

Sometimes the anecdotes about their spontaneous "translations" from the old tongue were hilarious, as when the émigré Viennese actress proclaimed to the poultry butcher: "Behold it, I let it, I can become a chicken much cheaper elsewhere!" But these were also cautionary tales. Such people seemed so sad and helpless without the proper tools of their trade, flotsam between the two worlds which my mother had wished to claim as her own – even while eloquently acknowledging her underlying sense of homelessness in either.

Language could be tortuous or tortured in many ways, as I learned from her after her return to Vienna in the 1960s. There were words in German to be avoided at all costs, like *verkraften* or *betreuen*, whose origins or associations had become contaminated, even though people used them all the time. Words used casually at dinner parties had become like suspicious objects in a minefield.

My parents were often delighted by the subtle absurdities of original word coinage that we as very small children could so effortlessly produce. But the process of growing up was for me fraught with the need to take responsibility for one's choice of words, for their accuracy, charm, and lack of equivocation, where one could slip up so easily.

Command of language was what mattered above all, in our household as in the wide world outside. As a small boy I could of course find this intensely oppressive (in the manner of "watch your tongue!"); today I can appreciate the importance of the lesson, now that the whole of Europe, as a continent and political entity, is learning it too. Language then was the key to assimilation, and the Holocaust and the Exile changed the face of Europe so much that the barriers between the nations had to begin to fall. Living in Vienna, I too have brought up both my children to be bilingual.

I am not an uncritical admirer of my mother's work. Her early novels, and indeed some of the later ones, seem to me to verge on the superficial or even veer toward kitsch. My favorite is *The Darkened Room* (published later in German as *Lisas Zimmer*), perhaps because in discovering her own personal America she had also found the ideal vantage point for contrasting the nostalgia for prewar Europe with the struggle to make a new life in a new world, from an acute perspective which still illuminates both even today. But for me it is as an essayist that she excels, in portrayals of people, places, books, cultural disputes, and curious occurrences which show her brightest and warmest side, her enthusiasms and antagonisms.

Take, for instance, a brief passage from her essay "The Psychology of Exile" (1977):

> However much we may brag about being good Europeans, cosmopolitans, humanitarians, associates of one "Internationale" or another: that we are rooted in our birthplace, where we grew up and learned to live, is more than just a metaphorical image. No one who has been transplanted after the end of childhood can quite deny the traits of the *déraciné*, of the uprooted. Let us listen to them, the successful Hungarians in Hollywood, when a sudden sentiment makes them fall back into their melodious mother tongue, so

impossible to learn. Let us observe them, the masterly writers of the English language in New York, sitting over a dish of blinis in the Russian Tearooms on 57th Street, when they suddenly recollect their childhood in St. Petersburg. Only in one particular case can exile to a foreign country be felt as a real homecoming – in the land of Israel, which the Ahasverian people have for thousands of years seen as their native abode promised to them by Providence.

My mother bequeathed me a dual legacy in Vienna – as a feted *grande dame* of Austrian letters for the general public, and as an unpopular and suspect personage for the close-knit Jewish community of the city, who saw her unwillingness to be called a "Jewish writer" as a sign of her disinclination to seem Jewish at all. As in most animosities there was a grain of truth in this, since part of her had always wanted to be mysteriously absorbed by a kind of cultural osmosis into the local Catholic aristocracy – she could on occasion be a bit of a snob, in Hugo von Hofmannsthal fashion. In my debates with her she would never accept my view that, unfortunately perhaps, those loony Zionists had had more political foresight than most of the "enlightened" Jewish intelligentsia of her day, and that her generation's wish for assimilation had been made impossible for mine by the Shoah, at least in Central Europe. In England it may be possible, at least it seems so for my sister, but here in Vienna where I live and work, it is not.

Zionism as a creed or a mission was not something Hilde Spiel could genuinely identify with, although her sentimental ties with Israel remained strong. It could be no solution to one leitmotiv of her life, the problem of belonging. And it added to another, the lifelong intellectual conflict between sentimental attachments and a sceptical rationalism which could not leave such sentiments unexamined, once their primal sway over the human heart was acknowledged. It was her writing, her sense of identity as a writer, which demanded she remain critical of all national enthusiasms, whether Israeli, Austrian, British or American, much as she loved all four countries in different ways.

When I lived for a while in Israel, my mother begged me to come to Vienna. When I later settled in Vienna, she sometimes begged me to go to the United States. She knew for herself that she was unhappy with Vienna, with living in Vienna, but that living away from it would have been far worse, and that there was no solution to this dilemma other than writing about it – in the same way that all other dilemmas of more than a merely daily nature could only genuinely be solved for her by writing.

My mother did not confide intimacies to me in the way she did to my sister, although I lived closer to her for the last twenty-five years up to her death and was more involved in the daily politics of her private and public life. During my training as a psychoanalyst – of which she also disapproved, perhaps on intellectual grounds put forward by the Vienna Circle school of analytic philosophy, perhaps because my father had allegedly once had an affair with the psychoanalyst Emmy Szabó! – I did of course spend quite a few years on the couch talking a great deal about her. In the course of this exploration of my relationship to her, I had to come to terms with painful childhood experiences of sudden abandonment by her, of her fragile touchiness and often staggering lack of empathy towards feelings of dependency, even when she was demanding utter devotion. At the same time I came to admire more and more her inner sense of devotion, her subtle insistence on the marriage of ethics and aesthetics, her courageous willingness to accept contingencies as fate and still use them creatively rather than cavil or succumb, along with her consistently generous support of those to whom fate had been much harder.

This book itself is the best testimony to that most important of her human qualities – she was a woman who could speak for herself. With her great charm, her intellectual acumen and uncluttered poetic sensibility, her love of life and her deep sadnesses which she tried so hard to keep not only from the world but from herself, in her pursuit and defence of an always essential freedom of spirit, she lived an exemplary life and gave it an original voice.

Felix de Mendelssohn is a psychoanalyst in private practice and director of the Department of Psychoanalytic Studies at the Sigmund Freud University, Vienna.

Postscript: A Compliment to Hilde Spiel

by Ingrid Schramm

"Every life becomes a legend," wrote Hilde Spiel in her book *Fanny von Arnstein*. It can be neither grasped nor exhausted. Does this statement apply to Hilde Spiel herself? Has her life too become a legend in her autobiography?

I believe I can answer this. To write her autobiography, Hilde Spiel brought to life many of the memories from her diaries and thus made possible for us a very vivid insight into her life. This naturally leads me to the question: as biographer and administrator of her literary estate, what can I add, in this postscript to the English version of her autobiography, that the author has not already related? What is there left to say that Hilde Spiel has not herself already reported about her life, one that was not always easy, but that she lived to the full?

When working on a literary estate, one will inevitably discover hidden sides of an author and perhaps come to know her better than she might have wished. Reading the diary of her Aunt Lonny, written before Hilde Spiel's birth, gave me an insight into her life before she had even come into the world. Is it surprising, then, that I feel as close to Hilde Spiel as to a member of my own family?

With every item in her literary estate that I examined, a more complex image of Hilde Spiel appeared before my eyes. I came to know her as a woman who fought courageously for her path in life during an extremely difficult period of world history. She made it very easy for me to respond with boundless admiration to her work as an essayist, novelist, critic, and translator. Her qualities have already been praised by many others, for example by the German literary critic known as the "pope of literature," Marcel Reich-Ranicki, to name only one. Nevertheless, I feel justified in adding one more comment. Hilde Spiel not only had the admirable quality of beginning her texts with a brilliant first sentence; she is also a master of the closing sentence. As examples, I would like to mention here the last paragraph of her autobiography, and that of her favorite among her own books, *Fanny von Arnstein*.

And so we may assume that after her death, Hilde Spiel was able to give a similar answer to God as the wise Rabbi Hillel. Hasidic legend reports that when the rabbi briefly regained consciousness shortly before his death, he was able to report to his pupils that God had asked him who he had been in life. God had assured him that he need not be Abraham or Moses, but simply Rabbi Hillel. The wise rabbi was able to answer God's question accordingly.

In these terms, the greatest thing one can say of Hilde Spiel is that during her life she was the best possible Hilde Spiel.

Dr. Ingrid Schramm administers the literary estate of Hilde Spiel, which is in the Austrian Literary Archive of the Austrian National Library.

Hilde Spiel: A Biographical Note

1911   Born in Vienna on October 19, the daughter of the scientist Dr. Hugo F. Spiel and his wife Marie (Mimi).

1930   After attending the Frauenerwerbverein and Eugenie Schwarzwald's Frauenoberschule, began studies at the University of Vienna under Moritz Schlick and Karl Bühler.

1933-35   Work at research center for industrial psychology directed by Paul Lazarsfeld.

1936   Graduation with Dr. phil. degree. Left Vienna for London; marriage to Peter de Mendelssohn.

1937   Joined English PEN Center.

1939   Contributions to *Daily Express*. Birth of daughter Christine.

1941   Acquired British nationality.

1944   Contributions to *New Statesman* (until 1958). Birth of son Anthony Felix.

1946   First return to Vienna as correspondent for *New Statesman*.

1946-8   Resident in Berlin. Theater reviews for Berlin edition of *Die Welt*.

1948   Return to London. Cultural correspondent for *Die Neue Zeitung*, then *Süddeutsche Zeitung, Tagesspiegel, Weltwoche, Haagse Post, Neues Österreich* and several German radio stations.

1955   Acquired house in St. Wolfgang, Salzkammergut.

1963   Final return to Austria. Cultural correspondent in Vienna for *Frankfurter Allgemeine Zeitung*.

1963   Cultural correspondent in Vienna for *Weltwoche* (until 1972) and *Guardian* (until 1970).

1965-72   General secretary, then vice president of Austrian PEN.

1971   Marriage to Hans Flesch von Brunningen.

Publication of memoirs in Germany, 1989

1970-72   Founder (with Milo Dor) and first president of Interessengemeinschaft österreichischen Autoren.

1972   Member of Darmstadt Academy.

1974-76   Member of committee of West German PEN. For many years member of International PEN's Writers in Prison committee.

1980   Elected member of Grazer Autorenversammlung.

1983   Member of Bavarian Academy.

1983-84   Resident in London as cultural correspondent for *Frankfurter Allgemeine Zeitung*.

1990   Died in Vienna on November 30.

Bibliography

Kati auf der Brücke (novel), Vienna, Paul Zsolnay Verlag, 1933. Reprinted in *Frühe Tage*, Munich, Albrecht Knaus Verlag, 1986.

Verwirrung am Wolfgangsee (novel), Vienna, Höger, 1935. Reprinted as *Sommer am Wolfgangsee*, Hamburg, Rowohlt Verlag, 1961; reprinted under original title in *Frühe Tage*.

Flute and Drums (novel), London, Hutchinson, 1939. German version: *Flöte und Trommeln*, Vienna, and Hamburg, W. Krüger, 1949; reprinted in *Frühe Tage*.

Der Park und die Wildnis (essays), Munich, Beck, 1953.

London (text to photographs by Elisabeth Niggemeyer), Munich, 1956.

Laurence Olivier (memoir), Berlin, 1958.

Welt im Widerschein (essays), Munich, Beck, 1960.

The Darkened Room (novel), London, Methuen, 1961. German version: *Lisas Zimmer*, Munich, Nymphenburger Verlag, 1965; paperback, DTV, 1968, 1984.

Fanny von Arnstein oder Die Emanzipation (biography), Frankfurt, S. Fischer Verlag, 1962. English version: *Fanny von Arnstein: A Daughter of the Enlightenment* (tr. Christine Shuttleworth), Oxford, Berg Publishing, 1991.

"Shakespeare's König Richard III" (essay accompanying edition of A. W. von Schlegel's translation of *Richard III*), Frankfurt am Main/Berlin, Ullstein, 1964.

Der Wiener Kongress in Augenzeugenberichten, Düsseldorf, 1965.

Verliebt in Döbling (text to photographs by Franz Vogler), Vienna, 1966.

Rückkehr nach Wien (journal), Munich, Nymphenburger Verlag, 1968.

Städte und Menschen (essays), Vienna and Munich, Jugend und Volk, 1972.

Kleine Schritte (articles and stories), Munich, Edition Spangenberg, 1976.

Mirko und Franca (novella), Munich, Nymphenburger Verlag, 1980.

In meinem Garten schlendernd (essays), Munich, Nymphenburger Verlag, 1981.

"Virginia Woolf: Bildnis einer genialen Frau" (essay introducing volume of essays by Virginia Woolf: *Augenblicke* (*Moments of Being*), Stuttgart, Deutsche Verlagsanstalt, 1981 (paperback, Frankfurt, Fischer Taschenbuch Verlag, 1984).

Englische Ansichten (essays), Stuttgart, Deutsche Verlags-Anstalt, 1984.

Der Mann mit der Pelerine (stories), Bergisch Gladbach, Gustav Lübbe Verlag, 1985.

Frühe Tage (collection of three early novels), Munich, Albrecht Knaus Verlag, 1986.

Vienna's Golden Autumn: 1866–1938 (cultural history), London, Weidenfeld and Nicolson, 1987. German version: *Glanz und Untergang: Wien 1866–1938* (tr. Hanna Neves), Vienna, Kremayr & Scheriau, 1987; Munich, Paul List Verlag, 1988.

Die hellen und die finsteren Zeiten: Erinnerungen 1911–1946 (memoirs), Munich, Paul List Verlag, 1989.

Anna und Anna (screenplay adapted for the stage), Vienna, Kremayr & Scheriau, 1989.

Welche Welt ist meine Welt? Erinnerungen 1946-1989 (memoirs), Munich, List Verlag, 1990.

Die Dämonie der Gemütlichkeit (ed. Hans A. Neunzig) (essays and other prose), Munich, Paul List Verlag, 1991.

Das Haus des Dichters (literary essays, interpretations, reviews), Munich, Paul List Verlag, 1992.

Briefwechsel (ed. Hans A. Neunzig) (correspondence), Munich, Paul List Verlag, 1995.

Edited and introduced by HS:
England erzählt (short stories), Frankfurt am Main and Hamburg, S. Fischer Verlag, 1960.

Edited and co-written by HS:
Wien – Spektrum einer Stadt, Vienna and Munich, Jugend und Volk, 1971.

Die zeitgenössische Literatur Österreichs, Volume IV of Kindler's *Literaturgeschichte der Gegenwart* (Contemporary Literary History) series, Munich, Kindler, 1976.

Contributions by HS to multi-author volumes in German and English include:
    Genius in the Drawing-Room (ed. Peter Quennell) (essay on Rahel Varnhagen), London, Weidenfeld & Nicolson, 1980.
    Lebenslernzeit, Erzählungen und Gedanken, Munich, 1989.
    Venedig: Theater der Träume, Munich, 1988.

Translations into German by HS include works by:
    John Arden, W. H. Auden, Nigel Balchin, Elizabeth Bowen, Christopher Fry, Rumer Godden, Graham Greene, David Mercer, Joe Orton, James Saunders, Tom Stoppard, Emlyn Williams

Works published in periodicals:
    "Der kleine Bub Desider" (short story), *Neue Freie Presse,* October/November 1929.

From 1929 to 1937 onward, over 40 short stories (some published under pseudonyms), and numerous reports, travel articles, essays, and interviews in various Austrian and Swiss periodicals and *Prager Tagblatt.*

Publications in the British press (from 1937 onward) include essays in the *New Statesman* on Marie Bashkirtseff (1944) and Henri Alain-Fournier (1946).

Honors
    In addition to many awards from the governments of Austria and the German Federal Republic, HS was the recipient of several literary prizes:

1934	Julius Reich Prize of the City of Vienna (for *Kati auf der Brücke*)
1976	Prize of the City of Vienna
1981	Roswitha von Gandersheim Prize
	Johann Heinrich Merck Prize (German Academy, Darmstadt)
1986	Ernst Robert Curtius Prize
1987	Grand Literary Prize (Bavarian Academy)
1990	Goethe Medal (Goethe Institute) (for services to the German language)

Felix with his family – left to right: Anna, Jutta, Arif, Felix

The grandchildren in St. Wolfgang:
Arif, Anna, Beckie

Index

by Christine Shuttleworth

412

315
and Lonny 324
and Thomas Mann 309
marriage to HS 335, 359
and Georg von Mendelssohn 258
and Mimi 274
and PEN 131, 207, 261
personality 111, 252-253, 369-370
quoted 182, 221, 235, 257
relationship with HS 3, 252-253, 312, 334
return to Austria 315
in St. Wolfgang 273, 324, 362-370
and Torberg 310
in USA 362
in Venice 337-338, 379
in Vienna 318, 347
as writer 157-158
Die Frumm 365
Perlen und schwarze Tränen 253, 316
Flesch von Brunningen, Tetta 123, 126, 176, 206, 220
Florence
Albergo Porta Rossa 274
Bargello 92
Uffizi 92
Fluss, Bergrat 87, 88
Fondi 210
Fontane, Theodor 221
Forster, E. M. 251, 261
Forster, Rudolf 31, 206
Forte dei Marmi 220, 258
Forum 277, 313, 345
Foster-Cooper, Jeanne 360
Fowey, Cornwall 125
France 315-316
see also Paris
La France libre 130, 176

Francis I, Emperor of Austria 17, 80
Franck, Walter 222
Franckenstein, Baron Georg (Sir George) 115, 116, 122, 171
Franco, Francisco 68, 93
Frank, Bruno 101, 102
Frank, Hans 339
Frankfurt 322, 368
Frankfurter Allgemeine Zeitung 325, 369
Franz Joseph, Emperor 339
funeral 13, 27
Fraser, Lady Antonia (née Pakenham) 128, 383
Frauenerwerbverein 30, 34, 35, 39-40, 42
Frederick II (the Great), King of Prussia 310
Fredericksborg 240
Freud, Anna 374, 377
Freud, Sigmund 55, 89, 122, 249, 255
Freytag, Gustav, *Soll und Haben* 60
Fried, Erich 305
Friedburger, Kurt 320
Friedell, Egon 44
Friedensburg, Ferdinand 226
Friedenthal, Richard 129, 262
Friedmann, Hermann 209
Friedmann, Werner 317
Frischauer, Mariza 113
Frischauer, Paul 113
Fry, Christopher 256, 379
Fuchs, Albert 64, 70, 114
Fürstenberg, Tassilo von 155
Furtwängler, Wilhelm 198-201, 206, 231, 241, 265
Fuschl 299
Gadol, Annie 157
Gaitskell, Dora (née Frost, later Baroness Gaitskell) 70, 71, 382

Seipel, Ignaz 17, 40
Seitz, Karl 40-41
Selsdon Park, Surrey 17
Sernau, Lola 290
SHAEF 137, 138, 143
Shakespeare, William 135, 223, 378
  Hamlet 111
  Henry V 111
  Julius Caesar 259
  Measure for Measure 244
  The Merchant of Venice 31, 33
  A Midsummer Night's Dream 224
Shaw, George Bernard 44, 60
  The Doctor's Dilemma 31
Shaw-Taylor, Desmond 104
The "She-Youth" 364-365, 366, 367, 379
Shuttleworth, Christine (née de Mendelssohn) 174, 202, 248, 388
  in Belfast 360-361
  in Berlin hospital 243, 245
  birth of daughter 368
  and bomb attack in Wimbledon 136
  childhood 26, 127, 132, 140, 146, 151, 168, 174, 182-183, 209, 214, 234
  first marriage 359
  and great-grandfather 121
  and Henrietta Leslie 169
  letter to HS 161
  and Robert Maxwell 322
  at Oxford 315, 318, 323-324
  and Peter's last days 369
  relationship with HS 340, 376, 385, 387, 388, 401
  schooldays 207, 256, 303
  second marriage 367
  in Venice 259-260
Shuttleworth, Frank (son-in-law) 367, 376, 387
Shuttleworth, Rebecca (grand-

daughter) 156, 368, 369, 376, 385, 387, 388, 388, 410
Sibylle, Frau 185, 221, 255
sie 176, 189
Siebert, Grete 121
Siebert (Singer), Leo (great-uncle) 19, 121, 164
Siepi, Cesare 228
Silone, Darina 209, 258
Silone, Ignazio 52, 209, 258, 265
Simplizissimus 204
Sims, Mrs. 129-130
Simson, Kathleen von 208
Singer, Fanny (née Benedict) (great-grandmother) 18-19
Singer, Gustav (great-uncle) 17-18, 23, 40, 115
Singer, Irene (great-aunt) 19
Sinowatz, Fred 354, 382
Sintenis, Renée 267
Siodmak, Robert 294, 320
Sitwell, Osbert 160, 261
Skoda, Adele von 252
Slovenia 348
Smith, Joseph 291
Smith, Stevie 153
  Novel on Yellow Paper 104
Smolka, Peter (later Smollett) 109-110, 112, 113, 125, 145, 153, 157, 158, 167, 249, 292
  Forty Thousand Against the Arctic 109
Smolka, Thomas Garrigue 109
Social Democratic Party (Germany) 195
Social Democratic Party (SPÖ) (Austria) 382
Social Democratic Workers' Party (SDAP) 56, 66, 71, 72
Socialist Party (Austria) 215
Socialist Unity Party (SED) (Germany) 195, 231

442

444